Bloomsbury Keys

Good English

Bloomsbury Keys

Good English Guide

Edited by Martin Manser

First published in 1988 as *Bloomsbury Good Word Guide*. This edition first published in 1994.

10 9 8 7 6 5 4 3 2 1

British Library Cataloguing in Publication

A CIP record for this book is available from the British Library.

ISBN 0 7475 1777 0

Acknowledgments
The editor expresses his thanks to the following: Rosalind Desmond and Gloria Wren for careful checking, Kathy Rooney and Tracey Smith, of the Publishers, for encouragement at every stage of the book's production, and on the first edition, Sarah Peasley for help in compiling the text and Margaret McPhee for advice on Australian English.

Typeset by Watermark, Cromer, Norfolk
Printed in Britain by HarperCollins Manufacturing, Glasgow

INTRODUCTION

These days the term 'communicative skills' has become a vogue expression, being much in evidence in situations vacant columns and playing an important role in educational rethinking. In common with many voguish expressions of the age overuse has left it in danger of not being taken seriously. This is a great pity since the phenomenon which the term describes is of paramount importance in modern life.

Failure to communicate effectively is at the root of many social ills and misfortunes, from war to missed career opportunities, from industrial strife to broken relationships. If only we had been able to persuade the other party of our real intentions, what misunderstandings and conflict might have been averted.

Nowadays there is little excuse for poor communicative skills in those with a basic education, even in those who feel that they missed out at school in this particular area of education. Articulacy is not necessarily inborn; it can be acquired. Never before has there been such a wealth of self-help English language material available to ease the process of this acquiral.

The proliferation of English language reference books is a relatively recent occurrence. Not long ago the average family bookshelves probably stocked, if any reference books, an ancient Bible, a dog-eared, somewhat elderly dictionary, and perhaps a set of out-of-date encyclopedias. In many cases this state of affairs must have changed radically, judging from current sales of English language reference books.

Something of a revolution hit reference book publishing, brought about partly by the arrival of computerization and the new technology and partly by the realization among publishers that reference books, although expensive to produce, represented less of a risk than other branches of publishing. There was probably also an element of response to demand as people came to realize the need for articulacy in the modern world.

For whatever reasons bookshop shelves have become positively crammed with a wide range of attractive, up-to-date English language reference books, most of them extremely reasonably priced. At first most of these were English language dictionaries but soon a wider selection of books joined them. The net result was that the promotional activities involved in bringing these reference wares to the notice of the public made it difficult for people not to be aware of an important fact — that language is subject to change. Newspapers revelled in providing their readers with selected lists of the 'new English', the more bizarre the better.

The speed at which new words are added to the language nowadays is overwhelming, but it is not only the vocabulary that is subject to change. As attitudes and conventions change other areas of language change with them — stylistics, usage, and even, in some cases, pronunciation.

It is all too easy to feel marooned in this sea of change. While the importance of communicative skills cannot be denied, many people find it difficult to set about acquiring them. Getting to grips with something as amorphous as the English language can be a daunting task, particularly for those whose formal education omitted to convey much about the structure or grammar of the language.

Dictionaries obviously provide a great deal of self-help with regard to language but their contribution is frequently restricted to meaning, spelling, or pronunciation. People seeking to extend their competence in the use of English require more varied and in-depth assistance.

Thesauruses are another great boon to those wishing to improve their standard of articulacy but here again they are far from providing all the solutions. Although would-be writers or speakers will undoubtedly find in thesauruses a wide range of inspirational words with which to clothe ideas, they might well feel in need of some guidance as to how exactly these words should be used.

In the present age much more emphasis than hitherto is placed on the importance of being able to produce a high standard of English, whether oral or written. Formerly this aspect tended to be neglected in favour of highly developed reading and interpretative skills but this is now being rectified in these days of mass communication.

Participation in the communication media, for example, is no longer restricted to a few highly educated experts. Audience participation has extended from the realms of the stage to the realms of radio and television. Indeed one wonders what local low-budget radio stations would do without the phone-in contributions of the man/woman in the street, not to mention the chat show featuring the local celebrity who has published a first novel, climbed Everest, or lost more weight than anyone else in the community. All manner of things are of interest to the media.

In order to improve one's oral and written skills it is important to have more than just a dictionary and a thesaurus as self-help material. Of immense help are books that offer guidance in the use of language, particularly those which show language in action by including example sentences or phrases.

Such books provide very valuable ground rules on which to base one's own English usage. Few of us can rely entirely on instinct or even on memory when it comes to the English language for it is full of quirks and inconsistencies. Even the most educated benefit from having a standard authority to fall back on.

Language reference books these days are less didactic than they were. In general we have moved on from the times when they were entirely prescriptive in their comments on language. Now most of them adopt a more descriptive role, restricting themselves to stating what is actually happening in language rather than dictating what ought to be happening.

Inevitably there are people who are unhappy with this change of emphasis. There is a school of thought prevalent mainly among older people which seeks to impose a kind of restriction on language that is no longer imposed on other areas of life. It is as if, in an age of uncertainty and kaleidoscopic change, they look to language to provide a safe, unchanging structure.

This places an impossible burden on language. It does not exist in a vacuum but simply reflects what is happening in society and the world around. If we do not like the words, we probably do not like the events but it is difficult to hold back the tide of change.

At the very least we cannot stem the flow of vocabulary additions which are created in response to new inventions, new discoveries, and new concepts. New labels have to be found and so are born *camcorders, E-numbers, genetic engineering*, and *teleshopping*, to name but a few of the new words that are invading the language from every area of human activity.

Language change is not confined to new vocabulary additions. Sometimes the old gets recycled in a new form as words alter their meaning in some way. The classic example is, of course, the word *gay*, which has almost entirely lost its 'merry' associations — except in literature written before the present day — in favour of the modern meaning of 'homosexual'.

There are, however, a growing number of other instances of language change, several based on misconception or error. *Hopefully* was an early example when it came to mean 'it is to be hoped that' as well as 'with hope'. Now *disinterested* is frequently to be found meaning 'not interested' as well as 'unbiased'. There is now a very fine line to be drawn between error and alternative usage — and sometimes the former becomes the latter.

Data, for example, as the plural of *datum* should come accompanied by a plural verb but it is now frequently seen in the presence of a singular verb, particularly in the field of information technology. The same fate has befallen *media*. It is no longer thought of as simply the plural of *medium* but as a word in its own right. As such it is increasingly accompanied by a singular, rather than a plural, verb.

Educational trends frequently have an effect on the state of the language. With the virtual demise of the teaching of classics in schools a knowledge of Latin and Greek in relation to the English language is now quite a rare phenomenon among younger people. So is born the puzzlement over *medium/media* and *datum/data* and the confusion over *stadia/stadiums* and *referendums/referenda*.

The creative writing phase in primary schools was the forerunner of many spelling problems and even more grammatical problems. It is, of course, a good thing to encourage creativity and self-expression, but some knowledge of the structure of the language is necessary if one is to use it with confidence and skill. Attempts are now being made to revive grammar, at least in some form, but what is done cannot be undone and there remain generations to whom it is a closed book.

This has undoubtedly affected modern English as it is used by the man/woman in the street. It may offend purist ears but *less bottles of milk* is challenging *fewer bottles of milk* for supremacy in terms of frequency.

Then there is the nervousness about *me* and *I*. There is a general — and erroneous — feeling that *I* is much more polite and more correct than *me* in all contexts. This accounts for the *between you and I* which so offends those brought up on a diet of parts of speech and parsing.

Prepositions in English are the source of much confusion. Should it be *different from* or *different to*? For that matter should *accompanied* be followed by *with* or *by*? Is either possible and, if so, which is correct in which context?

As formal language training has diminished and public communication has increased, language has become less and less rigid and the distinction between the linguistically correct and the linguistically incorrect has become blurred. But we are not yet at the stage where anything goes; let us hope we never reach it. I think that most of us would prefer a few guidelines to a linguistic free-for-all.

The trouble is that it is difficult to establish such guidelines when the language is in a state of flux. As has already been suggested it is difficult to pigeonhole language into the correct and the incorrect. The categories are often too black and white; some shades of grey are sometimes necessary.

In any area where extremes are involved it is often advisable to take the middle course. So it is with language, provided the rationale and the terms of reference are clearly explained. By taking such a course and explaining the options you may not please everyone but, on the other hand, you are unlikely to offend everyone.

The *Bloomsbury Key Good English Guide*, one of the most wide-ranging English language reference books available, presents the reader with the facts associated with the relevant words and makes recommendations rather than laying down didactic rules. Where a supposed alternative is in fact still generally considered wrong this is clearly stated, but where acceptable alternatives exist these are also stated together with the justifications for these.

Sometimes distinctions have to be made between the habits of the consciously careful users who wish to achieve absolutely correct and elegant English and those of the run-of-the-mill users who simply wish to get their basic message across as speedily and as painlessly as possible. A distressing number of us fall into this latter category although on special occasions, when we are out to impress, we try to mend our ways.

The said special occasions are usually formal occasions when we dress up not only ourselves but our language also. Forms of language associated with particular social situations are called registers. Thus in a formal situation a formal register of language is used.

Many of the entries in the *Bloomsbury Key Good English Guide* distinguish between formal and informal registers. The formal/informal distinction is often, although not always, between written and spoken English. We tend to be at our most formal, linguistically speaking, when we are writing letters of a business nature, while informal English is kept for chatty letters to friends and family or everyday conversation. It is important to remember that informal English is neither incorrect nor less correct as long as it is the appropriate register for the context.

The *Bloomsbury Key Good English Guide* takes language as it finds it and acts as a navigator through the many potential hazards. All problematic areas are dealt with and explained in a way that is readily understandable by all users. Giving help with language is of very little use if the help itself is more difficult to comprehend than the original linguistic problem.

It tackles two types of **spelling** difficulty — words that for some reason present problems in themselves and words which are problematic because they are likely to be confused with other words that resemble them. Into the first category come such words as *antihistamine, disappoint, innocuous, privilege*, and *wilful*, while the second category covers such duos as *bloc/block, dual/duel, principal/principle*, and *stationary/stationery*. This edition of the *Guide* also includes words and expressions of foreign origin which frequently present spelling and pronunciation problems. Examples include *bête noire* and *tête-à-tête*.

Of course the *Guide* does not confine its help with **pronunciation** to foreign words. The editor has been conscious of the fact that knowing how to pronounce words correctly is essential for confident public speaking, whether in the area of business or leisure. Thus words such as *Celtic, dynasty, flaccid, irrevocable, status*, and many more are listed to save you from red-faced stumbling.

Many people find difficulty with **punctuation** and so hesitate to launch into print. The *Good English Guide* gives advice on many aspects from the basic comma and paragraph to the more esoteric semicolon. Potential authors will find it invaluable.

Grammar is a cause of nervousness in many, mostly because they have never been taught the rudiments of it. One of the great advantages of this book is that the grammatical information is presented in an easily comprehensible, rapid-to-use form as it unfolds the mysteries of the preposition, the conjunction, and the rest.

If your particular linguistic problem centres on **usage** you will find that the *Bloomsbury Key Good English Guide* gives sensible answers to a wide range of possible queries, often incorporating examples of the particular words showing the usual context. Should you use *converse* or *inverse*, *impinge* or *infringe*, *soluble* or *solvable*? A quick scan through the alphabetical listing will reveal the answer. Although mindful of the fact that print gives a kind of credence to any statement the editor has sensibly given examples of incorrect usage on occasion to contrast with the correct form.

One of the most innovative features of this book is the concentration on what are known as **buzz words** or vogue words, expressions which, however much we may deprecate them, suddenly leap into fashionable prominence in the general language, often from specialist sources. In many cases objections to buzz words lie not with the words themselves but with their overuse, the user rather than the word being at fault. Too many of us jump on the linguistic bandwagon and reach for the vogue word of the day instead of spending time and effort in finding the more appropriate expression.

What is to be done with buzz words? Should we ignore them and hope they will fade rapidly? Should we embrace them enthusiastically and risk heaping criticism on ourselves? Should we take the middle course and use them sparingly and effectively? The choice is of course yours but this particular volume advocates this last course of action. Appreciate their merits but do not abuse them by overusing them.

If you find yourself tempted by any of them put temptation behind you by consulting the *Guide* for suggested suitable alternatives. Armed with it you will have no excuse for peppering your prose with *the bottom line*, *catalyst*, *gravitas*, *downsizing*, *leading-edge*, *parameter*, *matrix*, and so on unless the context demands it. Many of them are best left to their specialist use. A severe head injury is *traumatic*; missing a bus is just annoying.

In this edition of the *Guide*, two additional tables have been included: *Countries and Peoples*, giving guidance on the spelling of words derived from the names of countries – what do you call a person who comes from *the Seychelles*; what is the adjective that derives from *Burkina Faso*? – and *Prepositions*, showing which preposition to use with certain verbs, adjectives, and nouns – do you use *for* or *to* with *liable*; *between* or *with* with *alternate*?

The *Bloomsbury Key Good English Guide* is a book for everyone and truly is an invaluable ready reference to English today. Whether you are using it for guidance with spelling, punctuation, pronunciation, or usage — or simply to settle or cause language disputes — you will quickly come to regard it as an old friend. Just remember one thing. Do not blame the book for what is happening to the language.

BETTY KIRKPATRICK
Edinburgh

HOW TO USE THIS BOOK

Entries, listed in a single alphabetical ordering, cover five main areas of the English language: spelling, pronunciation, grammar and punctuation, usage, and buzz words. Two tables, of Countries and Peoples and Prepositions, are also included in the main alphabetical listing.

Spelling

accommodation The word *accommodation* is often misspelt. Note the *-cc-* and *-mm-*.

Pronunciation

controversy In the traditional pronunciation of this word, the stress falls on the first syllable [*kon*-trŏversi]. The variant pronunciation, with stress on the second syllable [kŏn-*trov*ĕrsi], is widely heard, but is disliked by many users. See also STRESS.

Grammar and punctuation

dangling participles Participles are often used to introduce a phrase which is attached to a later-mentioned subject: □ *Startled by the noise she dropped her book.* □ *Being by now very tired, we stopped at a pub.* There is a tendency, though, for such introductory participles to become apparently attached to the wrong noun: □ *Startled by the noise, her book fell to the floor.* □ *Being by now very tired, a pub was a welcome sight.* It was not the book that was startled or the pub that was tired. Then there is the sentence where the participle appears to have no subject at all, which is the thought behind the term *dangling participle* (also known as *unattached*, or *unrelated participle*): □ *Lying in the sun, it felt as though it had always been summer.* Who, or what, was lying in the sun?

semicolon The semicolon is a useful punctuation mark but, unlike many of the other punctuation marks, there is no occasion when its use is compulsory. It is mainly used between clauses that are linked by sense but are not joined by a conjunction, and that could each stand as a separate sentence: □ *I am very tired; I am also hungry.* □ *The night was dark; the rain fell in torrents.* It is frequently used before such phrases as *however, none the less, nevertheless.* The semicolon can be replaced by a comma, but in sentences where clauses already contain commas, the semicolon is often used to separate the clauses. It can also be used to establish subjects in a long list or series separated by commas.

Usage

he or she The use of *he/him/his* as pronouns of common gender, with reference to a person of unspecified sex, is widely considered to be misleading and sexist, as is the use of *she/her/hers* for the same purpose with reference to jobs or activities that are traditionally associated with women: □ *The candidate must pay his own travelling expenses.* □ *This book will be of great value to the student nurse preparing for her examinations.* The most acceptable substitutes for these pronouns are the cumbersome and pedantic expressions *he or she, he/she, (s)he, his or her,* etc.: □ *If a child is slow to learn, he or she will be given extra tuition.*

In some cases, the problem may be avoided by restructuring the sentence, making the subject plural, or both: □ *Travelling expenses must be paid by the candidate.* □ *Children who are slow to learn will be given extra tuition.*

Buzz words—vogue expressions, often originally from specialist subjects

hi-tech The adjective *hi-tech* specifically refers to high technology, or sophisticated electronics; its indiscriminate application to basic electrical appliances or to anything remotely connected with computing is disliked by many careful users: □ *a beautiful hi-tech modern home* □ *high-tech benefits* [a reference to the computerization of the social security benefits system] □ *This transition of the cycle from leisure 'toy' to hi-tech pedal machine.*

The word hi-tech has a number of variant spellings: *high-tech, high tech, hi-tec, high-tec,* etc. It is also used as a noun: □ *Reflecting the world of high tech* [spelt *hi-tech* in the headline], *the first museum devoted to the chemical industry opens today.*

Examples of the use of words are preceded by □. Many of the examples are drawn from actual quotations of contemporary usage.

market forces The phrase *market forces* refers to anything that affects or influences the free operation of trade in goods or services, such as competition or demand, as opposed to (artificially imposed) government controls. It is in danger of becoming overused as a vogue term: □ *The printing of this holy work* [the Bible] *should be subjected to market forces* (*The Bookseller*). □ *The Government yesterday unveiled plans to shift the financing of universities and polytechnics away from block grants and towards higher tuition fees in an attempt to expand student numbers through emphasis on market forces* (*The Guardian*). □ *Green market forces are working in the appliance manufacturers' favour* (*Daily Telegraph*).

Indications of incorrect usages are sometimes shown to contrast with the correct forms.

your or **you're**? These two words may be confused. *Your* means 'belonging to you': □ *your house* □ *your rights*. *You're* is a contraction of *you are:* □ *Hurry up, you're going to be late!* Note also the spelling of *yours*: □ *That's mine not yours*; the spelling with an apostrophe, *your's*, is wrong.

A distinction is made between the use of many words in informal and formal contexts.

outside of Many people dislike the prepositional phrase *outside of*, in which the word *of* is incorrect. The phrase is best avoided in formal contexts: □ *There was a taxi outside* [not *outside of*] *the house.*

et al. *Et al.* is an abbreviation of *et alii* and means 'and other people'. It is used particularly in writings of a formal technical nature to indicate the omission of other names: □ *Similar findings have been recorded by Jones, Bernstein, et al.*

Differences between British English and American English spelling, usage, etc., are highlighted.

worship The single final *p* doubles in front of most suffixes beginning with a vowel in British English: □ *worshipped* □ *worshipper* □ *worshipping*. American English retains the single *p*. *Worshipful* retains the single *p*.

At many entries advice is given to avoid overusing a particular word or expression.

aggravate The use of the verb *aggravate* and its derivatives in the sense of 'annoy', 'irritate', or 'exasperate' dates back to the early 17th century but is still disliked by some people. It is therefore best restricted to informal contexts and the offending word replaced by one of its synonyms: □ *I was aggravated by the noise.* □ *She has a number of aggravating habits.* □ *His lackadaisical attitude is a constant source of aggravation.*

Cross-references are used to show where an entry may be found or where there is additional information.

uninterested see DISINTERESTED OR UNINTERESTED?

challenged *Challenged* is a vogue word used to form euphemisms for disability or disadvantage: □ *physically challenged.* See also ABLED; POLITICAL CORRECTNESS.

GUIDE TO PRONUNCIATION

a as in b*a*d
ă as in *a*rrest
ah as in f*a*ther
air as in d*are*
ar as in c*ar*pet
ăr as in burgl*ar*
aw as in s*aw*
ay as in m*ay*
b as in *b*ed
ch as in *ch*eese
d as in *d*ig
dh as in *th*ese
e as in g*e*t
ĕ as in op*e*n
ee as in s*ee*
eer as in h*ere*
er as in b*ir*d
ĕr as in butch*er*
ew as in f*ew*
ewr as in p*ure*
f as in *f*it
g as in *g*o
h as in *h*at
i as in *i*t
ĭ as in penc*i*l
ī as in tr*y*
j as in *j*am
k as in *k*eep
kh as in lo*ch*
ks as in mi*x*
kw as in *qu*iz
l as in *l*ie
m as in *m*ad
n as in *n*od
ng as in si*ng*
n(g) as in restaura*nt*
o as in h*o*t
ŏ as in cann*o*n
ō as in n*o*
oi as in b*oy*
oo as in z*oo*
oor as in c*ure*
or as in t*ore*
ŏr as in doct*or*
ow as in n*ow*
p as in *p*at
r as in *r*im
rr as in ma*rr*y
s as in *s*at
sh as in *sh*ip
t as in *t*ake
th as in *th*in
u as in *u*p
ŭ as in croc*u*s
uu as in p*u*sh
v as in *v*an
w as in *w*ater
y as in *y*es
yoo as in *u*nite
yoor as in *ur*ine
yr as in t*ire*
z as in *z*oo
zh as in trea*s*ure

stressed syllables are shown in italics: [*sis*tĕr].

A

a or **an**? *A* is the form of the indefinite article used before words or abbreviations that are pronounced with an initial consonant sound, regardless of their spelling; *an* is used before words that begin with a vowel sound: □ *a light* □ *an LP* □ *a unit* □ *an uncle* □ *a horse* □ *an heir* □ *a one-armed bandit* □ *an ostrich* □ *a seat* □ *an SOS* □ *a ewe* □ *an egg* □ *a UFO* □ *an IOU*.

abbreviations Abbreviations are useful space-saving devices. They are used heavily both in informal writing and in technical or specialized writing, but less in formal writing. Some abbreviations stand for more than one thing, and it is better to spell these out unless the context makes the meaning clear. □ *He was a CO in the war* is confusing, as the abbreviation means both 'commanding officer' and 'conscientious objector'. See also ACRONYMS.

aberration This word, meaning 'deviation from the norm': □ *a temporary mental aberration*, is sometimes misspelt. Note the spelling: a single *b* and *-rr-*, as in *error*.

ability see CAPABILITY, CAPACITY, OR ABILITY?

-able or **-ible**? Both forms of this suffix are added to words to form adjectives, *-able* being the suffix that is productive and the more frequently used: □ *washable* □ *comfortable* □ *collapsible*.

abled The term *abled* is sometimes used as a synonym for 'ablebodied'; it is also used as an alternative for 'disabled' or 'handicapped': □ *otherly abled* □ *Marshall rejects the term 'disabled' for these children. ... She calls them 'uniquely differently abled'* (*Daily Telegraph*). Users feel that such phrases project a more positive image of people with disabilities, but these alternatives are widely disliked as much by the supposed beneficiaries as by the public at large. See also ABLEISM; CHALLENGED; POLITICAL CORRECTNESS.

ableism The term *ableism* refers to discrimination against people with disabilities, especially in employment and in the provision of facilities in public places. See also POLITICAL CORRECTNESS.

about see AROUND OR ABOUT?

above or **over**? The preposition *above* means 'at a higher level than'; *over* means 'vertically or directly above', 'on top of', or 'across': □ *He raised his hand above his head.* □ *She held the umbrella over her head.* □ *There's a mark on the wall above the radiator.* □ *I've put my towel over the radiator.* □ *The aeroplane flew above the clouds.* □ *The aeroplane flew over Southampton.*

abridgment or **abridgement**? This word, meaning 'a shortened version of a work such as a book', may be spelt *abridgment* or *abridgement*. Both spellings are fully acceptable.

abscess This word, meaning 'a collection of pus surrounded by inflamed tissue', is often misspelt. Note the *sc* at the beginning of the second syllable.

absence This word is sometimes misspelt, the most frequent error being the substitution of *-sc-* for the *-s-*, as in *abscess*. Note also the *-ence* ending.

absolutely Some users dislike the frequent use of *absolutely* in place of *yes*. Others feel that the adverb is overused as an intensifier, in the sense of 'completely': □ *it's absolutely disgraceful!*

absorption Note the spelling of this word. The final *-b* of the verb *absorb* changes to *-p-* in the derived noun.

abstention or **abstinence**? Both these nouns are derived from the verb *abstain*, meaning 'refrain' or 'refrain from voting'. The noun *abstention* is chiefly used in the second of these senses: □ *24 votes for the motion, 16 against, and 5 abstentions. Abstinence* refers to the act or practice of abstaining, often from something that is enjoyable but possibly harmful: □ *abstinence from alcohol* □ *total abstinence from sexual intercourse.*

abstractedly or **abstractly**? *Abstractedly* is derived from the adjective *abstracted,* meaning 'lost in thought': □ *He stared abstractedly out of the window.* The adverb *abstractly,* meaning 'in the abstract', is less frequent in usage.

abuse or **misuse**? The noun *abuse* denotes wrong, improper, or bad use or treatment; the noun *misuse,* denoting incorrect or unorthodox use, is more neutral: □ *the abuse of power* □ *child abuse* □ *the misuse of words* □ *misuse of the club's funds.*

abysmal This word, meaning 'very bad; dreadful': □ *abysmal weather,* is sometimes misspelt. The word comes from *abyss,* hence the *y* in the spelling.

academic The adjective *academic* is widely used in the sense of 'theoretical': □ *an academic question* □ *of academic interest only,* but some people object to its frequent use in place of *irrelevant:* □ *Whether he wins this race or not is academic, because he is already several points ahead of his nearest rival.*

accede or **exceed**? *Accede,* used in formal contexts, means 'agree'; *exceed* means 'go beyond' or 'be greater than': □ *They will accede to our demands.* □ *Do not exceed the speed limit.*

accelerate The word *accelerate,* meaning 'speed up', is sometimes misspelt. Note the *-cc-* and single *l*.

accent or **accentuate**? Both verbs can be used in the sense of 'to emphasize'. *Accent* usually refers to the act of stressing a sound in speech or music, whereas *accentuate* is used in a wider range of visual and abstract contexts: □ *He accented the word 'life'.* □ *to accent the first beat in the bar* □ *to accentuate an outline/a problem.*

accents Accents are sometimes used on words that are now accepted into English, though the tendency is increasingly to omit them.

accentuate see ACCENT OR ACCENTUATE?

accept or **except**? These two verbs should not be confused, being virtually opposite in meaning. *Accept* means 'receive' or 'admit'; *except,* used in formal contexts, means 'exclude' or 'leave out': □ *She was accepted for the job.* □ *He was excepted from the team.* The two words are similar but not identical in pronunciation: *accept* is pronounced [ăk*sept*] and *except* is pronounced [ik*sept*].

access The use of the word *access* as a verb is best restricted to the field of computing, where it means 'gain access to (stored information or a computer memory)'.

access or **accession**? The noun *access* refers to the act, right, or means of approaching, reaching, entering, or using: □ *Access to the laboratory is restricted.* The noun *accession* is derived from the verb *accede* (see ACCEDE OR EXCEED?) and is most frequently used in the sense of 'becoming monarch': □ *Elizabeth II's accession (to the throne) in 1952.*

accessory or **accessary**? In British English, the spelling of this word in the sense 'supplementary attachment' is *accessory*: □ *car accessories.* In the legal sense of 'a person who incites another to commit a crime', the spelling is usually *accessory, accessary* being an older variant.

accommodation The word *accommodation* is often misspelt. Note the *-cc-* and *-mm-*.

accompany The passive verb *to be accompanied* may be followed by the preposition *by* or *with*, depending on the sense in which it is used: □ *She was accompanied by her friend.* □ *His words were accompanied with/by a gesture of impatience.* In the first example the verb *accompany* means 'go somewhere with someone as a companion; escort', in the second it means 'supplement'.

accountable The adjective *accountable*, meaning 'answerable', should be applied only to people: □ *Union leaders are accountable to the rank-and-file members.* □ *We were accountable for their welfare.*

accumulative or **cumulative**? The adjective *cumulative* refers to something that gradually increases with successive additions: □ *the cumulative total* □ *a cumulative effect.* It should not be confused with *accumulative*, an adjective that is derived from the verb *accumulate* but is rarely used.

acetic see AESTHETIC, ASCETIC, OR ACETIC?

acknowledgment or **acknowledgement**? This word may be spelt with or without the *e* after the *g*; both spellings are fully acceptable.

acoustics The word *acoustics* is often misspelt, the most frequent error being the doubling of the first *c*.

acquaint The verb *acquaint* is best avoided where *tell* would be adequate or more appropriate: □ *He acquainted me with his plans*, for example, may be more simply expressed as *he told me his plans*.

acquirement or **acquisition**? In the sense of 'something acquired' *acquirement* is largely restricted to abilities or skills and *acquisition*, the more frequent word, to material things or people: □ *Fluency in spoken and written Japanese is one of her many acquirements.* □ *He showed me his latest acquisition.*

acronyms An *acronym* is a word formed from the initial letters or syllables of other words: □ *OPEC* (Organization of Petroleum Exporting Countries) □ *radar* (radio detecting and ranging). See also DINKY; NIMBY; YUPPIE.

acrylic This word is sometimes misspelt. Note particularly the *yl*, not *il* in the middle of the word.

act or **action**? Both these nouns mean 'something done', but *action* tends to emphasize the process of doing whereas *act* denotes the deed itself: □ *Terrorist action has increased.* □ *It was an act of terrorism.*

active An active verb is one in which the SUBJECT performs the action of the verb (compare PASSIVE). The sentence □ *The mechanic mended my car* contains the active verb *mended*.

actualize The verb *actualize*, meaning 'make actual', is disliked by some users as an example of the increasing tendency to coin new verbs by adding the suffix -*ize* to nouns and adjectives: □ *They have actualized their plans.*

actually Many people object to the frequent use of the adverb *actually* where it adds nothing to the meaning of the sentence: □ *Actually, I prefer coffee to tea.*

□ *We weren't actually very impressed by his performance.* □ *She doesn't live here, actually.*

See also IN FACT.

acumen In the traditional pronunciation of this word, which means 'the ability to make good judgments': □ *sound business acumen*, the stress falls on the second syllable [ă*kyoo*mĕn]. The pronunciation with the stress on the first syllable [*ak*yoomĕn] is, however, more frequently heard.

AD and **BC** The abbreviation *AD*, which stands for *Anno Domini*, is traditionally placed before the year number; *BC*, which stands for *before Christ*, always follows the year number: □ *The custom dates back to AD 1462.* □ *The city was destroyed in 48 BC.*

address Note the spelling of this word, particularly the *-dd-* and the *-ss* ending. See also LETTER WRITING 1.

adherence or **adhesion**? Both these nouns are derived from the verb *adhere*, meaning 'stick'. *Adhesion* is largely confined to the literal sense of the word, whereas *adherence* is used for the figurative senses of 'loyalty' or 'obedience': □ *the adhesion of the tape to the fabric* □ *their adherence to the cause* □ *strict adherence to the rules.*

ad hoc The Latin phrase *ad hoc* denotes something that is made or done for a particular purpose, rather than as a general rule. It is most frequently used as an adjective: □ *an ad hoc decision* □ *on an ad hoc basis.*

adjectives An *adjective* is a word which provides information about a noun: □ *fat* □ *blue* □ *happy* □ *intelligent* □ *dirty*. The main division of adjectives corresponds to the position that they take. Attributive adjectives come before a noun: □ *a stupid boy*. Predicative adjectives follow a verb: □ *the sky is grey*. Postpositive adjectives follow a noun: □ *the chairman elect.* Some adjectives can be used in all three positions, and most can be used attributively and predicatively. Nouns can also be used as attributive adjectives: □ *a glass bowl*. Adjectives can be used in the place of adverbs, and such words as: □ *fast* □ *late* □ *early* function as both adjectives and adverbs.

Absolute adjectives are such words as: □ *entire* □ *unique*, which cannot be used in the comparative or superlative and cannot be modified by words like *very* or *totally*. See also COMPARATIVE AND SUPERLATIVE; NOUNS.

adjourn This word, which means 'stop for a short time' and 'go', is sometimes misspelt. Note the *d* in front of the *j*, and the *our*, as in *journey*.

administer or **administrate**? Either verb may be used in the sense of 'manage', 'supervise', 'control', or 'direct', with reference to the work of an administrator: □ *She has administered/administrated the company since the death of her father.*

admission or **admittance**? Both these nouns mean 'permission or right to enter'. *Admission* is the more frequent, *admittance* being largely restricted to formal or official contexts: □ *Admission is by ticket only.* □ *No admittance.*

admit In the sense of 'confess' or 'acknowledge' *admit* is generally used as a transitive verb: □ *He admitted his mistake.* □ *I admitted that I had lied.* The insertion of the preposition *to* in such contexts is disliked by many users: □ *He admitted to his mistake. Admit* is followed by *to* in the sense of 'allow to enter' or 'give access'. In the formal sense of 'be open to' or 'leave room for' *admit* is followed by *of*: □ *The phrase does not admit of a different interpretation.*

admittance see ADMISSION OR ADMITTANCE?

adolescence This word is sometimes misspelt. Note particularly the *sc* and the *nc*.

adopted or **adoptive**? The adjective *adopted* is applied to children who have been adopted; *adoptive* relates to adults who adopt another person's child: □ *their adopted daughter* □ *her adoptive parents.*

adult The noun *adult* may be stressed on either syllable, but the pronunciation [adŭlt] is heard more frequently than [ădult] in British English.

advance or **advancement**? The noun *advance* means 'forward motion' or 'progress': □ *the advance of the enemy.* The noun *advancement* is chiefly used in formal contexts to refer to 'promotion' or 'increased status': □ *opportunities for personal advancement.*

advantage or **vantage**? *Advantage* means 'superiority' or 'benefit': □ *to have the advantage over one's rivals* □ *the advantages of coeducation. Vantage* is chiefly found in the phrase *vantage point,* meaning 'a place that affords a good overall view'.

advantageous This word is sometimes misspelt, the most frequent error being the omission of the *-e-*. Note also the pronunciation of this word, stressed on the third syllable [advăn*tay*jŭs].

adverbs Adverbs modify other parts of speech and answer questions such as how? (adverbs of manner): □ *quietly* □ *greedily*, when? (adverbs of time): □ *then* □ *tomorrow*, where? (adverbs of place): □ *there* □ *outside. See also* ADJECTIVES.

adversary The pronunciation of this word with stress on the second syllable [ăd*ver*sări] is disliked by many users, who prefer the traditional pronunciation with stress on the first syllable [*ad*vĕrsări]. See also STRESS.

adverse or **averse**? *Adverse,* meaning 'unfavourable', 'antagonistic', or 'hostile', usually precedes an abstract noun; *averse*, meaning 'disinclined', 'unwilling', or 'having a strong dislike', usually relates to people and is never placed before the noun it qualifies: □ *adverse criticism* □ *an adverse effect* □ *The committee was not averse to the proposal.* □ *They are averse to all publicity.*

advertise This word, meaning 'promote or publicize': □ *a brochure advertising holidays*, is sometimes misspelt. This is one of the words ending in *-ise* that cannot be spelt *-ize*; see also -IZE OR -ISE?

advise The use of the verb *advise* as a synonym for 'tell', 'inform', 'notify', etc., is widely regarded as COMMERCIALESE and is best avoided in general usage.

adviser or **advisor**? This word, meaning 'person who gives advice', may be spelt either *adviser* or *advisor*. Both spellings are fully acceptable.

-ae- and **-oe-** In such words as *archaeology* and *amoeba*, the vowel combinations *-ae-* and *-oe-* were once represented by the symbols æ and œ. They are now usually written or printed as separate letters and there is an increasing tendency for the *-a-* and *-o-* to be omitted.

aerial This word, meaning 'of the air; from an aircraft' and 'device that receives or sends out broadcast signals', is sometimes misspelt. Note particularly the *ae-* at the beginning of this word.

aero or **air**? Both these words may be used adjectivally or as prefixes in the sense of 'relating to aeroplanes or aircraft': □ *aerobatics* □ *airliner* □ *aerodrome* □ *airport* □ *an aero engine* □ *the air force* □ *aerospace* □ *airspace.*

aeroplane see AERO OR AIR?; PLANE.

aerosol Note the spelling of this word, particularly the *ae-* at the beginning and the *-ol* at the end. An *aerosol* is a fine spray dispensed from a pressurized container; the noun may refer to the container or the contents.

aesthetic, ascetic, or **acetic**? These three words should not be confused. The adjective *aesthetic* means 'relating to beauty or good taste': □ *aesthetic value.* An *ascetic* is a person who practises self-denial; *acetic acid* is the main component of vinegar.

affect or **effect**? The noun *effect* means 'result'; the verb *affect* means 'influence' or 'have an effect on', hence its frequent confusion with the verb *effect*, which means 'bring about' or 'accomplish': □ *The new legislation may have an effect on small businesses.* □ *The new legislation may affect small businesses.* □ *We have effected a number of improvements. Affect* and *effect* are often misused, one in place of the other: □ *Officials said yesterday the downturn could effect the future of the scheme* (*The Guardian*). □ *'It will have very little affect.'*

affectation or **affection**? *Affectation* is false behaviour that is intended to impress; *affection* means 'fondness' or 'tenderness'. The two nouns are related to the different meanings of the verb *affect.*

affinity The use of the preposition *for* with the noun

affinity, in the sense of 'liking' or 'attraction', is disliked by some but acceptable to most: □ *He has a natural affinity for young children*. Those who object to this usage restrict the noun to the meaning 'reciprocal relationship or similarity', in which sense it is followed by *between* or *with*.

afflict or **inflict**? To *afflict* is to distress or trouble, to *inflict* is to impose: □ *He afflicted the prisoners with cruel torture.* □ *He inflicted cruel torture on the prisoners.*

affront or **effrontery**? *Affront* may be used as a noun or as a verb, meaning 'insult': □ *an affront to his pride* □ *I felt affronted.* The noun *effrontery* means 'impudence': □ *She had the effrontery to suggest we were mistaken.*

afters see DESSERT, SWEET, PUDDING, OR AFTERS?

afterward or **afterwards**? In British English *afterwards* is the usual form of the adverb meaning 'subsequently', the variant *afterward* being more frequently used in American English: □ *I'll do the washing-up afterwards.* □ *His foot was sore for days afterwards.*

again This word may be pronounced either [*ăgen*] or [*ăgayn*]. The first of these is probably the more frequently used.

aged This word is pronounced [*ay*jid] in the sense 'very old': □ *his aged uncle* □ *looking after the aged.* When the word is used with a specific age: □ *She was aged twenty*, it is pronounced [ayjd].

ageing or **aging**? This word, meaning '(the process of) becoming old', may be spelt *ageing* or *aging*.

ageism *Ageism* is discrimination against people on the grounds of age, especially in employment, or the offensive use of images of old people. In the first sense the noun is not restricted to old age: any job advertisement that puts an upper (or lower) limit on the age of applicants may be described as *ageist*. See also POLITICAL CORRECTNESS.

agenda The word *agenda* is used as a singular noun, with the plural form *agendas*: □ *The agenda for tomorrow's meeting has been changed.* □ *This item has appeared on a number of* *previous agendas.*

aggravate The use of the verb *aggravate* and its derivatives in the sense of 'annoy', 'irritate', or 'exasperate' dates back to the early 17th century but is still disliked by some people. It is therefore best restricted to informal contexts and the offending word replaced by one of its synonyms: □ *I was aggravated by the noise.* □ *She has a number of aggravating habits.* □ *His lackadaisical attitude is a constant source of aggravation.*

aggressive The use of the adjective *aggressive* in the sense of 'assertive' or 'forceful' is best avoided where there is a risk of confusion with its principal meaning of 'belligerent' or 'hostile': □ *an aggressive salesman* □ *an aggressive approach.*

aging see AGEING OR AGING?

ago or **since**? It is wrong to place *ago* and *since* side by side: □ *It was a fortnight ago that* [not *since*] *I posted the letter.* □ *It is a fortnight* [not *a fortnight ago*] *since I posted the letter.*

agoraphobia This word, describing a fear of open spaces, is sometimes misspelt. Note the *o* after the *ag-*.

-aholic The suffix *-aholic* (or *-oholic*), derived from the noun *alcoholic*, is being attached to an increasing number of words to denote a person who is obsessed by or addicted to something: □ *golfaholic* □ *shopaholic* □ *spendaholic* □ *chocoholic.*

aid The noun *aid* is specifically used to denote a tangible source of help, assistance, or support, such as a device: □ *hearing aid* □ *teaching aids* □ *audiovisual aids* or money, supplies, equipment, etc., given to those in need: □ *overseas aid.*

ain't As a contraction of *are not, is not, have not,* or *has not, ain't* is wrong. It is however generally widely used in speech and in such jocular expressions as: □ *Things ain't what they used to be.* □ *You ain't heard nothing yet.*

air see AERO OR AIR?

air miss or **near miss**? An *air miss* is the near collision of two aircraft in the sky. Such a situation is traditionally called a *near miss,* and both terms are in current use: □ *The Civil*

Aviation Authority has launched an investigation into a near miss 33,000 feet over Exmoor (Daily Telegraph). □ *The Civil Aviation Authority is investigating an air miss over Sussex this morning (BBC South Today).* The expression *near miss* is also used figuratively to describe something that almost succeeds.

aisle This word is sometimes misspelt, the most frequent mistake being the omission of the silent *s*.

alibi The use of the noun *alibi* as a synonym for 'excuse' or 'pretext' is disliked by many people and is best restricted to informal contexts: □ *He used the power cut as an alibi for not finishing his essay.*

align This word, meaning 'bring or come into line; support', is sometimes misspelt. Note the single *l* and also the silent *g*.

all The use of the preposition *of* between *all* and *the, this, that, these, those,* or a possessive adjective is optional, *all* being preferred in British English and *all of* in American English: □ *All (of) the birds have flown away.* □ *I can't carry all (of) that.* □ *Do all (of) these books belong to you?* □ *All (of) her children are right-handed.* □ *They spent all (of) their leave in France.* See also ALL RIGHT OR ALRIGHT?; ALTOGETHER OR ALL TOPGETHER?; NOT.

allege The verb *allege*, meaning 'state without proof', is sometimes misspelt, the most frequent error being the substitution of *-edge* for the *-ege* ending.

all right or **alright**? The spelling *all right* is correct; the spelling *alright* is wrong.

all together see ALTOGETHER OR ALL TOGETHER?

allude The verb *allude* means 'refer indirectly'; it should not be used in place of the verb *refer* itself: □ *He was alluding to the death of his father when he spoke of the loss of a lifelong friend.* □ *She referred* [not *alluded*] *to 'the spectre of redundancy' in her speech.*

allure or **lure**? Both these words may be used as a noun or as a verb. The verbs *allure* and *lure* are virtually synonymous in the sense of 'entice', 'tempt', or 'attract', but *lure* is by far the more frequent: □ *They tried to lure her away.* The verb *allure* is most frequently found in the form of the present participle, used as an adjective: □ *an alluring proposition.*

allusion, illusion, or **delusion**? An *allusion* is an indirect reference (see ALLUDE); an *illusion* is a false or misleading impression or perception; a *delusion* is a false or mistaken idea or belief: □ *an allusion to his schooldays at Eton* □ *an optical illusion* □ *to destroy one's illusions* □ *delusions of grandeur* □ *to labour under a delusion.*

allusive, elusive, or **illusive**? The adjectives *allusive* and *illusive* relate to the nouns *allusion* and *illusion* respectively (see ALLUSION, ILLUSION, OR DELUSION?); *elusive* means 'difficult to catch, find, achieve, describe, define, remember, etc.': □ *an allusive style* □ *an illusive hope* □ *an elusive quality.*

almond This word is sometimes mispronounced. The *-l-* is silent, as in calm; the correct pronunciation is [*ah*mŏnd].

alone or **lone**? *Alone* and *lone* are both used in the sense of 'solitary' or 'by oneself', but *alone* is always placed after the verb and *lone* before the noun: □ *She was alone.* □ *a lone cyclist* □ *The house stood alone.* □ *a lone tree. Lone* tends to be used more in literary or poetic contexts. There is also some difference in meaning: *alone* is more likely to suggest loneliness or a desire for solitude, whereas *lone* usually describes a person or thing that simply happens to be on his/her/its own.

along with In the phrase *along with,* the word *along* is often superfluous: □ *The package was delivered along with the rest of the mail* could be changed to: □ *The package was delivered with the rest of the mail* without affecting the meaning.

alright see ALL RIGHT OR ALRIGHT?

also The use of the adverb *also* in place of the conjunction *and* is disliked and avoided by many users, especially in formal writing: □ *Please send me a copy of your new catalogue and a list of local stockists* [not ... *a copy of your new catalogue, also a list* ...].

altar or **alter**? These words are sometimes confused. An *altar* is a place where sacrifices are offered to a god and also the table on which the bread and wine are blessed in Communion services: □ *The priest approached the altar. Alter* with an *e* means 'change': □ *a scheme for radically altering the whole tax system.*

alternate or **alternative**? The adjective *alternate* means 'every other' or 'occurring by turns'; the adjective *alternative* means 'offering a choice' or 'being an alternative': □ *on alternate Saturdays* □ *alternate layers* □ *alternative routes* □ *an alternative suggestion.*

alternative medicine see COMPLEMENTARY MEDICINE OR ALTERNATIVE MEDICINE?

although or **though**? As conjunctions, meaning 'despite the fact that', *although* and *though* are interchangeable in most contexts: □ *We bought the table, although/though it was damaged.*

altogether or **all together**? The adverb *altogether* means 'in all' or 'completely'; *all together* means 'at the same time' or 'in the same place': □ *She has nine pets altogether.* □ *Your system is altogether different from ours.* □ *They disappeared altogether.* □ *They arrived all together.* □ *We keep our reference books all together on a separate shelf.*

a.m. and **p.m.** Full stops are often retained in the abbreviations *a.m.* (for *ante meridiem*, meaning 'before noon') and *p.m.* (for *post meridiem*, meaning 'after noon') to distinguish *a.m.* from the verb *am.*

amateur This word, meaning 'person who follows an activity as a pastime rather than as a profession': □ *an amateur golfer*, has several pronunciations, the most frequent being [*am*ătĕ]. The pronunciations [*am*ăchĕ], [*am*ătewr], and [amă*ter*] are also heard.

ambience Some people object to the frequent use of the noun *ambience* as a pretentious synonym for 'atmosphere': □ *the ambience of the restaurant.*

ambiguous or **ambivalent**? *Ambiguous* means 'having two or more possible interpretations or meanings' or 'obscure'; *ambivalent* means 'having conflicting emotions or attitudes' or 'indecisive': □ *The phrase 'a French horn player' is ambiguous.* □ *Many people are ambivalent about the* *issue of disarmament: they recognize the importance of the nuclear deterrent but feel that the money spent on nuclear weapons could be put to better use.*

amen The word *amen*, meaning 'so be it', may be pronounced [*ay*men] or [*ah*men]. Both pronunciations are correct.

amend or **emend**? Of these two verbs *amend*, meaning 'correct', 'improve', or 'alter', is the more general, *emend* being restricted to the correction of errors in a printed or written text: □ *The ambiguous wording of the opening paragraph has been amended.* □ *They have amended the rules.* □ *The manuscript was emended by an eminent scholar.*

amenity The noun *amenity* is ultimately derived from the Latin word for 'pleasant'. A few users prefer to restrict the term, which is generally used in the plural form *amenities*, to what is conducive to comfort or pleasure, objecting to its extended application to what is merely useful or convenient: □ *The amenities of the hotel include a sauna, swimming pool, licensed restaurant, and 24-hour room service.* □ *The town lacks some of the basic amenities, such as public toilets and a rubbish dump.*

America The word *America* is most frequently used with reference to the United States of America, although it strictly denotes the whole landmass comprising Canada, the USA, Central America, and South America.

Americanisms For many years American English has had a significant influence on British English. Although many British purists dislike American English, in some respects its differences arise from greater conservatism than British English. Such words as: □ *gotten* □ *fall* (autumn) as well as many American spellings, were originally the British forms and have changed in Britain but not in the United States. American English is also a fertile ground for new words and idioms and there is no reason why British English should not borrow the more striking ones. Such American words as: □ *truck* □ *commuter* □ *teenager* have become part of British vocabulary.

amiable or **amicable**? *Amiable* means 'friendly', 'pleasant', 'agreeable', or 'congenial'; *amicable* means 'characterized by friendliness or goodwill': □ *an amiable man* □ *an amicable agreement* □ *She smiled at me in an amiable manner.* □ *The dispute was settled in an amicable manner.*

amid, **amidst**, **mid**, or **midst**? *Amid* and *amidst* are synonymous, and are used in formal or poetic contexts, but *amidst* is used more rarely. Both mean 'in the middle of' or 'among': □ *amid the crowd* □ *amidst the waving reeds.* The word *mid* also means 'in the middle of'; in modern usage it is chiefly found in combination with nouns: □ *mid-September* □ *mid-air. Midst* is most frequently used as a noun, in the phrases *in the midst of*, meaning 'in the middle of' and *in our/their/etc. midst*, meaning 'among us/them/etc.': □ *in the midst of the election campaign* □ *There is a traitor in our midst.*

amok or **amuck**? The work *amok*, pronounced [ă*muk*] or [ă*mok*] and used especially in the phrase *run amok*, 'behave in a violent manner; go berserk', has the rarer spelling *amuck*, pronounced [ă*muk*].

among or **amongst**? The words *among* and *amongst* are interchangeable in all contexts, *among* being the more frequent in modern usage: □ *They hid among/amongst the bushes.* See also BETWEEN OR AMONG?

amoral or **immoral**? *Amoral* means 'not concerned with morality' or 'having no moral standards'; *immoral* means 'not conforming to morality' or 'infringing accepted moral standards': □ *an amoral matter* □ *an amoral politician* □ *immoral behaviour* □ *an immoral young man* □ *Some people consider vivisection to be immoral, others have an amoral attitude to the issue.*

amuck see AMOK OR AMUCK?

an see A OR AN?

anaesthetic This word, meaning 'a substance that produces a loss of feeling', is sometimes misspelt. Note the *ae* in the middle of the word.

analogous The adjective *analogous* is best avoided where *similar, equivalent, comparable, corresponding,* *like*, etc., would be adequate or more appropriate: □ *The new system is analogous to that used in the electronics industry.*

analyse The *s* of *analyse* should not be replaced with *z* in British English, *analyze* being the American spelling of the word.

analysis see ANALYSE.

ancillary This word, meaning 'supplementary or subsidiary': □ *ancillary services*, is sometimes misspelt. Note particularly the *c*, the *-ll-*, and the ending *-ary*, not *-iary*.

and The use of *and* at the beginning of a sentence is disliked by some users but acceptable to most. And it can sometimes be an effective way of drawing attention to what follows.

and/or The phrase *and/or* should only be used where three possibilities are envisaged: □ *cash and/or postage stamps*, for example, means 'cash, postage stamps, or both'.

angle Some people object to the frequent use of the noun *angle* in place of *point of view, standpoint*, etc.: □ *The report has been written from a unilateralist angle.*

annex or **annexe**? In British English *annex* is a verb meaning 'add' or 'appropriate'; *annexe* is a noun that denotes a building built or used as an extension: □ *to annex a state* □ *a room in the annexe.*

anonymous This word, meaning 'of unknown origin or identity': □ *an anonymous donor*, is sometimes misspelt, the most frequent error being to replace the *y* with an *i*.

anorexic or **anorectic**? The words *anorexic* and *anorectic* are interchangeable. Either may be used as a noun or as an adjective to describe a person suffering from the disorder anorexia nervosa, although *anorexic* is used more frequently.

-ant or **-ent**? The suffixes *-ant* or *-ent*, identical in pronunciation, cause frequent spelling problems. Either suffix may be used to form nouns and adjectives: □ *the defendant* □ *a superintendent* □ *a defiant child* □ *an irreverent remark.* However, in many cases where both *-ant* and *-ent* forms exist, *-ant* is the usual form for the noun and *-ent* for the adjective (see CONFIDANT OR CONFIDENT?; DEPENDANT OR DEPENDENT?; PENDANT OR PENDENT?).

ante- or **anti-**? These two prefixes are sometimes confused. *Ante-*, from Latin, means 'before': □ *antenatal* □ *anteroom* □ *antecedent*. *Anti-*, from Greek, means 'against; opposite to': □ *anti-apartheid* □ *anti-aircraft* □ *anti-American* □ *anticlockwise*.

antennae or **antennas**? The noun *antenna* has two plural forms, *antennae* and *antennas*. The plural form *antennae*, pronounced to rhyme with *my* or *tree*, is used to denote an insect's or crustacean's feelers; when *antenna* is used to mean 'aerial' (this sense being of American origin) the plural form *antennas* is preferred.

anti- see ANTE- OR ANTI-?

anticipate The verb *anticipate* is widely used as a synonym for 'expect': □ *We do not anticipate that there will be any problems.* □ *Oil prices showed their expected leap yesterday .... But the rally was not as strong as some traders anticipated* (*Daily Telegraph*). This usage is disliked by many people, who restrict the verb to its accepted more formal senses of 'forestall', 'act in advance of', etc.: □ *Preventative medicine anticipates disease.* □ *They anticipated the attack by boarding up their doors and windows.* □ *You must learn to anticipate his needs.*

antihistamine The word *antihistamine*, which denotes a medicinal substance that is used to treat allergies, is sometimes misspelt. Note the third syllable, *-hist-* (not *-hyst-*), and the *-ine* ending.

antique or **antiquated**? The adjective *antique* is used to describe a piece of furniture or a work of art that is old and valuable: □ *a beautiful antique vase.* The adjective *antiquated*, meaning 'old-fashioned' or 'obsolete', is usually derogatory: □ *an antiquated washing machine* □ *antiquated procedures.*

antisocial, asocial, unsocial, or **unsociable**? These four adjectives are sometimes confused. Both *antisocial* and *unsociable* can mean 'unfriendly', describing somebody who avoids the company of others: □ *Our* *new neighbours seem rather antisocial/unsociable. Antisocial* is the stronger of the two and may also describe behaviour that causes harm or inconvenience to others: □ *an antisocial act/habit. Asocial,* a much rarer word, implies a deeper hostility to or withdrawal from society; *unsocial* is chiefly used in the phrase *unsocial hours*, referring to the time when most people are not at work: □ *You must be prepared to work unsocial hours.*

any The use of a singular or plural verb with the pronoun *any* depends on the sense and context in which it is used: □ *Is any of the furniture damaged?* □ *Ask him if any of his children watch/watches the programme. See also* SINGULAR OR PLURAL?

anybody or **anyone**? The pronoun *anybody* and its synonym *anyone* are interchangeable in all contexts.

apartheid The name of the South African political system *apartheid* may be pronounced in several different ways. Some users prefer the pronunciation [ă*part*hayt] following the Afrikaans original. Other frequently used pronunciations are [ă*part*hīt] and pronunciations in which the *h* is not sounded: [ă*par*tīt] and [ă*par*tīd].

apostrophe The apostrophe is used mainly to denote possession and other relationships: □ *Angela's house* □ *the Church of England's doctrines* □ *the rabbits' warren,* and to indicate omitted letters in contractions: □ *can't* □ *you're* □ *there's.* See also CONTRACTIONS; ITS OR IT'S?

appal Note the spelling of this verb, especially the *-pp-* and (in British English) the single *l*.

apparatus This word is usually pronounced [apă*ray*tŭs] or [*ap*ăraytus], though the pronunciation [apă*rah*tŭs] is also sometimes heard.

appendixes or **appendices**? The noun *appendix* has two accepted plural forms, *appendixes* and *appendices*.

applicable In the more traditional pronunciation of this word, the first syllable is stressed [*ap*likăbl]. The pronunciation with the second syllable stressed [ă*plik*ăbl] is probably more frequently heard, however. See also STRESS.

apposition A noun or phrase that is in apposition supplies further information about another noun or phrase. Both nouns or phrases refer to the same person or thing; they are equivalent in meaning. In the sentence □ *Mary Jones, an accountant, was elected,* the phrases *Mary Jones* and *an accountant* are in apposition. In the phrase □ *the accusation that he had stolen the car, the accusation* and *that he had stolen the car* are in apposition. See also COMMA 3.

appraise, apprise, or **apprize**? To *appraise* is to assess the quality or worth of something; *apprise* means 'inform': □ *She appraised their work.* □ *He apprised me of the details. Apprize* is listed in some dictionaries as a less frequent variant spelling of *apprise*; it is also an archaic verb meaning 'appraise'.

appreciate The frequent use of the verb *appreciate* in place of *realize* or *understand* is disliked by a few users: □ *I appreciate that the child's parents were unaware of the risk.* □ *Do you appreciate our problem?*

apprehend or **comprehend**? These two verbs are sometimes confused when they have the meaning 'understand'. *Comprehend* implies a complete understanding, sometimes emphasizing the mental activity needed to come to such knowledge: □ *They did not fully comprehend the motives that lay behind her decision. Apprehend,* which is used fairly rarely in this sense, implies a perception – not always complete – of the essential quality or significance of something: □ *to apprehend the nature of beauty.*

apprise, apprize see APPRAISE, APPRISE, OR APPRIZE?

a priori The Latin phrase *a priori,* which literally means 'from the previous', is applied adjectivally to deductive or presumptive reasoning, arguments, statements, etc.

apropos As a preposition meaning 'with regard to', *apropos* may be followed by *of*: □ *apropos (of) your enquiry* □ *apropos (of) the new development.*

apt see LIABLE OR LIKELY?

aqueduct The noun *aqueduct,* describing a structure that carries water, is often misspelt. Note that the word begins *aque-*, not *aqua-* (as in *aqualung, aquaplane,* etc.).

Arab, Arabian, or **Arabic**? The adjective *Arab* relates to the people of Arabia and their descendants, *Arabian* to Arabia itself, and *Arabic* to the language of Arabia and other Arab countries: □ *an Arab sheikh* □ *the Arab nations* □ *the Arabian peninsula* □ *the Arabian Sea* □ *an Arabic numeral* □ *Arabic literature.*

arbiter or **arbitrator**? An *arbiter* is a person who has the power to judge or who has absolute control; an *arbitrator* is a person who is appointed to settle a dispute: □ *an arbiter of fashion* □ *an arbiter of human destiny* □ *The arbitrator's decision proved acceptable to both parties.*

arbitrarily The adverb *arbitrarily* should be stressed on the first syllable [*ar*bitrărĕli].

arbitrator see ARBITER OR ARBITRATOR?

arch- and **archi-** The prefixes *arch-* and *archi-* are both derived from a Greek word meaning 'to rule'. In words beginning with the prefix *arch-* the *-ch-* sound is soft, as in *choose*; in words beginning with the prefix *archi-* the *-ch-* sound is hard, as in *chord*: □ *archbishop* [arch*bish*ŏp] □ *architect* [*ar*kitekt].

archaeology This word, describing the study of the material remains of ancient cultures, is spelt with the vowels *-aeo-* in the middle of the word in British English.

archetypal The adjective *archetypal* is best avoided where *typical, characteristic, classic, original,* etc., would be adequate or more appropriate: □ *an archetypal Yorkshire village.*

archi- see ARCH- AND ARCHI-.

Argentine or **Argentinian**? Either word may be used as an adjective, meaning 'of Argentina', or as a noun, denoting a native or inhabitant of Argentina. Though purists prefer *Argentine*, *Argentinian* is more frequent in both senses: □ *the Argentinian/Argentine flag* □ *an Argentinian/Argentine ship* □ *Her stepfather is an Argentinian/Argentine.*

argument Note the spelling of this word. The final *-e* of the verb *argue* is dropped when the suffix *-ment* is added to form the noun.

arise or **rise**? *Arise* means 'come into being', 'originate', or 'result'; *rise* means 'get up', 'move upwards', or 'increase': □ *A problem has arisen.* □ *The quarrel arose from a misunderstanding.* □ *He rose to greet her.* □ *The water level is rising.*

aristocrat In British English this word is usually stressed on the first syllable [aristŏkrat].

around or **about**? In British English *about* is preferred to *around* in the sense of 'approximately': □ *We have about/around 200 employees.* □ *He left at about/around eleven o'clock.*

around or **round**? *Around* and *round* are synonymous in most of their adverbial and prepositional senses, *around* being preferred in American English and *round* in British English: □ *I turned round/around.* □ *The wheels went round/around.* □ *They sat round/around the table.* □ *She wore a gold chain round/around her ankle.*

arouse or **rouse**? *Arouse* means 'stimulate' or 'excite'; *rouse* means 'wake' or 'stir': □ *Their curiosity was aroused.* □ *The ban on smoking has aroused widespread opposition.* □ *The noise of the aeroplanes roused the child.* □ *I was roused to anger by his accusations.*

artefact or **artifact**? Both spellings of this noun, referring to an object made by a person, e.g., a tool with special historical interest, are correct. *Artefact* is probably more frequent in British English and *artifact* in American English.

articles see A OR AN?; THE.

artifact see ARTEFACT OR ARTIFACT?

artist or **artiste**? An *artist* is a person who is skilled in one or more of the fine arts, such as painting or sculpture; an *artiste* is a professional entertainer, such as a singer or dancer: □ *the Dutch artist Vincent Van Gogh* □ *the music-hall artiste Marie Lloyd.*

as The *as … as* construction may be followed by a subject pronoun or an object pronoun: □ *She loves the child as much as he* [as much as he does]. □ *She loves the child as much as him* [as much as she loves him].

ascent see ASSENT OR ASCENT?

ascetic see AESTHETIC, ASCETIC, OR ACETIC?

as far as The phrase *as far as … is concerned* can often be replaced by a simple preposition: □ *The course is a waste of time for the more experienced students* [not *as far as the more experienced students are concerned*].

as for see AS TO.

as from The phrase *as from* is best avoided where *from, on, at,* etc., would be adequate or more appropriate: □ *I shall be available for work from* [not *as from*] *next Monday.* □ *Sunday deliveries will cease on* [not *as from*] *1 November.* □ *The increase will come into effect at* [not *as from*] *midnight.*

Asian or **Asiatic**? Either word may be used as an adjective, meaning 'of Asia', or as a noun, denoting a native or inhabitant of Asia. *Asian* is preferred in both senses, the use of *Asiatic* with reference to people being considered racially offensive: □ *an Asian/Asiatic country* □ *an Asian* [not *Asiatic*] *doctor* □ *an Asian* [not *Asiatic*] *living in Europe.* See also INDIAN.

as if or **as though**? *As if* and *as though* are interchangeable in most contexts: □ *The car looked as if/though it had been resprayed.* □ *She trembled, as if/though aware of our presence.* □ *He opened his mouth as if/though to speak.*

asocial see ANTISOCIAL, ASOCIAL, UNSOCIAL, OR UNSOCIABLE?

as of see AS FROM.

as per The use of the phrase *as per* in place of *according to* is widely regarded as COMMERCIALESE: □ *as per instructions* □ *as per the specifications.*

asphalt This word, used to describe a material used in road-surfacing, is often misspelt. Note particularly the *sph*. The preferred pronunciation is [*as*falt], although [*ash*falt] is also heard.

asphyxiate This word, meaning 'suffocate', is sometimes misspelt. Note particularly the *phy*, as in *physics*.

assassinate This word, meaning 'murder an important person': □ *The president was assassinated,* is often misspelt. Remember the *-ss-*, which occurs twice.

assent or **ascent**? These two

words are sometimes confused, being identical in pronunciation. The noun *assent* means 'agreement' (see ASSENT OR CONSENT?); the noun *ascent* means 'the act of ascending', 'a climb', or 'upward slope': □ *She gave her assent.* □ *the ascent of Everest.*

assent or **consent**? Either word may be used as a verb, meaning 'agree', or as a noun, meaning 'agreement'. The verb *consent* sometimes implies greater reluctance than *assent*: □ *They readily assented to our plan.* □ *After hours of persuasion they consented to end the strike.*

assertion or **assertiveness**? An *assertion* is a positive statement or declaration; *assertiveness* is the state of being dogmatic or aggressive: □ *to make an assertion* □ *assertiveness training.* Careful users maintain the distinction between the two nouns.

assignation or **assignment**? Both these nouns may be used to denote the act of assigning: □ *the assignation/assignment of household chores.*

assimilate This word, meaning 'absorb or integrate', is often misspelt. The only double letters are the *-ss-*.

assume or **presume**? In the sense of 'suppose' or 'take for granted' the verbs *assume* and *presume* are virtually interchangeable: □ *I assume/presume you will accept their offer.*

assurance or **insurance**? Both *assurance* and *insurance* are used to denote financial protection against a certainty, such as the death of the policyholder: □ *life assurance* □ *life insurance.*

assure, ensure, or **insure**? To *assure* is to state with conviction or to convince; to *ensure* is to make certain; to *insure* is to protect financially: □ *He assured me that the carpet would not be damaged.* □ *Please ensure that you do not damage the carpet.* □ *I insured the carpet against accidental damage.*

asthma This word, which describes the disorder that makes breathing difficult, is sometimes misspelt, the most frequent error being in the combination of the consonants *sthm*.

as though see AS IF OR AS THOUGH?

as to Many people object to

the unnecessary use of *as to* before *whether, what, why,* etc.: □ *There is some doubt (as to) whether she is suitably qualified.* □ *He offered no explanation (as to) why he was late.*

astrology or **astronomy**? These two nouns are sometimes confused. *Astrology* is the study of the movements of the planets and their effect on human affairs; *astronomy* is the scientific study of the universe.

astronomical The use of the adjective *astronomical* in the sense of 'very large' is best restricted to informal contexts: □ *an astronomical increase in crime* □ *astronomical prices.*

astronomy see ASTROLOGY OR ASTRONOMY?

as well as When two or more verbs are linked by the phrase *as well as,* in the sense of 'in addition to', the verb that follows *as well as* is usually an *-ing* form: □ *The burglar broke a valuable ornament, as well as stealing all my jewellery.* □ *As well as weeding the borders, the gardener pruned the roses and mowed the lawn.*

as yet The phrase *as yet,* meaning 'up to now' or 'so far', is best avoided where *yet* would be adequate: □ *Have you sold any tickets yet* [not *as yet*]*?* □ *I haven't sold any tickets (as) yet.* □ *No tickets have been sold (as) yet.* □ *Only a few tickets have been sold as yet.*

at or **in**? *At* is traditionally used before the name of a village or small town, *in* before the name of a large town, city, country, etc.: □ *He lives at Great Snoring.* □ *They stayed at Keswick.* □ *She works in Southampton.* □ *We have a house in Scotland.*

ate This word, which is the past tense of the verb *eat,* is pronounced [et] or [ayt] in British English.

-ate A number of words ending in *-ate* may be used as adjectives (and/or nouns) and verbs. In these adjectives and nouns the ending *-ate* is pronounced [-ăt]; in verbs it is pronounced [-ayt]. For example, the adjective *animate* is pronounced [*an*imăt] whereas the verb is pronounced [*an*imayt], and the noun *delegate* is pronounced [*de*ligăt], whereas the verb is pronounced [*de*ligayt].

attach This word, meaning

'join or fasten', is sometimes misspelt. Note the *-tt-* and the *ch*. There is no *t* before the *ch*.

at the sharp end To be *at the sharp end* of an activity is to be involved in the area in which there is the greatest difficulty or danger: □ *football referees at the sharp end of violence on the field and also criticism from the media* □ *'Nurses' ... a repeat of the* [television] *series on life at the sharp end of the National Health Service* (*The Guardian*). Care should be taken to avoid using this expression, which is best restricted to informal contexts.

at this moment in time Many people object to the frequent use of the cliché *at this moment in time* in place of *now*: □ *I am not in a position to comment on the situation at this moment in time.*

attribute The verb *attribute*, meaning 'ascribe', is generally used with the preposition *to*: □ *They attributed the accident to careless driving.* □ *To what do you attribute your success?* □ *The idea was attributed to his colleague.*

attributive see ADJECTIVES.

au fait *Au fait* means 'familiar', 'informed', or 'competent': □ *Are you au fait with the procedure?*

aural or **oral**? These two words are sometimes confused, partly because they both often have the same pronunciation [*awrăl*]. *Aural* means 'of the ear or the sense of hearing', *oral* means 'of the mouth; expressed in speech'. An *aural comprehension* tests a person's ability to understand a spoken language; an *oral examination* is one in which the questions and answers are spoken, not written.

Australianisms There are fewer differences between Australian and British English than between American and British English, probably because until comparatively recently nearly all settlers in Australia were British or Irish. The words that were adopted by the early settlers from the Aboriginal languages: □ *koala* □ *boomerang*, are now in general use, and most British people are familiar with those Australian words which were coined in the context of the early days of European settlement: □ *outback* □ *bushranger* □ *swagman* □ *digger* □ *walkabout.*

author The use of the word *author* as a verb, in place of *write*, is disliked and avoided by careful users in all contexts: □ *She has written* [not *authored*] *a number of books on the subject.*

authoritarian or **authoritative**? The adjective *authoritarian* means 'favouring obedience to authority as opposed to individual freedom'; *authoritative* means 'having authority' or 'official': □ *an authoritarian father* □ *an authoritarian regime* □ *an authoritarian policy* □ *an authoritative voice* □ *an authoritative article* □ *an authoritative source.*

avenge see REVENGE OR AVENGE?

averse see ADVERSE OR AVERSE?

avoid, evade, or **elude**? *Avoid* means 'keep away from'; *evade* and *elude* mean 'avoid by cunning or deception': □ *He avoided the police by turning down a side street.* □ *He evaded the police by hiding in the cellar.* □ *He eluded the police by using a series of false names.*

avoidance see AVOID, EVADE, OR ELUDE?

await or **wait**? *Await* is principally used as a transitive verb, meaning 'wait for' or 'be in store for'; *wait* is chiefly used intransitively, often followed by *for*, in the sense of 'remain in readiness or expectation': □ *They awaited the verdict of the jury with trepidation.* □ *I wonder what adventures await you in your new career.* □ *She asked us to wait outside.* □ *He waited for the rain to stop.*

awake, awaken, wake, or **waken**? All these verbs may be used transitively or intransitively in the literal senses of 'rouse or emerge from sleep' and the figurative senses of 'make or become aware': □ *Please waken me at six o'clock.* □ *He wakes earlier in the summer.* □ *Her sister's plight awakened her to the problems faced by single parents.* □ *They awoke to the dangers of drug abuse. Wake* and *waken* are preferred in literal contexts and *awake* and *awaken* in figurative contexts.

award-winning The adjective *award-winning*, which is frequently used in advertising, is meaningless unless the nature of the award is specified: □ *an award-winning design* □ *an award-winning writer*. It is therefore best avoided or replaced with a more precise synonym, such as *excellent* or *remarkable*.

aware The use of the adjective *aware* before the noun it qualifies, in the sense of 'knowledgeable' or 'alert', is disliked by many users: □ *one of our more aware students* □ *financially aware individuals*.

awesome The adjective *awesome* is used as a slang term of approval, especially by young people: □ *'What was the party like?' 'Awesome!'* In formal contexts it should be restricted to the sense of 'inspiring admiration or dread': □ *an awesome responsibility*.

awful see AWFULLY.

awfully The use of the adverb *awfully* as an intensifier is best restricted to informal contexts: □ *I'm awfully sorry.* □ *It's awfully difficult to decide which to buy.*

axe In journalese the verb *axe* is frequently used in the sense of 'dismiss', 'terminate', 'remove', etc.: □ *Britain's biggest teaching union, the National Union of Teachers, is to axe a third of its head office staff* (*Sunday Times*). □ *Coloroll, the wallpaper and furnishing company, is to axe 120 jobs* (*Daily Telegraph*). □ *Saturday Review, the BBC's current arts magazine programme ... will be axed after a final series starting in October* (*Sunday Times*).

axes *Axes* is the plural of *axe* or *axis*: □ *axes for chopping wood* □ *the horizontal and vertical axes*. The plural of *axe* is pronounced [*ak*siz] and the plural of *axis* is pronounced [*ak*seez].

B

-babble Many people dislike the increasing use of the suffix *-babble* to coin new words for particularly incomprehensible types of jargon: □ *technobabble*. See also -SPEAK.

bachelor This word, meaning 'unmarried man': □ *a confirmed bachelor*, is sometimes misspelt. The most frequent error is to insert a *t* before the *ch*.

back burner The phrase *on the back burner* is often used, especially in informal contexts, in the figurative sense of 'deferred' or 'postponed': □ *'Priorities will be made, and some things will be put on a back burner.'* (*The Guardian*). Care should be taken not to overuse this phrase.

back formation Back formation is a way of creating new words, usually verbs, by removing an affix from an existing word: □ *donate* (from *donation*) □ *extradite* (from *extradition*). Many such words have been used for so long that they are no longer recognized as back formations: □ *edit* (from *editor*) □ *laze* (from *lazy*) □ *burgle* (from *burglar*) □ *enthuse* (from *enthusiasm*).

background Some people object to the use of the word *background* to mean 'the circumstances that relate to, lead up to, or explain an event or experience', preferring to use such words as *circumstances, conditions, context,* or *setting* instead.

backlash *Backlash* is used metaphorically to describe a strong adverse reaction to a recent event or political/social development or tendency: □ *the backlash against the Government's radical new changes in education policy*.

backward or **backwards**? In British English *backward* is principally used as an adjective, *backwards* being the usual form of the adverb meaning 'towards the back' or 'in reverse': □ *a backward step* □ *a backward child* □ *walking backwards* □ *written backwards*. *See also* -WARD OR -WARDS?

bacteria The term *bacteria* refers to all microorganisms exhibiting certain characteristics. They are thought of as disease-bearing, but in fact many are harmless and some essential to human life, although others do cause disease.

bad The adjective *bad* is used as a slang term of approval, especially by young people. The potential ambiguity of this usage is obvious. See also WICKED.

bade *Bade* is a form of the past tense of the verb *bid*: □ *He bade them farewell.* Its traditional pronunciation is [bad], but [bayd] is also acceptable.

bail or **bale**? The spellings of these words are often confused. The primary senses of these words are as follows. *Bail* is the security deposited as a guarantee of the appearance of an arrested person; a *bale* is a large quantity of hay, old newspapers, etc. The associated verbs also follow these spellings: □ *Davies was released on £10,000 bail.* □ *His friends bailed him out for £10,000.* □ *bales of old papers* □ *to bale hay.*

baited or **bated**? These two words are occasionally confused. *Baited* means 'provoked or teased' or 'hooked or trapped with food to attract a fish or animal'. *Bated* is used only in the expression *with bated breath*, meaning 'tense with anxiety or excitement'.

balance Some people dislike the frequent use of the noun *balance* in the sense of 'remainder', especially in nonfinancial contexts: □ *The balance of the work will be completed by the end of the month.*

bale see BAIL OR BALE?

baleful or **baneful**? The adjective *baleful* means 'harmful' or 'menacing': □ *a baleful stare.* It should not be confused with the adjective *baneful*, meaning 'destructive' or 'fatal', which is very rare in modern usage.

balk or **baulk**? Either spelling may be used for this word: □ *He balked* [or *baulked*] *at paying such a high price.* □ *The horse* *balked* [or *baulked*] *at the fence.* □ *As usual she was balked* [or *baulked*] *in her ambitions by a man.*

ball game or **ballpark**? Both these terms have informal idiomatic uses, of American origin. In the phrase *a whole new ball game*, *ball game* means 'state of affairs'; in the phrases *in the right ballpark* and *not in the same ballpark*, *ballpark* means 'range' or 'area': □ *a ballpark figure* is an estimate or approximate figure.

balmy or **barmy**? These words are sometimes confused. *Balmy* means 'mild and pleasant': □ *a balmy evening*. *Barmy,* an informal word in British English, means 'foolish'.

baneful see BALEFUL OR BANEFUL?

banister A *banister*, a handrail supported by posts fixed alongside a staircase, has the less common variant spelling *bannister*.

baptismal name see FIRST NAME, CHRISTIAN NAME, FORENAME, GIVEN NAME, OR BAPTISMAL NAME?

barbarian, barbaric, or **barbarous**? *Barbaric* means 'crude, primitive, uncivilized': □ *They discovered a barbaric tribe living in the bush*; or sometimes 'uncultured, unsophisticated': □ *Most teenagers have barbaric tastes in music. Barbarian* as a noun means 'someone living barbarically' and as an adjective is synonymous with *barbaric*. *Barbarous* means 'cruel, harsh, or inhuman': □ *Torture is condemned as a barbarous practice.*

barbecue The word *barbecue* is often misspelt. The most frequent error is the substitution of *-que* for the *-cue* ending, perhaps influenced by advertisements that use the nonstandard phonetic spelling *bar-b-q*.

barely see HARDLY.

barmy see BALMY OR BARMY?

base or **basis**? Both *base* and *basis* mean 'a foundation, substructure, or support'. *Base* is usually used to refer to the bottom support of a tangible object: □ *the base of a pillar*, while *basis* is used for abstract or theoretical foundations: □ *on the basis of all the evidence received* □ *The new pay scale provides a sound basis for the new contract.*

basically The literal sense of *basically* is 'concerning a base or basis, fundamentally': □ *His argument has a superficial persuasiveness but it is basically flawed.* □ *I believe she is basically a good person.* It is often used to mean no more than 'importantly'. It has recently become fashionable to put it at the beginning of a sentence, where its presence is often superfluous: □ *Basically, I don't think he should have been offered the job.*

basis see BASE OR BASIS?

bated see BAITED OR BATED?

bath or **bathe**? In British English the verb *bath* means 'have a bath (in a bathroom)', or 'wash someone else in a bath': □ *bath the baby,* while the noun means 'the vessel in which one baths, or the act of washing in a bath'. *Bathe* means 'immerse in liquid, apply water or soothing liquid to (a wound)', or 'swim, usually in the sea, for pleasure': □ *Who's coming for a bathe?* In American English *bathe* is used to mean 'to have a bath' and does not have the transitive use of *bath*.

bathroom see TOILET, LAVATORY, LOO, OR BATHROOM?

battalion The word *battalion*, denoting a military unit, is sometimes misspelt. Note the consonants *-tt-* and *-l-*, which are the same as those in the word *battle*.

baulk see BALK OR BAULK?

BC see AD AND BC.

be The infinitive *be* is used in some British dialects in place of other parts of the verb: □ *It be a fine day*. In standard speech it is used mainly in imperatives: □ *Be quiet!*, after *to*: □ *You ought to be careful*, and after an auxiliary verb: □ *He should be home soon.*

beat or **beaten**? *Beat* is the past tense and *beaten* the past participle of the verb *beat*: □ *He beat the eggs.* □ *She has beaten the champion.*

beautiful This word, meaning 'delightful to the senses': □ *a beautiful woman* □ *a beautiful sunset,* is sometimes misspelt. Note particularly the first letters *beau-*.

because The conjunction *because* means 'for the reason that': □ *You're cold because you need warmer clothes.*

because, as, for, or **since**? All these words are used to introduce clauses which give the reason for whatever has been said in the main clause. *As* and *since* are used more often at the beginning of a sentence than *because*, and tend to be used when the reason is already well known or when the reason is not considered as important as the main statement. Ambiguity in the use of *as* should be avoided, since it can mean both 'while' and 'because'. *For* always comes between the elements it joins and places equal emphasis on the main statement and the reason.

because of see DUE TO, OWING TO, OR BECAUSE OF?

befriend Some people dislike the increasing use of the verb *befriend* in the sense of 'make friends with': □ *She soon befriended her new neighbours.* The traditional meaning of the verb is 'act as a friend to (by giving assistance or showing kindness)'.

beggar This word, describing a person who begs, is sometimes misspelt. Note the ending *-ar*, not *-er*.

beg the question To *beg the question* is sometimes used as if it meant 'evade the question skilfully' or even 'raise the question'. In fact it means 'base an argument on an assumption whose truth is the very thing that is being disputed'.

behalf To speak or act *on behalf of* someone else is to act as the representative of that person or those people: □ *I am speaking on behalf of my union.*

beige This word, describing a very pale brown colour, is sometimes misspelt. Note the *ei* and the soft *g*. See also SPELLING 5.

bells and whistles The phrase *bells and whistles* is used in informal English to refer to the nonessential facilities and special features that are used to promote sales of a particular computer, software package, or similar product: □ *This system's got fewer bells and whistles, but it's half the price.* The phrase should not be overused.

beloved This word, meaning 'dearly loved', may be pronounced [bi*luv*id] or [bi*luvd*]. Either is acceptable.

below, beneath, under, or **underneath**? These words all mean 'lower than', and the distinctions between them are subtle. *Below* and *under* are often synonymous; *below* is contrasted with *above,* and *under* with *over. Below* alone is used to refer to written material following: □ *See chapter 5 below,* and is more often used in comparison of levels: □ *She lives in the flat below.* □ *He was below me in rank. Under* is used in reference to being subject to authority: □ *He served under Montgomery. Underneath* is used mainly for physical situations, and often suggests proximity: □ *She kept her savings underneath her mattress. Beneath* can be synonymous with *underneath* but sounds either old-fashioned or poetic; it is now used mainly to mean 'unworthy of': □ *beneath contempt.*

beneficent, beneficial see BENEVOLENT, BENIGN, BENEFICENT, OR BENEFICIAL?

benefit Note the single *-t-* in the spelling of the past tense: □ *benefited* and the present participle: □ *benefiting.*

benevolent, benign, beneficent, or **beneficial**? These are all adjectives suggestive of doing or intending good. *Benevolent* means 'disposed to do good; charitable': □ *a donation from a benevolent well-wisher. Benign* means 'kind, mild, and well-disposed' and can be used of things as well as people: □ *a benign climate*; it is also used as a medical term meaning 'non-cancerous': □ *a benign tumour. Beneficent* means 'doing good; promoting good' and is used of people, while *beneficial* means 'promoting good or well-being' and is often used of things: □ *The waters are said to be beneficial to one's health.*

bereft *Bereft* was formerly synonymous with *bereaved* but is now used mainly to suggest loss or deprivation of any nonmaterial thing: □ *He was now bereft of all hope.*

beside or **besides**? *Beside* means literally 'by the side of': □ *Come and sit beside me*, and is also used in the expression *beside oneself*, meaning 'extremely agitated': □ *He was beside himself with grief. Besides* can mean 'moreover': □ *I won't be able to go; besides, I don't want to*, 'as well as': □ *Besides the usual curries,* *the restaurant offers some unusual tandoori specialities*, and 'except for; other than': □ *He's interested in nothing besides cricket.*

best-before date see SELL-BY DATE.

best-selling *Best-selling* is the adjective derived from *best-seller*, which is applied to anything which has sold very well, but particularly a book which has sold a great number of copies: □ Sue Townsend, author of the best-selling *Adrian Mole* books.

bet or **betted**? *Bet* is the usual form of the past tense and past participle: □ *They bet me £10 I wouldn't do it.*

bête noire A *bête noire* is something that a person fears or hates: □ *Rock music is her bête noire.* The phrase is of French origin and is sometimes written or printed in italics in English texts.

betted see BET OR BETTED?

better The phrase *had better* means 'ought to' or 'should': □ *You had better close the window.* □ *She'd better stay here.* Careful users do not drop the word *had* (or its contraction *'d*), even in informal contexts: □ *I'd better apologize*, not *I better apologize*. This last form, without *had* or *'d*, is common in informal speech, but it should be avoided when writing.

between The preposition *between* is used either before a plural noun: □ *the interval between the acts* or in conjunction with *and*; it should not be used with *or*: □ *You must choose between your family life and* [not *or*] *your work.*

between or **among**? *Between* is traditionally used when speaking of the relationship of two things, and *among* of three or more: □ *There was a clear hostility between George and Henry.* □ *There was dissent among the committee members.*

bi- The prefix *bi-* always means 'two' but sometimes in the sense of doubling: □ *bicycle* □ *bifocal*, and sometimes halving: □ *bisection.* This is particularly confusing with words like *biweekly*, which sometimes means 'every two weeks' and sometimes 'twice a week'. It is probably best to avoid *biweekly* and *bimonthly* and express in a fuller form what is intended.

bias The doubling of the final *s* of the word *bias* before a suffix beginning with a vowel is optional. Most dictionaries give *biased*, with *biassed* as an acceptable alternative.

Bible or **bible**? The noun *Bible* is spelt with a capital *B* when it refers to the sacred writings of the Christian religion: □ *the first book of the Bible* □ *a Bible reading.* When the noun refers to a copy of the book containing these writings, it may be spelt with a lower-case *b*-: □ *I bought her a bible for Christmas.* The noun is also spelt with a lower-case *b*- when it refers to an authoritative book on a particular subject: □ *the gardener's bible.*

bid The noun *bid*, normally meaning 'an offer', takes on a new meaning in popular journalism, where it is used, particularly in headlines, to mean 'an attempt or effort': □ *Athlete's bid for title* □ *Rescue bid fails* □ *Vicar's bid to cut family breakdowns.*

big bang The *big-bang theory* is a cosmological theory that suggests that the universe originated in an explosion of a mass of material. The term is increasingly used in general contexts to denote any sudden radical change or reform.

billion *Billion* has traditionally meant 'one million million' in Britain. However, in the United States it means 'one thousand million' and this usage has been increasingly adopted in Britain and internationally.

bimbo *Bimbo* is a slang term used in a derogatory manner, especially by the media. It is applied to an attractive but unintelligent young woman, especially one who has a much-publicized affair with somebody who is in the public eye.

bio- The prefix *bio-* comes from the Greek word *bios*, meaning 'life', and words beginning with it have a connection with life or living organisms: □ *biology* □ *biography* □ *biopsy.*

bivouac The verb *bivouac* adds a *-k-* before the suffixes *-ed* and *-ing*: □ *We bivouacked halfway up the mountain.* See also SPELLING 1.

bizarre Note the spelling of this word, meaning 'eccentric or odd', particularly the single *-z-* and the *-rr-*.

black *Black* is the word now usually applied to dark-skinned people of Afro-Caribbean origins and is the term most black people themselves prefer: □ *black power* □ *black consciousness.* In Britain it is sometimes extended to include other nonwhite races. *Coloured* is considered offensive as it groups all non-Caucasians. In South Africa it is a technical term used to refer to South Africans of mixed descent. The terms *Negro* and *Negress* are also considered offensive.

black hole The term *black hole,* originally used in astronomy, is increasingly found in figurative contexts, where it is used with a variety of meanings: □ *an economic black hole* □ *It is likely that many of the 'black holes' in BCCI's accounts ... can be put down to transactions connected with the nuclear bomb project* (*The Guardian*).

blame *Blame,* as a verb, means 'hold responsible; place responsibility on': □ *He was blamed for the accident.* The expression *blame (it) on:* □ *They all blame it on me* is disliked by some careful users, who would substitute: □ *They blame me for it* or: *They put the blame on me.* However, the usage is well-established and is acceptable in all but very formal contexts.

blanch or **blench**? Both these verbs mean 'make or become white' or 'make or become pale'. *Blanch* may be applied to people or things and is more frequently used as a transitive verb: □ *The sun had blanched the rug.* □ *Her face was blanched with fear. Blench* is chiefly applied to people and is more frequently used as an intransitive verb: □ *He blenched with shock.*

blatant or **flagrant**? *Blatant* and *flagrant* are both concerned with overtly offensive behaviour but their usage is not identical. *Blatant* means 'crassly and conspicuously obvious': □ *The article was blatant propaganda. Flagrant* means 'conspicuously shocking or outrageous': □ *The European parliament sees the tougher measures as a 'flagrant violation of human rights and justice'* (*Sunday Times*).

blench see BLANCH OR BLENCH?

blends A *blend*, also known as a *portmanteau word*, is a new word that is formed by joining parts of two other words, usually the beginning of one and the end of the other, such as: □ *brunch* (*br*eakfast + l*unch*) □ *motel* (*mo*tor + ho*tel*). Many of these words fill a genuine gap in the English language; others are best restricted to informal contexts.

blessed This word sometimes causes problems with pronunciation. The word *blessed*, the past tense of the verb *bless*: □ *He blessed the child*, is pronounced [blest]. The noun or adjective *blessed*: □ *the Blessed Sacrament*, is usually pronounced [*bles*-id] but is occasionally pronounced [blest].

blip *Blip*, a term used in radar, has developed the figurative sense of 'sudden change or interruption; temporary minor problem'.

bloc or **block**? The noun *bloc* denotes a group of people or nations that have political aims or interests in common: □ *the Communist bloc*. *Block* has a wide range of meanings and uses: □ *a block of wood* □ *a mental block* □ *a block of flats*.

blond or **blonde**? These two spellings of the word meaning 'light in colour' are sometimes confused. *Blond* is used when the subject is masculine: □ *He has blond hair; blonde* is used when the subject is feminine: □ *She is a blonde*.

blue The verb *blue* has the slang sense 'squander': □ *He blued the prize money on drink*. It is synonymous with the verb *blow*, used in the slang sense 'spend freely or recklessly': □ *She blew her inheritance*. The two verbs are virtually interchangeable; neither should be used in formal contexts. Ambiguity or confusion may arise from the fact that *blue* (present tense of *blue*) and *blew* (past tense of *blow*) are identical in pronunciation.

blue-chip *Blue-chip* is originally a Stock Market term referring to a share issue which is considered to be both reliable and profitable: □ *a blue-chip investment*. It is extended to companies and any extremely worthwhile asset or property; it can also mean 'fashionable and exclusive' or 'of the highest standard', but many people dislike this last use of the word.

blueprint A *blueprint* is literally a print used for mechanical drawing, engineering, and architectural designs. The word is used metaphorically to mean any plan, scheme, or prototype: □ *a blueprint for a successful life* □ *the London launch of a policy document, 'A Blueprint for Urban Areas'* (*The Times*). Although a literal blueprint is a finished plan, the metaphorical use, very popular as a jargon and journalistic term, is just as often applied to preliminary schemes. Care should be taken, however, not to overuse this word.

blush or **flush**? Both these verbs mean 'go red in the face'. To *blush* may be a sign of modesty, embarrassment, shame, or guilt; to *flush* may indicate any of these emotions as well as stronger feelings, such as anger, or the effects of alcohol or physical causes.

boat or **ship**? The use of *boat* or *ship* is mainly a matter of size. *Boat* is usually applied to smaller vessels, especially those that stay in shallow or sheltered waters: □ *a rowing boat* and: □ *lifeboat*, and *ship* to larger vessels that travel the open seas: □ *steamship* □ *warship*.

bona fide *Bona fide* is an adjective meaning 'of good faith; genuine or sincere': □ *I will accept any bona fide offer. Bona fides* is a singular noun, meaning 'good faith, sincerity, honest intention': □ *He had no documentary proof but we did not doubt his bona fides.*

born or **borne**? These two spellings are sometimes confused. *Borne* is the past participle of the verb *bear*: □ *They had borne enough pain.* □ *The following points should be borne in mind.* □ *His account is simply not borne out by the facts.* □ *It was borne upon him that the decision was irrevocable.* □ *airborne supplies*. In the sense of 'giving birth', *borne* is used in phrases where the mother is the subject: □ *She has borne six children*, and also in the passive with *by*: □ *borne by her*. *Born* is used for all other passive constructions without *by*: □ *He was born in Italy.* □ *Twins were* *born to her.* □ *a born leader* □ *his Burmese-born wife.*

born again The term *born again* was originally confined to the context of evangelical Christianity, to mean 'converted': □ *a born-again believer.* The term is now often used generally to refer to a conversion to any cause or belief, particularly when accompanied by extreme enthusiasm or fervour.

borne see BORN OR BORNE?

borrow Besides its literal meaning of 'take something for a limited period with the intention of returning it': □ *I borrowed this book from the library, borrow* can also be used metaphorically to refer to words, ideas, etc., taken from other sources: □ *Wagner borrowed this theme from Norse mythology.* □ *Some American slang is borrowed from Yiddish.* One borrows *from,* not *off* someone.

both *Both* is used as a determiner, a pronoun, and a conjunction: □ *Both legs were amputated.* □ *I like both.* □ *He is both an artist and a writer.* It should not be used where more than two elements are involved, as in: □ *She's both selfish, mean, and malicious.*

bottleneck *A bottleneck* is a term originally applied only to narrow stretches of road which cause traffic hold-ups. It is now extended to anything that holds up free movement or progress.

bottom line *Bottom line* is a vogue expression, taken from financial reports where the final line registers the net profit or loss. It can mean 'the most important or primary point of consideration'. Care should be taken not to overuse this phrase.

bottom out To *bottom out* was formerly used to describe a levelling out of something that has reached its lowest point: □ *Industrial output is now bottoming out.* It is more recently being used to suggest that the low point is prior to an upsurge: □ *The market has now bottomed out and is expected to improve by the spring.*

bouquet Some users prefer to pronounce the first syllable of this word [boo-] rather than [bō-], and to stress the second syllable [boo*kay*].

bourgeois This word, meaning 'middle class': □ *a bourgeois mentality*, is sometimes misspelt. Note the first syllable *bour* and the *e* which softens the *g* in the second syllable.

bow The word *bow* has two pronunciations. The noun and verb *bow*, referring to the bending of (part of) the body as a sign of respect, etc., are pronounced to rhyme with *how*. The same pronunciation is used for the noun meaning 'front of a boat or ship'. The noun *bow*, meaning 'looped knot', the *bow* that is used as a weapon, the *bow* that is used to play a violin, and the verb *bow*, meaning 'curve', are pronounced to rhyme with *toe*.

boy A *boy* is a male child or adolescent. The use of the noun as a synonym for 'man' is largely restricted to informal contexts: □ *one of the boys* □ *a local boy*.

boycott This word, meaning 'refuse to deal with': □ *boycott the Olympic games*, is sometimes misspelt. Note the *-tt* at the end of the word.

bracket Some people object to the frequent use of the noun *bracket* in place of *group*, *level*, *range*, etc.: □ *the 25–35 age bracket* □ *a lower income bracket*.

brackets The most frequently used kind of brackets are round brackets, also known as parentheses. They are used to enclose supplementary or explanatory material that interrupts a complete sentence: □ *He asked his scout (as college servants are called in Oxford) to wake him at nine*. The material in parentheses could be removed without changing the meaning or grammatical completeness of the sentence. Round brackets are used, in preference to commas or dashes, when the interruption to the sentence is quite a marked one.

brake or **break**? These words are sometimes confused. A *brake* is a device to slow something down: □ *the handbrake on a car*. *Break* has many meanings including '(cause to) fall into pieces', 'stop', and 'transgress': □ *break a vase* □ *break for lunch* □ *break the law*.

bratpack The noun *bratpack*, often spelt *brat pack*, is a slang term applied (especially by the media) to any group of young people, usually precociously rich and famous, noted for their rowdy or ill-mannered behaviour.

bravado, bravery, or **bravura**? These three nouns are sometimes confused. *Bravery* means 'courage'; *bravado* is a false or outward display of courage or daring; *bravura* is an ostentatious or brilliant display of daring, skill, etc.

breach or **breech**? The word *breach* means 'the breaking or violating of a rule or arrangement': □ *a breach of the peace. Breach* should not be confused with *breech*, 'the rear part of the body' and 'the part of a gun behind the barrel': □ *a breech birth.*

break see BRAKE OR BREAK?

breakthrough *Breakthrough* as a metaphor meaning 'a sudden advance in (particularly scientific or technological) knowledge' has become something of a journalistic cliché. One reads, for example, of: □ *a major breakthrough in cancer research* so frequently that it has lost all impact.

breech, breeches see BREACH OR BREECH?

Brit The noun *Brit*, meaning 'British person', is often used derogatorily. It should be restricted to informal contexts. A British person may be called a *Briton*, but this term is most frequently found in newspaper reports about the British abroad: □ *A coach carrying 58 Britons ... was preparing last night to spend a third night trapped in a motorway service area south of Paris* (*Daily Telegraph*). The informal term *Britisher* is chiefly used by people of other English-speaking nations, not by the British themselves.

Britain The expression *Britain* is often used vaguely, sometimes as a substitute for *Great Britain*, sometimes for the *United Kingdom* or the *British Isles*. As an abbreviation of *Great Britain* it means England, Scotland, and Wales.

Briticisms British English is the basis on which the English of America, Australia, New Zealand, South Africa, the West Indies, and the rest of the English-speaking world is built. To greater or lesser degrees the English of these countries has gone its own way, producing distinct varieties of English, while the English spoken in Britain has its own characteristics, known as Briticisms.

Britisher, Briton see BRIT.

Brittany *Brittany*, the English name of a region of northwest France, is often misspelt. Note the *-tt-* and single *-n-*, unlike *Britannia*.

broach or **brooch**? A *brooch* is a piece of jewellery that is pinned to a garment: □ *a diamond brooch. Broach*, a rare variant spelling of this noun, is most frequently used as a verb, meaning 'introduce' or 'mention': □ *to broach a subject.* Both words are pronounced [brōch].

brochure This word is usually pronounced [*brō*shĕr], although the French-sounding [brō*shoor*] is also possible.

brooch see BROACH OR BROOCH?

brownie points *Brownie points* are notional marks of approval for an action or achievement, especially something that is deliberately or ostentatiously done to win favour: □ *You should get some brownie points for that.*

buffet In the senses 'a counter where food is served' and 'food set out on tables': □ *a buffet car* □ *a buffet lunch, buffet* is pronounced [*buu*fay]. In the sense 'strike sharply': □ *buffeted by the wind*, the pronunciation is [*bu*fit].

bulk *Bulk* means 'thickness, volume, or size; a heavy mass': □ *the vast bulk of the castle walls.* It is also used in the expression *in bulk* to mean 'in large quantities': □ *We buy rice in bulk. Bulk* is frequently used to mean 'the greater part of, the majority'.

bulletin This word, meaning 'statement of news': □ *No further bulletin will be issued this evening*, is sometimes misspelt. Note the *-ll-* and single *t*, as in *bullet*.

bulwark This noun, meaning 'fortification', is sometimes mispronounced. The second syllable is unstressed; the *-ark* ending has the same pronunciation as the *-ock* ending of *hillock*.

buoy The noun and verb *buoy*, meaning 'type of float' or 'keep afloat', and the derived adjective *buoyant*, are sometimes misspelt. The most frequent mistake is to place the *-u-* and the *-o-* in the wrong order.

bureaucracy Note the spelling of this word: the first *u*, the vowels *eau*, and the suffix *-cracy* (not *-crasy*).

burgle, **rob**, or **steal**? To *steal* is to take other people's possessions without permission: □ *He stole her jewellery*. *Burgle* is a back formation from *burglar* and means 'break into a building in order to steal': □ *Their house was burgled when they were on holiday*. *Burglary* always involves unlawful entry. To *rob* is to steal money or property from a person or place, often with violence: □ *rob a bank*. *Rob* is sometimes incorrectly used in place of *steal*: □ *to rob a car* is to take things from a car, not to take the car itself.

burned or **burnt**? Either word may be used as the past tense and past participle of the verb *burn*. In transitive contexts *burned* is preferred in American English and *burnt* in British English; in intransitive contexts *burned* is the preferred form in both: □ *We burnt/burned the letters*. □ *He has burnt/burned his hand*. □ *She burned with anger*. □ *The fire had burned all night*.

bus Although the noun *bus* was originally short for *omnibus* it is now never spelt with an apostrophe. The word was rarely used as a verb until the 1960s.

business This noun, meaning 'occupation', 'commercial activity', or 'matter', is sometimes misspelt. The most frequent mistake is the omission of the letter *-i-*, which is silent in speech.

but There are various problems with the usage of the word *but*. As a conjunction it is used to link two opposing ideas: □ *He lives in Surrey but works in London*. It should not be used to link two harmonious ideas: □ *She is not British-born, but originates from Kenya*, and should not be used in a sentence with *however*, which conveys the same meaning: □ *But their suggestions for improvement, however, were ill-received*. See also CONJUNCTIONS; HELP; NOTHING BUT; NOT ONLY ... BUT ALSO.

buyout A *buyout* is the purchase of a company, often by a group of managers: □ *MFI Furniture, the independent company resulting from the management buy-out from Asda-MFI* (*The Guardian*). □ *And ... certainly in the UK... management buyouts are currently a very popular flavour* (*The Bookseller*).

buzz word A *buzz word* is a vogue word or expression, especially one that is first used in technical jargon and subsequently enters everyday language, usually in a figurative sense. Examples of buzz words that are dealt with in this dictionary are: *bottom line, gravitas, matrix, traumatic.*

by or **bye**? These spellings are sometimes confused. Note the spelling of the following compounds and expressions: □ *by-election* (occasionally, *bye-election*) □ *by-law* (sometimes, *bye-law*) □ *by-pass* □ *by-product* □ *by and by* ('later') □ *by and large* ('generally') □ *by the bye* (occasionally, *by the by*, 'incidentally') □ a *bye* in sports, and □ *bye-bye* (informal for *goodbye*).

by the same token *By the same token* is a fashionable expression meaning 'for the same reason; in a similar way': □ *Middle-aged men should avoid overworking because of the effects of stress on the heart; and by the same token they should avoid fatty foods.* Care should be taken to avoid overusing this phrase.

C

cadre Note the pronunciation of this noun, which means 'unit or nucleus of personnel'. Of French origin, *cadre* is usually pronounced [*kah*dĕ], rhyming with *larder,* in British English. The variant pronunciation [*kah*drĕ], which is closer to the French original, is less frequent but not incorrect.

Caesarean This word, meaning 'of or relating to any of the Caesars', is used particularly in the expression *Caesarean section*, 'the surgical operation for the delivery of a baby by cutting through the wall of the mother's abdomen and into the womb'. The variant spellings *Caesarian*, and, in American English, *Cesarean* or *Cesarian*, are also used. Note, too, that any of these spellings may be written with a lower-case *c*: □ *She had a caesarean.*

café or **cafeteria**? The noun *café* refers to any small restaurant or coffee-bar serving nonalcoholic drinks, snacks, light meals, etc.: □ *a seaside café.* The noun *cafeteria* is more specific, meaning 'self-service restaurant': □ *There is a cafeteria on the third floor.*

caffeine *Caffeine*, pronounced [*ka*feen], is a stimulant substance found in tea and coffee. Note the spelling of the word, especially the *-ff-* and the vowel sequence *-ei-*. It is an exception to the '*i* before *e*' rule (see SPELLING 5).

calendar, **calender**, or **colander**? These words are often confused. A *calendar* tells the date, a *calender* is a machine used to smooth paper or cloth, and a *colander* is a perforated bowl used for draining food.

callous or **callus**? *Callus* is a noun, denoting a hardened or thickened area of skin, especially on the hand or foot. The adjective *callous* is related to this noun, but is most frequently used in the figurative sense of 'unfeeling' or 'insensitive': □ *a callous attitude to the poor.*

calorie Note the spelling of this word, which is a unit for measuring the energy value of food and also a measurement of heat.

calvary see CAVALRY OR CALVARY?

camouflage This word, meaning 'disguise': □ *The trees provided excellent camouflage*, is sometimes misspelt. Note the *ou* and the soft *g*.

can or **may**? The verb *can* means 'be permitted' or 'be able'; the verb *may* means 'be permitted' or 'be likely'. In the sense of 'be permitted', *may* is preferred in formal contexts and *can* is best restricted to informal contexts: □ *Can I come to your party?* □ *May I borrow your pen, please?*

candelabra The word *candelabra*, meaning 'a branched candlestick or lamp', was originally a plural noun, from the singular *candelabrum*. Purists therefore consider it incorrect to speak of: □ *a valuable candelabra* or to say: □ *There were candelabras in every room*, although such usage is widespread.

cannon or **canon**? These two words are sometimes confused. A *cannon* is a large gun and a shot in billiards, a *canon*, with a single *n*, is a ruling laid down by the church, or a title given to a clergyman.

cannot and **can't** In American English *can not* is sometimes written as two words but in British English *cannot* is standard. It may be necessary to write *can not* when the *not* is stressed: □ No, I can *not* lend you any more money, or in sentences like: □ *It can not only blend vegetables but also grind coffee beans*, where the *not* goes with *only*, rather than *can*.

canon see CANNON OR CANON?

can't see CANNOT AND CAN'T.

canvas or **canvass**? *Canvas* is a certain type of woven cloth: □ *a canvas bag* □ *a painting on canvas. Canvass*, with *-ss* at the end, means 'solicit votes'.

-cap The suffix *-cap* relates to restrictions imposed by central government on local council spending and taxation. Under the system of domestic rates, councils could be *rate capped*; the introduction of the community charge (or poll tax) led to such terms as *charge-capping*. The verb is sometimes used independently: □ *The government threatened to cap some councils.*

capability, **capacity**, or **ability**? These words all refer to the power to do something. *Capability* suggests having the qualities needed to do something: □ *She has the capability to handle the work.* *Capacity* suggests being able to absorb or receive: □ *Children are born with the capacity to acquire language.* *Ability* can sometimes suggest above-average skills: □ *He has considerable mathematical ability.*

capital letters Capital letters are used to draw attention to a particular word. They are used to mark the first word of a sentence, a direct quotation, or a direct question within a setence (see also QUESTION MARK; QUOTATION MARKS; SENTENCES). They are sometimes used after a colon (see COLON). They are used for the first word of each line of poetry, and for the major words of titles of literary, musical and artistic works. Capitals are used for proper nouns, including days of the week, months, religious holidays, and historical and cultural periods. Italics, and not capitals, should be used for emphasis.

carat or **caret**? These words are sometimes confused. A *carat* is a unit for measuring the weight of precious stones and a unit for measuring the purity of gold; in this second sense, the spelling *karat* is usually used in American English. A *caret*, spelt with an *e*, is a character used in written or printed matter to indicate that an insertion should be made.

carburettor Note the spelling of this word, particularly the *-u-*, the *-tt-*, and the *-or* ending.

carcass This word, which describes the body of a dead animal: □ *a chicken carcass*, may be spelt *carcass* or *carcase* in British English.

caret see CARAT OR CARET?

caring *Caring* has been used in recent years in such phrases as: □ *the caring professions*, to describe people professionally involved in various kinds of social work, sometimes also including health care and education.

case *Case* is very often loosely used to mean 'state of affairs, the truth' in sentences where it is either redundant or could be replaced by simpler or more specific wording: □ *Is it the case that you are his aunt?* could be changed to: *Are you his aunt?* □ *Teenage pregnancies are now less common than was the case ten years ago* could be changed to: ... *than they were ten years ago*. The expression is acceptable in sentences like: □ *This rule applies in your case*.

caster or **castor**? For the senses 'a swivelling wheel on furniture' and 'a container from which sugar may be shaken', the spelling may be either *castor* or caster.

Finely granulated white sugar is usually *caster sugar*, although the spelling *castor sugar* is also found. The medicinal or lubricating oil, *castor oil*, is, however, always spelt with an *o*.

catalyst A *catalyst* is a scientific term that applies to a substance which speeds up a chemical reaction though itself remaining chemically unchanged. It is also used as a metaphor to apply to a person or event that, by its action, provokes significant change: □ *The shooting of Archduke Ferdinand acted as the catalyst for the outbreak of World War I*. Overuse of the word *catalyst* is disliked by some.

catarrh This word, which describes an inflammation of the throat and nasal passages, is sometimes misspelt. Note particularly the single *t* and the *rrh*.

catastrophic The adjective *catastrophic* comes from *catastrophe* which was originally used in Greek drama to describe the denouement of a tragedy. The word should be applied to extremely severe disasters and tragic events: □ *the catastrophic earthquake in Mexico City*.

catch-22 In Joseph Heller's novel *Catch 22*, published in 1961, the catch in question was that airmen could be excused from flying missions only if they were of unsound mind, but concern for personal safety in the face of danger was evidence of a rational mind, so it was impossible to escape flying missions. *A catch-22 situaion* is any such circular dilemma or predicament from which there is no escape.

Catholic or **catholic**? The word *catholic*, with a lower-case *c-*, is an adjective meaning 'general, wide-ranging, or comprehensive': □ *It is a catholic anthology which includes poems by Shelley, Auden, and Allen Ginsberg. Catholic*, with a capital, as a noun or adjective, usually refers to the Roman Catholic Church: □ *They go to a Catholic school.*

cavalry or **calvary**? These words are sometimes confused. *Cavalry* is used to refer to soldiers trained to fight on horseback and the branch of the army that uses armoured vehicles. *Calvary* is the hill near Jerusalem where Christ was crucified.

caviar or **caviare**? Both of these spellings are acceptable for the word which describes the salted roe of the sturgeon.

ceiling *Ceiling* is frequently used, particularly in economic jargon, to mean 'an upper limit': □ *The organization is urging the Government to put a ceiling on rent rises.* As the word *ceiling*, in its literal meaning, is in constant use, it can sound odd to speak of *increasing* or *reducing a ceiling*, an *unworkable ceiling*, and so on.

celibate *Celibacy* means 'the state of being unmarried, often because of a religious vow'. *Celibate* is used as a noun to describe a person living in a state of celibacy and, by implication, chastity: □ *As celibates, priests find it difficult to give advice on marital problems*, and as an adjective: □ *She never married but chose a celibate life.*

Celsius, **centigrade**, or **Fahrenheit**? All these terms denote scales of temperature. The Celsius and centigrade scales are the same; the degree Celsius is now the principal unit of temperature in both scientific and nonscientific contexts.

Celtic The word *Celtic*, referring to a language or people of Scotland, Wales, Ireland, or Brittany, is usually pronounced [*kel*tik], with a hard initial *C-*.

censure, **censor**, or **censer**? The verbs *censure* and *cen-*

sor are often confused. *Censure* means 'to blame, criticize strongly, or condemn': □ *The judge censured them for the brutality of the attack. Censor* means 'examine letters, publications, films, etc., and remove any material which is considered obscene, libellous, or contrary to government or official policy': □ *All prisoners' mail is censored.* The person who examines letters, etc., in this way is also known as a *censor. Censer* means a vessel used for burning incense.

centenary or **centennial**? Both *centenary* and *centennial* are used to mean a hundred-year anniversary: □ *1982 was the centenary of Joyce's birth. Centennial* is used more frequently in American English and can also be used as an adjective: □ *a centennial celebration.*

centigrade see CELSIUS, CENTIGRADE, OR FAHRENHEIT?

centre or **middle**? *Centre* and *middle* are sometimes used virtually synonymously: □ *Put it in the centre/middle of the table. Centre* is used as a precise geometrical term: □ *the centre of the circle,* whereas *middle* is more often used generally in situations where the geometric centre is not obvious or measurable: □ *the middle of the sea.*

centre on or **centre around**? The verb *centre* can be used with *on* or *upon* or (of a place) *at*: □ *His argument centres on Marxist theory.* □ *The European Parliament is centred at Brussels. Centre round* and *centre around* are frequently used, although they are disliked by many careful users who argue that a centre cannot be *around* anything.

centrifugal There are two pronunciations for this word. The traditional pronunciation stresses the second syllable [sen*tri*fyoogăl], but the alternative pronunciation [sentri*fyoo*găl] is widely used in contemporary English.

centuries People often become confused about when centuries start and end and how one should refer to them. As there was no year 0 AD, we calculate in hundred years from the year 1 AD. This means that the twentieth century began on 1 January 1901 (not 1900) and will end on 31 December 2000.

cereal or **serial**? These two words are sometimes confused. A *cereal* is a plant that produces grain for food: □ *breakfast cereals*. A *serial* is a novel or play produced in several parts and at regular intervals.

ceremonial or **ceremonious**? The adjectives *ceremonial* and *ceremonious* are sometimes confused. Ceremonial means 'marked by ceremony or ritual': □ *The Queen wears her crown only on ceremonial occasions like the opening of Parliament. Ceremonious* means 'devoted to formality and ceremony' and usually carries a slightly pejorative suggestion of overpunctiliousness or pomposity: □ *She presided over the dinner table with a ceremonious air*.

certainty or **certitude**? Both these nouns mean 'the state of being certain'. *Certainty* is by far the more frequent, and is used in a wider range of contexts: □ *a feeling of certainty* □ *the certainty of death*. *Certitude* is a formal or literary word, largely restricted to the state of mind of somebody who is certain: □ *Nothing could disturb his certitude*.

cervical There are two pronunciations for this word, both of which are perfectly acceptable: [*ser*vikăl] and [sĕr*vī*kăl].

cession or **cessation**? These two nouns should not be confused. *Cession* is derived from the verb *cede*, meaning 'yield'; *cessation* is derived from the verb *cease*, meaning 'stop': □ *the cession of territory* □ *the cessation of warfare*.

cession or **session**? *Cession* is the act of yielding (see CESSION OR CESSATION?); a *session* is a meeting or a period of time devoted to a specific activity: □ *the cession of rights/property* □ *a parliamentary session* □ *The court is in session*.

chafe or **chaff**? The verb *chafe* means 'rub'; the old-fashioned verb *chaff* means 'tease': □ *These boots chafe my ankles*. □ *She was chaffed by her colleagues*.

chain reaction *Chain reaction* is an expression from scientific terminology that refers to a chemical or nuclear reaction which creates energy or products that cause further reaction. It is now more often used to mean any series of events where each one sets off the next one, though this usage is disliked by some: □ *The shooting started a chain reaction which culminated in the street riots.*

chair The noun *chair* is sometimes used to denote a person presiding over a meeting, committee, etc., to avoid the potentially sexist terms *chairman* and *chairwoman* and the controversial neologism *chairperson*: □ *The new chair will be elected next week.*

challenge Some people object to the frequent use of the word *challenge* in the sense of 'stimulate' or, as a noun, 'something that is stimulating or demanding': □ *Gifted children need challenging work.*

challenged *Challenged* is a vogue word used to form euphemisms for disability or disadvantage: □ *physically challenged*. See also ABLED; POLITICAL CORRECTNESS.

chamois This word may cause problems with pronunciation and spelling. The antelope *chamois* is pronounced [*sham*wah]. The leather *chamois* made from the skin of this animal or a sheep is usually pronounced [*shami*].

changeable This word, meaning 'liable to change': □ *changeable weather*, is sometimes misspelt. Note the *e* of *change* which is retained before the suffix *-able*.

chaperon or **chaperone**? An older woman who accompanies a young unmarried woman on social occasions is known as a *chaperon* or a *chaperone*. The noun, and its derived verb, may be spelt with or without the final *e*.

character The word *character* can be used of the distinguishing qualities that make up individual people or things, of people with unusual traits, of people portrayed in works of fiction, and of moral firmness and integrity: □ *Such behaviour did not seem consistent with what I knew of her character.* □ *It is a lively town with a great deal of character.* □ *Everyone knows him – he's a real character.* □ *Mrs Gamp is a minor character in* Martin Chuzzlewit. □ *Anyone who takes this job on will need character and determination.*

charisma The word *charisma* was originally used only in theological contexts to refer to supernatural spiritual gifts of healing, speaking in tongues, etc. A *charismatic church* is one where emphasis is placed on the exercise of these gifts. *Charisma* and *charismatic* are now often used to describe a person with unusual qualities of leadership, personal appeal, and magnetism, though care should be taken to avoid overusing these words: □ *Lange is planning to run a presidential-style election campaign, based on his own charisma* (*Sunday Times*).

charted or **chartered**? A *chartered accountant/surveyor/engineer*/etc. is a person who has the required professional qualifications and experience. A *chartered yacht* is a hired yacht. *Chartered* should not be confused with *charted* (derived from the word *chart*): □ *charted territory*.

chattering classes The *chattering classes* are educated middle- and upper-class liberals who frequently air their opinions in the media: □ [Rupert] *Murdoch is contemptuous of the views of those to whom he and … Andrew Neil obsessively refer as the 'chattering classes'* (*The Bookseller*). This vogue term is generally used in a derogatory manner.

chauvinism The word *chauvinism* means 'excessive or fanatical patriotism' and comes from Nicolas *Chauvin*, a soldier of Napoleon's army who was noted for his overzealous patriotism. It is used more loosely to describe any prejudiced belief in the superiority of a group or cause, particularly in the term *male chauvinism* which is often applied by feminists to male supremacists. *Chauvinist* is not synonymous with *sexist*. *Chauvinist* should not be used in this sense unless preceded by *male*.

chequered Note the spelling of this adjective, meaning 'varied; marked by many changes in fortune', most frequently used in such phrases as a *chequered career* and *chequered past*. In British English the adjective is spelt *chequered*; *checkered* is the American English spelling.

chick or **chicken**? A *chick* is a young bird: □ *The chicks have hatched.* □ *eagle chicks*. A *chicken* is a type of domestic fowl and *chicken* is the meat of this fowl: □ *He keeps geese and chickens.* □ *roast chicken.* Either noun may be applied to the young of a domestic fowl: □ *a hen and her chicks* [or *chickens*].

chihuahua Note the unusual spelling of this word, which denotes a breed of tiny dog. These dogs are named after the state of *Chihuahua* in Mexico; the noun is sometimes written with a capital *C*-.

chilblain A sore that is caused by exposure to the cold is known as a *chilblain*. The word is sometimes misspelt, the most common error being to retain the second *l* of *chill*, which has been lost in the formation of this compound noun.

childish or **childlike**? *Childish* is almost always used in a pejorative sense to indicate immaturity and the less endearing characteristics of childhood: □ *She refused to tolerate his selfish behaviour and childish outbreaks of temper.* □ *The drawings looked like childish scribbles. Childlike* is usually applied to the attractive qualities of childhood, such as enthusiasm and innocence: □ *At 85, she retains a childlike curiosity about her environment.*

Chinese *Chinese* as an adjective means 'of or from China': □ *Chinese writing*; it is also used as a singular or plural noun for a person or people of Chinese nationality: □ *I took a party of Chinese around London.* □ *There is a Chinese studying at my college.*

chiropodist This word, describing a person who treats and looks after people's feet, may be pronounced [ki*ro*pŏdist] or [shi*ro*pŏdist], although the first of these is preferred by many users.

cholesterol This word is sometimes misspelt. The most frequent error is the omission of the second *e*, often silent in speech.

chord or **cord**? These spellings are sometimes confused. In the musical or mathematical senses the spelling is *chord. Chord* is also used when describing an emotional reaction: □ *He struck the right chord.* In the anatomical sense: □ *umbilical cord* □ *spinal cord,* either spelling is acceptable, although in vocal cords the word is nearly always spelt without the *h*. The word which describes any type of string is spelt *cord*: □ *nylon cord*.

Christian name see FIRST NAME, CHRISTIAN NAME, FORENAME, GIVEN NAME, OR BAPTISMAL NAME?

chronic *Chronic* means 'long-standing; permanently present': □ *She has suffered from chronic asthma all her life.* □ *Malnutrition is a chronic problem in the Third World.* It is often confused, in its medical context, with *acute*, which means 'intense and of sudden onset'. It is sometimes used in informal British English to mean 'bad' or 'dreadful'.

chutzpah *Chutzpah* or *chutzpa* is a Yiddish expression now in general use which, in one word, conveys 'cheek, gall, effrontery, audacity, cool nerve, brazen self-confidence, arrogance'.

circumstances *In the circumstances* and *under the circumstances* are used in slightly different ways. *In the circumstances* is more general, and merely acknowledges the existence of a situation: □ *In the circumstances you had better do nothing. Under the circumstances* suggests more of a connection between the circumstances and the action: □ *He was starving and under the circumstances cannot be blamed for stealing food.*

cirrhosis This word, denoting a disease of the liver, is sometimes misspelt. Note particularly the *-rrh-* combination.

city or **town**? In general a *city* is a place that is larger and more important than a *town*.

civic, civil, or **civilian**? These words all refer to citizenship but have different meanings. *Civic* means 'of a city': □ *civic centre*, or is used of the attitudes of citizens to their city: □ *a sense of civic pride. Civil* relates to citizens of a state, rather than a city: □ *civil rights*, or is used as distinct from criminal, religious, or military: □ *civil law* □ *civil marriage* □ *civil defence. Civilian* refers to a person who is not a member of the armed forces, police, or other official uniformed state organization.

clad or **clothed**? *Clad* means the same as *clothed* but, except in expressions like *thinly clad* or *ill-clad*, is considered archaic or poetic. It can be used of things other than clothes: □ *rose-clad trellises*, or of clothes where the note of archaism is appropriate: □ *clad in armour*, but for ordinary dress, *clothed* is used.

claim The verb *claim* means 'demand something as a right': □ *The dismissed workers are claiming redundancy pay*; 'take something one rightfully owns or that is one's due': □ *He claimed his father's estate.* □ *She claimed the prize*, and 'assert forcefully, especially when faced with possible contradiction': □ *He claims that there have been no composers of genius since Beethoven.*

clandestine This word, meaning 'secret', is generally stressed on the second syllable [klan*des*tin], although it is acceptable to stress the word on the first syllable [*klan*dĕstin].

classic or **classical**? There is some overlap in the meanings of *classic* and *classical*, but they have distinct separate meanings. *Classic* means 'typical of or unusually fine in its class': □ *classic symptoms of diabetes* □ *a classic example of 1960s pop art. Classical* essentially means 'of the classics, i.e. the literature, history, and philosophy of ancient Greece and Rome'.

clause A *clause* is a group of words, including a finite verb, within a compound or complex sentence. A *main clause* can stand alone as a sentence in its own right; it is expanded by a *subordinate clause.* A *relative clause* modifies the subject or object of a sentence.

claustrophobia The fear of being in confined spaces is known as *claustrophobia*. Note the *claustro-* in the spelling.

clean or **cleanse**? While *clean* functions as adjective, noun, adverb, and verb, *cleanse* is used only as a verb. The two words are almost synonymous but *cleanse* has more of a suggestion of very thorough cleaning which also purifies: □ *I'll just clean the flat quickly.* □ *The wound must be cleansed before a dressing is applied.*

clench or **clinch**? These two words are sometimes confused. The verb *clench* means 'close tightly' or 'grasp firmly': □ *to clench one's teeth* □ *She clenched the key in her hand.* The verb *clinch* is most frequently used in the sense of 'settle definitely': □ *to clinch a deal.*

clichés The word *cliché*, referring to a phrase or idiom that has become stale through overuse, is almost always used pejoratively. Examples of clichés are: □ *from time immemorial* □ *as old as the hills* □ *last but not least.*

client or **customer**? A *client* is someone who receives the services of a professional person or organization, while a *customer* is someone who buys goods from a shop or other trading organization: □ *The solicitor had several Asian clients.* □ *She was a regular customer at the fish market.*

clientele The preferred pronunciation of this word, which means 'clients' (see CLIENT OR CUSTOMER?): □ *an exclusive clientele*, is [kleeon*tel*]. Note also the spelling, particularly the *-ele* (not *-elle*) ending.

climactic or **climatic**? These two words have completely different meanings. *Climactic* is the adjective from *climax*: □ *This aria marks the climactic point of the opera. Climatic* is the adjective from *climate*: □ *The climatic conditions are unsuitable for outdoor activities.*

climate The word *climate* has been extended in meaning to embrace not just the atmosphere as regards the weather, but atmosphere in general: □ *a climate of hope.* It is used rather more specifically of the prevailing state of affairs or the attitudes and opinions of people at a particular time: □ *the economic climate.*

climatic see CLIMACTIC OR CLIMATIC?

clinch see CLENCH OR CLINCH?

clique The noun *clique*, often used pejoratively to denote a small exclusive group of people, may be pronounced to rhyme with *teak* or *tick*.

clone *Clone* is a word taken from genetic science, where it means 'the asexually, and often artificially, produced offspring of a parent, which are genetically identical to the parent and to each other'. Despite the dislike of some people, the word is now used popularly to suggest anything very similar to something else. It is also used synonymously with *lookalike*: □ *a dozen Elvis Presley clones*.

close or **closed**? Confusion between these two words sometimes arises when they are used in compounds, especially *close/closed season* (the period of time when the killing of certain animals, birds, or fish is forbidden). In British English *close season* is preferred; in American English, *closed season*.

close proximity *Proximity* means 'being close or near in space or time': □ *Its proximity to the station made the house particularly convenient*. As 'close' is part of the meaning of the word, it is never necessary to add *close* before *proximity*.

clothed see CLAD OR CLOTHED?

clout Some people object to the overuse of the noun *clout* to mean 'influence; political power'. This usage is best restricted to informal contexts.

co- The prefix *co-* is increasingly attached without a hyphen in modern usage. Some users prefer to retain the hyphen when the prefix is attached to a word beginning with *o-*: □ *co-ordinate* □ *co-operate* (see also HYPHEN 1). Some dictionaries retain the hyphen in words referring to a person who does something jointly with another: □ *co-author* □ *co-star*, but the spellings *coauthor*, *costar*, etc., are acceptable.

coarse or **course**? These words are sometimes confused. *Coarse* means 'rough or crude': □ *coarse behaviour* □ *coarse cloth*. The noun *course* means 'progression of events': □ *in the course of time*, or 'route': □ *The ship steered a difficult course*. The verb *course* means 'hunt or pursue'; *coursing* is the sport in which hares are hunted with dogs.

cocoon This word, which means 'protective covering': □ *The butterfly emerged from its cocoon*, is sometimes misspelt. Note the second *c* and the *-oo-*.

coherent or **cohesive**? *Coherent* and *cohesive* have the same roots in the verb *to cohere*, but they are used differently. *Coherent* means 'logically consistent; comprehensible': □ *a coherent argument* □ *coherent speech*.

Cohesive means 'clinging or sticking together': □ *the cohesive properties of the mortar*, but is more frequently used figuratively of anything that holds together or has unity: □ *Union members should think of themselves as a cohesive group*.

coiffure This word, meaning 'hairstyle', is usually pronounced [kwah*fewr*]. This should be clearly distinguished from the pronunciation of *coiffeur* meaning 'hairstylist' [kwah*fer*].

colander see CALENDAR, CALENDER, OR COLANDER?

collaborate or **cooperate**? Both *collaborate* and *cooperate* mean 'work together for a common purpose': □ *The two scientists have collaborated/cooperated for years on various projects*. *Collaborate* has the extra sense of working with or assisting an enemy, particularly an enemy occupier of one's country.

collective nouns The term *collective noun* applies to such nouns as: □ *flock* □ *gang* □ *troop*, which are usually followed by *of* and another noun: □ *a flock of sheep*, to other nouns which apply to groups, such as: □ *audience* □ *orchestra* □ *crowd*, and to 'class' collectives, which include various things of a certain kind: □ *furniture* □ *underwear* □ *greengrocery* □ *cutlery*. Class collectives always take a singular verb; words for people in general or a particular class of person take a plural verb. It is with group nouns such as: □ *audience* □ *jury* □ *committee* that problems arise. British English treats such words as plural, while American English treats them as singular. See also SINGULAR OR PLURAL?

colon A *colon* introduces a clause or word which amplifies, interprets, explains, or reveals what has gone before it: □ *He was beginning to be anxious: they had been gone for five hours*. □ *Only one party cares: Labour*. Its other main uses are to introduce lists: □ *The Thames Valley Police Authority covers three counties: Berkshire, Buckinghamshire, and Oxfordshire*, and to introduce lengthier quotations, often when quotation marks are not used and the quoted material is indented. Capitals should be used after colons only if the word following is a proper noun.

colonnade Note the spelling of this noun, meaning 'row of columns', particularly the *-l-* (as in *column*) and the *-nn-*.

coloration Note that the *u* of *colour* is omitted in this derived form of the word, which refers to a pattern or arrangement of colours: □ *the distinctive coloration of the feathers.*

coloured see BLACK.

colourize The verb *colourize* refers to the process of adding colour to black-and-white films: □ *the controversial practice of colourizing classic films.* Note that the verb is spelt *-our-* in British English (the American spelling is *colorize*), unlike the verb *decolorize*, meaning 'remove the colour from', which is spelt *-or-* in British and American English.

columnist The *n* of this word is sometimes not sounded in speech. The pronunciation [*kŏl*ŭmnist] is strictly correct, but [*kol*ŭmist] is becoming increasingly common; [*kol*ŭmist] reflects the pronunciation of *column*, with its silent *n*.

comic or comical? *Comic* and *comical* are not quite synonyms. *Comic* means 'of comedy, intended to cause laughter or amusement': □ *a comic actor* □ *a comic poem. Comical* means 'having the effect of causing laughter or amusement': □ *a comical sight.*

comma Of all the punctuation marks, the comma is the most likely to cause confusion or ambiguity through its misuse, overuse, or omission. Excessively long sentences containing many clauses separated by commas are best divided into shorter units; short sentences that require many commas for clarity should be reworded if possible. The principal uses of the comma are listed below.

1 The individual items of a series of three or more are separated by commas; the final comma preceding *and* or *or* is optional. The same conventions apply to series of longer units: □ *I closed the window, drew the curtains, and went to bed.* Omission of the final comma may cause confusion if the last or penultimate item contains *and.*

2 The use of a comma between adjectives that precede the noun they qualify is optional in most cases. When the final adjective has a closer relationship with the noun, it should not be preceded by a comma: □ *a picturesque French village.* Sometimes omission of the comma could cause ambiguity or confusion: □ *bright, blue curtains.*

3 Commas separate nondefining or parenthetical clauses and phrases from the rest of the sentence: □ *The mayor, who is very fond of gardening, presented the prizes at the flower show.* □ *My diamond necklace, a valuable family heirloom, has been stolen.*

Commas are not used around defining or essential clauses or phrases: □ *The classical guitarist Andrés Segovia has died.* □ *The skirt that I bought last week has a broken zip.*

In some cases, the removal or insertion of parenthetical commas can alter the meaning of a sentence: □ *My daughter Elizabeth is a doctor* implies that the speaker has two or more daughters, one of whom is called Elizabeth; □ *My daughter, Elizabeth, is a doctor* implies that the speaker has only one daughter.

4 The use of the comma or commas to separate such words and phrases as *however, therefore, nevertheless, of course, for example,* and *on the other hand* from the rest of the sentence is optional.

5 Commas are always used to separate terms of address, interjections, and closing quotation tags from the rest of the sentence: □ *I'm sorry to have troubled you, madam.* □ *It's cold today, isn't it?*

6 The main clause of the sentence may be separated from a preceding subordinate clause or participial phrase by a comma, but the comma is often omitted after a short clause or phrase: □ *When it stops raining we will go out.* See also DANGLING PARTICIPLES.

7 Two or more main clauses linked by a coordinating conjunction (*and, or, but,* etc.) may be separated with a comma if necessary. The comma is usually omitted if the clauses have the same subject or object. Where such clauses are not linked by a coordinating conjunction, they should be separated by a SEMICOLON.

commandant, commander, or **commandeer?** *Commandant* and *commander* are nouns; *commandeer* is a verb. The noun *commandant* refers to an officer in command of a particular group or establishment, such as a military academy or prisoner-of-war camp; the noun *commander* refers to an officer in command of a military operation, ship, etc. *Commander* is also the name of a rank in the Navy and is used in nonmilitary contexts to denote anybody who is in command: □ *the commander of the expedition.* The verb *commandeer* means 'seize, especially for military or public use'.

commemorate This word, meaning 'remember with a ceremony': □ *They commemorated their 50th anniversary*, is sometimes misspelt. Note the *-mm-* followed by a single *m*.

commence *Commence* means the same as *begin* or *start* but should be used only in formal contexts, where its opposite is *conclude*, rather than *end*: □ *The meeting will commence at 9.30 a.m. and conclude at noon.*

commensurate *Commensurate* means 'equal in measure or extent; proportionate': □ *The rent charged is commensurate with the flat's current value.* The word is frequently used in connection with job salaries: □ *Remuneration will be commensurate with the importance of this key role* (*Executive Post*).

commercialese *Commercialese* is a usually pejorative term applied to the jargon used in the business and commercial world.

commissionaire This word, meaning 'attendant in uniform': □ *the commissionaire at the theatre*, is sometimes misspelt. Note the *-mm-*, *-ss-*, single *-n-*, and the *-aire* ending.

commitment The sense of *commitment* which means 'loyalty to a cause or ideology' is an increasingly popular one: □ *a genuine Christian commitment* □ *his commitment to the animal rights movement* □ *As my commitment to the struggle for racial justice intensified,*

I wanted to go further in my relationship with the black community (Jim Wallis, *The New Radical*). Many users dislike this word's overuse.

committee The noun *committee* may be singular or plural: □ *The committee meets on Thursdays.* □ *The committee were unable to reach a unanimous decision.*

common see MUTUAL, COMMON, OR RECIPROCAL?

communal This word, meaning 'of a community': □ *communal living*, has two different pronunciations. Both [*kom*yuunăl] and [kŏ*mew*năl] are widely used. Careful speakers, however, prefer the first of these pronunciations.

community *Community* has become a vogue word in two different ways. The application of the word to a recognizable group within a larger society: □ *the Jewish community* □ *the black community*, has given the word an association with minority racial groups. *The community* is also used in a much vaguer sense to mean 'society in general': □ *cared for in the community*.

comparable The traditional pronunciation of this word is [*kom*părăbl]. The variant [kŏm*par*răbl] is avoided by careful speakers. See also STRESS.

comparative and **superlative** The *comparative* form of an adjective or adverb is used when two things or people are compared: □ *Anne is smaller than her sister*, while the *superlative* is used as the highest degree of comparison between three or more things: □ *Anne is the smallest girl in her class.*

comparatively *Comparatively* means 'relatively, as compared with a standard': □ *It was comparatively inexpensive for vintage champagne.*

compare to or **compare with**? *Compare to* and *compare with* are not interchangeable. *Compare to* is used when things are being likened to each other: □ *He compared her skin to ivory. Compare with* is used when things are being considered from the point of view of both similarities and differences: □ *Tourists find London hotels expensive compared with those of other European capitals.* When *compare* is used intransitively, *with* should always be used: □ *His direction compares with early Hitchcock.*

compel or **impel**? Both these verbs mean 'force', but they differ in usage. *Compel* is used with human and non-human subjects and implies strong obligation: □ *They compelled us to take part.* □ *Financial necessity compelled him to accept the job. Impel* is chiefly used with non-human subjects and implies an urge rather than an obligation: □ *She felt impelled to protest.* □ *Fear impelled him to turn back.*

competition or **contest**? *Competition* and *contest* both involve rivalry with an opponent or opponents and can be synonymous: □ *At 18 she won a contest/competition for young musicians.* However, *contest* is restricted to the sense of organized competitive events or exertions to achieve victory over opponents: □ *the contest for nomination as candidate. Competition* is used more generally of rivalry: □ *There will be keen competition for tickets*, and is also used of the people or organization against which one is competing: □ *We must assess the strengths and weaknesses of the competition.*

complacent or **complaisant**? A *complacent* person is smug or self-satisfied; a *complaisant* person is obliging or willing to comply. Both adjectives may be applied to the same noun: □ *'We can't lose,' she said with a complacent smile.* □ *He opened the door with a complaisant smile.*

complement The *complement* of a clause or sentence provides essential additional information about the SUBJECT or OBJECT. A complement may be a noun, adjective, pronoun, or phrase.

complement or **compliment**? These two words are often confused. Both as a noun and a verb, *complement* suggests the addition of something necessary to make something whole or complete: □ *a ship's complement* □ *The flowers complemented the room's decor perfectly. Compliment* is used as a noun and verb to refer to an expression of praise, respect, or admiration: □ *She complimented her host on the excellent meal.* □ *with the compliments of the management.* To avoid mistakes remember the *e* of *complement* is also in *complete*.

complement or **supplement**? *Complement* and *supplement* have a distinct difference in meaning. Both as noun and verb, *complement* suggests the addition of something necessary to make something whole or complete: □ *The closures were forced by the hospital's inability to recruit 92 nurses out of its full complement of nearly 800* (*Daily Telegraph*). □ *The music complemented the mime aptly. Supplement* suggests an addition to something that is already complete: □ *Her fees for private tuition supplemented her teacher's salary.* □ *Most Sunday newspapers publish a colour supplement.*

complementary medicine or **alternative medicine**? *Complementary medicine* is the treatment of illnesses by such techniques and systems as osteopathy, acupuncture, and homoeopathy. The term *complementary medicine* suggests that the treatments and therapies complement – fit in with and work alongside – orthodox medicine; the term *alternative medicine* emphasizes that such treatments, etc., are completely different from those of 'conventional' medicine.

complete When used to mean 'total' *complete* is an absolute adjective (see ADJECTIVES) and many people dislike any modification of it: □ *We were in almost complete darkness.* However, *complete* also has the meaning of 'thorough': □ *a complete overhaul*, and in that sense can be modified with *more* or *most*: □ *This is the most complete study of the period yet published.*

complex The noun *complex* is taken from psychoanalysis, where it means 'a set of subconscious repressed ideas and emotions which can cause an abnormal mental condition': □ *an Oedipus complex* □ *an inferiority complex.* The term has been taken up and used popularly to mean any behavioural problem or obsession, even if it is completely conscious. This usage is disliked by some. □ *She's got a complex about spiders.* □ *'You're crazy,' Clevinger shouted ... 'You've got a Jehovah complex'* (Joseph Heller, *Catch 22*).

complex or **complicated**? *Complex* and *complicated* are very similar in meaning and the differences in usage are subtle ones. Both mean 'consisting of many parts which are intimately combined': □ *This is a complex/complicated problem.*

compliment, complimentary see COMPLEMENT OR COMPLIMENT?

compose, comprise, or **constitute**? All these verbs are concerned with parts making up a whole. *Compose* and *constitute* are both used to mean 'come together to make (a whole)' but *compose* is usually used in the passive and *constitute* in the active: □ *The team is composed of several experts.* □ *the commodities that constitute the average household diet.* *Comprise* can only be used to mean 'consist of': □ *The house comprises three bedrooms, a living room, kitchen, and bathroom.* Its use in place of *constitute*: □ *Eleven players comprise a team* is not generally considered acceptable; its use in place of *compose*: □ *The team is comprised of eleven players* is wrong.

compound A *compound* is a word that consists of two or more other words joined together, with or without a space or hyphen: □ *breakdown* □ *forget-me-not* □ *dining room.* The plural of a compound noun is usually formed by making the noun element plural: □ *passers-by.* There are no absolute rules governing the use of spaces and hyphens in many compounds (see HYPHEN 2). The coining of new compound verbs, such as *to drug-test*, is disliked by some people: see also VERBS.

comprehend see APPREHEND OR COMPREHEND?

comprehensible or **comprehensive**? These two adjectives are derived from different senses of the verb *comprehend* (see APPREHEND OR COMPREHEND?). *Comprehensible* means 'understandable'; *comprehensive* means 'including all or most things': □ *The explanation must be comprehensible to the average reader.* □ *fully* *comprehensive car insurance.*

compulsive or **compulsory**? Both these adjectives are derived from the verb *compel*, meaning 'force'. *Compulsive* refers to something that one is forced to do by an internal or psychological urge; *compulsory* refers to something that one is forced to do by an external rule or law: □ *a compulsive gambler* □ *a compulsory payment.*

computerate The word *computerate* means 'able to operate a computer; experienced in computing'. It is a blend of the synonymous phrase *computer literate* (see LITERAL, LITERARY OR LITERATE?) and is often used in job advertisements: □ *Applicants must be computerate and able to work under pressure.*

concede This verb, meaning 'admit' or 'yield', is sometimes misspelt. Note the -*cede* ending, as in the verb *cede,* which is similar in meaning.

concept The precise meaning of *concept* is 'an idea of a category or thing which is formed by generalization from particular instances'. The meaning has widened to embrace ideas in general, and is often now used to mean 'an accepted idea of a particular thing': □ *the concept of alternative medicine.* It is frequently used very loosely to mean little more than 'an idea or notion', particularly in advertising. Many people dislike this usage: □ *a new concept in slimming.*

concerned The adjective *concerned* may be followed by *about* or *for* when it means 'anxious' and by *with* when it means 'on the subject of': □ *We are very concerned about pollution.* □ *The article is concerned with pollution.* □ *They are concerned for his health.* □ *The organization is concerned with public health.*

concerning *Concerning* means 'relating to, on the subject of, or about': □ *The head teacher is available to talk to people concerning their career choices.*

condition or **precondition**? A *condition* is a requirement or stipulation on which an agreement or contract depends: □ *I will let you go on condition that you are back before mid-*

night. While a condition can be fulfilled either before or after the agreement is made, a *precondition* is a requirement that must be satisfied in advance of an agreement being made: □ *Assent to the manifesto was a precondition of membership.*

conduit This word, which describes a pipe or channel conveying liquid, has various pronunciations. The most widely used is [*kon*dit], but [*kun*dit], [*kon*dyuuit], and [*kond*wit] are also heard.

confidant or **confident**? A *confidant*, feminine *confidante*, is someone in whom one can confide. Both words are pronounced either [*kon*fidant] or [konfi*dant*]. These nouns should not be confused with the adjective *confident* which means 'assured or certain': □ *a confident young man.*

confrontation A *confrontation* is a face-to-face meeting, especially in the context of opposition, challenge, or defiance: □ *St George's confrontation with the dragon.* Popular journalism has now weakened the meaning so that any disagreement or conflict of ideas is now inevitably referred to as *a confrontation.*

congenial, genial, congenital, or **genetic**? Both *congenial* and *genial* mean 'pleasant'; *congenial* is usually applied to abstract nouns and *genial* to people: □ *a congenial atmosphere* □ *He finds the work congenial.* □ *a genial host. Congenial company* refers to people who share one's interests or attitudes; *genial company* refers to people who are friendly and cheerful.

Congenital means 'existing from birth'; *genetic* means 'relating to genes': □ *congenital brain damage* □ *genetic engineering*. A *congenital defect* is not hereditary or inherited; a *genetic defect* is hereditary or inherited.

conjunctions *Conjunctions* are words which link two or more words, clauses, or sentences: □ *and* □ *but* □ *or* □ *because* □ *when.*

conjurer or **conjuror**? Either spelling is perfectly acceptable.

connection or **connexion**? This word, meaning 'a relationship between two things; joint': □ *His death must have had some connection with the stormy weather.* □ *faulty electrical connections*, is usually spelt *connection*. *Connexion* is a rarer variant spelling, especially in British English.

connoisseur A person who is an expert within a certain field is called a *connoisseur*. Note the *-nn-*, *-oi-*, and *-ss-*.

connote or **denote**? These two verbs are sometimes confused. *Denote*, the more frequent of the two, refers to the literal or primary meaning of something: □ *The word 'bachelor' denotes an unmarried man.* □ *Tears do not always denote sadness. Connote*, a more formal word, means 'imply' or 'suggest', referring to secondary meaning or association: □ *For some people, the word 'bachelor' connotes freedom.*

conscience Note the spelling of this word, particularly the *-sci-* in the middle and the *-ce* ending. The second syllable is identical in spelling (but not in pronunciation) with the noun *science*.

conscientious This word, meaning 'diligent and careful': □ *She was a conscientious worker*, is sometimes misspelt. Note in particular the *t*.

consensus *Consensus* means 'opinion shared unanimously, a view generally held or accepted': □ *He had broken the pro-nuclear consensus shared by all post-war leaders* (*Sunday Times*).

consent see ASSENT OR CONSENT?

consequent or **consequential**? *Consequent* means 'following as a direct result': □ *She was knocked down by a lorry and her consequent injuries left her a permanent invalid. Consequential*, a rarer word than *consequent*, is also used to mean 'following as a direct result': □ *the improvement in the local economy and the consequential loss of the area's special status. Consequential* also means 'important': □ *Their decisions were becoming increasingly consequential in determining the direction of the company.* It is also used in legal expressions such as *consequential loss* to mean 'an indirect result' and has the additional meaning of 'self-important; pompous': □ *His manner was pretentious and consequential.*

consequent or **subsequent**? *Consequent* and *subsequent* are sometimes confused. While *consequent* means 'following as a direct result', *subsequent* simply means 'occurring after': □ *her bereavement and consequent grief* □ *her bereavement and subsequent remarriage. Consequent* takes the preposition *on*, while *subsequent* takes *to*: □ *increase in salaries consequent on the pay review* □ *his behaviour subsequent to his arrival.*

consequential see CONSEQUENT OR CONSEQUENTIAL?

conservative or **Conservative**? The word *conservative* with a lower-case *c*- means 'tending to support tradition and established institutions, opposed to change, moderate, cautious, conventional': □ *The college has a reputation for being conservative and still refuses to admit women students.* □ *He has conservative tastes and dresses in sombre colours.* □ A *Conservative* is someone who supports or is a member of the Conservative Party in Britain or elsewhere; it is also used as an adjective: □ *a Conservative MP.*

consider *Consider* means 'regard as being': □ *I consider him a nonentity*, 'think about carefully': □ *I have considered all aspects of the problem*, and 'regard sympathetically': □ *We will not fail to consider your feelings on the matter.*

considerable *Considerable* means 'worth consideration; significant': □ *She has made a considerable contribution to biochemical research.* It has been extended to mean 'large in amount': □ *They have saved a considerable amount of money*, although some people dislike the imprecise nature of this use.

consist of or **consist in**? *Consist of* means 'comprise, be made up of': □ *Breakfast consists of bread, croissants, jam, and coffee. Consist in* means 'have its essence in': □ *The appeal of the writing consists in its use of language rather than its content.*

consonant A *consonant* is the sound represented by any of the letters *b, c, d, f, g, h, j, k, l, m, n, p, q, r, s, t, v,* *w*, *x*, *y*, and *z* in the English language. Compare VOWEL.

consortium or **consortia**? *Consortia* is a plural form of the noun *consortium*, which means 'association of companies': □ *a consortium of insurance brokers*. The plural form *-ia* is sometimes wrongly used in place of the singular noun: □ *Now only Phonepoint, a consortia led by British Telecom, and Byps, owned by Hutchison Telecom UK, are keen to offer the mobile phone service* (*The Guardian*).

constable A police officer of the lowest rank is known as a *constable*. The word has two pronunciations: [*kun*stăbl] or [*kon*stăbl], both of which are acceptable.

constitute see COMPOSE, COMPRISE, OR CONSTITUTE?

constrain or **restrain**? Both these verbs mean 'hold back' or 'limit', but there are differences of usage and application between them. *Constrain* is more formal and implies an abstract or undesirable restriction; to *restrain* may involve physical force: □ *Such strict guidelines constrain creativity*. □ *He struggled to restrain the dog*.

contact The meanings of *contact* as a noun include 'the state of touching': □ *He avoided all physical contact with dogs*, 'link or relationship': □ *The two towns have commercial contacts*, and 'communication': □ *I am in regular contact with her*. A modern use is 'a person one knows who may be useful to one': □ *I have a good contact at the Home Office*.

contagious or **infectious**? *Contagious* and *infectious* are both used of diseases that can be passed on to others. *Contagious* diseases are those that are passed on by physical contact, like venereal diseases or impetigo; *infectious* diseases are those passed on by airborne or waterborne microorganisms, like measles or influenza.

containerize *Containerize* is a verb formed from the noun *container* in its sense of a large packing case in which goods are transported by road and sea, being handled mechanically throughout. To *containerize* means both 'pack into containers for transport and transport in this method': □ *The beans must be containerized before the end of the week*; and 'change over to the use of containers': □ *We are containerizing our shipping procedures.*

contemporary The primary meaning of *contemporary* is 'happening or living at the same time as': □ *Joyce was contemporary with the Bloomsbury group, though not a member of it.* It has more recently been used to mean 'happening at the present time; current': □ *Contemporary values are materialistic and selfish.*

contemptible or **contemptuous**? Both *contemptible* and *contemptuous* are concerned with *contempt*, but they have distinctly different meanings. *Contemptible* means 'despicable; deserving scorn or contempt': □ *His meanness was contemptible. Contemptuous* means 'scornful, feeling or showing contempt': □ *She observed his feeble efforts with a contemptuous smile.*

contest see COMPETITION OR CONTEST?

contingency A *contingency* is 'something that happens by chance; something unforeseen that might possibly occur in the future': □ *We must prepare ourselves for every contingency.*

continual or **continuous**? *Continual* means 'frequently repeated'; *continuous* means 'without break or interruption': □ *Our neighbour's continual complaints forced us to move house.* □ *The continuous noise from the generator kept him awake all night.*

continuance, continuation, or **continuity**? All three nouns are derived from the verb *continue*. *Continuance* is the act of continuing, usually without a break, whereas *continuation* may be the act of continuing after a break: □ *the continuance of the strike* □ *a continuation of yesterday's discussion.* In some contexts, such as the first example above, *continuance* and *continuation* are interchangeable. *Continuity* is the state of being continuous (see CONTINUAL OR CONTINUOUS?): □ *the continuity of the action.*

continuous see CONTINUAL OR CONTINUOUS?

contractions The most common contractions in English are those of the verbs *am, are, is, have, has, had, will, shall, would,* and the word *not* combined with an auxiliary verb: □ *I'm* □ *you're* □ *she's* □ *we've* □ *he'll* □ *they'd* □ *can't* □ *shouldn't.*

contrary This word, meaning 'opposed in position': □ *On the contrary, I would like to go for a walk,* is stressed on the first syllable [*kon*trări]. Only in the sense 'perverse or stubborn': □ *such a contrary girl,* is it stressed on the second syllable [kŏn*trairi*].

contribute In the traditional pronunciation of this word, the stress is on the second syllable [kŏn*trib*yoot]; some users dislike the pronunciation with the word stressed on the first syllable [*kon*tribyoot].

controversy In the traditional pronunciation of this word, the stress falls on the first syllable [*kon*trŏversi]. The variant pronunciation, with stress on the second syllable [kŏn*trov*ĕrsi], is widely heard, but is disliked by many users. See also STRESS.

convalescence This word, meaning 'recovery after an illness', is sometimes misspelt. Note the combinations *sc* and *nc*.

converse, inverse, obverse, or **reverse**? These four words share the sense of 'opposite'; in some contexts they are interchangeable. The noun *converse* specifically denotes something that is opposite in meaning: □ *the converse of this statement. Inverse* is more frequently used as an adjective in such phrases as □ *in inverse proportion*; *obverse*, a formal word and the least common of the four, refers to a counterpart: □ *The obverse of the company's success is the failure of its rivals. Reverse,* the most frequent and general of the four words, may be used as a verb, noun, or adjective: □ *to reverse a decision* □ *to do the reverse* □ *in reverse order.*

convertible This word, meaning 'capable of being changed': □ *convertible car*, is sometimes misspelt. The ending is *-ible*, not *-able*.

cooperate see COLLABORATE OR COOPERATE?

cord see CHORD OR CORD?

co-respondent see CORRESPONDENT OR CO-RESPONDENT?

corps or **corpse**? The noun *corps*, meaning 'body of people', should not be confused with the noun *corpse*, meaning 'dead body': □ *the diplomatic corps* □ *The corpse lay undiscovered for several weeks.*

correspond There are two main meanings of *correspond*. One is 'communicate with someone by exchange of letters': □ *He met his Italian penfriend after they had corresponded for years.* The other meaning is 'match or be equivalent or comparable in some respect': □ *Your account corresponds exactly with the description of the other witnesses.* In this second meaning *correspond to* is considered correct by many careful users, although *correspond with* is often used.

correspondent or **co-respondent**? A *correspondent* is someone who communicates by letter: □ *She has correspondents in three continents*, or someone who contributes news reports to a newspaper or to radio or television programmes: □ *And now a report from our Middle East correspondent.* A *co-respondent* is the person cited in divorce proceedings as the lover of the husband or wife who has been accused of adultery: □ *Divorced couples hobnobbed with each other and with each other's co-respondents* (Noel Coward, *Present Indicative*).

cosmetic Some people dislike the use of *cosmetic* as an adjective to apply to anything that improves the outward appearance of something: □ *One supplier of decaffeinated coffee ... plans to switch from the chemical process ... although a spokesman insisted this was necessary for 'cosmetic' reasons only* (*Sunday Times*).

cost or **price**? *Cost* and *price* are often used synonymously as nouns to mean 'the amount paid or charged for something': □ *We were afraid the cost/price would be more than we could afford. Cost* is more likely to refer to an amount paid and *price* to an amount charged: □ *An increase in manufacturing costs will result in higher prices.*

couch potato The slang term *couch potato* originated in American English in the mid-1970s and entered British English in the later 1980s. It is applied to people who spend most of their leisure time watching television: □ *We are inexorably mutating into a coast-to-coast allotment of couch potatoes* (*The Guardian*). The term is best avoided in formal contexts.

could see CAN OR MAY?

council or **counsel**? The noun *council* means 'a body of people meeting for discussion and consultation': □ *the county council.* The noun *counsel* means 'advice': □ *She always gave wise counsel*, and has the corresponding verb *to counsel* meaning 'give advice to someone': □ *She was counselled about her future career.* □ *He was counselled against acting rashly.* □ *psychiatric counselling.*

counsel or **advise**? In many instances *counsel* and *advise* are synonymous, although *counsel* is rather more formal: □ *I would advise/counsel you not to drink any more if you're driving home. Advise* is more likely to be used in informal contexts and when the advice is not of great importance: □ *He advised me to go on the ring road. Counsel* is more appropriate when the advice is serious and when it is given by trained or professional counsellors: □ *He has been counselled by social workers, doctors, and clergy but he still can't sort out his problems.*

COUNTRIES AND PEOPLES

The right-hand column lists the words used as adjectives and nouns referring to the countries in the left-hand column and their people. A single item in the right-hand column, such as 'Albanian', indicates that the same word is used as adjective and noun. 'Argentinian *or* Argentine' indicates that either of these words may be used as an adjective or a noun.

Where the adjective and noun are not identical, they are separated by a semicolon, with the adjective first: 'Danish; a Dane' indicates that *Danish* is the adjective and *Dane* the noun.

Most of the nouns can be converted to plural or collective form by adding *-s*: □ *the Albanians* □ *a party of Danes*. However, the plural and collective form of nouns ending in *-ese* and *-ois* is identical to the singular form: □ *the Chinese* □ *the Seychellois*. Other irregular plurals and collective forms are separated from the singular noun by a second semicolon, as at 'Lesothan; a Mosotho ...; the Basotho ...' and 'Irish; an Irishman (*or* -woman); the Irish'.

Cross-references, e.g. see CHINESE, are also included to main entries in the *Good English Guide*.

Afghanistan	Afghan
Albania	Albanian
Algeria	Algerian
Andorra	Andorran
Angola	Angolan
Antigua and Barbuda	Antiguan
Argentina	Argentinian *or* Argentine
(see ARGENTINE OR ARGENTINIAN?)	
Armenia	Armenian
Austria	Austrian
Azerbaijan	Azeri *or* Azerbaijani
Bahamas, the	Bahamian
Bahrain	Bahraini
Bangladesh	Bangladeshi
Barbados	Barbadian
Belarus	*see* Byelorussia
Belgium	Belgian
Belize	Belizean
Benin	Beninese *or* Beninois
Bermuda	Bermudan *or* Bermudian
Bhutan	Bhutanese
Bolivia	Bolivian
Bosnia-Herzogovina	Bosnian
Botswana	Botswanan
Brazil	Brazilian
Brunei	Bruneian

Bulgaria	Bulgarian
Burkina Faso	Burkinabé
Burma	*see* Myanmar
Burundi	Burundian
Byelorussia	Byelorussian
Cambodia	Cambodian
Cameroon	Cameroonian
Canada	Canadian
Cape Verde	Cape Verdian *or* Cape Verdean
Cayman Islands, the	Caymanian; a Cayman Islander
Central African Republic, the	Central African
Chad	Chadian
Chile	Chilean
China (see CHINESE)	Chinese
Colombia	Colombian
Commonwealth of Independent States, the *or* the CIS	
Comoros, the	Comoran
Congo	Congolese
Costa Rica	Costa Rican
Côte d'Ivoire	Ivorian
Croatia	Croatian; a Croat *or* a Croatian
Cuba	Cuban
Cyprus	Cypriot
Czechoslovakia	Czech *or* Czechoslovak *or* Czechoslovakian
Denmark	Danish; a Dane
Djibouti	Djibouti
Dominica	Dominican
Dominican Republic, the	Dominican
Ecuador	Ecuadorean *or* Ecuadorian *or* Ecuadoran
Egypt	Egyptian
El Salvador	Salvadorean *or* Salvadorian *or* Salvadoran
England	English; an Englishman (*or* -woman); the English
Equatorial Guinea	Equatorial Guinean

Estonia	Estonian
Ethiopia	Ethiopian
Falkland Islands, the	Falklands; a Falkland Islander
Fiji	Fijian
Finland	Finnish; a Finn
France	French; a Frenchman (*or* -woman); the French
Gabon	Gabonese
Gambia *or* the Gambia	Gambian
Georgia	Georgian
Germany	German
Ghana	Ghanaian
Gibraltar	Gibraltarian
Great Britain (see **BRITAIN**; **BRIT**)	British; a Briton; the British
Greece (see **GREEK** OR **GRECIAN**?)	Greek
Grenada	Grenadian
Guatemala	Guatemalan
Guinea	Guinean
Guinea-Bissau	Guinea-Bissauan
Guyana	Guyanese *or* Guyanan
Haiti	Haitian
Holland	*see* Netherlands, the
Honduras	Honduran
Hong Kong	Hong Kong; a Hong Konger
Hungary	Hungarian
Iceland	Icelandic; an Icelander
India	Indian
Indonesia	Indonesian
Iran	Iranian
Iraq	Iraqi
Ireland, Republic of (Eire) (*see also* Northern Ireland *in table*)	Irish; an Irishman (*or* -woman); the Irish
Israel	Israeli
Italy	Italian
Ivory Coast	*see* Côte d'Ivoire
Jamaica	Jamaican

Japan	Japanese
Jordan	Jordanian
Kazakhstan	Kazakh
Kenya	Kenyan
Kiribati	Kiribati
Korea	Korean
(*see also* North Korea, South Korea *in table*)	
Kuwait	Kuwaiti
Kyrgyzstan	Kyrgyz; a Kyrgyzstani
Laos	Laotian *or* Lao
Latvia	Latvian *or* Lettish; a Latvian *or* a Lett
Lebanon	Lebanese
Lesotho	Lesothan; a Mosotho *or* a Lesothan; the Basotho *or* the Lesothans
Liberia	Liberian
Libya	Libyan
Liechtenstein	Liechtenstein; a Liechtensteiner
Lithuania	Lithuanian
Luxembourg	Luxembourg *or* Luxembourgian *or* Luxembourger; a Luxembourger
Macao	Macao; a Macanese
Macedonia	Macedonian
Madagascar	Madagascan *or* Malagasy; a Madagascan *or* a Malagasy
Malawi	Malawian
Malaysia	Malaysian
Maldives, the	Maldivian
Mali	Malian
Malta	Maltese
Mauritania	Mauritanian
Mauritius	Mauritian
Mexico	Mexican
Moldavia *or* Moldova	Moldavian
Monaco	Monacan *or* Monegasque
Mongolia	Mongolian *or* Mongol
Montenegro	Montenegrin

Montserrat	Montserratian
Morocco	Moroccan
Mozambique	Mozambican
Myanmar (Burma)	Myanmar *or* Burmese
Namibia	Namibian
Nauru	Nauruan
Nepal	Nepalese
Netherlands, the	Dutch; a Netherlander *or* a Dutchman (*or* -woman) *or* a Hollander; the Dutch
New Zealand	New Zealand; a New Zealander
Nicaragua	Nicaraguan
Niger	Nigerien
Nigeria	Nigerian
Northern Ireland	Northern Irish; a Northern Irishman (*or* -woman); the Northern Irish
North Korea	North Korean
Norway	Norwegian
Oman	Omani
Pakistan	Pakistani
Panama	Panamanian
Papua New Guinea	Papua New Guinean
Paraguay	Paraguayan
Peru	Peruvian
Philippines, the	Philippine; a Filipino
Poland	Polish; a Pole
Portugal	Portuguese
Puerto Rico	Puerto Rican
Qatar	Qatari
Romania	Romanian
Russia	Russian
Rwanda	Rwandan
St Lucia	St Lucian
St Vincent and the Grenadines	St Vincentian
San Marino	San Marinese *or* Sanmarinese
São Tomé and Príncipe	São Toméan
Saudi Arabia	Saudi Arabian *or* Saudi

Scotland	Scottish; a Scot *or* a Scotsman (*or* -woman); the Scots *or* the Scottish
(see SCOTCH, SCOTS, OR SCOTTISH?)	
Senegal	Senegalese
Serbia	Serbian *or* Serb
Seychelles, the	Seychellois
Sierra Leone	Sierra Leonean
Singapore	Singaporean
Slovenia	Slovenian
Solomon Islands, the	Solomon Islands; a Solomon Islander
Somalia	Somalian *or* Somali; a Somalian *or* a Somali
South Africa	South African
South Korea	South Korean
Spain	Spanish; a Spaniard; the Spanish
Sri Lanka	Sri Lankan
Sudan	Sudanese
Suriname	Surinamese
Swaziland	Swazi
Sweden	Swedish; a Swede
Switzerland	Swiss; a Swiss; the Swiss
Syria	Syrian
Tadjikistan	Tadjik
Taiwan	Taiwanese
Tanzania	Tanzanian
Thailand	Thai
Togo	Togolese
Tonga	Tongan
Trinidad and Tobago	Trinidadian *or* Tobagoan
Tunisia	Tunisian
Turkey	Turkish; a Turk
Turkmenistan	Turkmen
Tuvalu	Tuvaluan
Uganda	Ugandan
Ukraine	Ukrainian
United Arab Emirates, the	Emirian

United Kingdom, the *or* the UK	British; a Briton; the British
(*see also* Great Britain, Northern Ireland *in table*)	
United States of America, the *or* the USA *or* the US	American
Uruguay	Uruguayan
Uzbekistan	Uzbek
Vanuatu	Vanuatuan
Venezuela	Venezuelan
Vietnam	Vietnamese
Wales	Welsh; a Welshman (*or* -woman); the Welsh
Western Samoa	Western Samoan
Yemen	Yemeni
Yugoslavia	Yugoslavian *or* Yugoslav
Zaïre	Zaïrean *or* Zaïrian *or* Zaïrese
Zambia	Zambian
Zimbabwe	Zimbabwean

country or **countryside**? Both these words may be used to denote a rural area: □ *We went for a walk in the country/countryside. Countryside* is commonly preceded by *the* and usually only *country* occurs before a noun: □ *the English countryside* □ *a country cottage/lane*.

country or **nation**? These words are often used interchangeably: □ *the poorer countries/nations of the world*. Strictly speaking *country* should be used when the context is one of geographical characteristics: □ *Wales is a mountainous country*, and *nation* when speaking of the people or of social and political characteristics: □ *Wales is a nation of musicians and orators*.

countryside see COUNTRY OR COUNTRYSIDE?

course see COARSE OR COURSE?; OF COURSE.

crafted This word, meaning 'skilfully made', is sometimes used simply as a synonym for 'made' or 'produced' in exaggerated sales descriptions: □ *fitted cupboards crafted from the finest wood*. Many people dislike this usage.

crash The adjectival use of

crash in the sense of 'intensive' is best restricted to the few phrases in which it is most familiar: □ *a crash diet* □ *a crash course*.

creative The adjective *creative* traditionally refers to originality and imagination used for artistic purposes: □ *a creative mind* □ *She is very creative*. It is increasingly used in a less favourable sense, describing something that stretches the limits of convention, legality, or truth: □ *creative accounting/bookkeeping*.

-cred The slang term *-cred*, short for *credibility*, is derived from *street-cred* (or *street credibility*), meaning 'acceptance by young people or people who are familiar with the latest trends, fashions, topical issues, etc.' (see STREET-). It is occasionally attached to other nouns to denote acceptance by a specific group of people: □ *The new chief inspector has force-cred*. □ *Wearing last winter's looks ..., with precisely the same accessories, will do little for up-to-date morale and nothing for one's style-cred* (Daily Telegraph).

credence or **credibility**? *Credence* is the state of believing something; *credibility* is the state of being believable: □ *He gave credence to her explanation*. □ *Her explanation lacked credibility*. The two nouns should not be confused.

credibility gap *Credibility gap* is a fashionable expression used to describe the lack of trust created by a discrepancy between what is said officially and what is actually seen to happen: □ *The public cynically accepts the credibility gap between election promises and the Government's subsequent policies*.

credible, **creditable**, or **credulous**? The three adjectives *credible*, *creditable*, and *credulous*, and their corresponding nouns *credibility*, *credit*, and *credulity* are sometimes confused. *Credible* means 'believable': □ *My story may sound barely credible but I assure you it's true*. *Creditable* means 'deserving praise': □ *Her readiness to forgive her attacker is creditable*. *Credulous* means 'gullible; too ready to believe': □ *Only the most credulous person could* *believe such nonsense.*

creed see CREDENCE OR CREDIBILITY?

crescendo *Crescendo* is a musical term that is frequently misused in both its technical and figurative senses. In music it describes a gradual increase in volume: □ *The brass sections take up the theme as the crescendo builds up.* It can be used of other sounds or to describe any build-up of intensity: □ *The baby's whimpering increased in a crescendo to a howl.* □ *Public interest in the matter has risen in a crescendo.*

crisis *Crisis* literally means 'turning point' and it should be used for situations that have reached a turning point for better or worse, for decisive moments in dramas, for crucial states of affairs where significant changes are likely: □ *The illness had passed its crisis and it was clear that she would live.* □ *the worsening economic crisis* □ *It is feared that the crisis which resulted in the military coup may lead to civil war.*

criterion or **criteria**? The word *criterion*, meaning 'a standard by which to judge or evaluate something', is a singular noun: □ *Exam results were the only criterion for deciding whether candidates should be interviewed.* The plural of *criterion* is *criteria*: □ *on the condition that the basic criteria of the code are accepted and met (The Bookseller).*

critic or **critique**? A *critic* is someone who criticizes. The word is sometimes used in the sense of someone who finds fault or expresses disapproval: □ *Acupuncture has many critics in the medical profession.* It is also used of someone who is employed to evaluate works of art, music, or literature: □ *The public loved the play but the critics did not have a good word to say for it.* A *critique* is a work of criticism, usually applied to an academic work which analyses and discusses ideas in depth: □ *This is a thoughtful critique of logical positivism.*

critical *Critical* means 'inclined to judge severely': □ *My mother is so critical of the way I bring up the children*; 'involving careful or scholarly evaluation': □ *a* *critical account of Jung's work*; 'involving a turning point; crucial': □ *We are at a critical point in our negotiations.*

critique see CRITIC OR CRITIQUE?

crochet or **crotchet**? The noun *crochet* refers to a type of needlework; the noun *crotchet* is the name of a note in music.

cross-section A *cross-section* is a piece of something which has been cut off at right angles or a drawing of the dimensions revealed by such a cutting: □ *The diagram shows an artery in cross-section.* The expression is more often used popularly to mean 'a typical or representative sample': □ *Over five thousand people were interviewed as a cross-section of the general public.*

crotch or **crutch**? Either noun may be used to denote the angle between a person's legs (hence, the genital area) or the corresponding part of a garment (such as a pair of trousers). The term *crotch* is more frequently used in these senses, but *crutch* is not incorrect. The principal meaning of the noun *crutch* is 'support used by people with injured legs or feet'.

crotchet see CROCHET OR CROTCHET?

crucial The use of *crucial* as a synonym for *important* is best avoided in formal speech and writing, where it should be restricted to the sense of 'decisive' or 'critical': □ *constituencies where the self-employed vote could be crucial to the outcome of the election* (*Daily Telegraph*).

crutch see CROTCH OR CRUTCH?

cuisine The word *cuisine* is used to describe a style of cooking food, particularly one which is typical of a particular country or region: □ *Peppers and tomatoes are characteristic of Basque cuisine*; for the food itself: □ *Their cuisine is excellent*; and in various phrases which convey a particular style of cooking: □ *nouvelle cuisine* □ *cuisine minceur.*

cullender see CALENDAR, CALENDER, OR COLANDER?

culminate *Culminate* means 'form a summit; reach the highest or most crucial point': □ *The church culminates in a steeple.* □ *Her rise in society culminated in her marriage to an earl.*

cult Some people dislike the adjectival use of the word *cult* to refer to a particular person, idea, activity, etc., that arouses great popular interest, especially for a short period of time: □ *a cult movie* □ *a cult book* □ *a cult figure*. Care should be taken to avoid overusing the word in this way.

cultured or **cultivated**? *Cultured* and *cultivated* are almost synonymous in that they are both used to mean 'educated, refined'. *Cultured* is particularly applied to education in terms of an understanding and appreciation of the arts: □ *They were cultured people who attended concerts and art galleries*, while *cultivated* is applied to behaviour and speech: □ *He gradually dropped his Cockney twang and spoke in a soft, cultivated accent.* Both *cultured* and *cultivated* also have connections with things that are produced artificially: □ *cultured pearls* □ *cultivated plants*.

cumulative see ACCUMULATIVE OR CUMULATIVE?

curb or **kerb**? These two spellings may sometimes be confused. *Curb* means 'check or control': □ *He curbed his anger.* A *kerb* is the edge of a pavement; in American English this word is spelt *curb*.

currant or **current**? A *currant* is a small seedless dried grape used in cookery: □ *She always put lots of currants in her cakes*, or any of several different soft fruits: □ *redcurrant jam* □ *blackcurrant juice*. A *current* is a steady flow: □ *They did not swim because the current was very strong.* □ *250 volts, alternating current.*

current The adjective *current* means 'occurring in or belonging to the present time; presently existing or in progress': □ *Current techniques for treating the disease are acknowledged to be inadequate*; and 'accepted or prevalent at this time': □ *The current opinions of American Catholics are in conflict with the Vatican.*

curriculum This word, meaning 'programme of available courses in a school or college': □ *a wide-ranging sixth-form curriculum*, is sometimes misspelt. Note that the only double letters are *-rr-*, as in *current*.

curtsy or **curtsey**? The noun and verb *curtsy* refer to a formal greeting made by a girl or woman in which the head and shoulders are lowered, the knees are bent and the skirt is held outwards with both hands: □ *She curtsied to the Queen.* The alternative spelling *curtsey* is also acceptable.

customer see CLIENT OR CUSTOMER?

cutting edge Some people dislike the frequent use of the phrase *cutting edge* in the figurative sense of 'forefront': □ *at the cutting edge of information technology.* See also LEADING-EDGE.

cymbal or **symbol**? Note the spelling of these words, which have the same pronunciation [*sim*băl]. A *cymbal* is a circular brass percussion instrument; a *symbol* is a sign or design that represents something else: □ *the clash of cymbals* □ *The dove is a symbol of peace.*

cynical or **sceptical**? A *cynical* person is one who has a distrust of human nature and sincerity, believing others to be motivated by self-interest: □ *He had a cynical belief that nobody took up law or medicine for any reason but the money.* *Sceptical* (American English, *skeptical*) means 'doubtful, unwilling to believe without rational proof': □ *While accepting Jesus' moral teachings she remained sceptical about the miracles and the resurrection.*

czar see TSAR OR CZAR?

D

dais This word, meaning 'a raised platform', is usually pronounced [*day*is]. It was formerly pronounced as only one syllable [days], but this is now rarely heard.

dangling participles Participles are often used to introduce a phrase which is attached to a later-mentioned subject: □ *Startled by the noise she dropped her book.* □ *Being by now very tired, we stopped at a pub.* There is a tendency, though, for such introductory participles to become apparently attached to the wrong noun: □ *Startled by the noise, her book fell to the floor.* □ *Being by now very tired, a pub was a welcome sight.* It was not the book that was startled or the pub that was tired. Then there is the sentence where the participle appears to have no subject at all, which is the thought behind the term *dangling the term dangling participle* (also known as *unattached*, or *unrelated participle*): □ *Lying in the sun, it felt as though it had always been summer.* Who, or what, was lying in the sun?

dare The verb *dare* can be used in two different ways. It can be used as a full verb, followed by an infinitive with *to*: □ *I dare you to jump.* □ *We'll see if she dares to contradict him*; or it can be an auxiliary or modal verb, followed by an infinitive without *to*: □ *He dared not go there at night.* □ *How dare you say that?*

dash Dashes can be used both singly and in pairs. Though the dash is useful, most of its functions can be performed by other punctuation marks, and excessive use of the dash is sometimes considered to be a mark of a careless writer. A sentence should never contain more than one dash or pair of dashes.

data *Data* means 'facts, information that can be used as a basis for analysis, etc.': □ *We have data on road accidents for the past thirty years.*

dates It is usual to write dates in figures, rather than words, except in some very formal contexts, such as legal documents. There are various ways of expressing dates: □ *5 October 1994* is becoming the standard form in Britain in preference to *5th October, 1994* and *October 5th, 1994*. The standard form in the United States is *October 5 1994*.

de- The prefix *de-* is used to signify 'the opposite or reverse': □ *declassify*, 'removal': □ *descale*, or 'reduction': □ *degrade*.

deadly or **deathly**? *Deadly* means 'likely to cause death'; *deathly* refers to a characteristic of death: □ *a deadly weapon* □ *a deathly silence. Deadly* is sometimes used in place of *deathly* in figurative contexts: □ *'Goodbye,' she said, with a deadly finality.*

debris This word, meaning 'rubble or remains': □ *They removed the debris from the building site*, is stressed on the first syllable [*deb*ri]. The variant pronunciation [*day*bri] is widely used, and this pronunciation should be used when the word is written with an acute accent: □ *débris.*

debut *Debut*, meaning 'first appearance': □ *He made his debut in a James Bond film*, may be pronounced [*day*bew] or [*deb*ew]. If the word is spelt with an acute accent: □ *début*, the first pronunciation should be used.

deca- or **deci-**? The prefix *deca-* means 'ten times'; the prefix *deci-* means 'one tenth': □ *decagon* □ *decibel.* A *decametre* is ten metres; a *decimetre* is one tenth of a metre.

deceitful or **deceptive**? Both *deceitful* and *deceptive* imply misleading appearances or cheating. However, *deceitful* suggests an intention to deceive or mislead, even if not successful, and therefore carries negative moral overtones: □ *It was deceitful of you to pretend to be an orphan. Deceptive* applies to a misleading effect or result rather than dishonest motivation, and something might be unintentionally deceptive: □ *The* *ring's dull appearance was deceptive.*

decent or **decorous**? Both these adjectives can mean 'socially acceptable': □ *decent/decorous behaviour. Decorous*, a formal word, is largely restricted to this sense, whereas *decent* has the additional meanings of 'not obscene', 'adequate', 'morally correct', 'obliging; pleasant', etc.: □ *decent language* □ *a decent meal* □ *to do the decent thing.*

deceptive see DECEITFUL OR DECEPTIVE?

deceptively The adverb *deceptively* suggests misleading appearances and is used to indicate that something is not as it seems. *A deceptively healthy man* is actually a sick man; *a deceptively slimming meal* is, in fact, fattening. The word is frequently misused to mean 'surprisingly' or 'contrary to appearances'.

deci- see DECA- OR DECI-?

decidedly or **decisively**? *Decidedly* usually means 'definitely; unquestionably': □ *It was a decidedly welcome suggestion.* It is also sometimes used to mean 'firmly; resolutely', and *decisively* is used in the same way: □ *'I'm going ahead with it,' she said decidedly/decisively. Decisively* is also used to imply decision-making which is marked by firmness, confidence, and lack of wavering: □ *He studied the options briefly before decisively choosing the second one.*

decimate *Decimate* literally means 'destroy one in ten', from the Roman practice of killing every tenth soldier as a punishment for mutiny. The word is now used popularly to mean 'inflict considerable damage; destroy a large part of': □ *The weather decimated today's sports programme* (BBC TV). This use probably arises from the mistaken belief that the word means 'to destroy all but a tenth' and, although the usage is very widespread, many careful users still dislike it. *Decimate* should not be used to mean 'annihilate totally', or in such constructions as: □ *badly decimated* □ *utterly decimated* □ *Some 75 per cent of the cattle were decimated by the disease.*

decisively see DECIDEDLY OR DECISIVELY?

decolorize see COLOURIZE.

décor The noun *décor*, meaning 'interior decoration' or 'stage decoration', may be spelt with or without the acute accent in English. The pronunciation is [*day*kor] or [*de*kor].

decorous see DECENT OR DECOROUS?

decriminalize or **legalize**? These two verbs are virtually interchangeable in the sense of 'make no longer illegal': □ *to legalize* [or *decriminalize*] *the smoking of cannabis. Legalize* is the more frequent, and is used in a wider range of contexts in the sense of 'make legal': □ *to legalize independent radio stations.*

dedicated In technology, the word *dedicated* is applied to machines, parts, accessories, computer programs, etc., that are designed to fulfil a single specific function: □ *a dedicated word-processing package*. The term is increasingly used in more general contexts: □ *Three companies gave their proposals to the Commons select committee on broadcasting for a new 'dedicated' parliamentary channel* (*The Guardian*).

deduce or **deduct**? To *deduce* is to come to a logical conclusion; to *deduct* is to subtract: □ *I deduced that she was lying.* □ *He deducted £10 from the bill.* The two verbs have the derived noun *deduction* in common: □ *the deduction that she was lying* □ *a deduction of £10.*

defective or **deficient**? *Defective* means 'having a fault; not working properly': □ *The washing machine I bought yesterday turned out to be defective. Deficient* means 'having a lack': □ *She sings well but her voice is deficient in power.*

defence The noun *defence*: □ *the importance of the country's defence*, is spelt with a *c* in British English, while the adjective *defensive* is spelt with an *s*: □ *The players adopted a defensive strategy.*

deficient see DEFECTIVE OR DEFICIENT?

definite or **definitive**? These two words are sometimes confused, although their meanings are different. *Definite* means 'precise, exact, or unambiguous': □ *The rules draw a definite distinction between professionals and amateurs. Definitive* means 'final; conclusive': □ *This is the definitive game in the tournament*, and is frequently used in criticism in the sense of 'authoritative' to describe a work or performance that is unlikely to be improved on: □ *Painter has written the definitive biography of Proust.*

definite article see THE.

definitely This word, meaning 'certainly': □ *He was definitely going to win*, is sometimes misspelt, the most frequent error being the replacement of the second *i* with an *a*.

definitive see DEFINITE OR DEFINITIVE?

defuse or **diffuse**? To *defuse* is to remove the device that causes a bomb to explode; to *diffuse* is to spread: □ *The bomb was defused.* □ *The light was diffused.*

degree The phrase *to a degree* has two meanings, 'somewhat' and 'extremely': □ *The match was exciting to a degree.* This may give rise to ambiguity, as in the above example: how exciting was the match?

deity The pronunciation of *deity* is either [*day*iti] or [*dee*iti]. Although the former is widely used, the latter is the more traditional pronunciation.

delirious Note the spelling of this adjective, particularly the first two vowels *-e-* and *-i-*. The correct pronunciation is [di*lir*riŭs], with the short [i] of *squirrel*, not [di*leer*iŭs].

deliver Some people dislike the intransitive use of the verb *deliver* in the sense of 'fulfil a promise or commitment': □ *The government has failed to deliver on tax cuts.* □ *We don't just want people with good ideas; we want people who will deliver.*

deliverance or **delivery**? Both these nouns are derived from the verb *deliver*. *Deliverance* specifically refers to the act of delivering from danger, captivity, evil, etc., and is used in formal or literary contexts; *delivery* is used in the many other senses of the verb: □ *to pray for deliverance* □ *the delivery of a baby* □ *postal deliveries* □ *the delivery of a speech.*

delusion see ALLUSION, ILLUSION, OR DELUSION?

demi-, **hemi-**, or **semi-**? All three prefixes mean 'half': □ *demigod* □ *hemisphere* □ *semicircle*. *Semi-* is the most frequent, and may be used to form new words: □ *semiprofessional* □ *semi-independent*. *Hemi-* is found in a number of scientific terms: □ *hemihydrate* (a term used in chemistry) □ *hemiplegia* (paralysis of one side of the body). *Demi-* is chiefly found in words of French origin: □ *demitasse* (a small cup) □ *demilune* (a crescent-shaped formation).

demise The original meaning of *demise* was 'the transfer of an estate or of sovereignty', and because such a transfer was frequently the result of death, the word came to mean 'death': □ *We were sad to hear of the demise of your husband.* This usage is formal and somewhat outdated.

demonstrable This word may cause problems with pronunciation. The most widely used pronunciation is [di*mon*străbl] which is stressed on the second syllable. Some careful speakers prefer the traditional [*de*mŏnstrăbl] which is stressed on the first syllable.

denationalization see PRIVATIZATION OR DENATIONALIZATION?

denote see CONNOTE OR DENOTE?

denouement This word, meaning 'final outcome': □ *the stunning denouement of the novel,* may be spelt *denouement* or *dénouement*. Note the *oue* vowels in the middle of the word.

deny see REFUTE OR DENY?

depend *Depend* means 'be contingent': □ *It depends on the weather*, or 'be reliant on': □ *They depend on Social Security*. It is normally used with *on* or *upon*, except in certain constructions where *it* is the subject: □ *It depends whether I'm well enough.* □ *It depends what you mean by socialism.*

dependant or **dependent**? The adjective, meaning 'reliant', is spelt *dependent*: □ *industries that are dependent on North Sea gas* □ *He is completely dependent on other people's help.* The noun, meaning 'someone who relies on another person for financial support', is spelt *dependant*: □ *Apart from your children, do you have any dependants?* The two are often confused, as in a leaflet for *Exmoor Area Tourist Attractions*: □ *But this freedom will remain largely dependant upon visitors respecting the life of the countryside.*

dependence or **dependency**? Either noun may

be used to mean 'the state of being dependent', but *dependence* is the more frequent in this sense: □ *his dependence/dependency on his parents* □ *her dependence/dependency on alcohol.* See also DEPENDANT OR DEPENDENT?

dependent see DEPENDANT OR DEPENDENT?

deploy *Deploy* is a military term meaning 'organize troops or equipment so that they are in the most effective position': □ *the decision to deploy Cruise missiles at Greenham Common.* Careful users object to the frequent use of the word with reference to any utilization or organization of resources: □ *It will be up to you to set ambitious revenue targets and then train, develop, and deploy your team-members to ensure that those targets are met and surpassed* (*Daily Telegraph*).

deprecate or **depreciate**? *Deprecate* means 'express disapproval': □ *She deprecated the Government's record on equal opportunities. Depreciate* means 'reduce in value', where it is usually used intransitively: □ *It depreciates by about £100 every year*, and 'belittle or disparage': □ *He depreciated their attempts to talk English.*

deprived *Deprived* means 'having something taken away or withheld': □ *Brain damage can occur if a baby is deprived of oxygen during labour.* It should properly be applied to things which were once possessed or would be possessed in normal circumstances, but the modern tendency is to connect it with basic necessities and rights. As an adjective it has become a vogue word often meaning little more than 'poor': □ *It is always the most deprived women, usually with housing problems or of low intelligence, who are involved* (*The Times*).

derail Some people dislike the increasing use of the verb *derail* in a figurative sense: □ *The British Government ... would not be allowed to use its presidency of the European Community to derail progress to greater political union or a 'social Europe'* (*The Guardian*). This usage is best restricted to informal contexts.

derisive or **derisory**? *Derisive* means 'expressing derision; mocking or scornful': □ *His speech was received* *with derisive mirth. Derisory* means 'deserving derision': □ *It was a derisory performance.*

derived words Derived words are formed by adding fixed groups of letters at the beginning or end of another word. The noun □ *sadness* is derived from the adjective *sad*; the adjective □ *readable* is derived from the verb *read*; the adverb □ *boldly* is derived from the adjective *bold*; the noun □ *membership* is derived from the noun *member*.

deselect The verb *deselect*, referring to an MP who is not selected for re-election, is one of a number of new words formed with the prefix DE-: □ *a number of Labour MPs have been deselected by their local constituency parties.*

desert or **dessert**? These words are sometimes confused. *Dessert* is the last course of a meal (see DESSERT, SWEET, PUDDING, OR AFTERS?): □ *a deliciously sweet dessert* □ *a dessert spoon. Desert* is used in all other contexts: □ *the Sahara desert* □ *She got her just deserts.* □ *a deserted city.*

desiccated This word, meaning 'dried': □ *desiccated coconut*, is sometimes misspelt. Note the single *s* and *-cc-*.

design see INVENT, DESIGN, OR DISCOVER?

designer *Designer* has become a vogue adjective which is applied to clothes and other manufactured goods which are produced by a well-known company with a reputation for fashionable design: □ *designer jeans* □ *designer watches* □ *He won't wear anything without a designer label.* The use has been extended to mean 'chic', 'trendy' and is applied to anything that is in fashion.

desirable or **desirous**? *Desirable* means 'worth desiring or having': □ *a desirable residence* □ *Confrontation with the union is not desirable at this stage. Desirous,* which means 'desiring; wanting', is a more formal adjective, usually placed after the verb and followed by *of*: □ *to be desirous of peace* □ *The president is desirous of your opinion.* The two adjectives should not be confused.

despair or **desperation**? The noun *despair* means 'loss of hope': □ *a feeling of utter* *despair.* □ *She gave up in despair.* The noun *desperation* is often applied to a reckless act that results from despair: □ *In desperation he jumped out of the window.*

despatch or **dispatch**? Both of these spellings are acceptable for the verb meaning 'send quickly' or the noun meaning 'message or report'.

desperate This word, meaning 'having no hope': □ *a desperate man* □ *a desperate situation*, is sometimes misspelt. The middle part of the word is spelt *per*, not *par* as in *separate*.

desperation see DESPAIR OR DESPERATION?

despicable *Despicable*, meaning 'contemptible': □ *It was a despicable act,* is usually stressed on the second syllable [dis*pik*ăbl]. Careful users, however, prefer the traditional pronunciation with the stress on the first syllable [*des*pikăbl].

despite or **in spite of**? *Despite* and *in spite of* are completely interchangeable: □ *Despite/In spite of his injury, his playing was superb. In spite of* is used rather more frequently, although *despite* has the advantage of brevity.

dessert, sweet, pudding, or **afters**? The question of how the sweet (usually) last course of a meal is referred to in Britain is not fixed. Usage not only varies slightly from one individual, family, etc., to another, but also is probably currently changing. Generally, *dessert* is found in both spoken and written contexts: □ *For dessert we were offered ice cream and fruit. Sweet* is more informal, is found in spoken English, and is considered by some middle- and upper-class people to be unacceptable. Such users prefer the word *pudding*, but this may be becoming slightly old-fashioned to refer generally to the last course of a meal. *Afters* is used in very informal spoken English: □ *What's for afters, Mum?*

destined *Destined* means 'being determined or intended in advance; directed towards, or having a particular purpose or end': □ *She believed her son was destined to be the messiah.* □ *The convict ship was destined for Australia.*

desultory This word, meaning 'unmethodical', should be stressed on the first syllable [*des*ŭltri].

detach The verb *detach*, meaning 'separate', is often misspelt, the most frequent error being the substitution of *-tch* for the *-ch* ending.

detract or **distract**? *Detract* means 'to take away from; diminish' and is usually used figuratively to describe the diminishing of some desirable quality: □ *The new hotels can only detract from the resort's charm. Distract* means 'take one's mind off something; divert attention elsewhere': □ *I tried to concentrate but I was distracted by the noise outside.*

development Since Third World countries have been referred to as *underdeveloped countries*, and then *developing countries*, the word *development* has come to have a specialized meaning in terms of the economic growth and improvements in living conditions of these countries: □ *the World Development Movement* □ *The rich world need provide only $5 billion a year in development assistance* (Ronald Sider, *Rich Christians in an Age of Hunger*).

device or **devise**? These words are sometimes confused. *Device* is a noun meaning 'contrivance or gadget': □ *a device for opening bottles*, or 'scheme or ploy': □ *It was a cunning device to get his own way. Devise* is a verb meaning 'plan': □ *They devised a new method of classifying the books.*

devotee The noun *devotee*, meaning 'enthusiast', 'supporter', or 'follower', is sometimes mispronounced. The correct pronunciation is [devŏ*tee*], with the stress on the last syllable. The first two syllables rhyme with *clever*: they do not have the same vowel sounds as the verb *devote*.

dexterous or **dextrous**? This word, meaning 'skilful or nimble': □ *a dexterous artisan*, may be spelt *dexterous* or *dextrous* although the former is the more frequently used spelling.

diagnosis or **prognosis**? Both *diagnosis* and *prognosis* are most often used in medical contexts. A *diagnosis* is the identification of a disease, from studying the symptoms: □ *The doctor's diagnosis, based on her spots, was chicken-pox.* A *prognosis* is a forecast of the likely course of an illness and the prospect of recovery: □ *The doctor's prognosis is that he will never fully regain his eyesight.*

dialect *Dialect* usually refers to an established variety of a language, confined either to a region or to a social group or class.

dialectal or dialectic? *Dialectal* is an adjective, meaning 'relating to dialect': □ *a dialectal term. Dialectic* is a noun, meaning 'disputation'; it has a number of specialized uses in logic and philosophy.

dialogue *Dialogue* is now rarely used for an ordinary conversation between two or more people, but is increasingly applied to exchanges of opinion and high-level negotiation between organizations and individuals who are usually ideologically opposed or have a conflict of interest: □ *We must bring about meaningful dialogue between management and unions.* □ *Mr Gorbachev said, 'The meeting ... might start a peaceful chain-reaction in the sphere of strategic offensive arms ... and many other items on a possible agenda of international dialogue'* (*The Times*).

diaphragm A *diaphragm* is a separating membrane and especially refers to the partition that separates the chest from the abdomen. The word also refers to a contraceptive device. In spelling, note the *ph* and the silent *g*.

diarize Some people dislike the verb *diarize*, meaning 'write in one's diary', as an example of the increasing tendency to coin new verbs by adding the suffix *-ize* to nouns and adjectives: □ *to diarize one's appointments.* See also -IZE OR -ISE?

diarrhoea This word is often misspelt. Note particularly the *rrh* and also the *-oea* ending.

dice *Dice* was originally the plural form of a singular noun *die*, but this singular form is now almost never used except in the expression: □ *The die is cast. Dice* is used now both as a singular and as a plural: □ *He made a dice out of a sugar* *cube.* □ *You need two dice for that game.*

dichotomy A *dichotomy* is a division of two things which are sharply contrasted, especially if they are mutually exclusive, contradictory, or irreconcilably different: □ *the dichotomy between Christianity and atheism.* It has become a vogue word used generally to mean 'conflict, split, schism, or difference': □ *A new dichotomy is developing in the Church of England.* This usage is disliked by some people, both for its lack of precision and for its pretentiousness.

dietician or **dietitian**? A person who studies the principles of nutrition is known as a *dietician* or *dietitian*. Both spellings of the word are perfectly acceptable.

different from, different to, or **different than**? It is possible to follow *different* with *from, to,* or *than. Different from* is the most frequently used form and the most acceptable: □ *Your life is different from mine. Different to* is often used in informal British English: □ *The happy situation he finds himself in is very different to the experiences of graduates in the early 1980s* (*Sunday Times*). It is, however, disliked by some people and not used in American English. *Different than* is in frequent use in American English but is disliked by many users of British English and generally should be avoided.

differential *Differential*, as adjective and noun, is a term in mathematics and has the nontechnical meanings of 'based on a difference; a difference between comparable things'. It is now most frequently used in reference to differences in pay rates for various jobs in the same industry, based on differences in skills, work conditions, etc.: □ *Pay differentials between nursing and administrative staff have widened.*

different than, different to see DIFFERENT FROM, DIFFERENT TO, OR DIFFERENT THAN?

diffuse see DEFUSE OR DIFFUSE?

digital The adjective *digital* has specific technical uses in computing and sound recording: □ *a digital com-*

puter □ *a digital recording. Digital* also refers to the presentation of information in the form of digits rather than pointers on a dial or scale: □ *digital watch* □ *digital display.*

dilapidated This word, meaning 'falling into ruin': □ *a dilapidated cottage*, is sometimes misspelt, the most frequent mistake being to begin the word with *de-*, rather than the correct *di-*.

dilemma A *dilemma* is a situation where one is faced with two equally unsatisfactory alternatives: □ *It was a hopeless dilemma – she could stay with her husband and be miserable, or she could leave him and lose the children.*

dimension The literal uses of *dimension* are concerned with measurement, *dimensions* being also used figuratively to mean 'scope or extent': □ *They were now in a position to assess the dimensions of the tragedy.* The word is also fashionably used as a synonym for *aspect* or *factor*: □ *The fact that one of the applicants was black and one a woman added a new dimension to their decision.*

diminution This word means 'decrease in size, intensity, etc.': □ *the possible diminution in readers.* Note the spelling and the pronunciation [dimi*new*-shŏn].

dinghy or **dingy**? These words are sometimes confused. A *dinghy* is a small boat; *dingy* is an adjective meaning 'gloomy or shabby': □ *a dingy basement flat.*

dining room see LOUNGE.

dinky *Dinky,* an acronym of 'dual (or 'double') income, no kids', is used with reference to a childless couple earning above-average salaries. The final *-y* is sometimes interpreted as 'yet'. There is also the British adjectve *dinky*, 'pretty', 'neat'.

dinner, lunch, tea, or **supper**? The question of how meals and mealtimes are referred to in Britain is fraught with class and regional considerations. In general, middle- and upper-class people have their main meal in the evening and call it *dinner* or *supper*; *lunch* is taken around midday and is usually a light meal or snack, although Sunday lunch may be the main meal of the day. *Tea* (or *afternoon tea*), if it is taken, is eaten late in the afternoon and consists of small sandwiches and cakes. *High tea* is a meal eaten in the late afternoon rather than *dinner* or *supper* later in the evening. Some people, especially those living in Northern England and Scotland have *dinner* at midday, while *tea* is a substantial meal eaten at about six o'clock. *Supper* is always the last meal of the day and is sometimes a light bedtime snack for those who have had a large tea, or it can be the main evening meal for those who choose not to call the main evening meal *dinner* or *tea*.

diphtheria This word causes problems with spelling and pronunciation. Note the *phth* in the spelling. The *ph* sound is pronounced *f* by careful users [dif*theer*iă] or *p* [dip*theer*iă].

diphthong Note the *phth* in the spelling. The *ph* sound is pronounced *f* by careful users [*dif*thong] or *p* [*dip*thong].

direct speech *Direct speech* is a record of the actual words used by a speaker. These words are usually enclosed in QUOTATION MARKS and followed or preceded by a verb such as *said, whispered, shouted,* etc.: □ *'Get out!' he cried.* □ *She replied, 'I don't know.'* See also REPORTED SPEECH.

dis- or dys-? Confusion between these two prefixes can cause spelling mistakes. *Dis-* is the more frequent, indicating lack, reversal, negation, removal, etc.: □ *disagreement* □ *discontinue* □ *dissimilar.* *Dys-* means 'abnormal', 'faulty', 'difficult', or 'bad' and is chiefly found in technical words relating to physical or mental problems: □ *dyspepsia* □ *dyslexia* □ *dysfunction.*

disadvantaged Like UNDERPRIVILEGED and DEPRIVED, *disadvantaged* has become a fashionable euphemism for 'poor', with particular emphasis on the lack of a reasonable standard of housing, living conditions, and opportunities for gaining basic rights: □ *Up to 100 teachers from each country are to spend one or two months studying* *such matters as how to motivate disadvantaged children* (*The Times*).

disappear Note the spelling of this word, particularly the single *-s-* and the *-pp-*.

disappoint The verb *disappoint* and its derivatives are often misspelt, the most frequent error being the doubling of the *-s-*. Note also the *-pp-*.

disassemble see DISSEMBLE OR DISASSEMBLE?

disassociate see DISSOCIATE OR DISASSOCIATE?

disastrous This word is sometimes misspelt. Note that the *e* of *disaster* is dropped before the suffix *-ous* is added.

disc or **disk**? These spellings are sometimes confused. A *disc* is a flat round or circular shape: □ *a slipped disc* □ *compact disc*. In American English this word is usually spelt *disk*. In British English *disk* is reserved for use in computer science, to describe a thin plate on which data is stored: □ *a floppy disk*. This is occasionally spelt *disc*.

discipline Note the *c* following the *s* in the spelling of this word.

discoloration see COLORATION.

discomfit or **discomfort**? There is some overlap between these words and often confusion as to the distinction between them. *Discomfit* means 'defeat or thwart': □ *He discomfited his opponent*, and 'disconcert, confuse, or embarrass': □ *They were discomfited by his strange manner*. *Discomfort* means 'make uncomfortable or uneasy'. This might be physical distress: □ *The hard seats discomforted her*, or mental uneasiness, in which case the distinction between *discomfort* and *discomfit* often becomes blurred: □ *His ominous tone discomforted them.*

discover see INVENT, DESIGN, OR DISCOVER?

discreet or **discrete**? These two words are sometimes confused. *Discreet* means 'judicious or prudent': □ *You can confide in him; he is very discreet*; *discrete* means 'separate or distinct': □ *discrete elements in the composition*.

discrepancy or **disparity**? Both these nouns mean 'difference'. A *discrepancy* is a difference between things that should be the same; a *disparity* is a greater difference that suggests imbalance or inequality: □ *a discrepancy between the accounts of the two witnesses* □ *a disparity between the wages of factory and office workers.*

discriminating or **discriminatory**? Both these adjectives are derived from *discrimination* and are connected with 'distinguishing, making distinctions' but they are used in very different ways. *Discriminating* is applied to someone who is discerning in matters of taste and able to tell the difference between good and poor quality: □ *We'd better serve the Bordeaux because Paul is discriminating when it comes to wine. Discriminatory* is now almost always applied to discrimination that is unjust and based on prejudice: □ *Feminists are organizing a boycott of the bank because of its discriminatory practices.*

disinterested or **uninterested**? *Disinterested* means 'impartial; having no self-interest': □ *As a disinterested party he felt free to intervene in the dispute. Uninterested* means 'having no interest; indifferent; bored': □ *I was quite uninterested in their holiday photos.*

disk see DISC OR DISK?

disorganized or **unorganized**? Either adjective may be used in the sense of 'not organized'. As the past participle of the verb *disorganize, disorganized* specifically refers to something organized that has been thrown into confusion, but it is also used in a general informal sense: □ *I'm a bit disorganized this morning. Unorganized* is more neutral and less frequent: □ *an unorganized method of working.*

disorient or **disorientate**? *Disorient* and *disorientate* are interchangeable and mean 'cause to lose bearings or sense of identity; confuse': □ *They had organized a one-way traffic system since his last visit and he was completely disoriented/disorientated.* □ *After years of being institutionalized she was disoriented/disorientated after her discharge. Disorient* is preferred by some users as the shorter and simpler alternative; it is also the standard form in American

English, while *disorientate* is more frequently used in British English. See also ORIENT OR ORIENTATE?

disparity see DISCREPANCY OR DISPARITY?

dispassionate, impassioned, or impassive? The adjectives *dispassionate* and *impassive* are sometimes confused because of their similarity in meaning; *impassioned* and *impassive* because of their similarity in form. *Dispassionate* means 'not influenced by emotion; objective', whereas *impassive* means 'showing no emotion': □ *a dispassionate assessment of the problem* □ *She remained impassive, ignoring his cries. Impassioned* means 'full of passion': □ *an impassioned attack on the government.*

dispatch see DESPATCH OR DISPATCH?

dispel or disperse? *Dispel* means 'scatter; drive away' and is often used for abstract things: □ *He allowed them to see the original document so as to dispel their doubts about its authenticity. Disperse* means 'break up': □ *The family were dispersed over Europe*, 'spread over a wide area': □ *The gas dispersed over half the town*, and 'dissipate, evaporate, or vanish': □ *The mist had now dispersed and visibility was normal.*

dispute The noun *dispute* may be pronounced with the stress on the first syllable [*dis*pewt] or the second [dis*pewt*]. The first of these pronunciations is becoming increasingly frequently heard, although it is disliked by many users. The verb *dispute* is always stressed on the second syllable.

dissect This word, meaning 'separate or cut up for analysis', is spelt with *-ss-*, unlike *bisect*.

dissemble or disassemble? *Dissemble*, a literary word, means 'pretend' or 'conceal'; *disassemble* means 'take apart': □ *He dissembled his excitement.* □ *She disassembled the machine.* The two verbs should not be confused.

dissemble, dissimulate, or simulate? The verbs *dissemble* and *dissimulate*, both of which are formal, mean 'pretend not to have; conceal'; *simulate* means 'pretend to have; feign': □ *to dissemble* [or *dissimu-*

late] *one's anger* □ *to simulate enthusiasm.* See also SIMULATE OR STIMULATE?

dissension or **dissent**? The noun *dissension* refers to a state of disagreement, discord, or conflict: □ *The proposal caused much dissension.* The noun *dissent,* the opposite of *assent,* means 'difference of opinion'; it refers to the act of disagreeing or an expression of disagreement: □ *a voice of dissent.*

dissimulate see DISSEMBLE, DISSIMULATE, OR SIMULATE?

dissociate or **disassociate**? *Dissociate* and *disassociate* are interchangeable opposites of *associate*. Most careful users prefer the form *dissociate.*

distil In British English the verb *distil* ends in a single *l*, which is doubled before a suffix beginning with a vowel: □ *distilled* □ *distillery.*

distinct or **distinctive**? These two adjectives are frequently confused although they are not interchangeable. *Distinct* means 'definite; clearly perceivable or distinguishable': □ *There's a distinct taste of garlic in this stew. Distinctive* means 'characteristic, peculiar to, distinguishing': □ *He had the distinctive rolling gait of a sailor.*

distract see DETRACT OR DISTRACT?

distrust or **mistrust**? *Distrust* and *mistrust* are often used interchangeably: □ *Somehow I distrust/mistrust the whole business. Distrust* is more frequently used and has a far more emphatic suggestion of suspicion and lack of trust: □ *I have known him to be deceitful in the past and I have come to distrust everything he says. Mistrust* is rather more tentative and is used for a less positive lack of trust or when the doubt is directed against oneself: □ *There was something about her manner that made me uneasy and I found myself beginning to mistrust her.* □ *I mistrust my critical judgment when it comes to my own writing.*

disturb or **perturb**? *Disturb* can mean 'interrupt; inconvenience': □ *His reverie was disturbed by a ring at the doorbell.* □ *I hope I'm not disturbing you by phoning so late,* 'throw into disorder': □ *The cleaner had disturbed all her papers,* and 'upset;

destroy the mental composure of': □ *I was deeply disturbed by this revelation.* In this last use, *disturb* is virtually synonymous with the less frequently used word *perturb*, which means 'cause disquiet to; cause mental disturbance': □ *His violent language and abrupt departure had perturbed her.*

dived or **dove**? In British English the past tense of *dive* is almost always *dived*: □ *They all dived for cover.* However, the past tense *dove* exists in some British dialects and is the standard form in several regions of the United States and Canada: □ *She dove beautifully, and a moment later she was swimming back to the side of the pool* (Philip Roth, *Goodbye Columbus*).

divorcee A divorced person is known as a *divorcee* [divaw*see*]. A divorced man is called a *divorcé* [divaw*say*] or [divaw*see*], and a divorced woman is called a *divorcée* [divaw*see*].

do *Do* is used as an informal replacement for various different verbs, for example 'prepare': □ *Shall I do you a sandwich?*, 'clean': □ *I'm just going to do my teeth*, 'visit': □ *We're doing the British Museum tomorrow*, 'perform': □ The local rep are doing *The Cherry Orchard*, 'study': □ *She's doing maths at Cambridge*, 'provide': □ *Do they do breakfasts?* There are also the slang meanings of 'cheat' and 'arrest'. *Do* is also used informally as a noun to mean 'a party or social event'. A use such as: □ *They behaved just as I wanted them to do* is best reserved for informal use. *Do* is also used as an auxiliary verb in questions: □ *Do you like it?*, in negative sentences: □ *They don't want to go*, and for emphasis: □ *I do wish he'd phone!*

document *Document* is used as a verb to mean 'provide documentary evidence or information to act as factual support': □ *His essay was well documented with authoritative references.* It is also used in reference to the production of a written, filmed, or broadcast work that has plentiful detailed factual information: □ *The programme documents life in a women's prison.*

Domesday or **doomsday**? The *Domesday Book* is the survey of England carried out during the reign of William I. The noun *doomsday,* sometimes spelt with a capital *D-*, means 'Judgment Day; Last Judgment' in the Christian religion, and 'day of reckoning' or 'end of the world' in general usage. The phrase *till doomsday* means 'for ever': □ *You can wait till doomsday, but I won't change my mind.*

dominate or **domineer**? To *dominate* means 'rule, exert power or control over': □ *Her charm and energy were such that she came to dominate the whole company.* It can also mean 'occupy a preeminent position': □ *Our products dominate the pet-food market,* and 'overlook from a superior height': □ *The church is built on a hill and dominates the town. Dominate* is often used in a negative way that would be better reserved for *domineer* which means 'tyrannize, exert power in an arbitrary or overbearing manner'. It is most frequently used as a present participle that functions as an adjective: □ *his cruel domineering manner.*

doomsday see DOMESDAY OR DOOMSDAY?

doorstep The verb *doorstep* is disliked by some people as an example of the increasing tendency to use nouns as verbs. It originally referred to the practice of selling door-to-door, then to the practice of canvassing door-to-door, and later to the practice (favoured by investigative journalists, press photographers, etc.) of waiting outside the house or office of somebody in the public eye and accosting that person when he or she appears.

do's and don'ts In the phrase *do's and don'ts*, note that the apostrophe in *don'ts* comes after the *n* and not after the *t*. The apostrophe in *do's* is sometimes omitted.

double negative The double negative, as in: □ *I didn't do nothing.* □ *He hasn't had no tea*, is always avoided by careful users. The objection to such constructions is that the negatives cancel each other out and reverse the meaning of the sentence.

double whammy A *double*

whammy is a double blow, or any problem or difficulty that has a two-pronged effect: □ *We have been hit by a double whammy: a cut of £30 million below meagre expectations ... and major cost increases for equipment and international subscriptions following the devaluation of sterling* (*Daily Telegraph*).

doubling of consonants On the general rule of doubling consonants in such words as: □ *drop – dropped* □ *refer – referred*, see individual entries and SPELLING 1.

doubt The main problem with *doubt* is what preposition or conjunction to use with it. When *doubt* is used as a noun it is most often followed by *about*: □ *I have my doubts about it*, but it can be followed by *that* in a negative construction: □ *There is no doubt in my mind that he is telling the truth*. When *doubt* is used as a verb it can only be followed by *that* in negative constructions: □ *I don't doubt that you are right*, and in most other constructions it is followed by *whether*: □ *They doubted whether she would be welcome*.

doubtful or **dubious**? Both *doubtful* and *dubious* mean 'giving rise to doubt, uncertain, questionable' and they are often more or less interchangeable: □ *They were doubtful/dubious whether the car was safe*. *Doubtful* is more neutral and is more likely to be used when expressing uncertainty: □ *The eventual result remains doubtful*. *Dubious* carries more negative overtones and is often used to suggest a suspicion that a person or practice is underhand or dishonest in some way: □ *He was involved with some dubious export company*.

doubtless see UNDOUBTEDLY.

douse or **dowse**? Either spelling of this verb may be used in the sense of 'soak' or 'extinguish', pronounced [dows]. *Douse* is the more frequent: □ *doused with petrol* □ *to douse a candle*. The verb *dowse*, in the additional meaning 'search for water using a divining rod' and pronounced [dowz], should never be spelt *douse*.

dove see DIVED OR DOVE?

downside The vogue word *downside* means 'unfavourable aspect'; it is best avoided where *disadvantage* would be more appropriate: □ *the downside of the new system* □ *Every scientific breakthrough has its downside.*

downsizing *Downsizing* is the act of reducing in size. In America in the late 1970s it referred to the production of smaller cars: □ *With the whole industry downsizing, big-car addicts will find fewer alternatives* (*Time*). In Britain in the late 1980s it referred to redundancy: □ *downsizing the workforce* □ *In the case of the latest cuts – 55 jobs to go at US investment bank L.F. Rothschild – downsizing is something of an understatement* (*The Guardian*).

downward or **downwards**? In British English *downward* is principally used as an adjective, *downwards* being the usual form of the adverb meaning 'to a lower level': □ *a downward slope* □ *to look downwards.*

dowse see DOUSE OR DOWSE?

draft see DRAUGHT OR DRAFT?

dramatist or **playwright**? *Dramatist* and *playwright* are synonymous words, both dating from the late seventeenth century and meaning 'a person who writes plays': □ *He is a poet as well as a dramatist/playwright.*

draught or **draft**? These words are sometimes confused. A *draft* is a preliminary outline: □ *a rough draft of the essay.* A *draft* is also a money order and a group of soldiers. *Draught* is the spelling for: □ *draught beer* □ *draught animals* □ *a draught from an open door.* The American English spelling of *draught* is *draft*.

drawing room see LOUNGE.

dreamed or **dreamt**? Either word may be used as the past tense and past participle of the verb *dream*: □ *I dreamed/dreamt I was in Australia.*

drier or **dryer**? *Drier* is the usual spelling of the comparative form of the adjective *dry*; both are equally common for the noun derived from the verb *dry*: □ *These socks are drier/dryer than those.* □ *a hair-dryer/drier* □ *a spin-dryer/drier.*

drunk or **drunken**? Both *drunk* and *drunken* are adjectives applied to alcoholic intoxication, but *drunk* is normally used after a verb: □ *She got drunk on cheap white wine,* while *drunken* is normally used before a noun: □ *We were just sipping sherry – it was hardly a drunken orgy.* □ *the campaign against drunken driving.*

dryer see DRIER OR DRYER?

dual or **duel**? These two words are sometimes confused, being identical in pronunciation. *Dual* is an adjective, meaning 'double'; *duel* is a noun or verb referring to a rather formal fight between two people: □ *dual-purpose* □ *a dual carriageway* □ *the duel of the champions* □ *to settle a quarrel by duelling.*

dubious see DOUBTFUL OR DUBIOUS?

duel see DUAL OR DUEL?

due to, owing to, or **because of**? Although these phrases have roughly the same meanings they are not used in the same way. *Due to* should be used only adjectivally: □ *His shakiness is due to Parkinson's disease*; whereas *owing to* and *because of* can be used either adjectivally or as prepositions: □ *The delay was owing to an electrical fault on the line.* □ *Because of poor health he took early retirement.* □ *She was now rich, owing to her successful venture.*

duplication or **duplicity**? The noun *duplication* is derived from the verb *duplicate*, meaning 'copy' or 'repeat'; the more formal noun *duplicity* means 'deception' or 'double-dealing': □ *There may be some duplication in the text.* □ *They were unaware of his duplicity.* The two nouns should not be confused.

dwarfs or **dwarves**? Either spelling is acceptable as the plural of the noun *dwarf*, *dwarfs* being the more frequent.

dwelled or **dwelt**? Either word may be used as the past tense and past participle of the verb *dwell*. *Dwelled* is more frequent in American English than in British English, but *dwelt* is the preferred form in both: □ *He dwelt on her infidelity.*

dying or **dyeing**? These spellings are sometimes confused. *Dying* is the present participle of the verb *die*, meaning 'cease to live': □ *Her son is dying.*

□ *his dying words. Dyeing* is the present participle of the verb *dye*, meaning 'change the colour of': □ *She was dyeing her hair blonde.*

dynamic *Dynamic* is an overworked vogue word meaning 'lively, forceful, or energetic': □ *The Party needs young, dynamic leadership.*

dynasty The preferred British English pronunciation of *dynasty*, which means 'series of hereditary rulers', is [*din*ăsti]. The American English pronunciation [*dīn*ăsti] is sometimes also used in British English.

dys- see DIS- OR DYS-?

dyslexic or **dyslectic**? The words *dyslexic* and *dyslectic* are interchangeable; either may be used as a noun or adjective to describe a person suffering from dyslexia, though *dyslexic* is used much more frequently.

E

each When *each* is used as a determiner or as a pronoun which is the subject of a sentence, the rule is that subsequent verbs and pronouns should be singular: □ *Each man has his price.* □ *Each of the operas was sung in English.*

each or **both**? see BOTH.

each and every *Each and every* is used for emphasis in such phrases as: □ *Each and every person has a vital part to play.* □ *I am deeply grateful to each and every one of you.* It is disliked by most careful users as a cliché and as an unnecessarily wordy construction for which *each*, *everyone*, or *all* can often be substituted.

each other or **one another**? The traditional rule is that *each other* is used when two elements are involved and *one another* when more than two are involved: □ *Helen and Charles love each other deeply.* □ *All the people at the party already knew one another.* However, there is no particular reason for this rule and most people feel free to ignore it.

earthly or **earthy**? *Earthly* relates to the earth as opposed to heaven; *earthy* refers to earth in the sense of 'soil': □ *our earthly life* □ *an earthly paradise* □ *an earthy taste/texture.* The two adjectives are not interchangeable.

east, East, or **eastern**? As an adjective, *east* is always written with a capital *E* when it forms part of a place-name: □ *East Anglia* □ *the East End.* The noun *east* is usually written with a capital *E* when it denotes a specific region, such as the countries of Asia: □ *She has travelled extensively in the East.* □ *East-West relations.*

eatable or **edible**? *Eatable* means 'palatable', but with the suggestion of 'not actually tasting unpleasant' rather than 'delicious': □ *He had managed to get together a reasonably eatable meal. Edible* means 'suitable for eating as food': □ *Common sorrel is edible but wood sorrel is poisonous.*

EC or **EEC**? The abbreviation *EC* and its full form *European Community* have now replaced the abbreviation *EEC* and *European Economic Community.*

echelon *Echelon* is a military expression applying to the formation of units or to a division of a supply organization. It is now often used as a fashionable synonym for *grade, rank, level of power,* or to describe the people at that level: □ *the management echelon* □ *the higher echelons of the civil service.*

eco- The growing popularity of the science of *ecology*, the study of living things in their relation to the environment, has given rise to several words with the prefix *eco-*, some legitimate terms in ecology: □ *ecospecies* □ *ecotype* □ *ecosystem*, and some more modern coinages: □ *ecocatastrophe* □ *eco-freak*. New *eco-* words are being spawned all the time.

economic or **economical**? *Economic* is the adjective from *economics* or *the economy* and is concerned with the production, distribution, and structure of wealth: □ *Friedman's economic theories* □ *the Government's economic policies. Economical* is the adjective from *economy* and is concerned with thrift and the avoidance of waste: □ *an economical car* □ *a large economical pack.* An *economic price* is one that benefits the seller, but an *economical price* benefits the buyer.

economics see -ICS.

ecstasy This word, meaning 'intense emotion', especially of happiness, is sometimes misspelt. Note particularly the *cs* and the *-asy* ending, as in *fantasy*.

ecu The noun *ecu* is an acronym of *European Currency Unit,* the currency unit of the European Community. It is sometimes written *ECU*.

-ed or **-t**? The past tense and past participle of the verbs *burn, dream, dwell, kneel, lean, leap, learn, smell, spell, spill,* and *spoil* may end in *-ed* or *-t*. In most cases the *-ed* form is preferred in American English and the *-t* form is slightly more frequent in British English.

edible see EATABLE OR EDIBLE?

-ee or **-er**? In general, the suffix *-ee* can be applied to the recipient of an action denoted by the verb to which the suffix is attached, and the suffix *-er* is applied to the thing or person who performs the action: □ *employer–employee* □ *trainer–trainee*. However, this rule does not apply in all cases. The suffix *-ee* can sometimes indicate someone who behaves in a particular way: □ *absentee* □ *arrestee* □ *escapee*, and the suffix *-er* can be applied to something that is a suitable object for an action: □ *prisoner* □ *cooker* (type of apple).

EEC see EC OR EEC?

effect see AFFECT OR EFFECT?

effective, **effectual**, **efficacious**, or **efficient**? The distinction between these words is subtle. *Effective* means 'having or producing the desired effect': □ *The talks were effective in settling the dispute. Effectual*, a formal word, means 'capable of achieving the desired effect': □ *All plans to reduce the trade deficit have not so far proved effectual*, and in religious contexts: □ *effectual prayer* □ *God's effectual calling of his people. Efficacious*, also a formal word, means 'having the power to achieve the desired effect' and is usually applied to medical treatment: □ *an efficacious remedy. Efficient* is applied to people or things producing results through a good and economical use of resources: □ *an efficient machine* □ *an efficient secretary*.

effrontery see AFFRONT OR EFFRONTERY?

e.g. and **i.e.** The abbreviation *e.g.* stands for *exempli gratia* and means 'for example'. It is used before examples of what has previously been mentioned: □ *We could show you some of the sights, e.g. Buckingham Palace and the Tower of London.* The abbreviation *i.e.*, often used in error for *e.g.*, stands for *id est* and means 'that is'. It is used before amplifications or explanations of what has previously been mentioned: □ *They were vegans, i.e.*

vegetarians who also avoid eggs and dairy products.

egoism or **egotism**? The words *egoism* and *egotism* are frequently used interchangeably but there are differences between them. *Egoism* is applied to the ethical theory that all actions and motivation are based on self-interest. An *egoist* is a believer in this theory or, much more often, a person who is selfish and self-seeking: □ *His conduct was characterized by ruthless egoism. Egotism* means 'being self-obsessed; self-centred'. The typical *egotist* is vain, boastful, and uses the word *I* constantly: □ *Her egotism makes her oblivious to other people's concerns.*

egregious The adjective *egregious*, used in formal contexts and meaning 'very bad', is sometimes misspelt and/or mispronounced. Note the *-egi-* in the middle of the word. The correct pronunciation is [igreejŭs].

eighth Note that in the spelling of this word the letter *h* occurs twice: *eight* plus *h*.

either As an adjective or pronoun *either* is used with a singular verb: □ *Is either child left-handed?* □ *Is either of your children left-handed?* In the *either ... or* construction, a singular verb is used if both subjects are singular and a plural verb is used if both subjects are plural. When a combination of singular and plural subjects occurs, the verb traditionally agrees with the subject that is nearest to it: □ *Either his friends or his brother is responsible.*

eke out The original meaning of *eke out* is 'make something more adequate by adding to it': □ *She eked out the meal with extra rice.* It is frequently used in two other senses: 'make something last longer by using it economically': □ *They eked out the supplies over two weeks*, and 'make (a living) with laborious effort': □ *The children eked out a living by selling wild flowers to tourists.*

elder, **eldest**, **older**, or **oldest**? *Elder* and *eldest* are applied only to people, and usually within the context of family relationships: □ *my eldest brother* □ *She is the elder of my two daughters.* One cannot say: *Rachel is elder than Sarah* or: *He is elder/eldest* without adding *the*. *Older* and *oldest* can be used of things as well as people and in a far wider range of constructions: □ *I am older than David.* □ *It is the oldest church in Yorkshire.*

electric or **electrical**? *Electric* and *electrical* can both mean 'worked by electricity' although *electric* tends to be applied more to specific, and *electrical* to general things: □ *electric lighting* □ *an electric motor* □ *electrical appliances* □ *electrical equipment.*

elemental or **elementary**? *Elemental* means 'of or like the elements or forces of nature': □ *This evoked a flood of elemental passion.* It is also sometimes used to mean 'fundamental or essential': □ *an elemental truth of Christianity.* It should not be confused with *elementary* which means 'very simple; introductory'.

elicit see ILLICIT OR ELICIT?

eligible see ILLEGIBLE OR ELIGIBLE?

ellipse or **ellipsis**? An *ellipse* is an oval; *ellipsis* is a term used in grammar and linguistics (see ELLIPSIS). The two nouns share the derived adjective *elliptical*: □ *an elliptical shape* □ *an elliptical phrase. Elliptical* also means 'ambiguous' or 'obscure' in formal contexts: □ *an elliptical reference.*

ellipsis There are two meanings of the term *ellipsis* in grammar: one is for the punctuation marks ..., usually indicating omission; the other is for the omission of words in a sentence, as an abbreviation or in order to avoid repetition: □ *See you Friday.* □ *I ought to write some letters and make some phone calls.* The ellipsis ... is used mainly to indicate an omission from a quoted passage: it is always three dots, or four if a full stop is included. The ellipsis is also used in the same manner as the dash (see DASH).

elliptical see ELLIPSE OR ELLIPSIS?

else *Else* is often followed by either *than* or *but*: □ *Nothing else than revolution is possible.* □ *Anybody else but him would be preferable.* Some careful users object to following *else* with *but* and difficulties can be avoided by substituting such phrases as *nothing but* or *anyone other than.*

elude see AVOID, EVADE, OR ELUDE?

elusive see ALLUSIVE, ELUSIVE, OR ILLUSIVE?

embarrass This word, meaning 'cause to feel shy, ashamed, or self-conscious': □ *She was embarrassed by her brother's behaviour*, is often misspelt. Note the *-rr-*, the *-ss-*, and the last vowel, which is an *a*, not an *e*.

emend see AMEND OR EMEND?

emigrant or **immigrant**? An *emigrant* is someone who is migrating from his or her country: □ *Thousands of emigrants left Britain for Australia under the assisted passage scheme*. An *immigrant* is someone who is migrating into another country: □ *Some of the immigrants had only been in the country for a week*.

eminent, **imminent**, or **immanent**? *Eminent* means 'outstanding, notable, or distinguished' and is particularly applied to people who have achieved some distinction or fame in their profession, or in the arts or sciences: □ *an eminent barrister* □ *an eminent poet*. *Imminent* means 'impending; about to happen; threatening'. *Immanent* means 'inherent, indwelling' and is not frequently used.

emotive or **emotional**? *Emotive* means 'causing or arousing emotion, especially as opposed to reason': □ *Taxation is always an emotive subject* (*Mind Your Own Business*). *Emotional* means 'expressing emotion, showing excessive emotion': □ *an emotional meeting*.

empathy *Empathy* means 'an imaginative identification with another's feelings or ideas': □ *He read all he could about the king, and meditated on his character, so by the time he came to play the part he felt a real empathy with Henry*. It has recently become a fashionable word and its frequent use as a mere synonym for *sympathy* is disliked by some.

emulate *Emulate* means 'attempt to equal or do better than, especially by close imitation': □ *Since the company's success all our competitors are trying to emulate our products*.

encyclopedia or **encyclopaedia**? Both spellings of this word are acceptable, *encyclopaedia* being the more traditional in British English. In American English *encyclopedia* is the more frequent spelling and this spelling is becoming adopted in British English. See also -AE- AND -OE-.

endemic or **epidemic**? *Endemic*, a formal word, is most frequently used as an adjective, meaning 'occurring in a particular area': □ *an endemic disease* □ *The plant is endemic in* [or *to*] *Africa*. An *epidemic* is the widespread occurrence or rapid spread of a disease: □ *a flu epidemic*.

end product and **end result** *End product* usually means 'the final product of a process, or series of processes': □ *We use the best materials so that the end product is a quality item*.

enervate *Enervate* means 'weaken, to lessen vitality or strength': □ *It was an enervating climate and they felt listless most of the time*.

England see BRITAIN.

enhance *Enhance* means 'improve, increase the value or attractiveness of': □ *The new windows have enhanced the value of the house*. □ *This week's running debacle over Labour's defence policies has hardly enhanced Mr Kinnock's appeal to any Tories who might be wavering* (*Sunday Times*).

enormity or **enormousness**? *Enormity* means 'the quality of being outrageous or wicked, a very wicked act': □ *Those experiences alerted him to the enormity of what was being done to the Jews* (*The Guardian*). *Enormousness* means 'the quality of being extremely large': □ *They were daunted by the enormousness of the task*.

enquiry or **inquiry**? For many users of British English the spellings of the nouns *enquiry* and *inquiry* (and of the verbs *enquire* and *inquire*) are completely interchangeable. Some users, however, maintain that *enquire* and *enquiry* are used for simple requests for information: □ *He enquired after her health*. □ *an enquiry office* □ *directory enquiries*, and *inquire* and *inquiry* are used for investigations, especially official ones: □ *The police are now inquiring into the events that led up to his disappearance*.

enrol In British English the verb *enrol* ends in a single *l*, unlike the word *roll*. The *l* is doubled before suffixes beginning with a vowel: □ *enrolled* □ *enrolling*.

ensure see ASSURE, ENSURE, OR INSURE?

-ent see -ANT OR -ENT?

enterprise Some people dislike the overuse of the noun *enterprise* in the context of self-employment and the setting up of new small businesses: □ *the enterprise culture* □ *the government's Enterprise Allowance Scheme* □ *a network of Local Enterprise Agencies* □ *Britain's enterprise economy* □ *the enterprise initiative*.

enthral In British English the verb *enthral* ends in a single *l*, which is doubled before suffixes beginning with a vowel: □ *enthralled* □ *enthralling*.

enthuse The verb *enthuse* is a back formation from *enthusiasm* and means 'show enthusiasm': □ *The critics enthused over her new play*, or 'make enthusiastic': □ *Mr Neil Kinnock's achievement has been to mobilise and enthuse the traditional Labour vote* (*Sunday Times*).

entomology or **etymology**? *Entomology* is the study of insects; *etymology* is the study of the origin and development of words. The two nouns should not be confused.

entourage Of French origin, the noun *entourage*, meaning 'attendants; retinue', is pronounced [ontuu*rahzh*] in English.

entrepreneur Like ENTERPRISE, the noun *entrepreneur* is losing its traditional connotations of risk and initiative and is indiscriminately applied to any person who becomes self-employed or sets up a new small business: □ *Skills appear to be the main requirement for successful entrepreneurship ... in contrast with the simple traditional view of the entrepreneur as someone who is risk loving* (*The Guardian*).

E-numbers *E-numbers*, which appear on food labels as E401, E218, etc., denote additives that have been approved for use throughout the European Economic Community. The belief that E-numbers denote harmful artificial substances is a popular misconception: E440(a), for example, is pectin, which occurs naturally in ripe fruit and vegetables; E270 is lactic acid, which is found in dairy productsı and E150 is caramel. The term was popularized by Maurice Hanson in *E for Additives* (1984).

envelop or **envelope**? The verb *envelop* means 'enclose, surround, or enfold' and is used both literally and figuratively: □ *He was enveloped in a blanket and barely visible.* □ *She spent a happy childhood, enveloped in love and security.* The noun *envelope* means 'something that envelops, a wrapper (particularly for a letter)': □ *It arrived in a plain brown envelope.*

enviable or **envious**? Both these adjectives are derived from the word *envy* (see ENVY OR JEALOUSY?). *Enviable* means 'causing envy'; *envious* means 'feeling envy': □ *the enviable task of showing the film star around the building* □ *He was envious of his sister's success.* The two words are not interchangeable.

environment *Environment* can be applied to the surrounding conditions of people and other organisms and can include physical and social influences, though many people are careful not to overuse this word. *Environment* and its derived noun *environmentalism* have become fashionable words in the conext of ecology. See also -FRIENDLY; GREEN.

envisage or **envision**? Both *envisage* and *envision* mean 'have a mental image of, especially of something hoped for in the future': □ *They envisaged/envisioned a world where war and poverty no longer existed.* *Envisage* is more often used in British English and *envision* in American English.

envy or **jealousy**? *Envy* involves the awareness of an advantage possessed by someone else, together with a desire to have that advantage oneself: □ *She gazed at his car with envy.* □ *I envy your ability to relax.* *Jealousy* involves a concern to avoid the loss of something that one regards as one's own, and includes the tendency to be suspicious of rivalry and infidelity in relation to a person one is close to: □ *Her husband's jealousy forced her to conceal even the most innocent encounters with other men*, as well as vigilance in preserving a possession: □ *They guarded their professional* *reputation jealously.*

ephemeral This word, meaning 'lasting only a short time': □ *the ephemeral pleasures of life*, is sometimes misspelt. Note particularly the *ph*, pronounced [f], and the sequence of vowels.

epic *Epic* originally applied to long narrative poems on a grand, heroic scale, like Homer's *Iliad* and *Odyssey* or the Finnish *Kalevala*. It was extended to other works with some of these qualities or to series of events or episodes which might be fit subjects for an epic: □ *a marvellous epic novel* (*Newsweek*, review of Salman Rushdie's *Midnight's Children*) □ *the epic battle between Greenpeace and the whaling ships.*

epidemic see ENDEMIC OR EPIDEMIC?

epigram, epigraph, epitaph, or **epithet**? These four nouns should not be confused. An *epigram* is a short witty saying; an *epigraph*, the least common of the four words, is a quotation or motto printed at the beginning of a book or engraved on a monument. An *epitaph* is a commemorative statement about a dead person, often inscribed on a gravestone; an *epithet* is a short descriptive word or phrase applied to a person, such as *Lionheart* in *Richard the Lionheart.*

epitome This word, meaning 'typical example': □ *He is the very epitome of the absent-minded professor*, is sometimes mispronounced. Note that there are four syllables [i*pi*tŏmi].

eponyms An *eponym* is a person from whose name a word is derived: □ *sandwich* □ *quisling* □ *cardigan* □ *ampere.* There are eponymous nouns: □ *martinet* □ *salmonella* □ *listeria* □ *watt*, adjectives: □ *quixotic* □ *herculean*, and verbs: □ *bowdlerize* □ *guillotine.*

equable or **equitable**? *Equable* means 'regular, moderate, not given to extremes' and is frequently applied both to climates which are consistently mild and not subject to sudden changes, and to people who are placid and even-tempered. *Equitable* means 'fair, reasonable, impartial': □ *It was an equitable agreement which both parties found satisfactory.*

equally The word *equally* should not be followed by *as* in such sentences as: □ *She is a brilliant pianist, and her brother is equally talented* [not *equally as talented*].

equal to or **equal with**? When briefly indicating identity, equivalence, or similarity *equal* is used as a verb with no preposition: □ *x equals 5* or as an adjective followed by *to*: □ *x is equal to 5*. In longer constructions, using *equal* as an adjective, it is preferable to use *equal with*, rather than *equal to*: □ *The Bradford team have gained five points and are now equal with the team from Liverpool. Equal to* has the specific meaning of 'capable of meeting the requirements of': □ *He seemed too young and inexperienced to be equal to the task.*

equitable see EQUABLE OR EQUITABLE?

-er see -EE OR -ER?

-er or **-or**? The suffix *-er* is used to form nouns to indicate an occupation: □ *lawyer* □ *bricklayer*, or an action performed by a person: □ *steeple-chaser* □ *messenger* □ *enquirer*. The suffix *-or* is used in the same way with other words, normally those formed from Latin roots. Often these are words where there is no English verb base: □ *sponsor* □ *doctor* □ *author* □ *mentor*, but this is not always the case: □ *actor* □ *investigator* □ *sailor*.

erogenous *Erogenous* zones are the parts of the body that are sensitive to sexual stimulation. Note the spelling of the word *erogenous*: a single *r* and *-gen-*, not *-gyn-* as in *misogynist*.

erupt or **irrupt**? These two verbs (and their derived nouns *eruption* and *irruption*) are identical in pronunciation but different in meaning. *Erupt* means 'burst out; come or go out with force', whereas *irrupt*, a more formal word, means 'burst in; enter with force': □ *The crowd erupted onto the street.* □ *The police irrupted into the building.*

escalate *Escalate* is a back formation from *escalator*, and as a vogue word meaning 'expand, rise, intensify' tends to be overused. It is best confined to the description of an upward movement that increases step by step: □ *Rents have* *escalated over the last five years.* □ *Officials killed by mine as Tamil attacks escalate* (*The Times*).

especially or **specially**? These adverbs are often used interchangeably, but there is a difference in their meanings. *Especially* means 'more than usual, in particular, above all': □ *He was especially hungry.* □ *I hate dogs, especially big ones.* *Specially* means 'specifically, purposely, in this particular way': □ *The car is specially designed for handicapped people.* □ *I made it specially for you.*

-ess The use of the feminine suffix *-ess* is sometimes regarded as patronizing or sexist and is often unnecessary.

essentially *Essentially* should be used primarily to mean 'basically, inherently, or most importantly': □ *The play is essentially a tragedy although there is some comic relief.*

establishment *The Establishment* refers to the powerful figures in government (especially the civil service), the legal system, the established church, the armed forces, and the City of London, who are thought to control the country: □ *The Prime Minister, the Archbishop of Canterbury, and the Lord Chief Justice were among the Establishment figures present. The Establishment* (sometimes with a lower-case *e*) is thought to have a conservative outlook, generally opposing changes to the existing order, and as such is often used as a derogatory term.

esthetic see AESTHETIC, ASCETIC, OR ACETIC?

estimation, **estimate**, or **esteem**? *Estimation* is the act of estimating; an *estimate* is a figure, idea, etc., arrived at by the process of estimation: □ *an estimate of the time it will take. Esteem,* a more formal word, means 'great respect': □ *He held her in high esteem.*

et al. *Et al.* is an abbreviation of *et alii* and means 'and other people'. It is used particularly in writings of a formal technical nature to indicate the omission of other names: □ *Similar findings have been recorded by Jones, Bernstein, et al.*

etc. The abbreviation *etc.* stands for *et cetera*, which means 'and other things, and so forth': □ *The college* *offers several non-academic subjects – home economics, physical education, craft and design, etc.*

ethics see -ICS.

ethnic The original meaning of *ethnic* is 'to do with groups of people classed by common race, traits, or customs': □ *There are many different ethnic groups in the USA.* As a vogue word *ethnic* is now used to mean 'to do with race': □ *Shooting continued last night in Sukhumi, ... more than 24 hours after the start of ethnic clashes in which 11 people have been killed* (*Daily Telegraph*), 'foreign': □ *But a great deal of ethnic food is not hot, but spiced, with pronounced flavours* (*Sunday Times*), and 'nonwhite': □ *Labour now has three other ethnic MPs* (*Sunday Times*).

ethnic cleansing The phrase *ethnic cleansing* is a euphemism applied to the deportation and murder of thousands of Muslims and Croats living in Bosnia. It is sometimes used as a synonym for the extermination of the Jews by the Nazis in 1930s Germany.

etymology see ENTOMOLOGY OR ETYMOLOGY?

euphemisms A *euphemism* is an inoffensive term that is used as a substitute for one that might give offence. Euphemisms tend to be used particularly when referring to sexual and bodily functions: □ *private parts* (genitals) □ *smallest room* (toilet) □ *pass water* (urinate), and to death: □ *She passed away.* □ *I lost my wife two years ago.*

Euro- Although the United Kingdom is part of Europe, British people have traditionally spoken of *Europe* to mean all the continent apart from the United Kingdom. When United Kingdom membership of the European Community was mooted, it was often referred to as *going into Europe*, and *Europe* is now quite often used as a synonym for the EC.

evade, evasion see AVOID, EVADE, OR ELUDE?

even The position of the word *even* in a sentence can influence its meaning. Compare the following sentences and their implications: □ *Even I like opera on television* (so other people would like it still more). □ *I like even opera on television* (presumably I would prefer things other than opera). □ *I like opera even on television* (though it is inferior on television). In formal writing it is best to put *even* before the word it modifies, in order to make the meaning unambiguous, although in speech it is often more natural to put *even* before the verb: □ *He doesn't even stop working on holiday.*

eventuate *Eventuate* is used, usually in formal contexts, to mean 'result': □ *If the proposed merger takes place, this might eventuate in the new company having a monopoly of the market.* It is disliked by many people as pompous and affected, and conveying nothing that is not conveyed by simpler and more usual words.

ever The use of *ever* with superlatives in such constructions as: □ *the largest pie ever* □ *his fastest speed ever*, is disliked by some people as they feel that *ever* includes the future, as well as the past. The usage is well-established, but the criticism can be met by changing the constructions slightly: □ *the largest pie ever baked* □ *his fastest speed to date/the fastest he has ever run.*

every *Every* is used with singular nouns and all related words should be in the singular form: □ *Every machine is equipped with a safety device.* The temptation to use plurals arises when one wishes to avoid such gender-specific constructions as: □ *I hope every committee member has remembered to bring his agenda.* Rather than use the ungrammatical *their agendas* or the rather clumsy *his or her agenda* it is better to rephrase the sentence: □ *I hope all committee members have remembered to bring their agendas.*

everybody or **everyone**? The pronoun *everybody* and its synonym *everyone* are interchangeable in all contexts.

evince *Evince* is a formal verb meaning 'show clearly; make apparent': □ *Her writing evinces keen perception and skills of observation.* Some careful users believe it should be applied only to qualities, not to attitudes or emotions, although it is generally acceptable in such applications.

ex As a prefix, *ex-* means 'former' or 'outside': □ *the ex chairman* □ *an ex-directory telephone number.* It is usually attached with a hyphen. The noun *ex*, meaning 'former wife' or 'former husband', should be restricted to informal contexts: □ *She had a letter from her ex this morning.*

exaggerate This word, meaning 'represent as greater than is true', is sometimes misspelt. Note the *-gg-* and single *-r-*, as in *stagger.*

exalt or **exult**? *Exalt* means 'elevate' or 'praise'; *exult* means 'rejoice' or 'triumph': □ *She was exalted to the position of sales director.* □ *to exalt a hero* □ *He exulted at his success.* □ *to exult in victory.*

exceed see ACCEDE OR EXCEED?

except It is usually better to use *except* rather than *except for*: □ *We all went for a walk except Flora.* The exceptions are at the beginning of a sentence: □ *Except for Stuart, we are all under 40,* and when a whole statement is being qualified and *except for* means 'if it were not for': □ *The room was silent except for the occasional squeak of a pen.* See also ACCEPT OR EXCEPT?

exceptional or **exceptionable**? *Exceptional* means 'out of the ordinary; uncommon': □ *Apart from the exceptional quiet day, we've been kept busy all month,* and 'unusually good': □ *This is an exceptional wine.* In British English *exceptional* is often used of people to mean 'above average; superior; gifted': □ *an exceptional student* □ *an exceptional musician.* In American English, however, *exceptional* is applied to children of both below and above average ability, and is now applied particularly to physically or educationally handicapped children. *Exceptional* should not be confused with *exceptionable*, which means 'objectionable; something to which exception might be taken': □ *His words were not offensive in themselves but there was something in his manner that we found exceptionable.*

exclamation mark Exclamation marks are used to indicate strong feeling or urgency: □ *Hurray!* Exclamation marks may come at the end of a sentence, as a substitute for a full stop, or at the end of a quotation, within quotation marks: □ *'Ouch!' he cried.* Occasionally, they may occur in the middle of a sentence. They are used after interjections, oaths, words representing loud noises, commands, insults, and exclamations expressing surprise etc. They should be used sparingly.

exclamations Exclamations are words, phrases, or sentences that express a strong feeling, such as surprise, anger, shock, excitement, etc.: □ *Gosh!* □ *Get out!* □ *Oh dear!* They are always followed by an EXCLAMATION MARK.

exclude or **preclude**? *Exclude* means 'leave out' or 'prevent from entering'; *preclude* is used in formal contexts and means 'make impossible' or 'prevent from happening': □ *A number of items were excluded from the list.* □ *Lack of resources precluded further research.* The two verbs should not be confused.

executive An *executive* is a senior businessman or businesswoman. Many people object to the increasing use of the word in the sense of 'fashionable', 'luxurious', or 'expensive', describing items that are designed to appeal to those who aspire to the social level of an executive or the (supposed) high income of an executive: □ *an exclusive development of executive homes* □ *an executive bathroom.*

exercise or **exorcise**? These two words should not be confused. *Exercise* is a noun and verb with various meanings, including 'a set of energetic movements', 'a short piece of school work', and, in formal contexts, 'make use of': □ *You should take more exercise.* □ *He exercised his right to remain silent.* The verb *exorcise* means 'expel evil spirits from': □ *The house had been exorcised.*

exhausting or **exhaustive**? *Exhausting* means 'extremely tiring': □ *I find Christmas shopping very exhausting.* It should not be confused with *exhaustive*, which means 'thorough; comprehensive; considering all possibilities': □ *They made exhaustive enquiries but to no avail.*

□ *This is an exhaustive study, covering every aspect of the subject.*

exhilarate This word, meaning 'thrill or excite': □ *an exhilarating experience*, is sometimes misspelt. Frequent errors include the omission of the *-h-* and the substitution of *-ler-* for *-lar-*.

existential *Existential* usually means 'relating to existence, particularly human existence': □ *an existential statement*, or 'grounded in human existence; empirical': □ *an existential argument for the existence of God*. It is also sometimes used to mean 'existentialist, based on existentialist philosophy': □ *existential angst* □ *Sartre's existential theories*.

exorbitant This word, meaning 'excessive': □ *an exorbitant price to pay*, is sometimes misspelt. There is no *h* in the spelling, unlike *exhilarate*.

exorcise see EXERCISE OR EXORCISE?

exotic The original meaning of *exotic* is 'from another country, not native to the place it is found': □ *exotic flowers*. By this definition the potato would be an exotic vegetable in Britain but it is never spoken of as such, because *exotic* is now almost always used with the meaning of 'unusual, excitingly different, interestingly foreign': □ *exotic food* □ *exotic dances* □ *travel to distant exotic lands*.

expatriate The word *expatriate*, meaning 'a person who is living in a country that is not his or her native country', is sometimes misspelt. Note the spelling of the ending of this word: *-iate*, not *-iot* as in *patriot*.

expeditious or **expedient**? *Expeditious* and *expedient* come from the same root, but have quite different meanings. *Expeditious* means 'speedy; efficient': □ *Our courier service is the most expeditious method of sending parcels.* *Expedient* means 'convenient for a particular situation or aim': □ *It would not be expedient to change the law at the present time.*

explicable In the traditional pronunciation of this word, which means 'able to be explained': □ *no explicable reason for their behaviour*, the stress was on the first syllable [*ek*splikăbl]. It is now more usual and perfectly acceptable to stress the second syllable [ik*splik*ăbl]. See also STRESS.

explicate *Explicate* means 'explain in detail; analyse and explore the implications of': □ *This series of lectures aims to explicate Kant's critical philosophy philosophy and explore its influence on German idealism.* It is a formal word, usually confined to intellectual contexts, and it is pretentious to use it merely as a synonym for *explain.*

explicit or **implicit**? *Explicit* means 'clear; unambiguous, stated or shown in a direct manner': □ *He gave them explicit instructions so there was no question of their making a mistake. Implicit* means 'implied; understood although not directly expressed': □ *He detected an implicit criticism in her words,* and 'without reservation; unquestioning': □ *I have implicit faith in your organizational abilities.* Some people use *explicit* to mean 'frankly portraying (usually) sexual material'; it would be preferable to use *explicitly sexual* or *sexually explicit* if that is what is meant.

exquisite *Exquisite,* meaning 'very delicate and beautiful': □ *exquisite carvings,* may be pronounced in two ways. Some users prefer the stress to fall on the first syllable [*ek*skwizit]. Other users find this pronunciation slightly affected and prefer to stress the second syllable [ik*skwiz*it].

extant or **extinct**? *Extant,* a formal word, means 'surviving' or 'still in existence': □ *Seven of Sophocles' plays are extant.* □ *an extant law. Extinct* is usually applied to a species of animal or plant that has died out or to a volcano that is no longer active: □ *The African elephant is in danger of becoming extinct.* The two adjectives are virtually opposite in meaning.

extempore or **impromptu**? These two words have similar meanings but are not quite interchangeable. Both are applied to speeches and performances which are not rehearsed in advance. However, *extempore* suggests that nothing has been memorized or written down beforehand, although the speaker or performer may have thought about the content in advance: □ *He never wrote his sermons down but preached extempore. Impromptu* suggests something improvised on the spur of the moment, with no prior notice: □ *She was surprised to be asked to address them but managed a splendid impromptu speech.*

extemporize or **temporize**? To *extemporize* is to act, make a speech, play music, etc., without preparation; to *temporize* (a rarer word) is to gain time by delaying, stalling, or being evasive: □ *He extemporized an accompaniment on the piano.* □ *She temporized, being unable to think of a reasonable excuse.* The two verbs should not be confused.

extensive or **extended**? *Extensive* means 'large' or 'widespread'; *extended* means 'lengthened in time or space': □ *an extensive search* □ *an extended contract.* Both adjectives may be applied to the same noun: □ *an extensive discussion* covers a wide range of subjects; □ *an extended discussion* goes on for longer than usual or longer than planned.

exterior, **external**, or **extraneous**? *Exterior* means 'on the outside; relating to the outside': □ *The house needs some minor exterior repairs.* □ *Beneath his charming exterior he has a cold and selfish nature. External* means 'outwardly visible; suitable for the outside; coming from the outside; not essential': □ *He has a few external injuries.* □ *This ointment is for external use only.* □ *The paper will be marked by the external examiners.* □ *Do not be misled by these external details. Extraneous* means 'from the outside; not essential or relevant to the issue': □ *We try to impart our values to our children but they are influenced by extraneous pressures.* □ *Let's concentrate on the main issue and ignore those extraneous points.*

extinct see EXTANT OR EXTINCT?

extract or **extricate**? Both hese verbs have the sense of 'remove' or 'withdraw', but *extricate* is more formal and specifically refers to disentanglement or setting free from a difficult situation:

□ *to extract a tooth* □ *to extract information* □ *to extricate oneself from a complex relationship* □ *to extricate a ball from a thorn bush.*

extraordinary This word, meaning 'unusual or exceptional': □ *an extraordinary memory for details,* is sometimes misspelt, the most frequent mistake being the omission of the first *a*. Remember the two elements of the word: *extra* plus *ordinary*.

extrapolate Apart from specialized mathematical uses, *extrapolate* is usually applied to the estimation or prediction of unknown factors by the examination, analysis, and extension of known data and past experience: □ *We can extrapolate from the existing figures and our knowledge of the previous trends in mobility and birth control to produce an estimate of the populations of major cities in twenty years' time.* Careful users, however, are aware that this word is in danger of overuse.

extricate see EXTRACT OR EXTRICATE?

extrinsic see INTRINSIC OR EXTRINSIC?

extrovert or **introvert**? *Extrovert* and *introvert* are terms coined by the psychologist Jung that are now in general use. *Extroverts* are people who are more concerned with their environment than with their own inner selves; they are generally sociable, outgoing, and confident: □ *He is an extrovert and enjoys nothing better than a noisy, crowded party. Introverts* are primarily concerned with their own mental and emotional lives. They are withdrawn and quiet, and prefer reflection to activity: □ *She tends to be an introvert and is happiest in her own company.*

exuberant This adjective is sometimes misspelt, a common error being the insertion of *-h-* after the *-x-*. Note also the *-ant* ending.

exult see EXALT OR EXULT?

F

façade This word, which means 'front', as in: □ *the palace's ornate façade*, is usually spelt with a cedilla under the *c* in British English.

face or **face up to**? Some users object to *face up to* as an unnecessary extension of the verb *face*, meaning 'confront' or 'accept', but there is a slight difference in sense and usage between the two: *to face up to one's punishment* suggests a greater degree of effort and courage than *to face one's punishment*.

facetious This word, which means 'jocular' or 'flippant', as in: □ *a facetious remark*, is sometimes misspelt.

facia see FASCIA.

facile In the sense of 'easily achieved' or 'superficial', the adjective *facile* is often used in a derogatory manner: *facile prose* is produced with little effort and lacks substance; a *facile argument* is glib and lacks sound reasoning.

facilitate The verb *facilitate* means 'make easier'; it should not be used as a synonym for 'help' or 'assist': □ *His cooperation facilitated our task.* □ *We were helped* [not *facilitated*] *in our task by the information he gave us.*

facility or **faculty**? These two words are sometimes confused in the sense of 'ability'. *Facility* is ease or skill that is often gained from familiarity; *faculty* is more likely to denote a natural power or aptitude: □ *a facility for public speaking* □ *a faculty for understanding complex scientific concepts.*

faction This word, a blend of *fact* and *fiction*, was coined in the mid-1960s and is used especially by critics to denote a book, play, film, etc., that describes historically true events, using the techniques of fiction. Its more generally known sense is 'a minority group within a larger party'.

factitious or **fictitious**? Both these adjectives mean 'not genuine', but they differ in usage and application and should not be confused. *Factitious*, which is largely confined to formal contexts, means 'artificially created' or 'unnatural': □ *factitious enthusiasm. Fictitious* means 'false' or 'invented': □ *a fictitious address.* See also FICTIONAL OR FICTITIOUS?

factor A *factor* is a contributory element, condition, or cause; many people object to its frequent use as a synonym for 'point', 'thing', 'fact', 'event', 'constituent', etc.: □ *A rise in the cost of raw materials and a fall in demand were important factors in the company's collapse.* □ *We must discuss all the relevant points* [not *factors*].

faculty see FACILITY OR FACULTY?

Fahrenheit This word should always begin with a capital letter.

fail Some people dislike the frequent use of the verb *fail* as a simple negative: □ *Those who fail to pay the tax will be imprisoned.* The principal meaning of *fail* is 'try unsuccessfully (to do something)'; the verb should not be used with reference to something that is deliberately not done.

faint or **feint**? *Faint* means 'not clear' or 'not strong'; it is also a noun or verb referring to a brief loss of consciousness. *Feint*, derived from the verb *feign*, refers to an action or movement intended to distract or mislead: □ *On hearing the news she fell to the floor in a faint.* □ *The boxer made a feint with his left fist then struck with his right.*

fait accompli A *fait accompli* is something that has already been done and that therefore cannot be changed: □ *She was afraid he might not agree to her selling the car, so she decided to present him with a fait accompli* [i.e. She did not tell him until she had sold the car].

fallible or **fallacious**? These two adjectives, both of which are formal, are sometimes confused. *Fallible* means 'capable of making an error' or 'imperfect'; *fallacious* means 'containing an error' or 'illogical':

□ *All human beings are fallible.* □ *fallacious reasoning.* The adjective *fallible* may be applied to people; *fallacious* is applied only to abstract nouns.

falsehood, falseness, or **falsity**? All three nouns are formal and are derived from the adjective *false*, meaning 'untrue', 'not genuine', or 'disloyal'. *Falsehood* and *falsity* are largely restricted to the first sense: □ *the difference between truth and falsehood/falsity.* A *falsehood* is a lie; a *falsity* is an act of deception. *Falseness* may be used in all three senses, occurring most frequently in the sense of 'disloyalty': □ *the falseness of his statement/name/behaviour.*

fantastic The use of *fantastic* as a synonym for 'excellent' or 'very great' is best restricted to informal contexts: □ *a fantastic holiday* □ *fantastic wealth.*

farther, farthest, further, or **furthest**? In the sense of 'more (or most) distant or advanced', as the COMPARATIVE and SUPERLATIVE of *far*, *farther* is interchangeable with *further* and *farthest* with *furthest*: □ *London is farther/further from Manchester than it is from Bristol.* □ *Which of the three can run the farthest/furthest?*

fascia The noun *fascia* may be spelt *facia*, without the *-s-*, but many careful users prefer *fascia*, the spelling of the Latin noun from which the word is derived. The word is pronounced [*fay*shĕr].

fascinate This word, meaning 'attract and capture the interest of', as in *fascinating tales about her experiences in China*, is sometimes misspelt. The most frequent error is the confusion of the *-sc-*.

fast-forward Some people dislike the use of the word *fast-forward*, normally applied to video recorders, cassette players, etc., as a verb and adjective in figurative contexts: □ *Fast-forwarding through the years* (*Sunday Times*) □ *Fast-forward reviewers dependent on the index* (*The Guardian*).

fast lane The *fast lane* (or *fast track*) is the quickest and most competitive way to success. People who are *in the fast lane* or *in the fast track* or who are described as *fast-lane* or *fast-track* have great ambitions, are involved in a lot of intense hectic activity, and are promoted rapidly: □ *He tells Carol Price how he copes with the critics, the fame, the fortune and a career in the fast lane* (*TV Times*). □ *fast-track executives.* These fashionable modern expressions should not be overused and are best restricted to informal contexts.

fast-moving This expression is often used in commerce and advertising to describe products that sell quickly: □ *one of the world's most successful manufacturers and marketers of fast-moving consumer goods* (*Sunday Times*).

fast track see FAST LANE.

fatal or **fateful**? *Fatal* means 'causing death or ruin'; *fateful* means 'decisively important': □ *a fatal illness* □ *a fatal mistake* □ *their fateful meeting* □ *that fateful night.*

faux pas A *faux pas* is a social blunder: □ *Inviting her ex-husband to the party was a faux pas.*

fax The word *fax*, short for *facsimile* (a system for transmitting documents telegraphically), has established itself in the English language as a noun (referring to the system of transmission, the machine used for transmission, or the document transmitted) and as a verb: □ *by fax* □ *a combined fax, photocopier, and answering machine* □ *fax number* □ *a fax from head office* □ *I faxed the details to the agency.* This abbreviation is acceptable in most contexts.

faze or **phase**? *Faze* is a verb, meaning 'worry' or 'daunt': □ *She was not fazed by the accusation. Phase* is a noun, meaning 'stage': □ *the next phase of the development* □ *He went through a rebellious phase in his early teens*, or a verb, often found in the phrasal forms *phase in/out*, meaning 'introduce/withdraw gradually': □ *The benefit will be phased out over a period of five years.*

fearful or **fearsome**? Both adjectives can mean 'frightened' or 'frightening', but *fearful* is the more frequent and principally used in the sense of 'frightened': □ *fearful of what might happen* □ *a fearsome sight.*

feasible The use of *feasible* to

mean 'probable', 'likely', or 'plausible' is avoided by many careful users, especially in formal contexts, where the word is restricted to its original sense of 'practicable' or 'capable of being done': □ *The committee decided that the project was feasible.*

feature The verb *feature* is best avoided where *have*, *include*, *display*, *appear*, etc., may be more appropriate; to *feature* is principally used in the entertainment world: □ *The concert features such stars as George Harrison and Eric Clapton.* □ *a new leisure centre, featuring squash and badminton courts and an indoor swimming pool with flumes.*

February This month name causes problems of spelling and pronunciation, the most frequent being the omission of the first *r*.

feedback The use of *feedback* as a synonym for 'response' or 'reaction' is disliked by some people, who prefer to restrict the term to its scientific or technical usage.

feel Some people dislike the use of the noun *feel* in the sense of 'impression' or 'quality', as in the phrases *a nice feel about it*, *a different feel about it*, etc.: □ *The car has a strange feel about it.*

feel-good factor The phrase *feel-good factor* refers to a feeling of optimism amongst the general public about the state of the nation, for example the economic situation: □ *The 'feel-good factor' – as it has come to be known – has plummeted since the time of the General Election in April* (*Daily Telegraph*). The phrase is disliked by some people and should not be overused.

feet see FOOT OR FEET?

feint see FAINT OR FEINT?

fellow- The word *fellow* may be combined with other nouns to denote a person in the same category: *fellow passengers* are the people with whom one is travelling; *fellow workers* are people who work in the same place. The two words are sometimes hyphenated in British English: □ *fellow-students* □ *fellow-sufferers.* See also HYPHEN 2.

female or **feminine**? The adjective *female* refers to the sex of a person, animal, or plant; it is the opposite of MALE: □ *a female giraffe*

□ *female reproductive cells. Feminine* is applied only to people (or their attributes) or to words (see GENDER); it is the opposite of MASCULINE: □ *feminine charms.*

ferment or **foment**? These two verbs are virtually interchangeable in the sense of 'to stir up': □ *to foment/ferment trouble.*

fête This word, used as a noun or verb, is usually spelt with a circumflex accent over the first *e* in British English.

fetid or **foetid**? Both spellings of this adjective, which describes something that has a very unpleasant smell, are acceptable. The spelling *fetid* is preferred in British English and is standard in American English. See also -AE- AND -OE-.

fetus see FOETUS OR FETUS?

few The difference between *few* and *a few* is one of expectation or attitude rather than number; both expressions mean 'some, but not many': □ *They brought few books.* □ *They brought a few books.*

fewer or **less**? *Fewer*, the comparative of *few*, means 'a smaller number of'; *less*, the comparative of *little*, means 'a smaller amount or quantity of': □ *fewer cars* □ *less unemployment.* The general rule is that *fewer* (or *few*) is used with plural nouns and *less* (or *little*) with singular nouns, whether the nouns are concrete or abstract: □ *fewer pleasures* □ *few chairs* □ *less wood* □ *little hope* □ *fewer noises* □ *less noise.*

fiancé or **fiancée**? An engaged woman's future husband is her *fiancé*; an engaged man's future wife is his *fiancée*.

fictional or **fictitious**? *Fictional* means 'of fiction' or 'not factual'; *fictitious* means 'false' or 'not genuine': □ *a fictional detective* □ *his fictional works* □ *a fictitious address.*

fifth The second *f* in this word is sometimes not sounded in speech.

fill in or **fill out**? In British English, application forms and other official documents are usually *filled in* rather than *filled out*: □ *Fill in this form and give it to the receptionist.*

finalize The verb *finalize* is best avoided where *complete*, *finish*, *conclude*, *settle*, etc., would be adequate or more appropriate:

□ *The preparatory work must be finished* [not *finalized*] *as soon as possible.*

finite verb A *finite verb* is a in any of the forms that change according to the person or number of the subject or according to the tense in which the verb is used. □ She *helps.* □ The train *stopped.* □ I *am* cold. □ They *were* leaving. □ He *has* lost his key. The following verbs are not finite: □ *going* to school □ *covered* with dew □ I want to *leave*.

fiord or **fjord**? Both spellings of this word are acceptable.

first or **firstly**? *Firstly* may be used in place of the adverb *first* when enumerating a list: □ *There are three good reasons for not buying the house: firstly, it is outside our price range; secondly, it is too close to the railway; thirdly, the garden is too small.*

first name, Christian name, forename, given name, or **baptismal name**? All these expressions are used to denote the name or names borne in addition to one's surname; in British English *first name* is replacing *Christian name* as the most frequent choice: □ *a dictionary of first names. Christian name* and *baptismal name* are inapplicable to non-Christians. *Forename* is widely used on official forms, but rarely heard in informal speech. *Given name* is the preferred expression in American English.

fish or **fishes**? The plural of *fish* is *fish* or *fishes*; *fish* is used in a wider range of contexts than the alternative form: □ *Fish live in water and breathe through their gills.* □ *There are five fish in the pond.* □ *Dace, bream, roach, and burbot are all freshwater fishes/fish.*

fix or **repair**? Both these verbs are used in the sense of 'mend', *repair* being more formal than *fix*: □ *Have you fixed the radio yet?* □ *He was ordered to repair the damaged boat.*

fjord see FIORD OR FJORD?

flaccid The formal adjective *flaccid*, meaning soft and limp, may be pronounced [*flak*sid] or [*fla*sid]. The first pronunciation is more widely accepted than the second.

flagrant see BLATANT OR FLAGRANT?

flagship The noun *flagship*, which denotes the ship

that carries the commander of a fleet, is increasingly used in figurative contexts with reference to the most important of a group of products, projects, services, etc.: □ *The Labour leader, Mr Neil Kinnock, amid uproar, said the Government's flagship* [the community charge] *had been 'badly holed' and was 'sinking fast'* (*The Guardian*). □ *The* [Laura Ashley] *company has recently opened a furnishing flagship store.*

flair or **flare**? The noun *flair* means 'a natural aptitude or instinct'; *flare* is a noun or verb referring to a sudden burst of flame: □ *a flair for cookery* □ *the flare of the torch.*

flak The use of *flak* in the sense of 'heavy adverse criticism or opposition' is best restricted to informal contexts: □ *Civil-service bureaucrats come in for a lot of flak.*

flammable see INFLAMMABLE.

flare see FLAIR OR FLARE?

flaunt or **flout**? *Flaunt* means 'show off' or 'display ostentatiously'; *flout* means 'treat with contempt' or 'disregard': □ *to flaunt one's wealth* □ *to flout the rules.*

flavour of the month The phrase *flavour of the month* is applied to something that is popular or fashionable for a short time: □ *Political correctness is flavour of the month.* The phrase is often used in a derogatory manner. Its overuse should be avoided.

flee or **fly**? The rather literary verb *flee* means 'run away (from)': □ *You must flee the town.* □ *They have fled.* □ *I fled from the danger.* The verb *fly* is also occasionally used in this sense in literary contexts: □ *You must fly the town,* but is more frequently found in its principal sense of '(cause to) move through the air': □ *Most birds can fly.* □ *The children were flying a kite.* □ *We flew to Paris.*

fleshly or **fleshy**? *Fleshly* refers to the body as opposed to the spirit; *fleshy* refers to the flesh of a person, animal, fruit, or plant: □ *fleshly desires* □ *fleshly delights* □ *fleshy thighs. Fleshly* is occasionally used in place of *fleshy,* but some users prefer to maintain the distinction between the two adjectives.

flier or **flyer**? The spellings *flier* and *flyer* are interchangeable in the sense of 'person or thing that flies' and in such compounds as □ *high-flier/high-flyer*.

floor or **storey**? Both these nouns are used to denote a particular level of a building or the rooms on this level. The word *floor* is more frequently used with reference to the interior of the building, *storey* with reference to the exterior or structure. □ *He lives on the fourth floor.* □ *The new office block will be ten storeys high.* See also STORY OR STOREY?

flounder or **founder**? To *flounder* is to struggle, move with difficulty, or act clumsily; to *founder* is to fail, break down, collapse, or sink. Both verbs can be used literally or figuratively: □ *They floundered in the mud.* □ *She floundered on to the end of the speech.* □ *The project foundered through lack of support.* □ *The ship foundered at the harbour entrance.*

flout see FLAUNT OR FLOUT?

flu The word *flu* – the shortened form of *influenza* – is more frequent in general and some technical contexts than *influenza:* □ *She's off work with (the) flu.*

fluorescent This word, which is usually applied to light fittings, colours, paint, etc., may cause spelling problems.

flush see BLUSH OR FLUSH?

fly see FLEE OR FLY?

flyer see FLIER OR FLYER?

fob or **foist**? Both these verbs may refer to the disposal of something unwanted or worthless: □ *He fobbed the damaged toys off on Christmas shoppers.* □ *She always foists the boring jobs on her assistant.*

focus The doubling of the final *s* of the verb *focus* before a suffix beginning with a vowel is optional. Most dictionaries give *focused, focuses, focusing,* etc., as the preferred spellings, with *focussed, focusses, focussing,* etc., as acceptable variants.

foetid see FETID OR FOETID?

foetus or **fetus**? There are two possible spellings for this word. The first is more frequent in British English, and the second in American English. See also -AE- AND -OE-.

foist see FOB OR FOIST?

folk The use of the noun *folk* as a synonym for 'people' is generally considered to have slightly old-fashioned and sentimental associations: □ *country folk* □ *old folk* □ *a name that will be familiar to many folk*.

following The preposition *following* may be confused with the present participle; it is best avoided where *after* or *because of* would be adequate or less ambiguous: □ *They went home after* [not *following*] *the party*.

foment see FERMENT OR FOMENT?

foot or **feet**? The plural of *foot*, as a unit of measurement, may be *foot* or *feet*: □ *a six-foot fence* □ *five feet tall* □ *nine feet eight inches long* □ *a pane of glass measuring two foot six by four foot three*.

for see BECAUSE, AS, FOR, OR SINCE?

for- or **fore-**? The prefix *for-* usually indicates prohibition (*forbid*), abstention (*forbear*), or neglect (*forsake*). The prefix *fore-* means 'before': □ *foreboding* □ *forecast* □ *forefather*.

forbade *Forbade*, the past tense of the verb *forbid*, may be pronounced [fŏr*bad*] or [fŏr*bayd*].

forbear or **forebear**? *Forbear* is the only accepted spelling of the verb, which means 'to refrain': □ *I shall forbear from criticizing her appearance.* The noun, meaning 'ancestor', may be written *forebear* or *forbear*, the spelling *forebear* being the more frequent: □ *His forebears were wealthy landowners.*

forbid or **prohibit**? Both these verbs are used in the sense of 'refuse to allow', *prohibit* being more authoritative than *forbid*: □ *I forbid you to visit her.* □ *The rules prohibit us from visiting her.*

forceful or **forcible**? *Forceful* means 'having great force'; *forcible* means 'using force': □ *a forceful personality* □ *forcible expulsion*.

fore- see FOR- OR FORE-?

forebear see FORBEAR OR FOREBEAR?

forego see FORGO OR FOREGO?

forehead This word is usually pronounced [*for*rid], rhyming with *horrid*.

forename see FIRST NAME, CHRISTIAN NAME, FORENAME, GIVEN NAME, OR BAPTISMAL NAME?

forever or **for ever**? The adverb *forever* may be written as a single word in all contexts, but some people prefer to use the two-word form *for ever* for the principal sense of 'eternally': □ *We shall remember her for ever.* □ *Liverpool for ever!*

foreword or **preface**? Both these nouns are used to denote the statement or remarks that often precede or replace the introduction to a book. *Preface* is the older of the two words and the more frequent.

forgo or **forego**? *Forgo* is the usual spelling of the verb that means 'do without' or 'give up'; *forego* is an accepted variant spelling of this verb: □ *The union will not forgo the right to strike.*

formally or **formerly**? These two adverbs are sometimes confused, being identical in pronunciation. *Formally* means 'in a formal manner'; *formerly* means 'in the past': □ *formally dressed* □ *Sri Lanka, formerly called Ceylon.*

former and **latter** Of two previously mentioned items or people, *the former* denotes the first and *the latter* the second: □ *On Monday evening there will be a lecture on local history and a meeting of the chess club: the former will be held in the main hall, the latter in the lounge.*

formerly see FORMALLY OR FORMERLY?

formidable This word may be stressed on the first syllable [*for*midăbl] or the second syllable [fŏr*mid*ăbl].

formulae or **formulas**? The noun *formula* has two accepted plural forms, *formulae* and *formulas*.

forte The noun *forte*, denoting a person's strong point, may be pronounced as two syllables [*for*tay] or as a single syllable [fort].

fortuitous or **fortunate**? *Fortuitous* means 'happening by chance' or 'accidental'; *fortunate* means 'having or happening by good fortune' or 'lucky': □ *a fortuitous meeting* □ *a fortunate child.*

forward or **forwards**? As an adjective, *forward* is never written with a final *s*: □ *forward motion* □ *a forward remark* □ *forward planning.* In some of its adverbial senses, the word may be written *forward* or *forwards*: □ *He ran forward/forwards to greet his father.*

founder see FLOUNDER OR FOUNDER?

foyer In British English this word, meaning 'an entrance hall or lobby in a theatre, hotel, etc.', is usually pronounced [*foi*ay].

fraction Some people dislike the use of *a fraction* to mean 'a small part' or 'a little': □ *We flew there in a fraction of the time it takes to go by sea.* □ *Could you turn the volume down a fraction, please?*

fraught *Fraught with* means 'filled with' or 'charged with': □ *fraught with problems* □ *The expedition was fraught with danger.* The use of the adjective *fraught* alone, in the sense of 'tense' or 'anxious', is disliked by some people and is best restricted to informal usage: □ *a fraught evening* □ *He looked fraught.*

-free The adjective *free* is frequently used in combination to indicate the absence of something undesirable or unpleasant: □ *lead-free petrol* □ *rent-free accommodation* □ *additive-free food* □ *pollution-free water* □ *duty-free spirits* □ *a trouble-free life.*

freeze or **frieze**? The verb *freeze* means 'change from liquid into solid form': □ *Water freezes at 0°C.* The noun *frieze* denotes a decorative or ornamental band or strip on a wall: □ *a frieze depicting the history of the town.* The two spellings should not be confused.

friable The adjective *friable*, a technical term, means 'crumbly' or 'easily broken up': □ *friable soil.* It has no etymological connection with the verb *fry*.

-friendly Some people object to the vogue for attaching the adjective *friendly* to an increasing number of nouns, on the model of USER-FRIENDLY: □ *customer-friendly* □ *Readers ... voted M&S Britain's least parent-friendly high street store* (*Daily Telegraph*) □ *ozone-friendly* □ *dolphin-friendly*. See also ENVIRONMENT; GREEN.

frieze see FREEZE OR FRIEZE?

frolic The verb *frolic* adds a *k* before suffixes beginning with a vowel: □ *frolicked* □ *frolicking* □ *frolicky*. There is no *k* in the derived adjective *frolicsome.* See also SPELLING 1.

front-line In military contexts, the *front line* is the most advanced or exposed position in a battle. Some people dislike the use of the phrase in figurative or nonmilitary contexts: □ *a front-line defender of government policy* □ *front-line inner city areas.*

fuchsia Note the spelling of this plant name, particularly the silent *ch*. It is pronounced [*few*shă].

-ful For nouns ending in *-ful*, such as *cupful, spoonful, sackful, handful, mouthful*, etc., most users prefer the plural form *-fuls*: □ *two cupfuls* □ *three spoonfuls.* The plural form *-sful* is best avoided. It is important to recognize the difference between *-ful* and *full*: □ *a bucketful of water* denotes the quantity of water held by a bucket, but not the bucket itself; *a bucket full of water* denotes both the bucket and the water it contains. See also FULLNESS OR FULNESS?

fulfil Note the spelling of this word: in British English neither *l* is doubled.

full see -FUL.

fullness or **fulness**? Both spellings are acceptable, *fullness* being the more frequent in British English.

full stop The principal use of the full stop as a punctuation mark is to end a sentence that is neither a direct question nor an exclamation.

fulsome *Fulsome praise, fulsome compliments*, etc., are offensively excessive, exaggerated, or insincere.

fun The use of the word *fun* as an adjective, meaning 'enjoyable' or 'amusing', is disliked by some users and is best restricted to informal contexts: □ *a fun game* □ *a fun person* □ *a fun-size packet of sweets.*

function The verb *function* is best avoided where *work, perform, operate, serve, act*, etc., would be adequate or more appropriate, particularly in general, nontechnical contexts: □ *The machine never works* [not *functions*] *properly in very hot weather.* □ *The automatic lock serves* [not *functions*] *as a safety device.*

fundamental The adjective *fundamental* means 'basic', 'essential', 'primary', or 'principal'; it is best avoided where *important, major, great*, etc., would be more appropriate: □ *the fundamental difference between the two systems* □ *a major* [not *fundamental*] *improvement in East-West relations.*

funeral or **funereal**? The

adjective *funereal* means 'like a funeral; suggestive of death; mournful; gloomy': □ *funereal music* □ *The atmosphere was funereal.* It should not be confused with the noun *funeral* used adjectivally: □ *a funeral service* □ *a funeral cortege.*

fungi *Fungi*, one of the plural forms of *fungus*, may be pronounced to rhyme with *try* or *tree*; the *g* may be hard, as in *gum*, or soft, as in *germ*.

furore The final *e* of the noun *furore*, meaning 'uproar' or 'craze', can cause problems of spelling and pronunciation. In British English, the *e* is never omitted in spellingı *furor* is the usual American spelling of the word.

Furore is usually pronounced as a three-syllable word stressed on the second sullable [few*ror*i]. It is occasionally pronounced as a two-syllable word stressed on the first syllable [*fewr*or]; this it also the pronunciation of the American spelling.

further, furthest see FARTHER, FARTHEST, FURTHER, OR FURTHEST?

G

Gaelic or **Gallic**? *Gaelic* is a noun or adjective that refers to the Celtic languages of Scotland and Ireland: □ *to speak Gaelic* □ *a Gaelic word. Gallic* is an adjective, meaning 'of France or the French': □ *a Gallic custom.*

The pronunciation of *Gaelic* is [*gay*lik], with the alternative pronunciation [*gal*ik] used especially in regions where the language is spoken. This second pronunciation is identical to that of *Gallic*, and so may cause confusion or ambiguity in some contexts.

gaiety *Gaiety*, meaning 'a cheerful and carefree manner' or 'festivity', is sometimes misspelt.

gallant The adjective *gallant*, 'brave and courageous', as in: □ *put up a gallant fight*, is stressed on the first syllable [*gal*ănt].

Gallic see GAELIC OR GALLIC?

gallop Note the spelling of this verb, particularly the *-ll-* and the final *p*, which is not doubled before *-ed*, *-ing*, etc.: □ *The horse galloped across the field.* □ *galloping inflation.*

gamble or **gambol**? The verb *gamble* means 'take a risk on a game of chance'; *gambol* means 'skip and jump playfully'.

gaol see JAIL OR GAOL?

garage This word may be pronounced [*gar*ahzh] or [*gar*ij]. Many users prefer the former pronunciation.

gases or **gasses**? The plural of the noun *gas* is *gases* or, less commonly, *gasses*.

-gate The suffix *-gate*, derived from the *Watergate* affair (a scandal involving Richard Nixon, then President of the USA, in 1972), is sometimes attached to other words to denote a political scandal: □ *Irangate/Contragate* (an American scandal in 1987 involving the sale of arms to Iran and use of the profits to supply arms to the anti-Communist Contras in Nicaragua) □ *Yuppiegate* (a scandal involving five young Wall Street employees in 1986) □ *The 'Dianagate' scandal, the disclosure of tapes of conversations believed to be between the princess and James Gilbey, her close friend* (*Sunday Times*).

gauge This word, which means 'measure or standard', is frequently misspelt. The *u* comes after the *a* and not before it.

gay The adjective *gay* is so widely used as a synonym for 'homosexual' that its use in the original sense of 'cheerful', 'merry', or 'bright' may be open to misinterpretation in some contexts: □ *a gay party.*

gender The word *gender* refers to the grammatical classification of nouns as masculine, feminine, or neuter. The use of *gender* as a synonym for 'sex' is avoided by many users in formal contexts.

general or **generic**? The adjective *general* has a wide range of meanings, including 'widespread', 'overall', and 'not specialized or specific': □ *general opinion* □ *general knowledge. Generic* means 'referring to a whole class or group': □ *a generic term for products that do not damage the environment.*

genetic, genial see CONGENIAL, GENIAL, CONGENITAL, OR GENETIC?

gentleman *Gentleman* is used as a synonym for 'man' in some formal or official contexts and as a term of politeness: □ *Show the gentleman to his room.* □ *Ladies and gentlemen, may I introduce tonight's guest speaker?*

geriatric Many people object to the increasing use of the noun and adjective *geriatric* as derogatory synonyms for 'old person' or 'elderly': □ *These geriatric drivers should be banned from the roads.* □ *The country is governed by a bunch of geriatrics. Geriatrics* is the branch of medical science concerned with the diseases of old age and the care of old people; the use of *geriatric* in this context is acceptable to all users.

gerunds see INFINITIVE; -ING FORMS.

get In formal contexts *get* can often be replaced with an appropriate synonym, such as *become*, *buy*, *obtain*, *receive*, etc.: □ *It is becoming* [not *getting*] *increasingly difficult to obtain* [not *get*] *impartial advice on financial matters.* However, if the synonym sounds clumsy or unnatural in context, or causes ambiguity, *get* should be retained or the sentence restructured.

geyser The noun *geyser*, meaning 'hot spring' or 'water heater', is usually pronounced [*gee*zĕr] in British English and [*gī*zĕr] in American English.

gibe or **jibe**? The word *gibe*, or variant spelling *jibe*, means 'jeer or taunt': □ *gibes/jibes and insults.*

gild or **guild**? *Gild* is a verb, meaning 'cover with gold' (see also GILT OR GUILT?) or 'make golden in colour': □ *gilded picture frames* □ *The setting sun gilded the leaves. Guild* is a noun, denoting an organization of craftsmen, tradespeople, or other people with similar or related interests: □ *a guild of wine merchants* □ *She belongs to the Townswomen's Guild.*

gilt or **guilt**? *Gilt* is a variant form of the past participle of the verb *gild* (see GILD OR GUILD?) used as an attributive adjective in the sense of 'covered with gold': □ *a gilt candlestick.* As a noun, *gilt* denotes the gold or other substance used for this covering: □ *Some of the gilt had worn away.* It should not be confused with the noun *guilt*, meaning 'responsibility for wrongdoing': □ *a feeling of guilt* □ *He admitted his guilt.*

gipsy or **gypsy**? This word, meaning 'wanderer', has two spellings: *gipsy* and *gypsy*.

girl see WOMAN.

given name see FIRST NAME, CHRISTIAN NAME, FORENAME, GIVEN NAME, OR BAPTISMAL NAME?

glacier The first syllable of this word, which means 'a vast area of ice', may be pronounced to rhyme with *mass* [*gla*seer] or with *clay* [*glay*seer].

glamorous Some people object to the frequent use of the adjective *glamorous* as a synonym for 'beautiful', 'romantic', 'exciting', 'interesting', etc.: □ *a glamorous setting* □ *a glamorous career.*

glasnost *Glasnost*, a Russian word, is used to denote the increased openness, both in East-West relations and in internal policies and reforms, that became a characteristic of the Soviet statesman Mikhail Gorbachev's regime in the mid-1980s: □ *We need to maintain the atmosphere of openness in our society through glasnost, democratisation and criticism* (Mr Gorbachev, *The Guardian*). See also PERESTROIKA. The word is increasingly used outside this specific context.

global The adjective *global* is increasingly used with specific reference to ecological or environmental issues that affect the whole world: □ *global consciousness* □ *global politics* □ *The Clinton team is likely to be far more European-minded on global issues such as energy consumption* (*Daily Telegraph*). This usage is probably influenced by the phrase *global warming* (see GREENHOUSE EFFECT).

gobbledygook The noun *gobbledygook* is used in informal contexts to denote the pretentious or incomprehensible JARGON of bureaucrats, especially the circumlocutory language of official documents, reports, etc.

gobsmacked The adjective *gobsmacked*, meaning 'astounded; flabbergasted; speechless with amazement', is a slang term that should not be used in formal contexts: □ *I was gobsmacked when I found out how much it would cost.* □ *There was a long pause (maybe he was gobsmacked at the prospect of me staying at home for another year)*' (*The Guardian*).

god or **God**? A *god* is any of a number of beings worshipped for their supernatural powers. *God*, written with a capital *G*, is the supreme being worshipped in many religions as the creator and ruler of all: □ *the god of war* □ *the Greek gods* □ *to believe in God* □ *for God's sake.*

gold or **golden**? The word *gold* is used adjectivally to describe things that are made of gold or contain gold: □ *a gold medal* □ *a gold mine.* The adjective *golden* usually refers to the colour of gold: □ *golden hair* □ *golden syrup.*

goodwill or **good will**? The term meaning 'a feeling of kindness and concern', as in: □ *a gesture of good will*, can be written either as one word or as two.

gorilla see GUERILLA, GUERRILLA, OR GORILLA?

got *Got*, the past participle of *get*, is often superfluous in the expressions *have got* (meaning 'possess') and *have got to* (meaning 'must'): □ *He has (got) grey hair and a small moustache.* □ *They have (got) to win this match to avoid relegation.* In informal contexts, especially in negative sentences, questions and CONTRACTIONS, *got* is often retained: □ *We haven't got any milk.* Used alone, *got* is the past tense of *get*; it should not be used in place of *have* or *have got*.

gourmand or **gourmet**? A *gourmand* enjoys the pleasurable indulgence of eating, with or without regard to the quality of the food. *Gourmet*, the more common and also more complimentary of the two terms, refers only to a connoisseur of fine food or drink: □ *The size of the meals will satisfy the gourmand; their quality should please the most discriminating gourmet.* To avoid ambiguity, *gourmand* may be replaced by *glutton* in the sense of 'one who eats greedily or to excess'.

government In the sense of 'the group of people who govern a country, state, etc.', *government* may be a singular or a plural noun: □ *The government is blamed for the rise in unemployment.* □ *The government have rejected the proposal.*

graceful or **gracious**? *Graceful* refers to movement, actions, forms, shapes, etc., that have *grace*, in the sense of beauty, charm, or elegance: □ *a graceful dance. Gracious* means 'kind', 'courteous', 'benevolent', or 'compassionate': □ *a gracious gift.*

graffiti Nowadays very few people still object to the widespread use of *graffiti* as a singular noun: □ *Graffiti covers the walls of the community centre.* □ *Some of this graffiti is quite obscene.*

grammar The word *grammar,* which denotes the rules of a language or a type of school: □ *Latin grammar* □ *a grammar school,* is often misspelt. The most frequent error is the substitution of *-er* for the *-ar* ending.

grand- or **great-**? Both these prefixes are used to denote family relationships that are two or more generations apart. Either prefix may be used for the aunts and uncles of one's parents and the children of one's nephews and nieces, *great-* being more frequent than grand-: □ *great-niece* □ *grandnephew* □ *great-uncle* □ *grandaunt.*

grass roots Some people object to the widespread use of this term both in political or industrial contexts and as a noun meaning 'the fundamental level' or as an adjective 'fundamental' or 'basic': □ *the grass roots of the problem* □ *at the grass-roots level* □ *support for the party at the grass roots* □ *grass-roots opinion.*

gratuitous The adjective *gratuitous* is most frequently used in the sense of 'unwarranted' or 'uncalled-for': □ *gratuitous violence* □ *gratuitous criticism.*

gravitas The noun *gravitas,* meaning 'serious or solemn nature or manner; weight, substance, or importance', is a vogue word that is increasing in frequency: □ *The most mentioned attribute which best equips him* [Peter Sissons] *for sustained political encounters is the gravitas he clearly was born with* (*The Guardian*). □ [Jonathan] *Dimbleby is felt to be a safe pair of hands, with sufficient stature to give the book gravitas* (*Daily Telegraph*). Some users consider the word to be a pretentious and unnecessary synonym for 'seriousness'.

gray see GREY OR GRAY?

graze The verb *graze,* traditionally applied to animals in the sense of 'eat', is increasingly used in human contexts with three specific meanings: 'eat small amounts of food throughout the day', 'eat food from supermarket shelves while shopping', and 'eat standing up'. The first sense is the most frequent in British English: □ *doing away with family meals and replacing them ... with 'grazing ... eating'* (*Daily Telegraph*).

great- see GRAND- OR GREAT-?

Great Britain see BRITAIN.

Greek or **Grecian**? The adjective *Greek* means 'of Greece, its people, or its language'; *Grecian* means 'in the simple but elegant style of classical Greece': □ *Greek history* □ *a Grecian vase.*

green The adjective *green* is becoming overused in its application to any product, policy, or ideology that is connected with the protection of the environment: □ *green consumerism* □ *green issues* □ *to buy green* □ *to go green* □ *Ministers moved ... to restore the Government's 'green' credentials by introducing a range of environmental safeguards into plans to sell the electricity and water industries* (*Daily Telegraph*). □ *The Whole Thing is a mail order company dedicated to providing a wide range of over 150 of the greenest products available* (advertisement, *The Guardian*). See also ENVIRONMENT; -FRIENDLY.

greenhouse effect The *greenhouse effect* is the warming of the earth's atmosphere (*global warming*) caused by an accumulation of gases that trap the radiated heat from the sun: □ *Flood defences along Britain's coasts will fail to prevent large tracts of farmland from being flooded when sea levels rise because of the greenhouse effect* (*Daily Telegraph*). The gases thus function like the glass in a greenhouse, hence the name. Sometimes called *greenhouse gases,* they include carbon dioxide produced by the burning of coal, oil, stubble, and the tropical rainforests that would normally absorb carbon dioxide from the air.

grey or **gray**? This word can be spelt with an *e* or an *a*, although the former is far more frequent in British English.

grievous The correct pronunciation of this word, most frequently encountered in the phrase *grievous bodily harm,* is [*greevŭs*], not [*greeviŭs*]. Note the spelling of the word, particularly the order and position of the vowels.

grill or **grille**? A *grill* is 'a framework of bars used for cooking food'. A *grille* is a grating over a window or door.

grisly or **grizzly**? The spellings of these words may sometimes be confused. *Grisly* means 'gruesome'; *grizzly* means 'partly grey': □ *a grizzly bear*, or 'whining fretfully': □ *a grizzly toddler.*

growth The word *growth* is used adjectivally, in the sense of 'rapidly developing or increasing', in economic and commercial spheres: □ *a growth industry* □ *a growth economy*.

guarantee This word, which is often misspelt, means 'an assurance that a certain agreement will be kept': □ *The washing-machine was still under guarantee.*

guerilla, guerrilla, or **gorilla**? *Guerilla/guerrilla* means 'fighter within an independent army': □ *a guerrilla war*; a *gorilla* is a large ape. The spellings *guerilla* and *guerrilla* are both acceptable, although the latter is preferred by some users since it derives from the Spanish *guerra* 'a war', with *-rr-*.

guest The use of the word *guest* as a verb, in the sense of 'be a guest (on a television or radio show)', is disliked by some users and is best restricted to informal contexts: □ *She guested on his chat show last month.*

GUI The acronym *GUI*, used in computing, is short for *graphical user interface*, an on-screen interface using visual icons: □ *The increasing success of the so-called 'graphical user interfaces' or GUIs, which are supposed to be making using PCs easy and 'intuitive'* (*Daily Telegraph*).

guidelines Some people object to the increasing use of the plural noun *guidelines* in place of *advice*, *policy*, *instructions*, *rules*, etc.: □ *New guidelines to establish minimum sentences in rape cases* (*The Guardian*). □ *The series is within the BBC's guidelines on violence* (*Daily Telegraph*).

guild see GILD OR GUILD?

guilt see GILT OR GUILT?

gut The use of the word *gut* as an adjective, meaning 'instinctive', 'strong', 'basic', or 'essential', is best restricted to informal contexts: □ *a gut reaction* □ *a gut feeling* □ *gut issues.*

gymkhana This word, meaning 'competition for horses and their riders', is sometimes misspelt.

gynaecology This word, meaning 'the branch of medicine concerned with women's diseases', is frequently misspelt. Note the *y* and, in British English *ae*, or American English *e*. See also -AE- AND -OE-.

gypsy see GIPSY OR GYPSY?

H

haemorrhage This noun, meaning 'immense loss of blood', is often misspelt. Note the *-rrh-* and the British English *-ae-*, which is reduced to *-e-* in American English (see -AE- AND -OE-).

hail or **hale**? The noun *hail* means 'frozen rain'; the verb *hail* means 'call' or 'be a native of': □ *hail a taxi* □ *She hails from Scotland.* *Hail* should not be confused with *hale*, meaning 'vigorous and healthy': □ *hale and hearty.*

half Although *half* is a singular noun, it is followed by a plural verb when it denotes a number rather than an amount: □ *Half of the books are missing.* □ *Half of the water has evaporated.* In most cases the word *of* is optional: □ *Give him half (of) the money.*

half- or **step-**? One's *stepparent* (*stepmother* or *stepfather*) is the new spouse of a divorced or widowed parent. Any children of this step-parent by previous partners become one's *stepbrothers* or *stepsisters.* Any children of one's father or mother by this step-parent (or any other partner) are one's *half-brothers* or *half-sisters.*

hallo see HELLO, HALLO, OR HULLO?

handful Most users prefer to form the plural *-fuls*: □ *handfuls.* See -FUL.

handicap The final *p* of the word *handicap* is doubled before a suffix beginning with a vowel: □ *handicapped* □ *handicapping.* See also SPELLING 1.

hands-on This expression refers to practical or personal involvement in a task: □ *This is not a desk job. It is a 'hands-on' sales role* (*Daily Telegraph*). □ *The Prime Minister returned to London last night to resume hands-on control of the Gulf crisis* (*The Guardian*).

hangar or **hanger**? These words are often misspelt. A *hangar* is a building for storing aircraft; a *hanger* is an apparatus on which articles can be hung: □ *coat hanger*.

hanged or **hung**? *Hung* is the past tense and past participle for most senses of the verb *hang*; *hanged* is restricted to the meaning 'suspended by the neck until dead', in the context of capital punishment or suicide: □ *He hung his coat on the peg.* □ *The picture was hung up in the hall.* □ *The conspirators were hanged for treason.* □ *Her father hanged himself.*

hanger see HANGAR OR HANGER?

hang-up The noun *hang-up* is an informal name for a mental or emotional problem or inhibition: □ *She's got a hang-up about answering the phone.* The word should not be used in formal contexts.

hara-kiri *Hara-kiri* is the traditional spelling of this Japanese term, which refers to a ritual act of suicide by cutting open the abdomen: □ *to commit hara-kiri.* It is pronounced [*harră kirri*].

harangue This word, which means ' a vehement and lengthy speech', as in: □ *a long harangue about the state of the economy,* is sometimes misspelt.

harass This word, meaning 'trouble persistently', is spelt with a single *-r-* and ends in *-ss*. It is pronounced [*haräs*]. The American pronunciation [hă*ras*] has recently come into British English but is disliked by some people.

hardly In the sense of 'only just' or 'almost not' the adverb *hardly*, like its synonyms *scarcely* and *barely*, is used with negative force; it is unnecessary to add another negative to the clause or sentence: □ *I can* [not *can't*] *hardly see you.* See also DOUBLE NEGATIVE.

have got (to) see GOT.

he see HE OR SHE.

headed for or **heading for**? The phrase *be headed for* is sometimes wrongly used in place of *be heading for*. When the verb *head* is used intransitively, the correct phrase is *be heading for*: □ *We were heading* [not *headed*] *for Southampton.* □ *The government is heading* [not *headed*] *for defeat.*

head up Many people dislike the use of this phrasal verb in place of the simpler *head*, meaning 'lead' or 'be in charge': □ *to head up a team of workers.*

healthful or **healthy**? *Healthy* can mean 'having good health' or 'promoting good health': □ *a healthy child* □ *a healthy diet. Healthful* is a less frequent synonym of *healthy* in both these senses, but in modern usage it is largely restricted to the sense of 'promoting good health': □ *foods that are both healthful and relatively inexpensive.*

heaved or **hove**? *Heaved* is the usual form of the past tense or past participle of the verb *heave*: □ *He heaved the crate up the steps.* □ *She heaved a sigh of relief. Hove* is an archaic variant of *heaved* that is used facetiously or in nautical contexts, in the past tense or past participle of *heave to*, meaning 'stop', and *heave into sight* (or *view*), meaning 'appear': □ *We hove to for lunch.* □ *A ship hove into sight.*

heavy-duty The term *heavy-duty* should be restricted to articles, materials, etc., that are designed to withstand hard wear or frequent use: □ *heavy-duty overalls* □ *heavy-duty plastic sheeting.*

height This word refers to the distance from the base to the top of an object or person: □ *the height of the mountain.* It also means 'most intense point': □ *at the height of summer. Height* is sometimes misspelt with the ending *-th*, on the model of *length*, *width*, etc.

heinous This word, meaning 'extremely evil': □ *a heinous crime*, is often misspelt and mispronounced. Note the *ei* spelling and the stress on the first syllable [*haynĕs*].

hello, hallo, or **hullo**? This word of greeting has various spellings which are all acceptable. The first spelling is probably the most frequent in contemporary usage.

help Many people object to the phrases *cannot/can't/could not/couldn't help but*, as in: □ *I couldn't help but laugh*, preferring either *I couldn't help laughing* or, less frequently, *I couldn't but laugh.*

hemi- see DEMI-, HEMI-, OR SEMI-?

hence *Hence* means 'from

this time' or, more rarely, 'from this place'; it is therefore unnecessary to precede the adverb with *from*: □ *The concert will begin three hours hence.*

he or she The use of *he/him/his* as pronouns of common gender, with reference to a person of unspecified sex, is widely considered to be misleading and sexist, as is the use of *she/her/hers* for the same purpose with reference to jobs or activities that are traditionally associated with women: □ *The candidate must pay his own travelling expenses.* □ *This book will be of great value to the student nurse preparing for her examinations.* The most acceptable substitutes for these pronouns are the cumbersome and pedantic expressions *he or she*, *he/she*, *(s)he*, *his or her*, etc.: □ *If a child is slow to learn, he or she will be given extra tuition.*

In some cases, the problem may be avoided by restructuring the sentence, making the subject plural, or both: □ *Travelling expenses must be paid by the candidate.* □ *Children who are slow to learn will be given extra tuition.*

hereditary or **heredity**? *Hereditary* is an adjective, meaning 'genetically transmitted' or 'inherited'; *heredity* is the noun from which it is derived: □ *The disease is not hereditary.* □ *Is intelligence determined by heredity or environment?*

heritage or **inheritance**? The noun *heritage* most frequently refers to cultural items, natural features, or traditions of the past that are handed down from generation to generation and are considered to be of importance to modern society: □ *The pyramids are part of Egypt's heritage.* An *inheritance* is money or property that an heir receives from an ancestor who has died.

hesitance, **hesitancy**, or **hesitation**? The nouns *hesitance* and *hesitancy* refer to the state of being hesitant (i.e. wavering, irresolute, indecisive, reluctant, etc.). *Hesitancy* is the more frequent of these synonyms: □ *There was a note of hesitancy in her voice.* The noun *hesitation* refers to the act or an instance of hesitating: □ *after a slight hesitation.*

hiatus The noun *hiatus* is best avoided where *gap, break,* or *pause* would be adequate or more appropriate: □ *a hiatus in our discussions.*

hiccup or **hiccough**? Both spellings of this word are acceptable but *hiccup* is the more frequent.

hidden agenda The phrase *hidden agenda* is generally used in a derogatory manner, referring to a secret intention or ulterior motive concealed behind a public statement, political policy, etc.: □ *Ministers have assured their critics that there is no hidden agenda.* The phrase is regarded by some people as a vogue cliché and should not be overused.

high or **tall**? Both these adjectives mean 'of greater than average size, measured vertically', but there are differences of sense, usage, and application between them: □ *a high mountain* □ *a tall woman.* The adjective *tall* is largely restricted to people, animals, and plants and to things that are narrow in proportion to their height; it is the opposite of *short. High* has the additional meaning of 'situated at a great distance from the base'; it is the opposite of *low.*

high-profile see PROFILE.

hijack The verb *hijack,* meaning 'seize control of (a vehicle in transit)', is increasingly used in figurative contexts: □ *One of their most successful authors has been hijacked by a rival company.*

him or **his**? see -ING FORMS.

Hindi or **Hindu**? *Hindi* is a language of India; *Hindu* is a noun or adjective relating to the Indian religion of Hinduism: □ *She speaks Hindi.* □ *He is (a) Hindu.*

hire or **rent**? Both verbs mean 'have or give temporary use of something in return for payment': □ *He hired a suit for the wedding.* □ *We rented a flat in the town centre.* □ *They hire/rent (out) cars at competitive rates.* The difference in sense between the two verbs concerns the length of the period of temporary use, and the nature of the item in question.

his or her see HE OR SHE.

historic or **historical**? The adjective *historic* relates to events, decisions, etc., that are memorable or important enough to earn a place in recorded history; *historical* relates to the study of history and to the past in general: □ *a historic election* □ *historical records* □ *The king's visit to the town was not a historic occasion, it is of historical interest only.* The adjective *historical* is also applied to people, events, etc., that existed or happened in fact, as opposed to fiction or legend.

histrionic or **hysterical**? The adjectives *histrionic* and *hysterical* are both used of emotional outbursts but should not be confused: *histrionic* behaviour is a display of insincerity, being deliberately exaggerated for melodramatic effect; *hysterical* behaviour is the result of an involuntary loss of control.

hi-tech The adjective *hi-tech* specifically refers to high technology, or sophisticated electronics; its indiscriminate application to basic electrical appliances or to anything remotely connected with computing is disliked by many careful users: □ *a beautiful hi-tech modern home* □ *high-tech benefits* [a reference to the computerization of the social security benefits system] □ *This transition of the cycle from leisure 'toy' to hi-tech pedal machine.*

The word hi-tech has a number of variant spellings: *high-tech, high tech, hi-tec, high-tec,* etc. It is also used as a noun: □ *Reflecting the world of high tech* [spelt *hi-tech* in the headline], *the first museum devoted to the chemical industry opens today.*

hoard or **horde**? A *hoard* is 'a store reserved for future use'; a *horde* is 'a large crowd': □ *hordes of tourists.*

holey see HOLY, HOLEY, OR WHOLLY?

holistic The adjective *holistic* is used of any system, method, theory, etc., that deals with the whole rather than with individual parts or members: □ *holistic medicine.*

holocaust The use of the noun *holocaust* to denote any major disaster, especially one that involves great loss of life, is disliked by some users, who prefer to restrict the word to its original meaning of 'total destruction by fire': □ *the nuclear holocaust.*

holy, holey, or **wholly**?

These three spellings should not be confused. The adjective *holy* means 'sacred'; the adjective *holey*, only used facetiously or informally, means 'having holes'; the adverb *wholly* means 'completely': □ *holy relics* □ *holey socks* □ *wholly convinced.*

homely In British English the adjective *homely* is complimentary, meaning 'like home', 'unpretentious', or 'sympathetic'; in American English it has the derogatory sense of 'ugly' or 'unattractive': □ *a homely room* □ *a homely child.*

homogeneity The traditional pronunciation of this word, derived from *homogeneous* (see HOMOGENEOUS OR HOMOGENOUS?) is [homŏjĕ*nee*iti], although [homŏjĕ*nay*iti] is sometimes heard.

homogeneous or **homogenous**? These two adjectives are virtually interchangeable in the sense of 'similar, identical, or uniform in nature, structure, or composition', *homogeneous* being the more frequent: □ *a homogeneous mixture.*

homophobia The noun *homophobia*, meaning 'fear or dislike of homosexuals', and the derived noun *homophobe* and adjective *homophobic* are used with increasing frequency: □ *The Church has been accused of homophobia.* □ *a homophobic police officer.* Some people object to these coinages, on the basis that the *homo-* element can only mean 'same' (as in the word *homosexual* itself) or 'man'.

homosexual This word may be pronounced in several ways, two of the most frequent being [homŏ*seks*yool] and [hōmō*seks*yool]. See also GAY.

honorary or **honourable**? *Honorary* means 'given as an honour, without the usual requirements or obligations' or 'unpaid': □ *an honorary degree* □ *an honorary member of the society* □ *the honorary secretary.* *Honourable* means 'worthy of honour' or 'showing honour' and is also used as a title of respect: □ *an honourable man* □ *an honourable deed* □ *the Right Honourable Margaret Thatcher.*

hoofs or **hooves**? Either *hoofs* or *hooves* is acceptable as the plural of *hoof*, 'the hard bony part of the foot of a horse, cow, etc.'.

hopefully The use of *hopefully* to mean 'it is (to be) hoped (that)' or 'I/we hope (that)' is disliked by some users and is best restricted to informal contexts: □ *Hopefully the rain will stop before we leave.*

horde see HOARD OR HORDE?

horrible, horrid, horrific, or **horrendous**? *Horrible* and *horrid* are virtually interchangeable in the sense of 'very unpleasant'; *horrific* and *horrendous* convey a stronger sense of horror: □ *a horrid sight* □ *a horrible dream* □ *a horrific attack* □ *the horrendous prospect of nuclear war.*

hors d'oeuvre An *hors d'oeuvre* is an item of food served before or as the first course of a meal. Of French origin, the phrase is sometimes misspelt: note particularly the vowel sequence *-oeu-*. The two words are sometimes hyphenated: □ *hors-d'oeuvre.* The plural is usually *hors d'oeuvres,* but *hors d'oeuvre* is also acceptable.

hospitable This word may be stressed on the first syllable [*hos*pităbl] or the second syllable [hos*pit*ăbl]. Some users prefer the former, more traditional pronunciation.

hospitalize The verb *hospitalize*, meaning 'send or admit to hospital', is disliked by some users as an example of the increasing tendency to coin new verbs by adding the suffix *-ize* to nouns and adjectives: □ *She was hospitalized in the eighth month of her pregnancy.*

host The verb *host*, meaning 'act as host at' or 'be the host of', is disliked by some users: □ *He hosted the firm's Christmas party.*

-hostile see FRIENDLY.

hove see HEAVED OR HOVE?

however The principal adverbial senses of *however* are 'nevertheless', 'in whatever way', and 'no matter how': □ *The car doesn't have a large boot; it does, however, have plenty of room inside.* □ *However I wash my hair, and however carefully I dry it, it always looks untidy.* For the distinction between *however* and *how ever* see WHATEVER OR WHAT EVER?

hullo see HELLO, HALLO, OR HULLO?

human Some people dislike the use of *human* as a noun,

preferring *human being* (or *man*, *woman*, *child*, *person*, etc.): □ *This job can be done more efficiently by a robot than by a human (being).*

humanism or **humanity**? *Humanism* is a philosophy that values human beings and rejects the need for religion. The noun *humanity* refers to human beings collectively; it also means 'kindness': □ *for the sake of humanity.* The two nouns should not be confused.

humanist or **humanitarian**? A *humanist* is a person who supports the philosophy of humanism (see HUMANISM OR HUMANITY?); a *humanitarian* is a philanthropist, a person who works for the welfare of human beings.

humanity see HUMANISM OR HUMANITY?

humiliation or **humility**? *Humiliation* is a feeling of shame, embarrassment, or loss of pride sometimes caused deliberately by other people; *humility* is the quality of being humble or modest: □ *the humiliation of failure* □ *the nun's humility.*

humorist The noun *humorist*, meaning 'humorous writer, speaker, etc.' is often misspelt. As in the adjective HUMOROUS, the *-mour* ending of *humour* is changed to *-mor* before the suffix *-ist*.

humorous This word, meaning 'amusing or funny', is often misspelt. The second *u* of *humour* is dropped before the suffix *-ous*.

hung see HANGED OR HUNG?

hygiene This word, meaning 'science of ensuring good health', is often misspelt. Note *hy-* and not *hi-* at the beginning of the word, and the *-ie-* in the middle.

hype The word *hype*, used as a noun or verb with reference to extravagant and often deceptive publicity of books, films, etc., is generally regarded as a slang term: □ *The launch owed more to hype than to literary merit* (*Sunday Times*). □ *the biggest money-making hype in sports history* (*Publishers Weekly*) □ *Hyping books is big business* (*The Bookseller*).

hyper- or **hypo-**? These two prefixes are often confused. This may result in misunderstanding when each is joined to its relevant suffix. *Hyper-* means 'above or excessively': □ *a hyperactive child*; *hypo-* means 'beneath or under': □ *a hypodermic syringe.*

hyperbola or **hyperbole**? These two nouns should not be confused. *Hyperbola* is a technical term used in mathematics to describe a type of symmetrical curve; *hyperbole* means 'exaggeration used for effect in speech or writing': □ *I've warned him a million times* is an example of *hyperbole*. Both nouns originate from the same Greek word and they share the derived adjective *hyperbolic(al)*.

hypercritical see HYPOCRITICAL OR HYPERCRITICAL?

hyphen The principal uses of the hyphen in English are to join two or more words together, either as a fixed compound or to avoid ambiguity, and to indicate that a word has been broken at the end of a line through lack of space.

There are a number of other situations in which the use of the hyphen is optional.

1 Most standard prefixes are attached without a hyphen: □ *unimportant* □ *multicoloured*.

Some users prefer to hyphenate words prefixed with *non-* and words in which the absence of the hyphen would result in a doubled vowel: □ *non-flammable* □ *pre-eminent* □ *co-ordinate*. Such words are widely and increasingly accepted in the single-word forms. However, the double *i* of words prefixed by *anti-*, *semi-*, etc., is usually split by a hyphen.

Words prefixed with *ex-* (in the sense of 'former') and *self-* are usually hyphenated: □ *ex-wife* □ *self-sufficient*.

A hyphen is sometimes inserted after the prefix to avoid ambiguity or confusion; for example, to distinguish between the nouns *co-op* (a cooperative) and *coop* (an enclosure), and to clarify the pronunciation and meaning of such words as *de-ice*. See also CO-.

A hyphen is always used to join a prefix to a word beginning with a capital letter: □ *anti-British*.

See also -LIKE.

2 Many compounds can be written with or without a hyphen and there is a growing tendency towards minimal hyphenation.

Some fixed compounds of three or more words, such as *son-in-law*, *happy-go-lucky*, etc., are always hyphenated; two-word compound adjectives in which the second element ends in *-ed*, such as *light-hearted*, *blue-eyed*, *short-sighted*, etc., are usually hyphenated (see also 4 below).

3 Compounds of two or more words used adjectivally before the noun they qualify are usually hyphenated. These hyphens are often essential to avoid ambiguity: □ *a red-wine bottle* is a bottle for red wine; □ *a red wine bottle* may be a wine bottle that is red.

4 Adjectives of participles preceded by an adverb are not hyphenated if the adverb ends in *-ly*: □ *a neatly written letter*. Compounds containing other adverbs, especially those that may be mistaken for other adjectives (*well, ill, best, little* etc.) are usually hyphenated when they are used adjectivally before a noun, to avoid ambiguity: □ *a half-cooked loaf*.

5 A common element need not be repeated in groups of two or more hyphenated compounds but the hyphen must not be omitted: the same convention applies to solid compounds, in which the common element may be replaced by a hyphen: □ *long- or short-haired dogs* □ *salesmen and -women*.

6 A hyphen is inserted when numbers between 21 and 99 are written out in full: □ *twenty-one*. A hyphen is used when fractions are written out.

7 The other major use of the hyphen is at the end of a line, splitting a word that is to be continued at the beginning of the next line.

hypo- see HYPER- OR HYPO-?

hypocrisy The noun *hypocrisy* is sometimes misspelt, a common error being the substitution of *-cracy* (as in *democracy*) for the *-crisy* ending. Note also the prefix *hypo-*, not *hyper-*.

hypocritical or **hypercritical**? These two words are often confused. *Hypocritical* means 'insincere' or 'two-faced'; *hypercritical* means 'excessively critical': □ *It would be hypocritical of me to say I enjoyed the concert, when really I thought it was awful.* □ *He's so hypercritical about the way his wife lays the table.*

hysterical, hysterics see HISTRIONIC OR HYSTERICAL?

I

I or **me**? The subject pronoun *I* and the object pronoun *me* are sometimes confused in informal speech, especially in the phrases *It's me* and *Between you and I*; the latter is the preferred usage. After verbs and prepositions the object pronoun *me* should be used; before verbs the subject pronoun *I* should be used. The verb *to be* is an exception: in formal contexts the idiomatic *It is me* is unacceptable to a few careful users, who prefer *It is I*.

-ible see -ABLE OR -IBLE?

-ic or **-ical**? Many adjectives are formed by the addition of the suffixes *-ic* or *-ical*: □ *cubic* □ *symmetrical* □ *phonetic* □ *geographical*. Sometimes, when either suffix is added to the same root, the words may be interchangeable. Other word pairs may differ in meaning or usage: see CLASSIC OR CLASSICAL?; COMIC OR COMICAL?; ECONOMIC OR ECONOMICAL?; ELECTRIC OR ELECTRICAL?; HISTORIC OR HISTORICAL?; MAGIC OR MAGICAL?; POLITIC OR POLITICAL?

-ics A number of words ending in *-ics* may be singular or plural nouns, depending on the sense in which they are used: □ *Acoustics is the study of sound.* □ *The acoustics of the room have been improved.*

identical with or **identical to**? The adjective *identical* may be followed by *with* or *to*: □ *This picture is identical with/to the one we saw in the shop.*

identify Some people dislike the frequent use of *identify* as a synonym for 'associate', 'link', or 'connect': □ *They have been identified with a number of extreme right-wing organizations.*

idioms An *idiom* is a more or less fixed expression, such as *out of hand*, *in spite of*, *to come into one's own*, or *a storm in a teacup*, the meaning of which is distinct from the individual senses of the words it contains. See also **METAPHORS**; **SIMILES**.

idiosyncrasy This word is often misspelt, the most frequent error occurring when the ending *-asy* is replaced by *-acy*. The correct ending is like *fantasy* and not like *privacy*.

idle, idol, or **idyll**? The adjective *idle* means 'not active; lazy': □ *an idle machine* □ *an idle fellow* □ *He is never idle*. An *idol* is an object of worship or admiration: □ *a pop idol* □ *They bowed before the idol*. An *idyll* is (a piece of writing that depicts) a pleasant or idealized scene or situation: □ *an idyll of life on the Pacific island*.

idyllic The first *i* of *idyllic* is usually pronounced as in *ill*, although it may be pronounced as in *item*.

i.e. see **E.G. AND I.E.**

if The use of *if* in place of *though* often causes ambiguity. The use of *if* in place of *whether* may also be confusing.

if and when Many people object to the frequent use of the phrase *if and when*, which can usually be replaced by *if* or *when* alone: □ *We'll move to a larger house if and when we start a family*.

ignoramus The only plural form of the noun *ignoramus*, which means 'ignorant person', is *ignoramuses*. Although the word is of Latin origin, implying a possible *i* ending in the plural (see **PLURALS**), it is not a noun in Latin but a verb, meaning 'we do not know'.

ilk The use of *ilk* as a synonym for 'type' or 'sort', in the phrase *of that ilk*, is widely accepted in many contexts but is disliked by some users: □ *Barbara Cartland and other writers of that ilk*. *That* is sometimes replaced by *your*, *their*, *his*, *her*, etc.: □ *Barbara Cartland and other writers of her ilk*.

ill see **SICK OR ILL?**

illegal see **ILLICIT, ILLEGAL, OR ILLEGITIMATE?**

illegible or **eligible**? The adjective *eligible*, meaning 'qualified; suitable; worthy': □ *to be eligible for a competition* □ *an eligible bachelor*, should not be confused with *illegible* (see **ILLEGIBLE OR UNREADABLE?**).

illegible or **unreadable**? The adjective *illegible* describes something that cannot be deciphered and is therefore impossible to read; *unreadable* means 'uninteresting' or 'badly worded', describing something that cannot be read with enjoyment, ease, or understanding: □ *Her handwriting is illegible.* □ *He has produced another unreadable novel.* □ *The document is unreadable; it must be reworded.*

illegitimate see ILLICIT, ILLEGAL, OR ILLEGITIMATE?

illicit or **elicit**? The adjective *illicit* (see ILLICIT, ILLEGAL, OR ILLEGITIMATE?) should not be confused with the verb *elicit*, meaning 'draw out' or 'evoke': □ *illicit dealings* □ *to elicit the truth.*

illicit, illegal, or **illegitimate**? All these adjectives mean 'unlawful', but there are differences of sense, usage, and application between them. *Illicit* means 'not permitted or approved by law'; *illegal* means 'forbidden by law'; *illegitimate* is principally applied to children born of unmarried parents: □ *the president's illegitimate daughter.*

illusion see ALLUSION, ILLUSION, OR DELUSION?

illusive, illusory see ALLUSIVE, ELUSIVE, OR ILLUSIVE?

illustrative In British English the adjective *illustrative*, as in: □ *illustrative examples*, is stressed on the first syllable, [*il*ŭstrătiv]. In American English the second syllable is stressed, [i*lus*trătiv].

image The frequent use of *image* as a synonym for 'reputation' is disliked by some users.

imaginary or **imaginative**? *Imaginary* means 'unreal' or 'existing only in the imagination'; *imaginative* means 'having or showing a vivid or creative imagination': □ *an imaginary house* □ *an imaginative designer* □ *an imaginative story.*

imbroglio An *imbroglio* is a confused situation: □ *a political imbroglio.* Note the spelling of this word, particularly the silent *g*. It is used in formal contexts and is of Italian origin; the anglicized pronunciation is [im*brō*liō].

I mean The phrase *I mean* may be used in informal speech to clarify, expand, or correct a previous statement, question, etc.: □ *Is your foot very painful, I mean too painful to walk on?* □ *She lives in Plymouth, I mean Portsmouth.*

immanent see EMINENT, IMMINENT, OR IMMANENT?

immigrant see EMIGRANT OR IMMIGRANT?

imminent see EMINENT, IMMINENT, OR IMMANENT?

immoral see AMORAL OR IMMORAL?

immune from or **immune to**? The adjective *immune* is followed by *to* in the literal sense of 'protected against or resistant to disease' and figurative extensions of this sense: □ *The plant is immune to fungal disease.* □ *She is immune to criticism.* In the figurative sense of 'exempt', *immune* is followed by *from*: □ *Nobody is immune from punishment.*

immunity or **impunity**? *Immunity* is exemption or freedom from obligation or duty; *impunity* is exemption or freedom from punishment or harm: □ *Diplomatic immunity provides foreign ambassadors with immunity from taxation and enables them to infringe the law with impunity.*

impact The use of *impact* as a synonym for 'effect', 'impression', or 'influence' is best restricted to contexts in which the effect, impression, etc., is particularly powerful: □ *the impact of the government's resignation on the stock market* □ *The new packaging has had little effect* [not *impact*] *on sales.*

impasse The formal word *impasse,* meaning 'deadlock; stalemate': □ *to reach an impasse,* is of French origin and has a number of anglicized pronunciations. The first syllable may be pronounced [am-], [im-], or [om-]; the second syllable [-pahs] or [-pas]; and the stress may be on either syllable. The pronunciation [am*pahs*] is closest to the French.

impassioned, impassive see DISPASSIONATE, IMPASSIONED, OR IMPASSIVE?

impeccable This word, meaning 'faultless': □ *She spoke impeccable Italian*, is often misspelt. Note particularly the *-able* ending.

impel see COMPEL OR IMPEL?

imperial or **imperious**? The adjective *imperial* means 'of an emperor, empress, or empire'; *imperious* means 'overbearing' or 'arrogant': □ *the imperial palace* □ *an imperious gesture.*

impersonate, personate, or **personify**? To *impersonate* is to imitate or pretend to be somebody else: □ *The comedian impersonated Humphrey Bogart.* □ *It is a crime to impersonate a police officer.* To *personify* is to represent or embody something abstract or inanimate as a human being: □ *He personifies the greed of modern society.* The rare verb *personate* is sometimes used in place of *impersonate* or *personify*.

impinge or **infringe**? Either verb may be used in the sense of 'encroach': □ *They are impinging/infringing on our rights.* Note that both verbs are followed by *on* (or *upon*) in this sense. *Impinge* is used with more abstract nouns: □ *everything that impinges on our consciousness*.

impious This word should be stressed on the first syllable [*im*piŭs].

implement The verb *implement* is best avoided where *carry out*, *fulfil*, *accomplish*, or *put into action* would be adequate or more appropriate: □ *His absence will enable us to carry out* [not *implement*] *our plan.*

implicit see EXPLICIT OR IMPLICIT?

imply or **infer**? The verb *imply* means 'suggest' or 'hint at'; *infer* means 'deduce' or 'conclude': □ *She implied that there would be some redundancies in the factory.* □ *I inferred from what she said that there would be some redundancies in the factory.* To *imply* involves speech, writing, or action; to *infer* involves listening, reading, or observation.

important or **importantly**? *More important* (short for *what is more important*) is sometimes regarded as an adverbial phrase, the adjective *important* being changed to *importantly*: □ *His assistants are very conscientious and, more important(ly), they are utterly trustworthy.*

impostor or **imposter**? This word, meaning 'person who fraudulently pretends to be another person', has two spellings, though the spelling *impostor* is more frequently used than *imposter*.

impractical or **impracticable**? see PRACTICAL OR PRACTICABLE?

impresario An *impresario* is a theatrical producer or sponsor. Note the spelling of the word, particularly the single *s*, unlike *impress*.

The usual pronunciation is [imprĕsariō]; the variant [imprĕsairiō] is disliked by some people.

impromptu see EXTEMPORE OR IMPROMPTU?

impunity see IMMUNITY OR IMPUNITY?

in see AT OR IN?; INTO OR IN TO?

inaccessible Note the spelling of this adjective, particularly the single *-n-*, the *-cc-* and *-ss-*, and the *-ible* ending.

inapt or **inept**? The adjective *inapt* means 'inappropriate' or 'unsuitable'; its synonym *inept* is more frequently used in the sense of 'incompetent' or 'clumsy': □ *an inapt comparison* □ *an inept mechanic.*

inasmuch as This phrase may also be written *in as much as*, although *inasmuch as* is far more frequent. See also INSOFAR AS.

incident The noun *incident* is frequently used in the mass media to denote an action or occurrence that has or is likely to have serious, violent, or political consequences: □ *The latest terrorist attack was sparked off by an incident in Londonderry.*

incomparable This word, meaning 'without comparison', is often mispronounced. The stress falls on the second syllable and not the third. The correct pronunciation is [in*kom*pĕrĕbl].

incontrovertible The adjective *incontrovertible*, meaning 'undeniable; indisputable', and the derived adverb *incontrovertibly*, are sometimes misspelt. Note the *-ible* (not *-able*) ending. Another frequent error is the substitution of *-a-* for the second *-o-*.

incredible or **incredulous**? *Incredible* means 'unbelievable'; *incredulous* means 'disbelieving': □ *He told her an incredible story.* □ *She looked at him with an incredulous expression.*

indecent see DECENT OR DECOROUS?

indefinite article see A OR AN?

indefinitely This word is often misspelt, the most common error being the substitution of an *a* for the final *i*.

independence and **independent** These words are sometimes misspelt, the most frequent error being the substitution of an *a* for the final *e*.

in-depth The adjective *in-depth* is disliked by many users; it can usually be replaced by *thorough* or *detailed*, for which it is an unnecessary synonym: □ *an in-depth knowledge of the latest electronic equipment* □ *an in-depth study of child abuse.*

indexes or **indices**? The noun *index* has two accepted plural forms, *indexes* and *indices*. The use of the plural form *indices*, pronounced [*in*diseez], is largely restricted to mathematics, economics, and technical contexts.

Indian The adjective and noun *Indian* may refer to India and its inhabitants or to the indigenous peoples of America: □ *the Indian Empire* □ *an Indian reservation. American Indian* should be used where appropriate.

indicate In the field of medicine the verb *indicate* can mean 'require; show the need for or advisability of', usually in the passive: □ *A course of antibiotics was indicated.* Some people object to the use of *indicated* in this sense in non-medical contexts, in place of *shown to be necessary, advisable*, etc.: □ *Redundancies were indicated.*

indices see INDEXES OR INDICES?

indict or **indite**? The words *indict* and *indite* are both pronounced [in*dīt*], but they have different meanings. *Indict* – note the *c* that is not pronounced – means 'accuse; formally charge'; *indite* is an older word that means 'write down'.

indifferent The adjective *indifferent* should be followed by *to* or *as to*, not *for* or *about*: □ *He is indifferent to your criticism.* □ *I am indifferent as to the outcome of the trial.*

indigenous see NATIVE.

indirect speech see REPORTED SPEECH.

indiscriminate or **undiscriminating**? Both adjectives refer to a lack of discrimination (in the sense of 'discernment' rather than 'prejudice'); *indiscriminate* has the extended meaning of 'random' or 'unselective': □ *indiscriminate killings* □ *an undiscriminating palate.*

indispensable This word, meaning 'absolutely essential': □ *In this job, a car and a telephone are indispensable assets*, is sometimes misspelt.

indite see INDICT OR INDITE?

individual The use of the

noun *individual* in place of *person* is disliked by some users, who reserve *individual* for contexts in which a single person is contrasted with a group: □ *the rights of the individual* □ *the person* [not *individual*] *who wrote this article.*

indoor or **indoors**? *Indoor* is an adjective; *indoors* is an adverb: □ *an indoor aerial* □ *to go indoors* □ *Indoor games are played indoors.*

industrial or **industrious**? These two adjectives should not be confused. *Industrial* is derived from the noun *industry* in the sense of 'manufacturing or commercial enterprises'; *industrious* means 'hard-working' (from *industry* in the sense of 'diligence; assiduity'): □ *an industrial town* □ *an industrious student.*

industrial action The term *industrial action* may denote any of a number of measures (such as a strike, sit-in, go-slow, work-to-rule, or overtime ban) used by protesting or dissatisfied employees to put pressure on their employers: □ *Industrial action by electricity workers may result in power cuts.* The term is, however, misleading and contradictory, as a strike is characterized by a *lack* of action, rather than action.

industrious see INDUSTRIAL OR INDUSTRIOUS?

inedible see EATABLE OR EDIBLE?

ineffective, ineffectual, inefficient see EFFECTIVE, EFFECTUAL, EFFICACIOUS, OR EFFICIENT?

inept see INAPT OR INEPT?

inequality, inequity, or **iniquity**? *Inequality* is the state of being unequal or different; *inequity* means 'unfairness'; *iniquity* is wickedness: □ *the inequality of their ages* □ *the inequity of the law* □ *a den of iniquity.* *Inequity* and *iniquity* are much more formal words than *inequality.*

in fact The phrase *in fact* is largely used for emphasis or to expand on a previous statement: □ *This legislation will not in fact improve housing conditions in inner-city areas.* □ *I'm not familiar with the machine, in fact I've only used it once.*

infamous or **notorious**? Both adjectives mean 'well-known for something bad': *notorious* emphasizes the well-known aspect; *infamous* emphasizes the bad aspect: □ *the execution of this infamous/notorious criminal* □ *his notorious lack of punctuality* □ *That junction is notorious for accidents.* □ *one of Richard III's most infamous deeds.*

infectious see CONTAGIOUS OR INFECTIOUS?

infer, inference see IMPLY OR INFER?

infinite or **infinitesimal**? *Infinite* means 'having no limits' or 'extremely great'; *infinitesimal* means 'negligible' or 'extremely small': □ *She has infinite patience.* □ *The difference is infinitesimal.* An *infinite* amount is so great that it cannot be measured; an *infinitesimal* amount is so small that it cannot be measured.

infinitive The *infinitive* of a verb, often preceded by *to*, is its basic form, without any of the changes or additions that relate to tense, person, number, etc.: *(to) go* is the infinitive of the verb from which the past participle *gone* is derived.

inflammable The adjective *inflammable* describes something that will catch fire and burn easily: □ *This liquid is highly inflammable. Inflammable* may be wrongly interpreted as the opposite of its synonym *flammable* (by analogy with *sensitive–insensitive*; *visible–invisible*; *edible–inedible*; *capable–incapable*; etc.). The potential danger of such confusion has led to a preference, especially on warning signs and labels, for the less ambiguous terms *flammable* (denoting an inflammable substance) and *nonflammable* (denoting a substance that is not (in)flammable).

inflation Inflation is a general increase in the level of prices: □ *The rate of inflation has risen to 16%.* The word is widely used, especially in informal contexts, to denote the rate of inflation: □ *Inflation has risen to 16%.*

inflection *Inflection* is the term used for the change in form that words undergo in order to denote distinctions of number, tense, gender, case, etc. It is also used to describe the grammatical relation of a word to its root by inflection. See DERIVED WORDS.

inflict see AFFLICT OR INFLICT?

influenza see FLU.

info- Some people dislike the increasing use of *info-*, short for *information*, to form new blends and compounds, especially in informal contexts. □ *infotainment* (informative entertainment) □ *infomania* (preoccupation with information for its own sake) □ *infotech* (information technology).

inform The verb *inform* is best avoided where *tell* would be adequate or more appropriate: □ *Please tell* [not *inform*] *your husband that his car is ready for collection.*

informant or **informer**? An *informant* is a person who gives information; an *informer* is a person who gives the police information about criminals and their activities: □ *The professor was one of the author's most useful informants.* □ *The police were tipped off about the robbery by an informer.*

infringe see IMPINGE OR INFRINGE?

ingenious or **ingenuous**? *Ingenious* means 'clever' or 'inventive'; *ingenuous* means 'innocent', 'naive', or 'frank': □ *an ingenious idea* □ *an ingenuous smile.* The two adjectives are not interchangeable, but are sometimes confused.

-ing forms The *-ing* form of a verb may be a present participle or a gerund (verbal noun): □ *I am learning Japanese* [present participle]. □ *Learning Japanese is not easy* [gerund]. It is sometimes difficult, and often unnecessary, to distinguish between a gerund and a present participle.

inherent This word, meaning 'essential or intrinsic', has two possible pronunciations: [in*heer*ĕnt] or [in*herr*ĕnt]. The first of these is the more traditional and is preferred by many users.

inheritance see HERITAGE OR INHERITANCE?

inhuman or **inhumane**? Careful users maintain the distinction between *inhuman* and *inhumane*. *Inhumane*, the opposite of *humane*, means 'lacking in compassion and kindness; cruel; not merciful': □ *inhumane treatment.* *Inhuman*, the opposite of *human*, is stronger and has a wider scope than *inhumane*. To be *inhuman* means to lack all human qualities, not only compassion and kindness: □ *inhuman violence* □ *inhuman living conditions.*

iniquity see INEQUALITY,

INEQUITY, OR INIQUITY?

in-law The use of the plural noun *in-laws*, denoting a person's relatives by marriage, is best restricted to informal contexts: □ *My in-laws are coming for dinner on Saturday.*

in lieu The phrase *in lieu (of)* is best avoided where *instead (of)* would be adequate or more appropriate: □ *She drove to the airport instead* [not *in lieu*] *of taking the train.*

innocuous The adjective *innocuous*, meaning 'harmless': □ *a few innocuous remarks*, is sometimes misspelt. Note the *-nn-*, the single *c*, and the vowel sequence *-uou-*.

innovative Many people dislike the frequent use of *innovative* in place of *new, creative, imaginative, progressive,* etc.: □ *an innovative method of contraception* □ *an innovative sales manager.*

inoculate or **vaccinate**? The verbs *inoculate* and *vaccinate* are virtually synonymous in the sense of 'introduce a vaccine into the body of a person or animal to provide immunity': □ *She has been inoculated* [or *vaccinated*] *against whooping cough. Inoculate* has a wider range of usage: it may refer to the introduction of a substance other than a vaccine and is also used in figurative contexts in the sense of 'instil': □ *He inoculated his students with egalitarian ideals.*

inoculation This word is often misspelt, the most frequent error being the addition of an extra *n* as in *innocent*. Note the single *c* and the single *l*.

in order that and **in order to** The phrase *in order that* is followed by *may, might, shall*, or *should* rather than *can, could, will*, or *would*: □ *He moved his suitcase in order that we might* [not *could*] *open the door.* □ *She drove him to the station in order that he should* [not *would*] *not miss his train.*

input Many people object to the use of the noun *input* as a synonym for 'contribution': □ *We hope to have some input from the teaching staff at tomorrow's meeting.* □ *positive input* 'approval or encouragement' □ *negative input* 'criticism'.

inquiry see ENQUIRY OR INQUIRY?

inside of Many people dislike the prepositional phrase

inside of, meaning 'within' or 'in less than', in which the word *of* is incorrect. phrase should not be used in formal contexts: □ *There was a cheque inside* [not *inside of*] *the envelope.* □ *The job was completed inside* [not *inside of*] *two weeks.*

in so far as This expression may be written *in so far as* or *insofar as*, the latter being more frequent in American English.

in spite of see DESPITE OR IN SPITE OF?

install or **instal**? Both spellings of this word are correct, although the first is more frequently used.

instantly or **instantaneously**? The adverbs *instantly* and *instantaneously* are virtually interchangeable in the sense of 'immediately' or 'without delay': □ *He replied instantly/instantaneously.*

instil This word, meaning 'introduce gradually', is often misspelt. It ends in a single *l* in British English.

institute or **institution**? Both nouns are used to denote certain professional bodies and established organizations founded for research, study, charitable work, the promotion of a cause, etc.: □ *the Institute of Metals* □ *the British Standards Institution* □ *the Royal National Institute for the Blind* □ *the Royal National Lifeboat Institution.* The nouns also denote the buildings or premises used by these organizations.

instructional or **instructive**? *Instructional* is the rarer word and means 'providing instruction(s)'; *instructive* is used in the wider sense of 'informative; enlightening': □ *an instructional leaflet* □ *an instructive experience.*

insurance see ASSURANCE OR INSURANCE?

insure see ASSURE, ENSURE, OR INSURE?

integral Some people object to the frequent use of the phrase *integral part*, in which the adjective *integral* is often superfluous: □ *The study of local history is an integral part of the syllabus.* Most parts are *integral*, i.e. 'essential to the completeness of the whole', by definition.

integrate The verb *integrate* is widely used in the sense of 'make or become part of a social group': □ *One of the aims of our organization* *is to integrate ethnic minorities into the community.* □ *Newcomers to the village often find it difficult to integrate.*

intense or **intensive**? *Intense* means 'extreme' or 'very strong'; *intensive* means 'concentrated' or 'thorough': □ *intense pain* □ *intense heat* □ *intensive training* □ *an intensive search.* The two adjectives are not interchangeable, although both may be applied to the same noun: *intense/intensive study.*

inter see INTERMENT OR INTERNMENT?

inter- or **intra-**? The prefix *inter-* means 'between' or 'reciprocally'; *intra-* means 'within': □ *intercontinental* □ *interdependent* □ *intravenous* □ *intramural.*

interactive In computing, the adjective *interactive* refers to direct communication between the user and the computer: □ *The disks are interactive, which means that they pose questions on the screen, and you only get further information by answering* (*Daily Telegraph*). The term is also applied to television programmes, video games, etc., in which the viewer or player is physically involved in the progress or completion of the programme, game, etc.

intercede This verb, meaning 'mediate', is sometimes misspelt. Note the *-cede* ending, as in *concede, precede,* etc. (unlike *proceed, succeed,* etc.).

interface In science, computing, etc., the noun *interface* denotes a surface forming a common boundary or a point of communication. Its extended use as a synonym for 'interaction', 'liaison', 'link', '(point of) contact', etc., is disliked by many people: □ *the interface between professionals and lay people in the caring professions* □ *the interface of history and literature* □ *at the interface between design and technology.*

interjections see EXCLAMATIONS.

interment or **internment**? *Interment* means 'burial'; *internment* means 'imprisonment': □ *the interment of the corpse* □ *the internment of the terrorists.*

internecine The adjective *internecine* may refer to slaughter or carnage, mutual destruction, or conflict within a group:

□ *an internecine battle* □ *internecine warfare* □ *an internecine dispute.*

internment see INTERMENT OR INTERNMENT?

interpersonal The adjective *interpersonal,* meaning 'between people', is disliked by some people as a vogue term and can often be replaced by a synonym, such as *social,* or by a simple paraphrase: □ *interpersonal skills* are social skills; □ *in an interpersonal situation* means 'with people'.

interpretive or **interpretative?** Either adjective may be used, but *interpretative* is the more frequent: □ *The appendix contains interpretative/interpretive notes on the text.*

intestinal The adjective *intestinal* is usually stressed on the third syllable, [intestīnl]. The variant pronunciation [intestinl], with the stress on the second syllable, is also heard.

in that The phrase *in that* means 'because' or 'to the extent that': □ *He is unsuitable for the job in that he has no relevant experience.* □ *The two machines are different in that one is fully automatic and the other is manually controlled.*

in the fast lane, in the fast track see FAST LANE.

in the near future The phrase *in the near future* is disliked by some users as an unnecessarily wordy substitute for *soon:* □ *The electronics company is considering relocating to Swindon in the near future.*

in this day and age The cliché *in this day and age* is best avoided where *nowadays, today, now,* etc., would be adequate or more appropriate: □ *In this day and age a good education is not a passport to a successful career.*

into or **in to?** *Into* is a preposition with a variety of meanings; *in to* is a combination of the adverb *in* and the preposition or infinitive marker *to:* □ *I went into the house.* □ *I went in to fetch a book.*

intonation *Intonation* is a change in pitch that adds to the meaning of a spoken word, phrase, or sentence. It should not be confused with STRESS, which relates to loudness or emphasis, although the two are often used in combination.

in toto The Latin phrase *in toto* means 'entirely' or

'completely': □ *He did not disagree in toto.*

intra- see INTER- OR INTRA-?

intransitive see VERBS.

intrinsic or **extrinsic**? The adjective *intrinsic* means 'inherent', 'essential', or 'originating from within': □ *The discovery is of great intrinsic interest. Extrinsic*, the opposite of *intrinsic*, is less frequent in general usage.

introvert see EXTROVERT OR INTROVERT?

Inuit The term *Inuit* refers to the people of North America and Greenland traditionally known as Eskimos. The term *Inuit* (meaning 'people') is preferred to *Eskimo* (meaning 'eater of raw flesh'), by the Inuit themselves. It may also be used to distinguish this people from the Eskimos of the Aleutian Islands and Siberia.

invalid The adjectival sense of 'not valid' is pronounced with the stress on the second syllable [in*val*id]. The noun sense of 'someone who is ill' is pronounced with the stress on the first syllable, either as [*in*vălid] or [*in*văleed].

inveigh or **inveigle**? To *inveigh* is to protest strongly; to *inveigle* is to persuade cleverly: □ *She inveighed against the inequity of the law.* □ *He inveigled us into signing the form. Inveigh*, an intransitive verb, is followed by *against*, whereas *inveigle* is transitive and often used with *into*.

invent, design, or **discover**? *Invent* and *design* refer to the creation of something new; *discover* refers to the finding of something that is already in existence: □ *to invent a machine* □ *to design a new computer* □ *to discover a cure for cancer.*

inventory The noun *inventory*, unlike *invent* and *invention*, is stressed on the first syllable. The usual British pronunciation is [*in*vĕntri]; in American English the *-o-* may be sounded: [*in*vĕntori].

inverse see CONVERSE, INVERSE, OBVERSE, OR REVERSE?

inversion *Inversion* is a reversal of the normal order of the elements of a sentence or clause so that the subject follows the verb: □ *There goes the bus.* □ *In came Michael.* □ *At the bottom of the heap was the missing book.*

inverted commas see QUOTATION MARKS.

invite The use of the word *invite* as a noun, in place of *invitation*, is disliked and avoided by many users, even in informal contexts: □ *Have you had an invite to their party?* □ *Thank you for your invitation, which I am very pleased to accept.*

involve Some people object to the frequent use of the verb *involve* and its derivatives in place of more specific or more appropriate synonyms: □ *This proposal will entail* [not *involve*] *further cuts in expenditure.* □ *Some changes may be necessary* [not *involved*]. □ *I have a number of questions concerning* [not *involving*] *teaching methods and discipline.* □ *These fingerprints are evidence of his participation* [not *involvement*] *in the robbery.*

inward or **inwards**? In British English *inward* is principally used as an adjective, *inwards* being the usual form of the adverb meaning 'towards the inside': □ *inward feelings* □ *to push inwards.*

IQ This abbreviation for 'intelligence quotient': □ *The average IQ is one hundred,* must always be written with capital letters. The abbreviation may be written with full stops, *I.Q.*, but this form is becoming less frequent in modern usage.

irascible The formal word *irascible,* meaning 'easily angered', is sometimes misspelt. *Irascible* has a single *r* and ends in *-ible*, unlike its synonym *irritable*. Note also the *sc*.

iron out The phrasal verb *iron out* is widely used in the metaphorical sense of 'settle', 'resolve', 'solve', or 'remove': □ *We have a few more problems to iron out before work can begin.*

irony *Irony* is the use of words to express the opposite of their accepted meaning, often for satirical or humorous effect.

irrefutable This word, meaning 'impossible to be disproved': □ *irrefutable evidence,* may be stressed on the second or on the third syllable: [i*ref*yootăbl] or [iri*fyoot*ăbl]. The second pronunciation is becoming more common.

irregardless The word *irregardless* is a nonstandard blend of *irrespective* and *regardless.* Most dictionaries do not acknowledge its existence, but it is frequently heard in colloquial usage: □ *'Irregardless of what we say about Robbo, he done a good job,' was a near-miss by Elton Welsby for ITV in Bologna* (*The Guardian*). The word should be avoided in all contexts; either *irrespective* or *regardless* may be used in its place (see IRRESPECTIVE).

irrelevant This word is frequently misspelt. Note the *-rr-* and the vowels *i-e-e-a*.

irreparable This word, meaning 'unable to be repaired', is often mispronounced. The stress should fall on the second syllable and not the third [i*rep*ărăbl].

irresistible Note the spelling of this adjective, particularly the *-rr-* and the *-ible* (not *-able*) ending.

irrespective The word *irrespective* is most frequently used in the prepositional phrase *irrespective of*, meaning 'regardless of': □ *Applications are invited from all suitably qualified candidates, irrespective of age, sexual orientation, nationality, disability or religion.*

irrevocable In its general sense of 'not able to be changed': □ *an irrevocable decision*, the word *irrevocable* is stressed on the second syllable, [i*rev*ŏkăbl]. The pronunciation [irivō*kăbl*], stressed on the third syllable, is restricted to a few legal or financial contexts, where the sense is literally 'not able to be revoked': □ *irrevocable letters of credit.*

irrupt see ERUPT OR IRRUPT?

-ise see -IZE OR -ISE?

-ism Some people object to the increasing use of the suffix *-ism*, in the sense of 'discrimination', to coin new words modelled on the nouns *racism* and *sexism*: □ *legislation against ageism* □ *the controversial issue of heterosexism.*

-ist or -ite? Both these suffixes may be used to denote an adherent, follower, advocate, or supporter of a particular doctrine: □ *Stalinist* □ *Luddite* □ *Labourite* □ *communist.* The suffix *-ite* is sometimes used in a derogatory manner: people who call themselves *Trotskyists*, for example, may be described by opponents of Trotskyism as *Trotskyites*.

isthmus The noun *isthmus*,

meaning 'narrow strip of land', causes problems of spelling and pronunciation. Note the four adjacent consonants *-sthm-*. The [th] sound is not heard in the usual pronunciation [*is*mŭs]; the full pronunciation [*isth*mŭs] is no more or less correct.

it The pronoun *it* has a wide range of uses: to replace an abstract noun or the name of an inanimate object, as the subject of an impersonal verb, etc.: □ *He washed the towel and hung it out to dry.* □ *It hasn't rained for a week.* □ *I find it difficult to make new friends.* □ *It's obvious that she doesn't like him.* For this reason, the use of *it* may sometimes cause ambiguity or confusion: □ *She took her purse out of her handbag and put it on the table* [the purse or the handbag?]. □ *You can open the window if it gets too hot* [the window or the weather?].

italics The word *italic* denotes a sloping typeface that is used for a variety of purposes in English. The principal uses of italics are: for the titles of books, films, etc.; for the names of ships, aircraft, etc.; for foreign words or phrases; to indicate stress or emphasis.

In handwritten or typewritten texts, underlining is generally used to indicate italics.

-ite see -IST OR -ITE?

itinerary This word, meaning 'planned route of a journey', is sometimes misspelt. The careful pronunciation [ī*tin*ĕrări] should ensure its correct spelling.

its or **it's**? *It's*, a contraction of *it is* or *it has*, should not be confused with *its*, the possessive form of *it*: □ *It's easy to tell the difference.* □ *It's been raining for several hours.* □ *The lion has escaped from its cage.* See also APOSTROPHE; CONTRACTIONS; 'S OR S'?

-ize or **-ise**? In British English, the sound [-īz] at the end of many verbs may be spelt *-ize* or *-ise*: □ *baptize/baptise* □ *realize/realise* □ *recognize/recognise* □ *organize/organise*; etc. Most modern dictionaries, partly because of the American international influence, list *-ize* as the preferred spelling, giving *-ise* as an accepted variant. Not all *-ise* verbs can be spelt *-ize*.

J

jail or **gaol**? In British English these two spellings are both acceptable, although *jail* is preferred by many people. In American English *jail* is the only accepted spelling.

jargon *Jargon* is the technical language used within a particular subject or profession, such as science, computing, medicine, law, accountancy, etc. The term is also used to denote obscure or pretentious language used by estate agents, journalists, politicans etc. Jargon is acceptable in professional journals and in communications between members of the same group; however, it should not be used to mislead or intimidate the outsider.

jealousy see ENVY OR JEALOUSY?

jeopardize This word, meaning 'expose to danger', is often misspelt, the most frequent error being the omission of the letter *o*.

jewellery or **jewelry**? This word has two spellings in British English. Both are acceptable although *jewelry*, standard in American English, is less frequent in British English.

jibe see GIBE OR JIBE?

jodhpurs This word, meaning 'riding trousers', is often misspelt, the *h* being either incorrectly placed or omitted completely.

join or **joint**? The nouns *join* and *joint* are synonymous (but not interchangeable) in the sense of 'place where two parts are joined'. *Join* most frequently refers to the visual effect of the act of joining, the line or seam between two flat or flexible parts (such as paper, fabric, carpet, string, etc.): □ *You can hardly see the join.* A *joint* is more practical or functional, joining two rigid three-dimensional parts: □ *The pipe was leaking at one of the* *joints.* □ *the joint between the shaft and the head.*

journalese *Journalese* is a derogatory name for the style of writing or language that is considered to be typical of newspapers.

judgment or **judgement**? Either spelling of this word is acceptable, although *judgement* is probably more common in British English and *judgment* in American English.

judicial or **judicious**? *Judicial* means 'of judgment in a court of law' or 'of the administration of justice'; *judicious* means 'having or showing good judgment' or 'prudent': □ *judicial proceedings* □ *a judicious choice.*

juncture The phrase *at this juncture* refers to a critical point in time; many people object to its frequent use in place of *now*: □ *The leader's resignation at this juncture would have a disastrous effect on the members' morale.* □ *I suggest that we take a short break for refreshments now* [not *at this juncture*].

junta This word refers to a controlling political council and has various pronunciations. The preferred pronunciation is [*jun*tă].

just *Just* has a variety of adverbial senses: 'at this moment', 'exactly', 'only', etc. For this reason it must be carefully positioned in a sentence in order to convey the intended meaning: □ *Your son has just eaten two cakes* [i.e. a short time ago]. □ *Your son has eaten just two cakes* [i.e. not one or three, etc.]. □ *Just your son has eaten two cakes* [i.e. only your son; no one else]. Transposing *just* and *not* may also change the meaning of a sentence: □ *I'm just not tired.* □ *I'm not just tired; I'm hungry too.*

K

K The letter *K*, short for *kilo-*, is increasingly used to represent 1000, especially in sums of money: □ *a salary of £50K plus company car* □ *houses priced from £250K upwards.* The abbreviation is also used in spoken language: □ *She was earning a hundred K in the City.*

kaleidoscope This word is sometimes misspelt. Note particularly the *-ei-* and the first *o* from the Greek *eidos*, meaning 'form'.

karaoke The noun *karaoke*, denoting a form of entertainment in which people sing along with a prerecorded tape, causes problems of spelling and pronunciation. Of Japanese origin, the word may be pronounced [karrăōki] or [karriōki] in English.

kerb see CURB OR KERB?

key Some people object to the increasingly frequent use of the word *key* as an adjective, in the sense of 'fundamental', 'essential', 'crucial', 'most important', 'indispensable', etc.: □ *a number of key individuals to manage their top UK stores* □ *setting up a policy committee that will take key decisions* (*Sunday Times*).

kibbutzim *Kibbutzim* is the plural form of the noun *kibbutz*, denoting a collective community in Israel. *Kibbutz* is pronounced [ki*buuts*], rhyming with *puts*; *kibbutzim* is stressed on the final syllable [kibuut*seem*].

kick-start The figurative use of the verb *kick-start* in the sense of 'take action to set in motion (again)' is becoming rather hackneyed, especially in the phrase *kick-start the economy*: □ *Plans to balance income tax cuts with measures to boost business and kickstart the economy will form a key element in the chancellor's strategy* (*Sunday Times*). □ *to kick-start the housing market.*

kid The use of the noun *kid* as a synonym for 'child' or 'young person' is best restricted to informal contexts: □ *Things were very different when I was a kid.* □ *One of the local kids broke the window.* □ *Have you got any kids?*

kidnap The final *p* of the word *kidnap* is doubled before a suffix beginning with a vowel: □ *kidnapped* □ *kidnapper*. See also SPELLING 1.

kilo The word *kilo*, pronounced [*kee*lō], is most frequently used as an abbreviation for *kilogram*: □ *a kilo of sugar* □ *50 kilos of coal.*

kilometre This word may be stressed on the first syllable [*kil*ŏmeetĕ] or on the second syllable [ki*lom*itĕ].

kindly The word *kindly* may be used as an adjective, meaning 'kind' or 'sympathetic', or as an adverb, meaning 'in a kind way': □ *a kindly policeman* □ *a kindly smile* □ *They treated us kindly.*

kind of In formal contexts the phrases *kind of*, *sort of*, and *type of*, in which *kind*, *sort*, and *type* are in the singular, should be preceded by *this* or *that* (rather than *these* or *those*) and followed by a singular noun: □ *this kind of story* □ *that sort of biscuit.* The use of *kind of* or *sort of* in place of *rather* or *somewhat* is best restricted to informal contexts.

knee-jerk In figurative contexts, the term *knee-jerk* is applied to an automatic, predictable, and/or unthinking reaction, as opposed to a more considered response: □ *A knee-jerk reaction to the problem could make matters worse.* □ *Industrial action is the knee-jerk response of many union leaders.* The term should be confined to informal usage and not be overused.

kneeled or **knelt**? Either word may be used as the past tense and past participle of the verb *kneel*. *Knelt* is more frequent in British English: □ *He knelt on the grass*; *kneeled* in American English.

knit or **knitted**? *Knitted* is the more frequent form of the past tense and past participle of the verb *knit*, especially in the literal sense: □ *I (have) knitted a cardigan for the baby.* □ *She was wearing a knitted jacket.*

knock-on effect The phrase *knock-on effect* refers to a series of related causes and effects: □ *The reduction in taxes will have a knock-on effect throughout the economy.*

know see YOU KNOW.

knowledgeable This word, meaning 'having clear knowledge or understanding', is sometimes misspelt. Note that the final *-e* of *knowledge* is retained before the suffix *-able*.

L

laboratory The usual pronunciation of this word in British English is [lăborrătŏri], with the stress on the second syllable; the second *o* is sometimes not sounded. In American English the stress falls on the first and fourth syllables, [*lab*ŏrrători]; the first *o* is sometimes not sounded.

laborious The word *laborious* is sometimes misspelt, the most frequent error being the insertion of a *u* after the first *o*, as in *labour*.

lack When using the verb *lack*, *lack for* in place of *lack* is unacceptable to many people, and the superfluous *for* is best omitted: □ *She did not lack* [not *lack for*] *friends*.

lacquer This word is sometimes misspelt. Note that it has only one *-u-*: the word ends in *-er*, and not *-eur* as in *liqueur*.

laden or **loaded**? *Laden*, a past participle of the verb *lade*, is principally used as an adjective, meaning 'weighed down' or 'burdened'; *loaded* is the past tense and past participle of the verb *load*: □ *The tree was laden with apples.* □ *We overtook a heavily laden lorry.* □ *He (has) loaded the car*. The verb *lade*, meaning 'load with cargo', is rarely used in modern times in any other form, except in the term *bill of lading*.

lady see WOMAN.

lama or **llama**? The spelling of these words is sometimes confused. A *lama* is a Lamaist monk, the order of Lamaism being a form of Buddhism of Tibet and Mongolia. A *llama* is a South American mammal related to the camel. Note the *ll-* at the beginning of this word.

lamentable This word has two pronunciations. The traditional British English pronunciation is [*lam*ĕntăbl]. The stress may also fall on the second syllable [lă*men*tăbl], although this is disliked and avoided by some users.

languor Note the spelling of this word, particularly the unusual *-uor* ending. *Languor* is a formal word that means 'laziness; weariness'; the derived adjective is spelt *languorous*.

lasso A *lasso* is a rope with a noose, used for catching horses or cattle. There are two acceptable pronunciations although [la*soo*] is the more frequent in contemporary British usage: [*la*sō] was once standard but is now less frequent.

last To avoid ambiguity, the adjective *last* should be replaced, where necessary, with an appropriate synonym, such as *latest*, *final*, or *preceding*: □ *His latest* [not *last*] *novel was published in June.* □ *His final* [not *last*] *novel was published in June.* □ *The preceding* [not *last*] *chapter contains a list of useful addresses. Last* may be retained where the context makes its meaning clear.

late Used directly before a noun denoting a person, the adjective *late* may mean 'dead' or 'former': □ *The widow gave her late husband's clothes to charity.* □ *The late president has written his memoirs.* To avoid confusion, *late* (in the sense of 'former') is often better replaced by *ex-* or *former*.

lath or **lathe**? These two nouns should not be confused. A *lath* is a thin strip of wood; a *lathe* is a machine for shaping wood, metal, etc. Note that it is the noun *lath*, not *lathe*, that is used in the simile *as thin as a lath*.

lather This word has various pronunciations. The traditional pronunciation rhymes with *gather*, but the pronunciation rhyming with *father* is becoming more frequently used.

latter see FORMER AND LATTER.

launch The verb *launch* is widely used in the figurative sense of 'set in motion', 'start', or 'introduce': □ *They have just launched their new perfume. Launch* is also used figuratively as a noun.

lavatory see TOILET, LAVATORY, LOO, OR BATHROOM?

law and order Careful speakers pronounce this phrase without an intrusive [r] sound between the words *law* and *and*. Similar care should be taken with the pronunciation of other words and phrases containing the sound [aw] followed by a vowel, such as *drawing, awe-inspiring, I saw it.*

lawful, legal, or **legitimate**? All these adjectives mean 'authorized by law', but there are differences of sense, usage, and application between them. *Lawful* means 'allowed by law' or 'rightful'; *legal* is more widely used, having the additional meaning of 'relating to law'; the adjective *legitimate* is principally applied to children born in wedlock, but also means 'reasonable', 'logical', 'genuine' or 'valid'.

lay or **lie**? The verb *lay*, which is usually transitive – i.e. has an object – is often confused with *lie*, which is intransitive, i.e. does not have an object: □ *I'll lay the towel on the sand to dry.* □ *She's going to lie down for a while.*

lead or **led**? These two words are often confused. *Lead* means 'guide by going in front': □ *He was leading the walking party*, and is pronounced [leed]. The past tense of this verb is *led*. This is sometimes wrongly spelt as *lead* because the pronunciation is the same as that of the metal: □ *as heavy as lead*, pronounced [led].

leadership *Leadership* is the state or rank of a leader; it also denotes qualities associated with a good leader: □ *elected to the leadership* □ *to lack leadership potential.* The use of the noun in place of *leaders* is disliked by some people: □ *China's leadership.*

leading-edge The adjectival use of *leading-edge* is best avoided where *advanced* or *up-to-date* would be adequate or more appropriate: □ *leading-edge technology* □ *a leading-edge project.*

leading question A *leading question* suggests or prompts the expected or desired answer, such as: □ *Did you see the defendant stab his wife with a kitchen knife?*

leak The use of the verb and noun *leak* with reference to the unofficial, surreptitious, or improper disclosure of secret information is acceptable in most contexts: □ *Details of the report were leaked to the press.*

leaned or **leant**? Either word may be used as the past tense and past participle of the verb *lean*: □ *She leaned/leant forwards to open the window.*

leaped or **leapt**? Either word may be used as the past tense and past participle of the verb *leap*: □ *They leaped/leapt across the very wide ditch.*

learn or **teach**? The use of the verb *learn* in place of *teach* is wrong: □ *He's teaching* [not *learning*] *me to swim.*

learned or **learnt**? Either word may be used as the past tense and past participle of the verb *learn*: □ *Have you learned/learnt the words of the song?*

learning curve The phrase *learning curve* refers to the process of acquiring new knowledge or experience as if represented by a graph. (The rate of learning is usually not uniform: the curve may rise steeply at the beginning, when a large amount of knowledge is acquired in a relatively short time.) It is a vogue term, often found in business contexts, and should not be overused: □ *to help new employees up the learning curve* □ *Most schools have only just started their second year of LMS and head teachers admit to being on a steep learning curve* (*The Bookseller*).

learnt see LEARNED OR LEARNT?

lease see HIRE OR RENT?

leave or **let**? The use of the verb *leave* in place of *let*, especially in the expressions *let go* and *let be*, is regarded as incorrect and avoided by many users: □ *You mustn't let* [not *leave*] *go of the rope.* □ *I told the children to let* [not *leave*] *him be.* The expressions *leave alone* and *let alone*, however, are virtually interchangeable in the sense of 'refrain from disturbing, bothering, interfering with, etc.': □ *Leave/Let the dog alone.*

led see LEAD OR LED?

leeward This word has two possible pronunciations. The generally accepted pronunciation is [*lee*wărd] but [looărd] is used in nautical contexts.

legal see LAWFUL, LEGAL, OR LEGITIMATE?

legalize see DECRIMINALIZE OR LEGALIZE?

legendary The use of the adjective *legendary* in the sense of 'very famous or notorious' may be misleading or confusing: □ *The legendary Dick Turpin rode a horse called Black Bess.* □ *Listening to recordings of the legendary Andrés Segovia during the 1930s* ... (*Reader's Digest*).

legible or **readable**? The adjective *legible* describes something that can be deciphered and read; *readable* describes something that may be read with interest, enjoyment, or ease: □ *legible handwriting* □ *a very readable novel.*

legionary see LEGIONNAIRE.

legionnaire Note the spelling of this word, particularly the *-nn-*. A *legionnaire* is a (former) member of a military legion, such as the French Foreign Legion, the British Legion, or the American Legion; the noun also occurs in the name of a serious disease, *legionnaires' disease.*

legitimate see LAWFUL, LEGAL, OR LEGITIMATE?

leisure This word, meaning 'time spent free from work', is sometimes misspelt. Note the *-ei-* spelling.

leisurely The word *leisurely* may be used as an adjective or, more rarely, as an adverb, meaning 'without haste': □ *stroll at a leisurely pace* □ *She walked leisurely up the garden.*

lend or **loan**? The word *lend* is used only as a verb; in British English *loan* is used principally as a noun: □ *He lent me his pen.* □ *Thank you for the loan of your lawn mower.* The use of *loan* as a verb is widely regarded as an Americanism. It is becoming increasingly acceptable, however, with reference to the lending of large sums of money, valuable works of art, etc.: □ *The bank will loan us the money we need to finance the setting up of the new venture.* □ *This picture has been loaned to the gallery by the Duke and Duchess of Kent.*

lengthways or **lengthwise**? Either word may be used as an adverb in British English: □ *Fold the sheet lengthways/lengthwise before ironing it.*

lengthy The adjective *lengthy* means 'tediously, excessively, or unusually long'; it should not be used in place of *long* as a neutral antonym of *short*: □ *The children became very restless during the headmaster's lengthy speech.* □ *She has long* [not *lengthy*] *dark hair* *and brown eyes.*

leopard This word is sometimes misspelt. The most frequent error is the omission of the *o* which is not pronounced.

less see FEWER OR LESS?

let Used in the imperative, *let* should be followed by an object pronoun rather than a subject pronoun: □ *Let them try.* □ *Let him finish his meal first.* □ *Let Paul and me* [not *I*] *see the letter.* See also LEAVE OR LET?

letter writing There are a number of conventions relating to the style and layout of a formal or semiformal letter.

1 The sender's address, followed by the date, should appear at the top of the letter, usually in the right-hand corner. The recipient's name and address appear below this, on the left-hand side of the page. Punctuation of the address – a comma at the end of each line (except the final line, which has a full stop) and sometimes after the house number – is optional.

2 The salutation (*Dear Sir, Dear Madam, Dear Miss Jones, Dear Mr Brown*, or, increasingly, under American influence, *Dear James Chapman*, etc., where the writer wants to avoid the formality of *Dear Mr Chapman* and the informality of *Dear James*) is set on a separate line, beginning with a capital letter and ending with a comma in British English, a colon in American English. See also ABBREVIATIONS; MS, MRS, OR MISS?

3 The letter itself should be divided into paragraphs, with or without indentation. The style and content of the letter depend on the level of formality.

4 The letter is closed with any of a number of fixed phrases, the most frequent being *Yours sincerely* (if the recipient's name is used in the salutation) or *Yours faithfully* (if an impersonal salutation, such as *Dear Sir* or *Dear Madam*, is used). Like the salutation, this phrase is set on a separate line, beginning with a capital letter and ending with a comma.

5 The signature is usually followed by the sender's name, title, and office (if appropriate).

leukaemia This word is

sometimes misspelt. Note the three sets of vowels: *eu*, *ae*, and *ia* in British English. The American English spelling is *leukemia*.

level The noun *level* serves a useful purpose in a variety of literal and figurative senses but is sometimes superfluous or unnecessarily vague: □ *a high level of unemployment* (high unemployment) □ *an increase in the noise level* (more noise) □ *decisions made at management level* (decisions made by the management).

level playing field The phrase *level playing field* is increasingly used in figurative contexts, denoting a situation where all can compete on equal terms: □ *These* [the single European market rules] *are meant to establish a level playing field for competition between community countries in the single market* (*The Guardian*). □ *I don't mind trying to compete on a level playing field with the rest of the book trade, but ...* (*The Bookseller*).

liable or **likely**? Both adjectives are used to express probability, followed by an infinitive with *to*. *Liable* refers to habitual probability, often based on past experience; *likely* refers to a specific probability that may be without precedent: □ *The dog is liable to bite strangers.* □ *The dog is likely to bite you if you pull his tail.* □ *The shelf is liable to collapse when it is filled with books.* □ *The shelf is likely to collapse if it is filled with books. Liable* also means 'responsible (for)' or 'subject (to)'.

liaison The noun *liaison* and its derived verb *liaise* are often misspelt, the most frequent error being the omission of the second *i*.

libel or **slander**? Both words refer to defamatory statements: *libel* is written, drawn, printed, or otherwise recorded in permanent form; *slander* is spoken or conveyed by gesture.

library The pronunciation of this word is [*lī*brări]. Careful users avoid dropping the second syllable [*lī*bri], but this pronunciation is frequently heard.

licence or **license**? In British English, the noun is spelt *licence*, the verb *license*: □ *a television licence* □ *an off-licence* □ *poetic licence* □ *to* *license one's car* □ *(un)licensed premises* □ *licensing hours*. In American English, both the noun and verb are spelt *license*.

lichen This word has two pronunciations [*lī*kĕn] or [*li*tchĕn]. Some people prefer the first of these, which is the same pronunciation as *liken*.

licorice see LIQUORICE.

lie see LAY OR LIE?

lieu see IN LIEU.

lieutenant This word is often misspelt, the most frequent errors occurring in the first syllable: *lieu-*. The pronunciation of this syllable varies. The most frequent pronunciation in British English is as in *left*, in nautical contexts the pronunciation is as in *let*, and in American English, the pronunciation is as in *loot*.

lifelong or **livelong**? The adjective *lifelong* means 'lasting or continuing for a lifetime': □ *my lifelong friend* □ *his lifelong admiration for her work*. The adjective *livelong*, meaning 'very long' or 'whole', is chiefly used in the old-fashioned poetic expression *all the livelong day*.

lifestyle Some people object to the frequent use of the term *lifestyle*, a synonym for 'way of life', by advertisers, journalists, etc.: □ *urban lifestyle* □ *consumer lifestyle values* □ *lifestyle packaging* □ *The spread of Aids is likely to have tremendous effects on the personal lifestyles of many people.*

lighted or **lit**? Either word may be used as the past tense and past participle of the verb *light*. *Lit* is the more frequent in British English: □ *Have you lit the fire?* □ *He lit his pipe.* □ *The hall was lit by candles.*

lightning or **lightening**? These two words are often confused. *Lightning* is a flash of light produced by atmospheric electricity: □ *thunder and lightning*. *Lightning* is also used as an adjective to describe things that happen very quickly: □ *the lightning strike by postal workers*. *Lightening* is the present participle/gerund of the verb *lighten*: □ *lightening someone's load.*

light-year A *light-year* is a unit of distance, not time; careful users avoid such expressions as: □ *It happened light-years ago.*

likable see LIKEABLE OR LIKABLE?

like The use of *like* as a conjunction, introducing a clause that contains a verb, is disliked by many users and is best avoided in formal contexts, where *as*, *as if*, or *as though* should be used instead: □ *The garden looks as if* [not *like*] *it has been neglected for many years.* □ *As* [not *like*] *the headmaster said, corporal punishment is not used in this school.* The use of *like* as a preposition, introducing a noun, pronoun, or noun phrase, is acceptable in all contexts: □ *The garden looks like a jungle.* See also SUCH AS OR LIKE?

-like The suffix *-like* may be attached with or without a hyphen in British English: □ *autumnlike* or *autumn-like.*

likeable or **likable**? Both spellings of this word are acceptable. See SPELLING 3.

likely In British English the adverb *likely*, meaning 'probably', is not used on its own in formal contexts; it is usually preceded by *very, quite, more,* or *most*: □ *They will very likely arrive tomorrow morning.* See also LIABLE OR LIKELY?

limited Some people object to the use of the adjective *limited* as a synonym for 'small', 'little', 'few', etc.: □ *a limited income* □ *with limited assistance.*

lineage or **linage**? The noun *lineage*, pronounced [*lini-ij*], means 'line of descent' or 'ancestry'; the noun *linage*, pronounced [*līnij*], means 'number of printed or written lines': □ *the emperor's lineage* □ *payment based on linage.*

lineament or **liniment**? The noun *lineament,* meaning 'feature', is largely restricted to formal or literary contexts: □ *the noble lineaments of his face.* It should not be confused with the noun *liniment,* denoting a liquid rubbed into the skin to relieve pain or stiffness.

linguist The noun *linguist* may denote a person who knows a number of foreign languages or a specialist in linguistics, the study of language. □ *Mr Evans, an accomplished linguist, was a great help to us on our European tour.* □ *At yesterday's lecture the linguist Noam Chomsky expounded his theory of language structure.*

liniment see LINEAMENT OR LINIMENT?

liquefy or **liquify**? Both spellings of this word are acceptable, although the first is generally preferred.

liqueur or **liquor**? The spellings of these words are sometimes confused. A *liqueur* [li*kyoor*] or, less commonly, [*li*ker] is a sweet alcoholic drink taken after a meal. *Liquor* [*li*kĕ] is any alcoholic beverage.

liquidate or **liquidize**? The verb *liquidate* is used in finance: □ *to liquidate a company* □ *to liquidate one's assets*, and as an informal euphemism for 'kill': □ *He liquidated his rivals.* To *liquidize* is to make something liquid, usually in a blender or liquidizer: □ *Liquidize the fruit and add it to the whipped cream.*

liquify see LIQUEFY OR LIQUIFY?

liquor see LIQUEUR OR LIQUOR?

liquorice There are two possible pronunciations of this word. The traditional pronunciation [*lik*ŏris] is preferred by many, but [*lik*ŏrish] is also acceptable and widely used.

lit see LIGHTED OR LIT?

literal, literary, or **literate**? *Literal* means 'word for word; exact'; *literary* means 'relating to literature'; *literate* means 'able to read and write; (well-)educated': □ *a literal translation* □ *the literal meaning of the word* □ *literary works* □ *a literary critic* □ *They are barely literate.* □ *a highly literate candidate.*

literally The use of the adverb *literally* as an intensifier, especially in figurative contexts, is disliked by many users: □ *It literally rained all night.* □ *I was literally tearing my hair out by the time they arrived.*

literary, literate see LITERAL, LITERARY, OR LITERATE?

literature Some people object to the use of the noun *literature*, with its connotations of greatness, to denote brochures, leaflets, and other written or printed matter: □ *They're sending us some literature about holidays in the Far East.*

little see FEW; FEWER OR LESS?

live The adjective *live*, meaning 'not prerecorded': □ *a live broadcast* □ *live music*, is increasingly used in the extended sense of 'actually present': □ *They have never performed in front of a live audience.*

livelong see LIFELONG OR LIVELONG?

livid The adjective *livid* may be used to describe a range of colours, from the dark purple colour of a bruise, through the greyish-blue colour of a *livid* sky, to the pale complexion of somebody who is *livid* with fear. *Livid* is perhaps most frequently used in the sense of 'very angry'.

living room see LOUNGE.

llama see LAMA OR LLAMA?

loaded see LADEN OR LOADED?

loadsamoney The word *loadsamoney,* from the name of a character created by the alternative comedian Harry Enfield, is used as a noun or adjectivally with reference to excessive or ostentatious wealth: □ *the loadsamoney economy.*

loan see LEND OR LOAN?

loath, loth, or **loathe**? *Loath* and *loth* are adjectives, meaning 'unwilling' or 'reluctant'; *loathe* is a verb, meaning 'detest': □ *He was loath/loth to move to London.* □ *He loathes working in London. Loath* and *loathe* are frequently confused: □ *The Independent ... would be loathe to see Mr Kinnock turn the clock back* (*Sunday Times*). For this reason some users prefer *loth*, the more distinctive variant spelling of the adjective.

locale, locality, or **location**? All three nouns mean 'place', but they are not altogether synonymous. *Locale,* the most formal of the three, refers to a place that is connected with a particular event or series of events: □ *an unlikely locale for a human rights convention* (example adapted from COBUILD corpus). *Locality* often refers to a neighbourhood or geographical area: □ *There are a number of bookshops in the locality. Location* means 'site' or 'situation' and is often used as a formal or pretentious substitute for the nouns *place, position,* etc. (see also LOCATE): □ *to move to a different location* □ *the location of the town hall.*

locate The verb *locate* and its derived noun *location* are best avoided where *find, situate, place, position,* etc., would be adequate or more appropriate: □ *I can't find* [not *locate*] *my front-door key.* □ *The shrub should be planted in a sheltered position* [not *location*]. □ *Offices in a prestigious part of the City* [not *a prestigious City location*].

location see LOCALE, LOCAL-

ITY, OR LOCATION?

lone see ALONE OR LONE?

longevity This word, meaning 'long length of life', is usually pronounced [lon*jev*ĭti] although [long*jev*ĭti] is also frequently used.

longitude This word, referring to the distance west or east of the Greenwich meridian, may be pronounced with a *j*-sound [*lon*jityood] or a *g*-sound [*long*gityood].

loo see TOILET, LAVATORY, LOO, OR BATHROOM?

lookalike The noun *lookalike* denotes someone who closely resembles another person, usually a famous person: □ *a Prince Charles lookalike* □ *the Marilyn Monroe lookalike competition.*

loose or **loosen**? The verb *loose* means 'release', 'set free', or 'undo'; the verb *loosen* means 'make or become less tight': □ *She loosed the lion from its cage.* □ *He loosened his belt.* The two verbs are not interchangeable.

lot The expressions *a lot (of)* and *lots (of)* are best avoided in formal contexts, where they may be replaced by *many*, *much*, *a great deal (of)*, *a good deal (of)*, etc.: □ *We have many* [not *lots of*] *books.* □ *They received a great deal of* [not *a lot of*] *help.*

loth see LOATH, LOTH, OR LOATHE?

lots see LOT.

loud or **loudly**? *Loud* may be used as an adjective or adverb: □ *a loud noise* □ *He shouted as loud as he could.* The adverb *loudly* may be substituted for *loud* in all its adverbial uses except the phrase *out loud*, meaning 'audibly': □ *She read the poem out loud* (not *out loudly*). It is not always acceptable, however, to use the adverb *loud* in place of *loudly*: □ *They protested loudly* [not *loud*] *and angrily.* □ *loudly* [not *loud*] *dressed in a blue-and-yellow striped jacket.*

lounge The *lounge* of a private house or flat is the room used for relaxation, recreation, and the reception of guests, as opposed to the *dining room*: □ *She showed the vicar into the lounge.* Some people consider the synonyms *sitting room* and *living room* to be less pretentious than *lounge*.

low or **lowly**? The adjective *low*, the opposite of *high*, has a number of senses: □ *a low wall* □ *a low temperature* □ *a low voice* □ *low morale* □ *to feel low.* The adjective *lowly,* meaning 'humble' or 'inferior', is much more restricted in usage and is formal: □ *their lowly abode* □ *a lowly job.*

low-key Some people object to the frequent use of the adjective *low-key*, meaning 'of low intensity', in place of *modest, restrained, subdued, unassertive,* etc.: □ *The reception was a very low-key affair.*

lowly see LOW OR LOWLY?

low-profile see PROFILE.

lumbar or **lumber**? These two words are identical in pronunciation and are sometimes confused. *Lumbar* is an adjective used in medical contexts, referring to the lower part of the back and sides: □ *a lumbar puncture* □ *the lumbar vertebrae. Lumber* is used as a noun or verb. In the sense of 'unwanted articles', the noun *lumber* is chiefly found in British English: □ *the lumber room*; in the sense of 'timber' it is chiefly found in American English: □ *heaps of lumber.* The verb *lumber* means 'move heavily, awkwardly, etc.': □ *An elephant lumbered past*; in the sense of 'burden' it should be restricted to informal contexts: □ *I got lumbered with the job of delivering the leaflets.*

lunch or **luncheon**? Both nouns denote a midday meal: a *luncheon* is usually a formal social occasion; *lunch* is often a light informal meal or a fuller meal at which business is conducted: □ *The Princess of Wales was the guest of honour at the luncheon.* □ *We stopped at a pub for lunch.* □ *They discussed the terms of the contract at their business lunch.* See also DINNER, LUNCH, TEA OR SUPPER?

lure see ALLURE OR LURE?

luxuriant or **luxurious**? *Luxuriant* means 'profuse', 'lush', or 'fertile'; *luxurious* means 'sumptuous' or 'characterized by luxury': □ *luxuriant vegetation* □ *a luxurious hotel.* The two adjectives are not interchangeable: *luxuriant* is principally applied to things that produce abundantly; *luxurious* to things that are very comfortable, expensive, opulent, self-indulgent, etc.

M

mac see MACINTOSH OR MACKINTOSH?

macabre Note the spelling of this word, which ends in *-re* in both British and American English. It means 'relating to death; gruesome': □ *a macabre tale*. The *r* is not always sounded in speech, the pronunciations [mă*kah*bĕ] and [mă*kah*brĕ] being equally acceptable to most people.

machinations This word, meaning 'devious plots or conspiracies', is traditionally pronounced [mak*inay*shŏnz], although the alternative pronunciation [mash*inay*shŏnz] is becoming increasingly common.

machismo The noun *machismo*, denoting aggressive masculinity: □ *the machismo of the leader*, may be pronounced [ma*kiz*mō] or [ma*chiz*mō]. Note that the *ch* does not have the *sh* sound of *machine*.

macho The adjective *macho*, the Spanish word for 'male', has derogatory connotations in English, describing a man who displays his masculinity in an aggressive or ostentatious way: □ *a macho image* □ *the macho hero*. Like MACHISMO, *macho* should not be used in formal contexts or overused in informal contexts: it is sometimes better replaced by *masculine, virile, male*, etc.

macintosh or **mackintosh**? The noun *mac(k)intosh*, meaning 'raincoat', may be spelt with or without the *-k-*. Similarly, the informal abbreviation of the noun may be spelt *mac* or *mack*.

mack, **mackintosh** see MACINTOSH OR MACKINTOSH?

macro- and **micro-** *Macro-* means 'large'; *micro-* means 'small'. Both prefixes are used in scientific and technical terms, such as: □ *macroeconomics* □ *micro-*

organism □ *macrobiotic* □ *microwave* □ *macrocosm* □ *microcosm* □ *macroscopic* □ *microscopic* □ *microprocessor* □ *microchip*. The use of *macro-* and *micro-* in other contexts, e.g. □ *macrocontract* □ *microskirt*, in place of the adjectives *large, great, small, tiny,* etc., is best avoided.

Madam or **Madame**? *Madam* is a polite term of address for a woman; the word may be written with a capital or lower-case *m*: □ *Would madam like a cup of coffee?* □ *Can I help you, Madam? Madame*, written with a capital *M*, is the French equivalent of *Mrs*: □ *Wax models of famous people are displayed at Madame Tussaud's.*

magic or **magical**? The adjective *magic* is more closely related to the art or practice of magic than *magical*, which is used in the wider sense of 'enchanting': □ *a magic wand* □ *a magic potion* □ *a magic spell* □ *a magical experience* □ *the magical world of make-believe.*

magnitude The noun *magnitude* is best avoided where *size, extent, importance, greatness*, etc., would be adequate or more appropriate: □ *the magnitude of the problem.*

Mahomet see MUSLIM OR MOSLEM?

maintenance The noun *maintenance*, which is related to the verb *maintain*, is often misspelt, a common error being the substitution of *-tain-* for *-ten-* in the middle of the word. Note also the *-ance* ending.

major Some people dislike the frequent use of the adjective *major* in place of *great, important, chief, principal, serious,* etc.: □ *There was certainly major news interest in the details of the background of a man convicted of murdering five members of his family* (*Daily Mail*).

majority and **minority** *Majority* means 'more than half of the total number'; *minority* means 'less than half of the total number': □ *the majority of the books* □ *a minority of his friends.* The terms should not be used to denote a part of a single item.

male or **masculine**? The adjective *male* refers to the sex of a person, animal, or plant; it is the opposite of

FEMALE: □ *a male kangaroo* □ *male genital organs. Masculine* is applied only to people (or their attributes) or to words (see GENDER); it is the opposite of FEMININE: □ *masculine strength.*

malevolent, **malicious**, or **malignant**? All these adjectives mean 'wishing harm to others', but there are differences of sense, usage, and application between them. *Malignant* is the strongest of the three, describing an intense desire for evil. It is also common in medical contexts. *Malevolent* and *malicious* are interchangeable in many contexts.

man Many people consider the use of the noun *man* as a synonym for 'person' to be ambiguous and/or sexist. With reference to individual human beings of unspecified sex, it is usually possible to use *person, people, human being, individual, everyone, worker(s), citizen(s)*, etc., in place of *man* or *men*. Idiomatic expressions, such as *the man in the street*, should not be changed but may be replaced with a synonym or paraphrase. See also BOY; CHAIR; GENTLEMAN; MALE OR MASCULINE?

manageable This word, meaning 'able to be controlled': □ *manageable in small numbers*, retains the -*e*- to indicate the softness of the *g*.

mandatory The adjective *mandatory* is usually pronounced [*man*dătŏri].

mankind The use of the noun *mankind* to denote human beings collectively may be confused with its second sense of 'men in general' (as opposed to *womankind*, meaning 'women in general'): □ *the future of mankind.*

man-management The term *man-management* denotes the management of people rather than processes, usually in an industrial environment.

manoeuvre This word is sometimes misspelt. Note the vowel sequence *-oeu-* and the *-re* ending in British English. The American spelling is *maneuver*. See also -AE- AND -OE-.

mantel or **mantle**? A *mantel*, or more commonly a *mantelpiece*, is a shelf forming part of an ornamental structure round a fireplace. A *mantle* is a cloak or something that covers: □ *shrouded in a mantle of secrecy.*

many In formal contexts the adjective *many* may be used in place of the informal expressions *a lot (of)* and *lots (of)* (see LOT). *Many* is also used in informal contexts, especially in negative and interrogative sentences: □ *She doesn't buy many clothes.* □ *Have you got many pets?* In some positive sentences, however, *a lot of* and *lots of* are more idiomatic than *many* in informal contexts: □ *We have a lot of* [not *many*] *books.*

margarine The usual pronunciation of this word has a soft *g* [marjă*reen*].

marginal Some people object to the use of the adjective *marginal* as a synonym for 'small' or 'slight': □ *marginal changes* □ *a marginal improvement* □ *a marginal effect* □ *a student of marginal ability.*

marginalize The verb *marginalize* means 'treat as unimportant' or 'relegate to the fringes (of society, an organization, etc.)'. Sometimes spelt *marginalise* (see -IZE OR -ISE?), it is chiefly used in the passive: □ *Britain risks being marginalized in the EC.* □ *Peter Shore ... has paid the price for his consistent opposition to party orthodoxy by being marginalised* (*The Guardian*). □ *The arts are no longer marginalised* (*The Guardian*). A vogue term, *marginalize* is disliked by some as an example of the increasing tendency to coin new verbs by adding the suffix *-ize* to nouns and adjectives. It is best restricted to informal contexts.

marital see MARTIAL OR MARITAL?

market forces The phrase *market forces* refers to anything that affects or influences the free operation of trade in goods or services, such as competition or demand, as opposed to (artificially imposed) government controls. It is in danger of becoming overused as a vogue term: □ *The printing of this holy work* [the Bible] *should be subjected to market forces* (*The Bookseller*). □ *The Government yesterday unveiled plans to shift the financing of universities and poly-*

technics away from block grants and towards higher tuition fees in an attempt to expand student numbers through emphasis on market forces (*The Guardian*). □ *Green market forces are working in the appliance manufacturers' favour* (*Daily Telegraph*).

marquess or **marquis**? A *marquess* is a British nobleman who ranks below a duke and above an earl; a *marquis* is a nobleman of corresponding rank in other countries. The word *marquis* is sometimes used in place of *marquess*.

marshal see MARTIAL OR MARSHAL?

martial or **marital**? These two adjectives are sometimes confused, being similar in spelling. *Martial* means 'of or relating to war or military matters': □ *martial music* □ *martial arts* □ *martial law*. *Marital* means 'of or relating to marriage': □ *marital problems* □ *marital status* □ *marital vows*. The word *marital* is also found in the adjectives *extramarital*, *premarital*, etc., and *martial* in the compound noun and verb *court-martial*.

martial or **marshal**? The pronunciation of these two words is identical and they are sometimes confused. The adjective *martial* means 'of or relating to war or military matters' (see MARTIAL OR MARITAL?). *Marshal* may be used as a noun, meaning 'officer' or 'official', or as a verb, meaning 'arrange', 'assemble', or 'guide': □ *Field Marshal Montgomery* □ *One of the marshals pushed the damaged car off the racetrack.* □ *to marshal the facts* □ *We were marshalled into the courtroom.*

masculine see MALE OR MASCULINE?

massage The verb *massage* is increasingly used in the figurative sense of 'manipulate (figures, data, etc.) to make them more acceptable': □ *to massage the accounts* □ *to massage the results of the survey*. This usage is best restricted to informal contexts.

masterful or **masterly**? *Masterful* means 'domineering'; *masterly* means 'very skilful': □ *His masterful approach made him unpopular with the staff.* □ *West Germany reached their fifth World Cup final with a display of masterly efficiency*

(*The Guardian*).

mat, matt, or **matte**? The adjective *matt,* meaning 'not shiny', has the variant spellings *mat* and *matte. Matt* is the most frequent spelling in British English: □ *a matt finish* □ *matt black paint.* The spelling *mat* is preferred in American English.

materialize The use of the verb *materialize* in place of *happen* or *turn up* is disliked by some users: □ *The threatened strike is unlikely to materialize.*

mathematics see -ICS.

matrimony This word, describing the state of marriage, should be pronounced [*ma*trimŏni].

matrix The noun *matrix* denotes the substance or environment within which something originates, develops, or is contained. It is also a technical term in fields such as mathematics, computing, printing, anatomy, and linguistics. In general contexts *matrix* is disliked by many as a vogue word and often better replaced by *setting, background, framework, environment,* etc.

matt, matte see MAT, MATT, OR MATTE?

mattress Note the *-tt-* and the *-ss* in this word, which is often misspelt.

maximal, maximize see MAXIMUM.

maximum The noun and adjective *maximum* refer to the greatest possible quantity, amount, degree, etc.: □ *a maximum of twenty guests* □ *the maximum dose.* The adjective *maximum* is more frequent than its synonym *maximal.* The verb *maximize* means 'increase to a maximum'.

may or **might**? *Might* is the past tense of *may* (see CAN OR MAY?): □ *She may win.* □ *May we sit down?* □ *I thought she might win.* □ *He said we might sit down.* In the last two examples, *might* cannot be replaced with *may.* In the first two examples, however, *might* can be substituted for *may* with a slight change of meaning: □ *She might win* expresses a greater degree of doubt or uncertainty than *She may win.* □ *Might we sit down?* is a more tentative request than *May we sit down?*

maybe or **may be**? *Maybe,* meaning 'perhaps': □ *Maybe the letter will come tomorrow,* is often confused with the phrase *may be*, the verb *may* and the verb *be*: □ *It may be that she has missed the train.*

mayoress A *mayoress* is the wife of a male mayor or a woman who assists or partners a mayor of either sex at social functions and on ceremonial occasions. The use of *mayoress* to denote or address a female mayor is incorrect.

me see I OR ME?

mean see I MEAN.

meaningful The adjective *meaningful* should be avoided where *important*, *significant*, *serious*, *worthwhile*, etc., would be adequate or more appropriate: □ *a caring, loving, and meaningful relationship* □ *a meaningful experience.*

means In the sense of 'method', *means* may be a singular or plural noun; in the sense of 'resources' or 'wealth' it is always plural: □ *A means of reducing engine noise was developed.* □ *Several different means of transport were used.* □ *His means are insufficient to support a large family.* See also SINGULAR OR PLURAL?

meantime or **meanwhile**? *Meantime* is chiefly used as a noun, in the phrases *in the meantime* and *for the meantime*; *meanwhile* is chiefly used as an adverb: □ *He wrote a letter in the meantime.* □ *We have enough for the meantime.* □ *Meanwhile, I had phoned the police.*

medal or **meddle**? These two words should not be confused. *Medal* is a noun, denoting a metal disc, cross, etc., given as an award; *meddle* is a verb, meaning 'interfere'.

media The word *media*, frequently used to refer to television, radio, newspapers, etc., as means of mass communication, is one of the plural forms of the noun *medium*: □ *The media act as publicity agents for writers.* □ *Television is an influential medium.* The plural of *medium* in the sense of 'spiritual intermediary' is *mediums*. The use of *media* as a singular collective noun is best avoided.

mediaeval see MEDIEVAL OR MEDIAEVAL?

medicine The word *medicine* is sometimes misspelt, the most frequent error being the substitution of *e* for the first *i*. This letter is sometimes not sounded in speech, resulting in the two-syllable pronunciation [*med*sin]. Some users prefer the full pronunciation [*med*isin].

medieval or **mediaeval**? The two spellings of this word are both acceptable. The spelling *medieval* is far more frequent in British English and is standard in American English. See also -AE- AND -OE-.

mediocre This word, meaning 'of indifferent quality', is sometimes misspelt. Note the ending *-cre*.

Mediterranean Note the spelling of this word, particularly the single *t*, the *-rr-*, and the *-ean* ending. It may help to associate the central syllables with the Latin word *terra*, meaning 'earth; land', from which they are derived.

medium, **mediums** see MEDIA.

meet with In British English the phrasal verb *meet with* should be restricted to the sense of 'experience' or 'receive': □ *I hope he hasn't met with an accident.*

mega- Some people object to the increasing use of the prefix *mega-*, meaning 'great' or 'large', in non-technical contexts, as in : □ *mega-motorway* □ *mega-trend* □ *mega-merger* □ *mega-bid* □ *megabucks*. The prefix is increasingly used as an adjective in its own right.

meltdown In nuclear physics, the noun *meltdown* refers to the melting of the core of a nuclear reactor, caused by a defect in the cooling system. It is also used figuratively with reference to any disastrous event, especially a stock-market crash: □ *Meltdown Monday.*

melted or **molten**? *Melted* is the past tense and past participle of the verb *melt*; it is also used as an adjective: □ *The chocolate (has) melted.* □ *Serve the asparagus with melted butter. Molten* is used only as an adjective, meaning 'melted' or 'liquefied': □ *molten iron* □ *molten rock.*

membership *Membership* is the state of being a member: □ *to apply for membership.* The noun is also used to denote the number of members of an organization: □ *Membership has increased this year.* Its frequent use in place of *members*, however, is disliked by some people:

□ *We must consult the membership.*

memento The word *memento* is sometimes misspelt, the most frequent error being the substitution of *o* for the first *e*, through confusion with such words as *moment* and *momentum.* It may help to associate the *mem-* with *memory* and *remember*.

mental The use of the adjective *mental* as a synonym for 'stupid', 'foolish', 'mentally ill', 'mentally deficient', etc., should be restricted to very informal contexts: □ *They must be mental to set off in such terrible weather.* □ *Her youngest son's a bit mental, and the other children tease him.*

mentholated or **methylated**? These two words should not be confused. *Mentholated* refers to the addition of *menthol,* a medicinal substance found in peppermint oil; *methylated* refers to the addition of the poisonous substance *methanol*: □ *a mentholated lozenge* □ *methylated spirits.*

meretricious or **meritorious**? *Meretricious* means 'superficially attractive' or 'insincere'; *meritorious* means 'having merit' or 'praiseworthy': □ *meretricious glamour* □ *a meritorious deed.* Both adjectives are fairly formal in usage.

meta- Some people object to the increasing use of the prefix *meta-* in the sense of 'transcending' or 'of a higher order': □ *A suggestion of metafiction, of uncertainties found to be themselves fictionally productive* (*London Review of Books*).

metal or **mettle**? These two words, which have the same pronunciation, are sometimes confused. A *metal* is one of a group of mineral substances that are good conductors of heat and electricity. *Mettle* means 'strength of character': □ *He was given no chance to prove his mettle.*

metallurgy This word, meaning 'the science of metals', is usually pronounced [me*tal*ĕrji], although it can be stressed on the first and third syllables [*met*ălerji].

metamorphosis The usual pronunciation of this word is [metă*mawf*ŏsis] with the stress on the third syllable.

metaphors A *metaphor* is a figure of speech in which a word or phrase is used, not with its literal meaning, but to suggest an analogy with something else. The comparison is implicit, not introduced by *like* or *as*: □ *the winds of change* □ *an icy voice* □ *stone deaf*.

meter or **metre**? The spelling of these words is often confused, probably partly because the American spelling of the measurement *metre* is *meter*. In British English, a *meter* is a measuring instrument: □ *gas meter* □ *speedometer*. A *metre* is the basic metric measurement of length and is used in derived measurements: □ *kilometre* □ *millimetre*.

methodology The noun *methodology* denotes a body or system of methods, rules, principles, etc., used in a particular area of activity: □ *the methodology of teaching*.

methylated see METHOLATED OR METHYLATED?

meticulous The adjective *meticulous* is widely used and accepted as a synonym for 'painstaking' or 'scrupulous': □ *meticulous attention to detail* □ *a meticulous secretary*.

metre see METER OR METRE?

mettle see METAL OR METTLE?

mezzanine This word, meaning 'intermediate storey between two floors', is usually pronounced [*mez*ă-neen]. The alternative [*mets*ăneen] is sometimes used and is closer to the original Italian.

micro- see MACRO- AND MICRO-.

mid see AMID, AMIDST, MID, OR MIDST?

middle see CENTRE OR MIDDLE?

midst see AMID, AMIDST, MID, OR MIDST?

midwifery This word is sometimes mispronounced. In British English the correct pronunciation is [*mid*wif-ĕri].

might see CAN OR MAY?; MAY OR MIGHT?

migraine The usual pronunciation of this word, meaning 'a severe and recurrent headache', is [*mee*grayn].

mileage or **milage**? *Mileage* is the more frequent spelling of this word, *milage* being an accepted but rare variant: □ *The exceptionally low mileage makes this car a good buy*. See also SPELLING 3.

militate or **mitigate**? The verb *militate*, which is usually followed by the preposition *against*, means 'have a powerful influence or effect': □ *His left-wing opinions militated against his appointment as headmaster.* The verb *mitigate* means 'moderate' or 'make less severe': □ *The judge's decision did little to mitigate the suffering of the bereaved parents.* □ *mitigating circumstances.*

millennium This word is often misspelt, the most frequent error being the omission of the second *n*.

millionaire The word *millionaire* is sometimes misspelt. Note the *-ll-*, but only one *n*.

mimic This word, meaning 'imitate': □ *He likes mimicking the teachers*, is sometimes misspelt. Note that a *k* is added before the suffixes *-ed*, *-ing*, and *-er*. *Mimicry* does not, however, have a *k*. See also SPELLING 1.

mincemeat The noun *mincemeat* principally denotes the sweet mixture of dried fruit, suet, sugar, and spices that is used to fill mince pies, traditionally baked and eaten at Christmas. To avoid confusion, meat that has been minced (*minced meat*) is usually called *mince* in British English and *ground meat* in American English.

miniature *Miniature*, meaning 'small in size', is sometimes misspelt. Note the spelling *-iat-*.

minimal, **minimize** see MINIMUM.

minimum The noun and adjective *minimum* refer to the smallest possible quantity, amount, degree, etc.: □ *a minimum of four employees* □ *the minimum requirements.* The frequent use of *minimal* in the sense of 'very small' is disliked by some users. The verb *minimize* means 'reduce to a minimum'.

minority see MAJORITY AND MINORITY.

minus The use of the preposition *minus* in the sense of 'without' or 'lacking' is best restricted to informal contexts: □ *She came home minus her umbrella.*

minuscule This word is often misspelt, the most frequent error being the substitution of an *i* for the first *u*. The word is pronounced [*min*ŭskyool].

minutiae The plural noun *minutiae*, meaning 'small, minor, or trivial details', may be pronounced [min*ew*shiee] or [mī*new*-shiee]: □ *The minutiae of the problem are of no interest to me.*

miscellaneous This word, meaning 'of a variety of items', is sometimes misspelt. Note particularly the *-sc-*, the *-a-*, and the *-eous* ending.

mischievous The correct pronunciation of this word is [*mis*chivŭs].

misogynist Note the spelling of *misogynist,* which refers to a person who hates women. The word derives from Greek *misos* 'hatred' and *gynē* 'woman' as in *gynaecology,* the branch of medicine concerned with women's diseases.

Miss see MS, MRS, OR MISS?

miss The verb *miss,* meaning 'regret the loss or lack of', is sometimes wrongly used with *not*: □ *I miss not having a car* means 'I was happier before I had a car', not 'I wish I had a car'.

misspelled or **misspelt**? Either word may be used as the past tense and past participle of the verb *misspell*: □ *You have misspelt/misspelled my name.*

mistrust see DISTRUST OR MISTRUST?

misuse see ABUSE OR MISUSE?

mitigate see MILITATE OR MITIGATE?

mix Some people object to the increasing use of the noun *mix* in place of *range*: □ *A wide mix of subjects will be taught at the college.*

mnemonic The word *mnemonic,* referring to something that aids the memory (e.g. the spelling rule '*i* before *e* except after *c*'), causes spelling and pronunciation problems. The initial *m* is silent; the word is pronounced [ni*mon*ik].

moccasin This word, used to describe a soft leather shoe without a heel, is sometimes misspelt. Note the *-cc-* but single *s*.

modal see VERBS.

modern or **modernistic**? The adjective *modern* means 'of the present time' or 'contemporary'; *modernistic* means 'characteristic of modern trends, ideas, etc.' and is sometimes used in a derogatory way: □ *modern society* □ *modernistic architecture.*

modus vivendi The Latin phrase *modus vivendi* is principally used in formal English to denote an arrangement or compromise between conflicting parties:

□ *This modus vivendi enabled them to complete the job without disruption.*

Mohammed see MUSLIM OR MOSLEM?

molten see MELTED OR MOLTEN?

momentary or **momentous**? *Momentary* means 'lasting for a very short time'; *momentous* means 'of great significance': □ *a momentary lapse* □ *The Commons last night took the momentous step of opening its doors to the television cameras for the first time* (*The Guardian*).

mongoose The plural of the noun *mongoose* is *mongooses*; the word should not be treated as a compound of the noun *goose* (the plural of which is *geese*).

monogram or **monograph**? A *monogram* is a design made up of a person's initials: □ *There was a monogram on the corner of the handkerchief.* A *monograph* is a learned book, treatise, etc., about a single subject: □ *He wrote a monograph on Oliver Cromwell.*

moot The adjective *moot*, meaning 'debatable' or 'open to question', rarely occurs outside the fixed phrase *a moot point*.

moral or **morale**? These two spellings are sometimes confused. *Moral* means 'concerned with the principles of right and wrong': □ *the gradual erosion of moral standards. Morale* is the extent of confidence and optimism in a person or group.

more The adverb *more* is used to form the comparative of a number of adjectives and adverbs: □ *She is more intelligent than her sister.* □ *The trains run more frequently in the summer months. More* should not be used with adjectives that already have the comparative ending *-er*, such as *happier*, *older*, etc.

mortgage This word is sometimes misspelt, the most frequent error being the omission of the silent *t*.

mortgagee or **mortgagor**? A *mortgagor* is a person who borrows money by means of a mortgage; a *mortgagee* is the person or organization, e.g. a building society or bank, that lends the money. The two nouns should not be confused: the *mortgagors* are the people who are mortgaging their property, i.e.

using it as security for a loan; the *mortgagees* are those who receive this security, not the recipients of the loan itself.

Moslem see MUSLIM OR MOSLEM?

most The adverb *most* is used to form the superlative of a number of adjectives and adverbs: □ *This is the most expensive picture in the shop.* □ *The prize will be awarded to the child who writes the most neatly. Most* should not be used with adjectives that already have the superlative ending *-est*, such as *saddest*, *youngest*, etc. The use of *most* in place of *very* is generally best avoided. The adverb *mostly,* meaning 'mainly' or 'usually', should not be confused with *most*: □ *He writes mostly* [not *most*] *for children.* □ *Old people are most* [not *mostly*] at risk.

motif or **motive**? These words are sometimes confused. A *motif* is a recurrent feature which establishes a pattern throughout a work of art, etc.: □ *a design with a feather motif.* A *motive* is a reason for a course of action: □ *no apparent motive for the crime.*

motivation The use of the noun *motivation*, which means 'incentive' or 'drive', in place of *reason* or *motive* is disliked and avoided by many users: □ *his reason* [not *motivation*] *for deserting his wife and family.*

motive see MOTIF OR MOTIVE?

mouse The plural of the noun *mouse,* in the sense of 'small animal', is *mice.* In computing contexts, where a *mouse* is an electronic device used to move the cursor on the screen, the preferred plural form is *mice,* though the plural form *mouses* is used by some computer scientists.

mousse The noun *mousse* denotes a creamy or foamy preparation. Some types of mousse are for eating: □ *chocolate mousse* □ *salmon mousse*; some are for cosmetic purposes: □ *styling mousse* □ *body mousse.* The spelling should not be confused with the animals *moose* and *mouse*.

moustache This word is sometimes misspelt. The most frequent error is the substitution of *u* for *ou* in British English. The British English spelling is *moustache*; the American

English spelling *mustache*. Note also the *-che* ending.

movable or **moveable**? This word has two spellings. Both are acceptable although the first spelling *movable*, which omits the *e* before the suffix *-able*, seems to be more frequent in contemporary usage. See also SPELLING 3.

movers and shakers *Movers and shakers* is an expression used informally to refer to people who get things done, either through their own power and influence or by urging or encouraging others to take action: □ *the movers and shakers of the film industry*. The phrase should not be overused.

move the goalposts To *move the goalposts* is to change the rules, requirements, etc., usually to the advantage of the person or organization that sets and changes the rules: □ *The Government is moving the goalposts again from April 6, with the cut-off point* [for eligibility for income support] *reduced to 16 hours a week* (*The Guardian*).

mowed or **mown**? Either word may be used as the past participle of the verb *mow*: □ *Have you mowed/mown the grass yet?*

Mr see MS, MRS, OR MISS?

Ms, Mrs, or **Miss**? *Ms*, *Mrs*, and *Miss*, shortened forms of the archaic title *Mistress*, are used before the names of girls and women, according to age and marital status, in letter writing and as polite terms of address.

Miss is traditionally used for girls, unmarried women, and married women who have retained their maiden name: □ *Miss Mary Baker* □ *Miss Davies* □ *Miss Elizabeth Taylor*. In formal contexts, two or more girls or unmarried women with the same surname should be referred to as *the Misses Brown/Smith/* etc. rather than *the Miss Browns/Smiths/*etc.

Mrs, pronounced [*mis*iz], is used before a woman's married name: □ *Mrs Anne Johnson* □ *Mrs Peter Johnson* □ *Mrs Johnson*.

Ms, pronounced [miz] or [mĭz], is used before the name of a woman of unknown or unspecified marital status. It was introduced as a feminine equivalent of the masculine title *Mr*, which makes no distinction between married and unmarried men. Because of its feminist associations, however, the title *Ms* is disliked by some people. *Ms* is most frequently used in place of *Miss*, but is best avoided when referring to elderly unmarried women or young girls. See also SEXISM.

much The use of the adjective *much* in positive sentences is best restricted to formal contexts: □ *They own much land.* □ *There is much work to be done.*

mucous or **mucus**? These two words are sometimes confused. *Mucous* is the adjective from the noun *mucus*; *mucus* is the secretion produced by *mucous membranes*.

muesli The noun *muesli*, denoting a type of breakfast food, causes problems of spelling and pronunciation. Note the *-ue-* in the first syllable, and the *-li* ending. The usual pronunciation is [*mew*zli], with the first syllable pronounced as in *music*, but the pronunciation [*moo*zli] is also acceptable.

Muhammad see MUSLIM OR MOSLEM?

multi- Some people object to the increasing use of the prefix *multi-*, meaning 'many', to coin new words that are often better expressed by a paraphrase: □ *a multirole device* □ *a multistage process* □ *her outstanding multi-tasking abilities* ('her abilities to perform many tasks at the same time'). □ *Specialist skills are now ignored or swamped in the drive for multi-skilling* (*The Guardian*).

municipal The adjective *municipal* should be stressed on the second syllable [mew*nis*ipăl], not the first or the third.

Muslim or **Moslem**? Nowadays the preferred spelling for a follower of the Islamic faith is *Muslim*, rather than the older spelling *Moslem*. The most accepted spelling of the name of the prophet of Islam is *Muhammad*, rather than *Mohammed* or *Mahomet*.

must The auxiliary verb *must* expresses obligation, compulsion, necessity, resolution, certainty, etc.: □ *We must obey the rules.* □ *They must go.* □ *I must finish writing this letter.* □ *You must be* *very thirsty*. In other tenses, and in the negative, *must* is usually replaced by *have to*: □ *We had to obey the rules.* □ *They don't have to go.*

mutual, common, or **reciprocal**? A *mutual* action or emotion is done or felt by each of two or more people to or for the other(s): □ *mutual help/destruction/admiration/hatred*/etc. □ *The feeling is mutual.* The frequent use of *mutual* in place of *common*, meaning 'shared' or 'joint', is disliked by many users: □ *a mutual friend.* However, the other senses of *common* ('unsophisticated') can cause ambiguity. *Reciprocal* and *mutual* are synonymous in the principal sense of the latter: □ *reciprocal help. Reciprocal* can also be used to describe an action or emotion that is done or felt in return: □ *He praised her new novel, and she expressed reciprocal admiration for his latest film.*

myself The use of the pronoun *myself* for emphasis is acceptable to most users but disliked by some: □ *I disapprove of such behaviour myself.* □ *I myself have never met her.*

mythical or **mythological**? *Mythical* means 'imaginary'; *mythological* means 'of mythology': □ *a mythical danger* □ *a mythological kingdom.*

N

naff The adjective *naff* is a derogatory slang term meaning 'inferior or worthless; vulgar or tasteless; not stylish': □ *a naff film* □ *That tie is really naff.* The adjective should be restricted to informal contexts.

naive, naïve, or **naïf**? This word, meaning 'innocent' or 'credulous', is most commonly spelt *naive* or *naïve*.

naked or **nude**? A person wearing no clothes at all may be described as *naked* or *nude*. The adjective *naked* has a wider range of usage and application than *nude*, which is largely restricted to artistic or pornographic human nakedness or to nudism. *Naked* is also used as a synonym for 'bare' or 'uncovered' in other contexts.

naphtha This word, meaning 'petroleum', is sometimes misspelt. Note the consonant sequence *-phth-*.

nation see COUNTRY OR NATION?

native The word *native*, used in the sense of 'non-white person' (originally applied to the indigenous inhabitants of lands colonized by the West), is derogatory and offensive: □ *The settlers intermarried with the natives.*

naturalist or **naturist**? A *naturalist* is a person who studies animals and plants or an advocate of naturalism (in art, literature, philosophy, etc.); a *naturist* is a nudist: □ *Naturalists will appreciate the flora and fauna of the island; naturists can take advantage of its secluded beaches.*

nature Such phrases as *of this/that nature* and *in the nature of* are often better replaced by more concise or less vague expressions.

naturist see NATURALIST OR NATURIST?

naught or **nought**? These two words are sometimes

confused. *Naught* means 'nothing' and is used in idiomatic expressions such as *set at naught* 'consider unimportant' and *come to naught* 'produce no successful results': □ *All our plans came to naught.* In British English *nought* is used to represent the figure *0* (see also ZERO): □ *The number 100 has two noughts.*

nauseous The use of the adjective *nauseous* in the sense of 'nauseated' or 'suffering from nausea' is acceptable in American English but is best avoided in British English: □ *I feel sick* [not *nauseous*].

naval or **navel**? These two words are sometimes confused. *Naval* is used to describe something connected with the navy: □ *a naval officer* □ *naval warfare*. The *navel* is the small depression in the middle of the abdomen where the umbilical cord was formerly attached, and the word is also used in the phrase *navel orange*.

near or **nearly**? In the sense of 'almost', the adverb *near* is sometimes interchangeable with *nearly*: □ *I nearly* [or *near*] *forgot.* □ *It's near* [or *nearly*] *impossible.* This use of *near* may be considered informal or archaic, and *nearly* is a safer choice.

nearby or **near by**? There is often confusion as to whether this term should be one word or two. *Nearby* is the preferred form for both adjectival and adverbial senses.

nearly see NEAR OR NEARLY?

near miss see AIR MISS OR NEAR MISS?

necessarily There are two possible pronunciations for this word. In the traditional pronunciation, the first syllable is stressed [*nes*ĕsĕrĭli]. Many users dislike the alternative pronunciation, which has the main stress on the third syllable [nesĕ*ser*rĭli].

necessary This word, meaning 'essential', is often misspelt. Note the single *c* and the *-ss-*.

née *Née*, the feminine form of the French word for 'born', is used to indicate the maiden name of a married woman: □ *Mrs Susan Davies, née Eliot.*

need *Need* may be used as a full verb, in the sense of 'require' or 'be obliged', or as an auxiliary or modal verb, indicating necessity or obligation: □ *We need help.* □ *Your daughter needs to wear glasses.* □ *He need not leave.* □ *Need she reply?*

needless to say The idiomatic expression *needless to say* is frequently used for emphasis, especially in informal contexts: □ *Needless to say, the unions intend to campaign against the proposed legislation.*

negative A negative word is one that is used to deny or contradict something. Words such as *no, not, nobody, never,* and *nothing* make the clause in which they appear a negative one. Care must be taken as to where a negative word is placed in a sentence. □ *She didn't explain definitely* does not have the same meaning as: □ *She definitely didn't explain.* Usually the negative word is placed with the clause whose truth is being denied: □ *He said he had never been there.* □ *He never said he had been there.* The adjective *negative* is now often used in a general way to mean 'lacking in positive features' or 'pessimistic, unenthusiastic'. See also DOUBLE NEGATIVE.

neglectful, negligent, or **negligible**? Both *neglectful* and *negligent* mean 'careless' or 'heedless'; *negligible* means 'very small', 'trivial', or 'insignificant': □ *a neglectful mother* □ *a negligent driver* □ *a negligible effect.*

negotiate The usual pronunciation of this verb is [nigōshiayt]. The variant pronunciation [nigōsiayt], in which the *sh* sound is replaced by *s*, is disliked by some people.

Negress, Negro see BLACK.

neither As an adjective or pronoun *neither* is used with a singular verb: □ *Neither towel is clean.* □ *Neither of the towels is* [not *are*] *clean.* In the *neither ... nor* construction, a singular verb is used if both subjects are singular and a plural verb is used if both subjects are plural. When a combination of singular and plural subjects occurs in a *neither ... nor* construction, the verb traditionally agrees with the subject that is nearest to it. As a pronoun *neither* should be used only of two alternatives: □ *There are two cars outside, but neither is mine.*

nephew There are two different pronunciations for this word. Both [*nev*ew] and [*nef*ew] are acceptable, although some people prefer the first pronunciation.

nerve-racking see RACK OR WRACK?

net or **nett**? The word *net*, referring to what remains after the deduction of tax, expenses, loss, packaging, etc., is sometimes spelt *nett*: □ *net* [or *nett*] *income* □ *net* [or *nett*] *profit* □ *net* [or *nett*] *weight* □ *500 kg net* [or *nett*] □ *to net* [or *nett*] *£2000 a month*. Both spellings are acceptable in British English, but *net* is the more frequent.

network The word *network* is used as a verb in telecommunications, computing, and the media; it is also increasingly used in general contexts to mean 'communicate or make contact with other people in a similar situation': □ *to network with clients* □ *Women also often mentioned the help, advice and support they had received from networking with other women* (*The Bookseller*). □ *Those four people ... network extensively and draw on specialist help as appropriate* (*Alpha*). □ *Networking ... is one of the current buzz-words of the enterprise industry* (*The Guardian*).

never The use of *never saw/took/went*/etc. in place of *did not see/take/go*/etc., usually for emphasis, is avoided by careful users in all but a few informal spoken contexts: □ *I never said a word! Never* means 'at no time' and should not be used when referring to a single occasion: □ *I never met his wife.* □ *I did not meet his wife in town yesterday.*

nevertheless see NONE THE LESS OR NEVERTHELESS?

New Age The *New Age* movement, of American origin, is defined in the *Oxford Dictionary of New Words* as 'a cultural movement ... characterized by rejection of (modern) Western-style values and culture and the promotion of a more integrated or 'holistic' approach in areas such as religion, medicine, philosophy, astrology, and the environment': □ *New Age philosophy* □ *New Age music* □ *New Age publishing* □ *the widespread distrust of New Age travellers.*

next or **this**? The adjective *this* is often used in place of *next* with reference to days of the current week, months of the current year, etc.: □ *I'm not going to the club this Friday.* □ *She's getting married this September.*

nice The adjective *nice*, in the sense of 'pleasant', 'agreeable', 'kind', 'attractive', etc., is often better replaced by an appropriate synonym, especially in formal contexts: □ *an attractive* [not *nice*] *garden* □ *a pleasant* [not *nice*] *afternoon.*

niceness or **nicety**? Both these nouns are derived from NICE. *Niceness* is used in the general senses of 'pleasantness', 'kindness', etc.; *nicety* is restricted to the sense of 'subtlety; precision' and specifically refers to refined details: □ *the niceness of the weather/ his sister* □ *a nicety of grammar* □ *the niceties of etiquette.*

niche This word may be pronounced to rhyme with *pitch* or *leash*. The second of these pronunciations is closer to the French origin, but the anglicized [nich] is the more frequent.

-nik The suffix *-nik*, of Russian or Yiddish origin, is used to denote somebody who is connected with or does the word that precedes it: □ *beatnik* □ *peacenik* □ *refusenik.* It should not be indiscriminately attached to other nouns and verbs.

nil see ZERO.

nimby *Nimby*, an acronym of 'not in my back yard', is used with reference to a person or people who object to proposed new developments, such as roads or power stations, in the vicinity of their houses: □ *the Nimby syndrome* □ *If he has changed his mind, and is now a true non-Nimby, he should withdraw his objection to having homes at the bottom of his garden* (*The Guardian*).

no see NO ONE OR NO-ONE?; YES AND NO.

nobody see NO ONE OR NO-ONE?

noisome The adjective *noisome* means 'offensive' or 'noxious'; it has no connection, etymological or otherwise, with the noun *noise*: □ *a noisome smell.*

non- The prefix *non-* is used to form a simple or neutral antonym of the word to which it is attached: □*a nonprofessional golfer* □*non-Christian religions*. The prefix *un-*, attached to the same words, may have stronger negative force: □*unprofessional* □*un-Christian*. See also HYPHEN 1.

none The use of a singular or plural verb with the pronoun *none* depends on the sense and context in which it is used: □*None of the milk was spilt.* □*None of my friends has/have seen the film.* In the first of these examples *none*, like *milk*, must be used with a singular verb. In examples of the second type some people prefer a singular verb in formal contexts, especially if *none* is used in the sense of 'not one'. In informal contexts, or in the sense of 'not any', a plural verb is more frequent. See also SINGULAR OR PLURAL?

none the less or **nevertheless**? These two synonyms are sometimes confused. Traditionally *none the less* has been written as three separate words, although *nonetheless* is gradually being accepted. *Nevertheless* is always written as one word.

nonflammable see INFLAMMABLE.

no one or **no-one**? Many users prefer the two-word compound *no one* to the hyphenated form *no-one*. Unlike *anyone, everyone,* and *someone*, *no one* should not be written as a one-word compound.

nor *Nor* is used in place of *or* in the *neither ... nor* construction (see NEITHER) and to introduce a negative alternative that stands as a separate clause: □*I speak neither German nor Spanish.* □*She hasn't been to America, nor has her sister.* □*He never watches television, nor does he listen to the radio.* In many other contexts *nor* and *or* are interchangeable.

normalcy or **normality**? These two nouns are synonymous derivatives of the adjective *normal*. *Normality* is the preferred form in British English; *normalcy* is chiefly used in American English.

north, **North**, or **northern**? As an adjective, *north* is always written with a capital *N* when it forms part of a proper name: □*North America* □*the North Sea.* The noun *north* is usually written with a capital *N* when it denotes a specific region, such as the northern part of England: □ *House prices are lower in the North.* In other contexts, and as an adverb, *north* is usually written with a lower-case *n*: □ *We travelled north for ten days.* □ *They live in north London.* The adjective *northern* is more frequent and less specific than the adjective *north*; it is written with a capital *N* when it forms part of a proper name, such as *Northern Ireland.*

nostalgia The noun *nostalgia* and its derivatives are most frequently used with reference to a wistful or sentimental yearning for the past: □ *She remembered the seaside holidays of her childhood with a deep nostalgia.* □ *Listening to old records always makes me nostalgic.* Some people object to this usage, restricting the term to its original meaning of 'homesickness'.

not The position of the word *not* in a negative sentence may affect its meaning and can sometimes lead to ambiguity: □ *All children are not afraid of the dark.* □ *We did not go because it was raining.* □ *He is not trying to win.* □ *He is trying not to win.* The first of these examples, which literally means 'No children are afraid of the dark', is easily reworded: □ *Not all children are afraid of the dark.* The second example may be reordered or expanded for clarity: □ *Because it was raining we did not go.* □ *We did not go because it was raining, we went because we were bored.*

notable, noted, or **noteworthy**? *Noted* means 'famous': □ *a noted scientist* □ *The area is noted for its spectacular scenery. Notable* and *noteworthy* both mean 'worthy of notice or of being noted': □ *a notable* [or *noteworthy*] *achievement*, but *noteworthy* is usually used to describe facts or events rather than people: □ *It was noteworthy that the average price remained the same despite the effects of inflation.*

notable or **noticeable**? The adjective *notable* means 'remarkable' or 'worthy of note'; *noticeable* means 'perceptible' or 'obvious': □ *a notable achievement* □ *a* *noticeable change in temperaturc*. The two words should not be confused.

noted, noteworthy see NOTABLE, NOTED, OR NOTEWORTHY?

nothing but The phrase *nothing but* ... is used with a singular verb, even if the noun that follows *but* is plural: □ *Nothing but crumbs was* [not *were*] *left on the plate*.

noticeable see NOTABLE OR NOTICEABLE?

not only ... but also The words or clauses that follow *not only* and *but also* must be grammatically balanced: □ *I have lost not only my purse but also my car keys* [not *I have not only lost* ...]. □ *They not only broke the world record for long-distance swimming but also raised several thousand pounds for charity* [not *They broke not only* ...].

notorious see INFAMOUS OR NOTORIOUS?

nougat The standard pronunciation of this word is [*noo*gah], after the French. The alternative pronunciation [*nug*ăt] is widely used.

nought see NAUGHT OR NOUGHT?

nouns Nouns are the names of things, places, or people. The main division of nouns is into countable and uncountable nouns. Countable nouns are those which can be preceded by *a* or *the* or a number or word denoting number: □ *a goat* □ *three lemons* □ *the priest* □ *several books*. Uncountable nouns are not able to be counted because they are nouns of mass: □ *flour* □ *water*. Some words can be countable or uncountable, according to how they are used: □ *Have a beer*. □ *Beer is fattening*. Proper nouns refer to a single particular person or thing and begin with a capital letter: □ *Trevor Jones*. Nouns can be used as adjectives (see also HYPHEN 3), and as verbs (see also VERBS).

noxious or **obnoxious**? Both these adjectives can mean 'extremely unpleasant', but *obnoxious* usually refers to a person and *noxious* to something that is physically or morally harmful: □ *their obnoxious children* □ *noxious fumes*.

nubile The adjective *nubile*, derived from the Latin word for 'marriageable', is frequently applied to any sexually attractive young woman, especially in jocular or informal contexts: □ *His friend's nubile sister was sunbathing in the garden.* Some people object to this usage, restricting the term to its original meaning.

nuclear The occasional use of *nuclear* as a noun, meaning 'nuclear power': □ *a national debate about nuclear,* is disliked and avoided by most people. In the phrase *nuclear family* the adjective *nuclear* simply means 'forming a nucleus'.

nude see NAKED OR NUDE?

number The phrase *a number of ...* is used with a plural verb; the phrase *the number of ...* is used with a singular verb: □ *A number of pupils were late.* □ *The number of pupils has increased.*

numbers Numbers that occur in printed or written texts may be expressed in figures or written out in full, according to the nature of the work, the context, the writer's personal preference, or the publisher's house style.

nutritional or **nutritious?** *Nutritional* means 'relating to nutrition (the process of taking food into the body and absorbing it)'; *nutritious* means 'nourishing': □ *the nutritional requirements of a baby* □ *a very nutritious meal.*

nutritive see NUTRITIONAL OR NUTRITIOUS?

O

O or **oh**? *O*, always written with a capital, is a rarer, more poetic variant of the exclamation *oh*: □ *O come all ye faithful.* □ *O* [or *Oh*] *for the school holidays!* □ *'I can't come and see you later, I'm afraid.' 'Oh well, never mind.'*

obeisance *Obeisance* is a very formal word that means an attitude or gesture of deference or respect: □ *to pay obeisance* □ *to make an obeisance.* It is not synonymous with *obedience,* although both nouns are derived from Old French *obeir,* 'to obey'.

object The *object* of a clause or sentence is the noun, pronoun, or phrase that is affected by the verb. The object usually follows the verb. An object may be *direct* or *indirect.* In the sentence: □ *The dog buried the bone, the bone* is the direct object and there is no indirect object. In the sentences: □ *I gave the child a book* and □ *She bought the child a book, a book* is the direct object and *the child* is the indirect object. Many sentences that contain both a direct and an indirect object can be rephrased using the prepositions *to* or *for*: □ *I gave a book to the child.* □ *She bought a book for the child.* Compare SUBJECT.

objective or **subjective**? The adjective *objective* means 'not influenced by personal feelings, beliefs, or prejudices'; its antonym *subjective* means 'influenced by personal feelings, etc.'

objet d'art The plural of the phrase *objet d'art,* meaning 'small object of artistic worth', is formed by adding *-s* to the first word, *objets d'art.*

obliged or **obligated**? Both these adjectives may be used in the sense of 'morally or legally bound': □ *He felt obliged/obligated* *to report the accident.*

oblivious The adjective *oblivious* is often used in the sense of 'unaware' or 'heedless': □ *He remained in the shelter of the tree, oblivious of the fact that the rain had stopped.*

obnoxious see NOXIOUS OR OBNOXIOUS?

obscene Some people object to the increasing use of *obscene* as a general term of strong disapproval: □ *Recent large pay awards to some company directors are obscene, the Bishop of Manchester said.*

observance or **observation**? The noun *observance* denotes either the act of complying or a ritual custom or practice; *observation* denotes either the act of watching or noticing or a remark or comment: □ *observance of the rules* □ *religious observances* □ *their observation of human behaviour* □ *an observation made by his client.*

obverse see CONVERSE, INVERSE, OBVERSE, OR REVERSE?

obviate To *obviate* something is to make it unnecessary or to dispose of it: □ *A reduction in inflation would obviate the need for higher pay rises.* □ *The management's new proposals obviated our complaints.* It is largely restricted to formal contexts and should not be used as a pretentious synonym for 'remove' or 'get rid of'.

occasion The verb *occasion* is best avoided where *cause, bring about,* etc., would be adequate: □ *The accident was caused* [not *occasioned*] *by a fault in the braking system.*

occupied or **preoccupied**? Applied to a person, *occupied* means 'busy'; *preoccupied* means 'absorbed in a particular train of thought (often to the exclusion of all else)': □ *I was occupied with the preparations for the carnival.* □ *Try to keep everybody occupied.* □ *He was preoccupied with his marital problems.* □ *She seemed preoccupied.*

occurrence This word is often misspelt. A frequent error is the substitution of *-ance* for the *-ence* ending. Note also the *-cc-* and *-rr-*, as also in *occurred* and *occurring.*

octopus The plural of the noun *octopus,* denoting a sea animal with eight tentacles, is *octopuses.* As the word is ultimately of Greek origin, the plural form *octopi* is incorrect; *octopodes* is permissible but pedantic.

oculist see OPTICIAN, OPHTHALMOLOGIST, OPTOMETRIST, OR OCULIST?

odious or **odorous**? *Odious* means 'extremely unpleasant'; *odorous*, a very formal word, means 'having a particular smell': □ *an odious man* □ *an odorous room.* The two adjectives should not be confused.

-oe- see -AE- AND -OE-.

of The preposition *of* is sometimes wrongly substituted for the verb *have* or, more frequently, its contraction *'ve*: □ *They should have* [not *of*] *refused.* □ *She must've* [not *must of*] *forgotten.* This substitution, caused by the similarity in pronunciation between the two words when unstressed, is wrong.

of course The phrase *of course* serves a number of useful purposes, but should not be used to excess.

off The use of the preposition *off* in place of *from*, to indicate the source of an acquisition, is considered wrong by many people, even in informal contexts: □ *I bought it from* [not *off*] *my sister*.

offence This word, meaning 'action causing displeasure; illegal act', is sometimes misspelt. Note the *-c-* not *-s-* in British English (American English, *offense*).

offer or **proffer**? Both verbs mean 'present for acceptance': □ *He proffered* [or *offered*] his passport. □ *She offered* [or *proffered*] *her sympathy. Offer* has a much wider range of usage; *proffer* is largely restricted to formal contexts, and should not be used as a pretentious substitute for *offer*.

official or **officious**? The adjective *official* means 'authorized', 'formal', or 'of an office'; *officious*, which is generally used in a derogatory manner, means 'interfering', 'bossy', 'self-important', or 'offering unwanted advice or assistance': □ *an official strike* □ *an official visit* □ *an officious clerk*. The two words should not be confused.

officialese *Officialese* is a derogatory name for the style of writing or language that is considered to be typical of official forms, reports, memoranda, letters, leaflets, and other bureaucratic documents.

officious see OFFICIAL OR OFFICIOUS?

off-limits The term *off-limits, meaning 'out of bounds' or 'forbidden', originated in American military contexts and is now entering general British usage:* □ *This part of the factory is off-limits to visitors.* Many users prefer to retain the more traditional synonyms.

off-the-wall The adjective *off-the-wall* is used in informal contexts, especially in American English, to mean 'amusingly unusual; eccentric or unexpected; zany': □ *off-the-wall humour.* Care should be taken to avoid overusing this expression.

often The words *oftener* and *oftenest* are accepted comparative and superlative forms of the adverb *often*, but many users prefer *more often* and *most often*, especially in formal contexts: □ *It rains most often in the autumn.* □ *Which car do you use oftener?*

oh see O OR OH?

OK or **okay**? The term *OK* or *okay*, denoting agreement or approval, may be used as an adjective, adverb, noun, or verb: □ *That's OK.* □ *The meeting went OK.* □ *Has she given us the OK/okay?* □ *They are unlikely to okay/OK the suggestion.*

old age pensioner see SENIOR CITIZEN OR OLD AGE PENSIONER?

older, oldest see ELDER, ELDEST, OLDER, OR OLDEST?

omelette This word is sometimes misspelt. In British English the spelling is *omelette*, in American English *omelet*. Note the first *e*.

omission This noun, meaning 'the act of omitting' or 'something omitted', is often misspelt. The most frequent error is the substitution of *-mm-* for the single *-m-*. Note also the *-ission* ending (not *-ision* or *-ition*).

on see ONTO OR ON TO?; UPON OR ON?

one The pronoun *one*, representing an indefinite person, is usually followed in British English by *one's, oneself*, etc., rather than by *his, himself*, etc.: □ *One should be kind to one's friends.*

onerous This word, meaning 'demanding or troublesome': □ *onerous tasks*, has two acceptable pronunciations, [onĕrŏs] and [ōnĕrŏs].

one-stop The term *one-stop refers to the modern trend towards combining various related facilities or services in one place or package:* □ *a one-stop system* □ *The report … suggests local authorities can offer 'one-stop shops' where employers can find child-care, training and other contacts under one roof* (*Daily Telegraph*). It is a vogue word disliked by some people.

ongoing Many people object to the use of the adjective *ongoing* in place of *continuing, developing, in progress*, etc.: □ *ongoing research* □ *an ongoing investment programme in manufacturing technology*. The cliché *ongoing situation* is also widely disliked.

on-line The term *on-line*, which relates to equipment that is directly connected to and/or controlled by a central computer, is sometimes used in the extended sense of 'in direct communication with': □ *on-line to the president*. It should not be confused with ON-STREAM: □ *Rent A Film … will be getting in the party spirit to celebrate a very special service which has just come on line at their plush, newly-refurbished premises* (*Littlehampton Guardian*).

only In some written sentences the adverb *only* must be carefully positioned, as near as possible to the word it refers to, in order to convey the intended meaning: □ *She eats fish only on Fridays* [i.e. not on other days]. □ *She eats only fish* [i.e. nothing else] *on Fridays*. □ *Only she* [i.e. She is the only one who] *eats fish on Fridays*.

onomatopoeia *Onomatopoeia* is the formation of words that imitate the sound associated with an object or action: □ *cuckoo* □ *moo* □ *clang* □ *croak* □ *hiss* □ *twitter*.

on-stream The term *on-stream* relates to an industrial process or plant that is in production or about to go into production or operation or to the launching of a new advertising campaign, etc.: □ *Collections* [of mail on Sundays] *will start in five districts in October, …. A further five dis-*

tricts will be added next January with the rest of the country coming on stream by the end of 1990 (*The Guardian*).

onto or **on to**? The preposition *onto* may be written as one or two words: □ *She drove onto/on to the pavement. On to* may also be a combination of the adverb *on* and the preposition or infinitive marker *to*, in which case it should not be written as one word: □ *She drove on to London.* □ *She drove on to find a hotel.*

onward or **onwards**? In British English *onward* is principally used as an adjective, *onwards* being the usual form of the adverb meaning 'ahead': □ *onward motion* □ *to march onwards.*

operative The frequent use of the noun *operative* in place of *worker*, especially in nonindustrial contexts, is disliked by many users: □ *a strike by cleaning operatives at the hospital.*

ophthalmologist see OPTICIAN, OPHTHALMOLOGIST, OPTOMETRIST, OR OCULIST?

opposite The noun *opposite* is followed by *of*, not *to*: □ *Hot is the opposite of* [not *to*] *cold.* As a preposition, *opposite* may be followed by *to* (not *of*) but usually stands alone: □ *the car park opposite (to) the station.*

oppress, **repress**, or **suppress**? These verbs are similar in meaning: all three refer to subjugation or restraint. *Oppress* means 'subjugate by force, cruel treatment, etc.'; the direct object of the verb is usually a group of people: □ *a regime that oppresses women* □ *the oppressed workers.* The verb *repress* is also used in this sense, but more frequently refers to the act of concealing or controlling one's feelings: □ *I repressed the urge to hit him.* □ *a repressed desire.* In psychology, *repress* means 'banish or exclude (thoughts, feelings, etc.) from one's conscious mind or awareness', an act that may lead to psychological problems: □ *repressed sexuality.* The verb *suppress* has the more general meaning of 'restrain' or 'control': □ *She couldn't suppress her laughter. Suppress* also means 'withhold' or 'crush': □ *to suppress information* □ *to suppress a rebellion.*

optician, **ophthalmologist**, **optometrist**, or **oculist**? All four nouns denote people who are concerned with defects or diseases of the eye. The word *optician*, which is probably the most familiar, may denote an *ophthalmic optician* or a *dispensing optician*.

An *ophthalmic optician* is qualified to test eyesight and prescribe corrective lenses. A *dispensing optician* makes and sells glasses (and other optical equipment).

An *ophthalmologist* is a doctor who specializes in eye diseases. *Optometrist* is a less frequent name for an *ophthalmic optician*; *oculist* is synonymous with *ophthalmologist*.

optimal see OPTIMUM.

optimistic Many people object to the frequent use of the adjective *optimistic* as a synonym for 'hopeful', 'confident', 'cheerful', 'favourable', 'encouraging', etc.: □ *She is optimistic that the car will be found.* □ *They have produced an optimistic report on the company's prospects.*

optimize see OPTIMUM.

optimum The adjective and noun *optimum* refer to the most favourable or advantageous condition, amount, degree, etc.: □ *the optimum speed* □ *A temperature of 15°C is the optimum.* The verb *optimize* means 'make the most of' or 'make as efficient as possible'.

opt in see OPT OUT.

optometrist see OPTICIAN, OPHTHALMOLOGIST, OPTOMETRIST, OR OCULIST?

opt out *Opt out* means 'choose not to participate or be involved', with the implication that a person or organization that does not opt out is automatically included: □ *to opt out of society* □ *schools that have opted out (of local government control).* In the opposite situation, where people or organizations are automatically excluded unless they choose to participate, the verb *opt in* may be used: □ *A survey into public attitudes to kidney donation found that most people are willing to donate their kidneys but they are against a scheme to 'opt out' of donorship rather than the present scheme of 'opting in'* (*New Scientist*).

opus The formal noun *opus*, denoting a musical work or other artistic composition, may be pronounced [ōpŭs], with the long *o* of *open*, or [opŭs], with the short *o* of *operate*. Both pronunciations are acceptable, but the first is more frequent.

or When *or* connects two or more singular subjects a singular verb is used: □ *Perhaps Peter or Jane knows* [not *know*] *the answer*. A plural verb is used if both subjects are plural: □ *Carrots or parsnips are served with this dish.* In a combination of singular and plural alternatives the verb traditionally agrees with the subject that is nearest to it.

oral see AURAL OR ORAL?; VERBAL OR ORAL?

ordinance or **ordnance**? An *ordinance* is a decree or regulation; the noun *ordnance* denotes military supplies or artillery.

organic The adjective *organic* is applied to methods of food production that do not make use of chemical fertilizers, pesticides, etc.: □ *organic farming* □ *organically produced fruit.* Some people dislike the increasing tendency to apply the adjective directly to the produce itself: □ *organic food* □ *organic vegetables.*

orient or **orientate**? Both forms of the verb are acceptable: *orient*, the standard form in American English, is preferred by some users as the shorter and simpler alternative, but *orientate* is the more frequent in British English.

orthopaedic or **paediatric**? Both these adjectives are used in medical contexts and they are often confused. *Orthopaedic* refers to the treatment of bones, joints, muscles, etc.; *paediatric* refers to the treatment of children.

ostensible or **ostentatious**? *Ostensible* means 'apparent'; *ostentatious* means 'showy': □ *the ostensible reason for her absence* □ *an ostentatious display of grief.*

other than The use of *other than* as an adverbial phrase is disliked by some users: □ *They were unable to escape other than by squeezing through the narrow window.* Its adjectival use, however, is acceptable to all: □ *There was no means of escape other than the narrow window. Other than* is best avoided where *apart from* would be more appropriate: □ *There was a narrow window; apart from* [not *other than*] *that, there was no means of escape.* The construction *other ... than* should not be replaced by *other ... but* or *other ... except*: □ *He had no other friend than* [not *but*] *me.* □ *Every other card than* [not *except*] *yours arrived on time.* If the word *other* is omitted, however, *but* or *except* may be substituted for *than*.

otherwise Some people object to the frequent use of *otherwise* as an adjective or pronoun: □ *All essays, finished or otherwise, must be handed in tomorrow morning.* □ *The entire workforce, union members and otherwise, went on strike.* *Otherwise* may be replaced by *not* in the first of these examples and by *others* in the second.

OTT see OVER THE TOP.

ought The auxiliary verb *ought*, expressing duty, obligation, advisability, expectation, etc., is always followed by an infinitive with *to*: □ *They ought to visit her more often.* □ *Ought we to have invited your sister?* □ *You oughtn't to leave your car unlocked.* □ *The meat ought to be cooked by now.*

our or **us**? see -ING FORMS.

out The verb *out*, meaning 'expose the homosexuality of', is a relatively recent coinage derived from the phrase *come out (of the closet)*, meaning 'reveal one's homosexuality': □ *The militant gay group threatened to 'out' MPs.* The verb *out* and its associated noun *outing* are increasingly used in other contexts.

outdoor or **outdoors**? *Outdoor* is an adjective, *outdoors* is an adverb: □ *outdoor sports* □ *outdoor pursuits* □ *to play outdoors* □ *Outdoor clothes are worn outdoors.*

outing see OUT.

outlet Some people object to the frequent use of the noun *outlet* in place of *shop*: □ *The product is available at a number of retail outlets in London.*

outplacement The noun *outplacement* refers to advice and assistance given to people who have been made redundant (or who are about to be made redundant): □ *outplacement counselling* □ *Outplacement consulting came to Britain from the US in the 1970s and has grown from a £2 million turnover in 1978 to about £55 million now*

(*The Guardian*).

outrageous This word, meaning 'shocking or unconventional': □ *outrageous manners*, is sometimes misspelt. The *e* of *outrage* is retained before the suffix *-ous* to indicate the softness of the *g*.

outside of Many people dislike the prepositional phrase *outside of*, in which the word *of* is incorrect. The phrase is best avoided in formal contexts: □ *There was a taxi outside* [not *outside of*] *the house*.

outward or **outwards**? In British English *outward* is principally used as an adjective, *outwards* being the usual form of the adverb meaning 'towards the outside': □ *the outward journey* □ *to pull outwards*.

over see ABOVE OR OVER?

overall The word *overall* is best avoided where *total, whole, comprehensive, general, average, inclusive, altogether*, etc., would be adequate or more appropriate: □ *his general* [not *overall*] *appearance* □ *the total* [not *overall*] *cost of the project* □ *The journey will take five days altogether* [not *overall*].

overkill The frequent use of the noun *overkill* in the sense of 'excess' is disliked by some users: □ *In the coverage of the election the media have been accused of overkill.*

overly Many people object to the use of the adverb *overly* in place of *too, excessively*, etc.: □ *She was not overly enthusiastic about my idea.* □ *He is overly sensitive to the slightest criticism.*

over the top The cliché *over the top* and its slang abbreviation *OTT*, meaning 'excessive' or 'outrageous', should not be overused: □ *The restaurant sketch was a bit OTT.*

overtone or **undertone**? In the figurative sense of 'implicit shade of meaning or feeling', these two nouns are virtually synonymous, although *overtone* may convey an additional effect and *undertone* an underlying effect. Both are more frequently used in the plural: □ *overtones of malice* □ *undertones of discontent* □ *political overtones*.

overview The noun *overview* is best avoided where *survey, summary*, etc., would be adequate or more appropriate: □ *a general overview of the situation.*

owing to see DUE TO, OWING TO, OR BECAUSE OF?

P

pace The Latin word *pace,* usually printed in italics, means 'with due respect to' and is used when stating an opinion contrary to that of the specified person: □ *The teaching profession,* pace *George Bernard Shaw, is not a refuge for those who cannot do anything else.* It is a two-syllable word with at least two accepted pronunciations, [*pay*si] and [*pah*chay].

package The word *package* and the expression *package deal* are widely used to denote a set of proposals or offers that must be accepted or rejected as a whole.

paediatric see ORTHOPAEDIC OR PAEDIATRIC?

palate This word, meaning 'the top part of the inside of one's mouth' or 'sense of taste': □ *a cleft palate* □ *He has a sensitive palate*, is sometimes misspelt. It should not be confused with *palette*, the board on which an artist mixes colours, or *pallet*, a flat platform used in stacking and moving stored goods, and also a hard bed or straw mattress.

pallor The noun *pallor,* meaning 'paleness', is sometimes misspelt. Note the final *-or*.

palpable The use of the adjective *palpable* in the extended sense of 'easily perceived', in place of *obvious, manifest, plain,* etc., is disliked by some people: □ *a palpable lie.*

panacea The noun *panacea* denotes a universal remedy for all ills; it should not be used with reference to individual problems or troubles: □ *Efficient use of energy saves money but is not a panacea for solving carbon dioxide pollution* (*Daily Telegraph*).

panic The word *panic* adds a *k* before the suffix *-y* and suffixes beginning with an *e* or *i* such as *-ed*, *-er*, and *-ing*: □ *panicky* □ *They panicked.* □ *Stop panicking!* See also SPELLING 1.

paradigm The noun *paradigm* is best avoided where *example*, *model*, *pattern*, etc., would be adequate or more appropriate: □ *a paradigm of enterprise and initiative. Paradigm* specifically denotes a clear or typical example; the *g* is not pronounced.

paraffin This word is sometimes misspelt. Note the single *r* and *-ff-*, as in *raffle*.

paragraphs A *paragraph* is a subdivision of a written passage, which usually deals with one particular point or theme. It expresses an idea which, though it relates to the sense of the whole passage, can to some extent stand alone.

parallel This word is sometimes misspelt. Note the single *r*, *-ll-*, and then the single *l*.

paralyse This word is sometimes misspelt. The spelling in British English is *paralyse* [not *-yze*], in American English, *paralyze*. See also -IZE OR -ISE?

parameter Many people object to the frequent use of the noun *parameter*, a mathematical term, as a synonym for 'limit', 'boundary', 'framework', 'characteristic', or 'point to be considered': □ *A business must operate within the parameters of time, money, and efficiency.* □ *We keep on refining our mailing selection parameters* (*The Bookseller*). □ *What are the parameters of the problem?*

paranoid The adjective *paranoid* principally relates to a mental disorder (*paranoia*) characterized by delusions of persecution or grandeur. Some people object to the frequent use of *paranoid* and *paranoia* with reference to any intense suspicion, distrust, anxiety, fear, obsession, etc.

paraphernalia The noun *paraphernalia*, sometimes used with derogatory connotations, denotes all the miscellaneous items associated with a particular activity: □ *the paraphernalia of photography.* It is also used in more abstract contexts: □ *the paraphernalia of buying a new house. Paraphernalia* is a plural noun, but it is frequently used with a singular verb: □ *His camping parapher-*

nalia is stored in the attic. This usage is acceptable.

parenting The word *parenting*, which means 'being a parent' or 'parental care', is increasingly used to emphasize the joint responsibility of both parents in all aspects of a child's upbringing and to avoid the sexual stereotypes and traditional roles associated with the words *mother* and *father* and their derivatives: □ *the advantages of shared parenting* □ *a guide to parenting the gifted child.*

parliament The noun *parliament*, meaning 'legislative authority, assembly, or body', is usually written with a capital *P* when it denotes a specific parliament, especially that of the United Kingdom: □ *The issue will be debated in Parliament this afternoon.*

partially or **partly**? Both adverbs mean 'not completely' or 'to some extent', but there are differences. The words are often used interchangeably, but it can be helpful to think of *partly* as meaning 'concerning one part; not wholly', and *partially* as meaning 'to a limited extent; not completely'.

participles All verbs have *present participles*, which are formed with *-ing*: □ *seeing* □ *walking*, and *past participles*, formed with *-d* or *-ed* for regular verbs and in other ways for irregular verbs: □ *loved* □ *finished* □ *given* □ *gone* □ *thought.*

particular Used for emphasis, the adjective *particular* is often superfluous: □ *Do you have any particular preference?* □ *This particular dress was worn by Vivien Leigh in 'Gone with the Wind'.*

partly see PARTIALLY OR PARTLY?

passed or **past**? These spellings are sometimes confused. *Passed* is the past tense and past participle of *pass*: □ *We passed the station.* □ *The years have passed by so quickly. Past* is used for all other forms.

passive A passive verb is one in which the SUBJECT receives the action of the verb (compare ACTIVE). The sentence □ *The play was written by Oscar Wilde* contains the passive verb *was written.*

past see PASSED OR PAST?

patent This word may be pronounced [*pay*tĕnt] in all senses in British English: □ *to patent/apply for a patent*

patent for a new invention □ *patent leather shoes*, and as the adverb *patently* [*pay*tĕntli]: □ *It is patently obvious she's lying.*

pathetic The use of the adjective *pathetic* in the derogatory sense of 'contemptible' or 'worthless' is best restricted to informal contexts: □ *The comedian made a pathetic attempt to mimic the president.*

patriot This word, meaning 'one who loves his or her country', has two acceptable pronunciations [*pay*triŏt] or [*pa*triŏt].

patron see CLIENT OR CUSTOMER?

PC see POLITICAL CORRECTNESS.

peaceable or **peaceful**? The adjective *peaceable*, meaning 'disposed to peace', 'peace-loving', or 'not aggressive', is principally applied to people: □ *the peaceable inhabitants of the town* □ *a peaceable temperament. Peaceful*, the more frequent of the two adjectives, means 'characterized by peace', 'calm', or 'not violent': □ *a peaceful scene* □ *a peaceful demonstration.*

pedal or **peddle**? The word *pedal* relates to a foot-operated lever: □ *the soft pedal on a piano* □ *a pedal bin* □ *to pedal a bicycle.* To *peddle* is to sell small articles or illegal goods, such as drugs, or to put forward ideas or information. The verb *peddle* is a BACK FORMATION from the noun *pedlar*, a person who goes from place to place selling goods.

pedigree The noun *pedigree* denotes an ancestral line or line of descent, specifically that of a purebred animal; its use as a synonym for 'record' or 'background' is disliked by some users: □ *a pedigree of success spanning over 50 years in the radio and television rental and retail field* (*Executive Post*).

pedlar see PEDAL OR PEDDLE?

pejorative This word, meaning 'disparaging', can be pronounced in two ways. The pronunciation [pi*jor*rătiv] is used more frequently than the more traditional [*pee*jŏrătiv].

pence As *pence* is one of the plural forms of the noun *penny*, many people object to the use of the term *one-pence piece* to denote a penny coin: □ *Does the machine still take one-pence pieces?* The plural noun *pennies* is used with reference to a number of coins, whereas *pence* usually refers to a sum of money: □ *My purse is full of pennies.* □ *The envelopes cost four pence each.*

penchant The noun *penchant,* meaning 'inclination' or 'liking', is of French origin and is pronounced [*pon*(g)shon(g)], an anglicized form of the French pronunciation, in British English.

pendant or **pendent**? The noun *pendant,* denoting a type of necklace, has the rare variant spelling *pendent.* The word *pendent* is also used as an adjective, in the sense of 'hanging', with the (less frequent) variant spelling *pendant.*

peninsula or **peninsular**? These two spellings are sometimes confused. A *peninsula* is a long narrow section of land that is almost surrounded by water but which is joined to the mainland. The adjective is *peninsular*: □ *the Peninsular War of 1808 to 1814.*

pennies, penny see PENCE.

pensioner see SENIOR CITIZEN OR OLD AGE PENSIONER?

people *People* is usually a plural noun, but in the sense of 'nation', 'race', or 'tribe' it may be singular or plural: □ *a nomadic people of Africa* □ *all the peoples of the world* □ *The French people are renowned for their culinary expertise.* The alternative plural form *persons* to denote a number of human beings is best restricted to formal contexts: □ *No more than eight persons may use the lift.* □ *There are four people* [not *persons*] *in the waiting room.*

per The preposition *per,* meaning 'for each' or 'in each', is often better replaced by *a* or *an*: □ *four times a* [not *per*] *month* □ *60p a* [not *per*] *metre.* In some contexts, however, *per* must be retained: □ *Use two ounces of cheese per person.*

per-, **pre-**, or **pro-**? These three prefixes sometimes cause confusion in the spelling and usage of certain pairs of words. See PERSECUTE OR PROSECUTE?; PRECEDE OR PROCEED?; PREREQUISITE OR PERQUISITE?; PRESCRIBE OR PROSCRIBE?

per annum The Latin phrase *per annum,* meaning 'for each year', is best restricted to formal contexts: □ *You will be paid a salary of*

£12,000 per annum.

per capita The adverbial or adjectival phrase *per capita* is widely used in English in the sense of 'for each person': □ *the minimum cost per capita* □ *a per capita allowance of ten pounds.*

per cent The phrase *per cent* is used adverbially, in combination with a number, in the sense of 'in or for each hundred': □ *an increase of 25 per cent* □ *75 per cent of the students.*

percentage Many people object to the use of *a percentage* to mean 'a small part', 'a little', or 'a few': □ *Only a percentage of the workforce will be present.* A percentage may be as small as 1% or as large as 99%; in the sense of 'proportion' the noun often needs a qualifying adjective for clarity: □ *A small percentage of the money is used for administration costs.*

perceptible, perceptive, or **percipient?** The adjective *perceptible* means 'perceivable', 'noticeable', or 'recognizable'; *perceptive* means 'observant', 'discerning', or 'sensitive': □ *a perceptible change* □ *a perceptive remark. Percipient* is virtually synonymous with *perceptive* and is largely restricted to formal contexts.

peremptory or **perfunctory?** *Peremptory* means 'commanding; dogmatic; positive; decisive': □ *a peremptory order* □ *a peremptory man* □ *in a peremptory tone of voice* □ *a peremptory knock at the door. Perfunctory* means 'quick; careless; cursory; superficial': □ *a perfunctory glance at the letter.* Both adjectives are largely restricted to formal contexts; they should not be confused.

perestroika *Perestroika,* a Russian word, is used to denote the restructuring or economic and social reform programme in the Soviet Union under Mikhail Gorbachev in the late 1980s. *Perestroika* was also the title of a book by Gorbachev published in 1987. Like GLASNOST, *perestroika* is increasingly used in other contexts in the Western world.

perfect Many people avoid using such adverbs as *very, rather, more, most, less, least,* etc., to qualify the adjective *perfect,* meaning 'faultless', 'unblemished', 'complete', or 'utter': □ *This* *book is in less perfect condition than that one.* □ *It was the most perfect diamond that he had ever seen.* The expressions *nearly perfect* and *almost perfect*, however, are generally acceptable.

perfunctory see PEREMPTORY OR PERFUNCTORY?

perk see PREREQUISITE OR PERQUISITE?

permissible or **permissive**? These two adjectives are derived from the verb *permit*, meaning 'allow' or 'authorize'. *Permissible* means 'permitted'; *permissive* means 'tolerant': □ *the smallest permissible investment* □ *a permissive attitude.* *Permissive* sometimes implies disapproval of such tolerance (or of the thing tolerated), especially when it is used with reference to sexual indulgence: □ *the permissive society.*

perpetrate or **perpetuate**? *Perpetrate* means 'commit' or 'perform'; *perpetuate* means 'cause to continue' or 'make perpetual': □ *to perpetrate a crime* □ *to perpetuate a tradition.* The two verbs should not be confused.

per pro. see P.P.

perquisite see PREREQUISITE OR PERQUISITE?

per se The Latin phrase *per se*, meaning 'by itself' or 'in itself', is best restricted to formal contexts: □ *The discovery is of little importance per se.*

persecute or **prosecute**? *Persecute* means 'harass' or 'oppress'; *prosecute* means 'take legal action against': □ *They were persecuted for their beliefs.* □ *Trespassers will be prosecuted.* The two verbs should not be confused.

perseverance The noun *perseverance* is sometimes misspelt. A common error is the addition of an extra *r-* before the *-v-*. Note also the *-ance* ending.

person Many people prefer to use the noun *person*, rather than *man*, to denote a human being whose sex is unspecified. As a general rule the substitution of *person* for *man*, in any context, is best avoided if a simpler or more idiomatic solution can be found. See also CHAIR; MAN; SEXISM.

personage or **personality**? Both nouns are applied to famous people, but they are not synonymous. *Personage* is used in formal contexts to refer to an important or distinguished person; a *personality* is a famous person from the world of show business, sport, etc.: □ *members of the royal family and other personages* □ *a TV personality*.

personality see PERSONAGE OR PERSONALITY?

personally The use of the adverb *personally* for emphasis is disliked by some users: □ *I personally prefer to spend my holidays at home*.

personate, personify see IMPERSONATE, PERSONATE, OR PERSONIFY?

personnel Many people object to the frequent use of the noun *personnel* in place of *staff, workforce, workers, employees, people,* etc.: □ *They do not have enough personnel to cope with the increased workload*. The word *personnel* is principally used to denote the employees of a large company or organization, considered collectively, or the department that is concerned with their recruitment and welfare: □ *hospital personnel* □ *the personnel officer*. *Personnel* may be a singular or plural noun, but it should not be used with a specific number.

persons see PEOPLE.

perspective or **prospective**? *Perspective* is a noun, meaning 'view', 'aspect', or 'objectivity'; it should not be confused with the adjective *prospective*, meaning 'expected', 'likely', or 'future': □ *a different perspective* □ *a prospective employer*.

perturb see DISTURB OR PERTURB?

perverse or **perverted**? *Perverse* means 'obstinate' or 'contrary'; *perverted* means 'corrupt' or 'characterized by abnormal sexual behaviour': □ *a perverse refusal* □ *a perverted attack*. The two adjectives should not be confused: to call a man *perverted* is a more serious and offensive accusation than to call him *perverse*.

phase see FAZE OR PHASE?

phenomena see PHENOMENON OR PHENOMENA?

phenomenal The use of the adjective *phenomenal* as a synonym for 'extraordinary', 'remarkable', 'prodigious', or 'outstanding' is disliked by some: □ *a phenomenal achievement*.

phenomenon or **phenomena**? *Phenomena* is the plural form of the noun *phenomenon*: □ *This phenomenon is* of great interest to astronomers. □ *Such phenomena are not easy to explain.*

philosophy The noun *philosophy* is best avoided where *idea, view, policy,* etc., would be adequate or more appropriate: □ *My philosophy is that children should be seen and not heard.* □ *The company has a philosophy of sound management practices at the local level.*

phlegm This word causes problems with spelling and pronunciation. Note the initial *ph-* spelling, pronounced [f], and the silent *g*. The word is pronounced [flem].

phobia A *phobia* is an abnormal or irrational fear or aversion: □ *He has a phobia about flying.* □ *She has a phobia of spiders.*

phone The use of the noun and verb *phone* in place of *telephone* is becoming increasingly frequent and acceptable: the telephone directory is now officially entitled 'The Phone Book', the term long used to describe it in informal contexts. The shortened form *phone* is best avoided, however, in formal contexts.

phoney or **phony**? The more frequent spelling of this word, meaning 'fake', is *phoney* in British English, and *phony* in American English.

photo The use of the noun *photo* in place of *photograph* is best restricted to informal contexts: □ *Did you take a photo of the baby?* □ *This pass is not valid without a photograph of the holder.* The plural of *photo* is *photos*.

photo-opportunity *Photo-opportunity* (or *photocall*) is a vogue term used for an allegedly spontaneous but invariably prearranged event for press and television photographers. The *opportunity* is ostensibly for the camera operators, but in fact is created by and for the politician or media star being photographed in order to obtain favourable visual publicity.

phrase A *phrase* is a group of words that function together as a noun, verb, adjective, adverb, preposition, etc.: □ *the red car* □ *give up* □ *highly polished* □ *at the back of the room* □ *with reference to.* See also CLAUSE; SENTENCES.

physician or **physicist**? A

physician is a doctor of medicine; a *physicist* is a scientist who has specialized in physics: □ *the number of physicians in the National Health Service* □ *physicists involved in nuclear research.* The two nouns should not be confused.

physiognomy Note the spelling of this word, which means 'the outward appearance of a person considered to show the person's character'. The most frequent error is to omit the silent *g*.

picnic This word adds a *k* before the suffixes *-er, -ed, -ing*: □ *picnickers* □ *They picnicked in the woods.* See also SPELLING 1.

pidgin or **pigeon**? These two words may sometimes be confused. *Pidgin* is a language that is a mixture of two other languages: □ *pidgin English.* A *pigeon* is a grey bird with short legs and compact feathers.

pièce de résistance The phrase *pièce de résistance*, meaning 'main dish of a meal; most outstanding or impressive item', is of French origin and is sometimes written or printed in italics in English texts. Note the accents, which serve to distinguish *pièce*, pronounced [pyes], from the English word *piece* [pees], and *résistance* [rezistahns] from the English word *resistance* [rizistăns]; these accents should never be omitted.

pigmy see PYGMY OR PIGMY?

piteous, pitiable, or **pitiful**? All these adjectives mean 'arousing or deserving pity', in which sense they are virtually interchangeable in many contexts. There are, however, slight differences of usage and application between them: □ *a piteous cry* □ *a pitiable figure* □ *a pitiful sight.*

pivotal The frequent use of the adjective *pivotal* in the sense of 'crucial or very important' is disliked by some users: □ *to come to a pivotal decision.*

plain or **plane**? These words are sometimes confused. The main noun sense of *plain* is 'level, treeless expanse of land': □ *the vast plains of the prairies. Plane* as a noun is a shortened form of *aeroplane*, a carpenter's tool, or a surface in geometry. See also PLANE.

plaintiff or **plaintive**? These

words are sometimes confused. A *plaintiff* is the person who commences legal action in a court; *plaintive* means 'mournful and melancholy': □ *a plaintive song.*

plane The use of the noun *plane* as a shortened form of *aeroplane* is acceptable in most contexts: □ *What time does your plane leave?* □ *More than 250 people were killed in the plane crash.*

plastic The first syllable of the word *plastic* may be pronounced with the short *a* of *plan,* or with the long *a* of *plant.* The first of these pronunciations, [*plas*tik], is more frequent than the second, [*plah*stik].

platform The use of the noun *platform* to denote the declared policies and principles of a political party or candidate is disliked by some users as an Americanism but is acceptable to most: □ *Their unilateralist platform will win them few votes in the forthcoming election.*

playwright see DRAMATIST OR PLAYWRIGHT?

plc This abbreviation for *public limited company* is often written or printed in lower-case letters, without full stops.

pleaded or **pled**? In British English *pleaded* is the usual form of the past tense and past participle of the verb *plead:* □ *'Save my child,' she pleaded. Pled* is an American, Scottish, or dialectal variant of *pleaded.*

pleasantness or **pleasantry**? *Pleasantness* is an uncountable noun, meaning 'the state of being pleasant': □ *the pleasantness of the weather. Pleasantry* is chiefly used in more formal English in the plural form *pleasantries,* meaning 'polite, casual, friendly, agreeable, or amusing remarks': □ *to exchange pleasantries.*

plenitude *Plenitude* means 'abundance': □ *religious adornments in great plenitude.* A formal word, it is best avoided where *plenty* would be adequate or more appropriate.

plenty The use of *plenty* as an adverb, in place of *quite* or *very,* is regarded by some as nonstandard: □ *The house is plenty big enough for us.* □ *She was plenty upset when she heard the news.*

plethora The phrase *a plethora of* implies excess or

superfluity; it should not be used as a pretentious synonym for 'a large number of' or 'plenty of': □ *a plethora of houses for sale*, for example, describes a situation in which there are too many houses on the market, far more than the number of prospective buyers, with the result that many will remain unsold.

plurals The regular way of forming plurals for English words is to add an *-s*, except for words ending in *-s*, *-x*, *-ch*, *-sh*, and *-z*, where *-es* is added. Of course, there are many irregularly formed plurals. Words ending in a consonant and then *-y* have *-ies* in the plural: □ *fairies* □ *ponies*, except for proper nouns, which have *-s* or *-ies*: □ *I've invited the Joneses and the Hartys.* □ *the Two Sicilies.* Some words ending in *-f* or *-fe* have *-ves* in the plural: □ *halves* □ *wives*, while others simply add *-s*, and others allow a choice: □ *beliefs* □ *hoofs – hooves*. Some words ending in *-o* add *-es*, others just an *-s*. It is impossible to formulate a general rule here, although note the frequently used *potatoes* and *tomatoes*, which both end *-es*. Note also that shortened forms ending in *-o* just add *-s*: □ *photos* □ *pianos* □ *radios* □ *stereos* □ *videos*. Some nouns ending in *-s* are already plural and cannot be pluralized: □ *trousers* □ *spectacles* □ *scissors*. With various animal names the plural form is the same as the singular: □ *deer* □ *sheep* □ *bison*. Several English words have plurals not formed in any of the ways described above: □ *man – men* □ *mouse – mice*. There is no rule about these words and one cannot generalize from them. Foreign words sometimes take a regular English plural and sometimes the plural of the foreign language. Often either is regarded as correct: □ *châteaux/châteaus*. The *-is* ending of such nouns as *analysis* and *thesis* changes to *-es* in the plural. For other types of ending see APPENDIXES OR APPENDICES?; INDEXES OR INDICES?; FORMULAE OR FORMULAS?; MEDIA; PHENOMENON OR PHENOMENA?; FUNGI. Difficulties often arise with the plurals of compound nouns. The general rule is that when the qualifying word is an adjective then the noun is made plural: □ *poets laureate*, though in less formal usage the second word is made plural. If both are nouns the second word is made plural: □ *town clerks*, although *woman teacher* becomes *women teachers*. In compounds of a noun and a prepositional phrase or adverb, the noun is made plural: □ *mothers-in-law*. If no words in the compound are nouns, the *-s* is added at the end: □ *forget-me-nots*.

plus The prepositional use of *plus* in the sense of 'with the addition of' is acceptable in all contexts: □ *My savings, plus the money my grandmother left me, are almost enough to buy a car.*

p.m. see A.M. AND P.M.

pneumatic and **pneumonia** Note the spelling of these words, particularly the silent initial *p-* and the *-eu-* of the first syllable.

poetess see -ESS.

poignant This word, meaning 'distressing', is usually pronounced [*poy*nyănt] although [*poy*nănt] is also acceptable. The *g* is silent.

politic or **political**? *Politic* means 'prudent', 'shrewd', or 'cunning'; *political* means 'of politics, government, policy-making, etc.': □ *a politic decision* □ *a political party*. The two adjectives should not be confused.

political correctness *Political correctness*, or *PC*, is the avoidance of words, phrases, or actions that may be deemed offensive by a particular section of society, such as ethnic minorities, homosexuals, women, blind people, deaf people, or old people. The term is most frequently used in situations where this anxiety to avoid offence seems excessive: □ *The legions of the politically correct continue to direct their accusations of racism, sexism, stoutism and inappropriate body language at every area of our public and private life, sniffing out imaginary insults and creating antagonism in their wake* (*Daily Telegraph*). See also ABLED; ABLEISM; AGEISM; CHALLENGED; SEXISM.

politics see -ICS.

poltergeist The word *poltergeist*, denoting a mischievous spirit, is sometimes misspelt. Note the *er* in the middle and the *ei* in the ‹ial syllable. The word is pronounced [*pol*tĕrgīst].

pomegranate Note the spelling of this word, particularly the single *m* and the *-ate* ending (not *-ite*, as in *granite*). Note also the first *e*, which is usually sounded in British English [*pom*igranit], but is often dropped in the American English pronunciation [*pom*granit].

pore or **pour**? These spellings are sometimes confused. *Pore* as a verb means 'look intently': □ *They pored over the map*; *pour* means 'cause to flow': □ *She poured the tea.* The noun *pore* refers to a minute opening in the skin.

portmanteau word see BLENDS.

Portuguese This word is sometimes misspelt; note the *-e-* following the second *u*.

position To *position* is to put carefully and deliberately in a specific place; the verb is best avoided where *place, put, post, situate, locate,* etc., would be adequate or more appropriate: □ *She positioned the mat on the carpet to hide the stain.* □ *He put* [not *positioned*] *his dirty plate on top of the others.* □ *The offices are situated* [not *positioned*] *in the town centre.*

possessives The two ways of showing that a noun is one of possession are the apostrophe and the use of the word *of*: □ *Anne's car* □ *the rabbits' burrow* □ *soldiers of the Queen.* In cases of joint possession the apostrophe belongs to the last owner mentioned: □ *Tom and Lucy's house.*

post- Some people object to the frequent use of the prefix *post-*, meaning 'after', to coin new adjectives, often of a futuristic nature: □ *post-nuclear Britain* □ *post-feminist literature* □ *Mr Steel said the aim would be to create an 'effective and electable alternative to government in the post-Thatcher period'* (*Daily Telegraph*).

posthumous This word causes problems with spelling and pronunciation. In speech the *h* is silent [*pos*tewmŭs]; the first syllable is not as in *post*, but as in *possible*.

post-traumatic stress disorder The phrase *post-traumatic stress disorder* (or *syndrome*) denotes a combination of largely psychological symptoms, such as irrational fear, feelings of guilt, depression, nightmares, etc., resulting from the shock of being involved in a highly distressing situation, such as a rail or plane crash, a major fire, a terrorist bomb attack, or warfare: □ *The … constable has been diagnosed as having post-traumatic stress syndrome resulting from her experiences while on the Stevens investigation into links between the security forces and loyalist groups* (*Daily Telegraph*).

pour see PORE OR POUR?

power The word *power* is sometimes used adjectivally to refer to an important business occasion. For example □ *a power breakfast* [or *lunch*] is a meeting of influential people from e.g. politics, business, or the media that is held over breakfast (or lunch). This vogue usage is best restricted to informal contexts.

p.p. The abbreviation *p.p.* (or *per pro.*), short for the Latin phrase *per procurationem*, is used when signing a letter on behalf of somebody else. The Latin phrase means 'by proxy' or 'through the agency of', and the abbreviation should precede the name of the person signing the letter.

practical or **practicable**? The adjective *practical* has a wide range of senses; the principal meaning of *practicable* is 'capable of being done or put into practice'. A *practicable* suggestion is simply possible or feasible; a *practical* suggestion is also useful, sensible, realistic, economical, profitable, and likely to be effective or successful: □ *It may be practicable to create jobs for everyone but this would not be a practical solution to the problems of unemployment.*

practically The adverb *practically* is widely used as a synonym for 'almost', 'nearly', 'virtually', etc.: □ *I practically broke my ankle.*

practice or **practise**? The noun is *practice*, the verb is *practise*: □ *the doctor's practice* □ *the doctor who practises in our town.*

practitioner This word is sometimes misspelt, the most frequent error being the substitution of *c* or *s* for the final *t*.

pray or **prey**? These spellings are sometimes confused. The verb *pray* means 'speak to God': □ *pray for forgiveness.* The verb *prey*, which is usually followed by *on* or *upon*, means 'hunt' or 'obsess': □ *The lion preys on other animals.* □ *The problem is preying on my mind.* The noun *prey* means 'animals hunted for food': □ *birds of prey.*

pre- see HYPHEN 1; PER-, PRE-, OR PRO-?; PRE-WAR.

precautionary measure The phrase *precautionary measure* can usually be replaced by the noun *precaution*, which denotes a measure taken to avoid something harmful or undesirable: □ *The police closed the road as a precaution(ary measure) against flooding.*

precede or **proceed**? *Precede* means 'come before', 'go before', or 'be before'; *proceed* means 'continue', 'go on', or 'advance': □ *September precedes October.* □ *The text is preceded by an introduction.* □ *I am unable to proceed with this work.* □ *They proceeded to dismantle the car.*

precedence or **precedent**? The noun *precedence* means 'priority' or 'superiority'; the noun *precedent* denotes a previous example that may serve as a model (in a court of law or elsewhere): □ *Should this work take precedence over our other commitments?* □ *The guests were seated in order of precedence.* □ *The committee's decision has set a precedent for future claims.* □ *This result is without precedent.*

precipitate or **precipitous**? The adjective *precipitate* means 'rushing', 'hasty', 'rash', or 'sudden'; *precipitous* means 'like a precipice' or 'very steep': □ *a precipitate decision* □ *their precipitate departure* □ *a precipitous slope.*

preclude see EXCLUDE OR PRECLUDE?

precondition see CONDITION OR PRECONDITION?

predecessor The noun *predecessor* denotes the previous holder of an office, post, etc.: □ *Her predecessor had left the accounts in a mess.* Although the words *predecessor* and *decease* (meaning 'death') are both derived from the Latin verb *dēcēdere*, a predecessor is not necessarily dead: the Latin verb means 'go away', not 'die'.

predicative see ADJECTIVES.

predict or **predicate**? To *predict* is to foretell; the verb *predicate* means 'affirm', 'declare', or 'imply': □ *It is impossible to predict the result of tomorrow's match.* □ *They predicated that the accident had been caused by negligence.*

preface see FOREWORD OR PREFACE?; PREFIX OR PREFACE?

prefer The elements that follow the verb *prefer* should be separated by *to*, not *than*: □ *I prefer cricket to football.* □ *She prefers watching television to reading a book.*

prefix or **preface**? The words *prefix* and *preface* are most frequently used as nouns (see FOREWORD OR PREFACE?; PREFIXES AND SUFFIXES). As verbs, both can mean 'add at the beginning' or 'put before', although *preface* is more common: □ *She prefaced/prefixed her speech with a few words of welcome.*

prefixes and suffixes Prefixes and suffixes are elements attached to a word in order to form a new word. Prefixes are attached to the beginnings of words and include: □ *un-* □ *dis-* □ *anti-* □ *non-* □ *ex-* (see also HYPHEN 1). Suffixes are attached to the ends of words and include: □ *-ism* □ *-ful* □ *-dom* □ *-ology* □ *-ship*.

prelude The frequent use of the noun *prelude* in the sense of 'introduction' is disliked by some users: □ *The leaders had an informal meeting this morning as a prelude to next week's summit in Geneva.*

premier The adjective *premier* is best avoided where *foremost*, *principal*, *first*, etc., would be adequate or more appropriate: □ *We consulted one of the country's premier authorities on the subject.*

premiere Some people dislike the use of the word *premiere* as a verb, meaning 'give the first performance of': □ *The film will be premiered in New York.*

premises The noun *premises*, denoting a building (or buildings) and any accompanying land or grounds, is always plural: □ *Their new premises are on the other side of the railway line.*

preoccupied see OCCUPIED OR PREOCCUPIED?

preparation The noun *preparation* is sometimes misspelt, a frequent error being *the substitution of -per- for -par-*, as in *desperation*.

prepositions *Prepositions* are such words as: □ *at* □ *with* □ *of* □ *up* □ *before* that show the relation of a noun or noun equivalent to the rest of the sentence.

PREPOSITIONS

The following table lists mainly verbs, adjectives, and nouns that have a choice of two interchangeable prepositions. Entries are in alphabetical order, showing the preposition that is recommended for the particular meaning of the word shown. If you want further details on the meaning, context, and use of the expressions listed, then you should consult a good dictionary.

Where there is a fuller discussion, cross-references, e.g., see ADMIT, are also included to main entries in the *Good English Guide*.

abound to abound with *or* in: □ *The river abounds with* [or *in*] *salmon.*

absolve to absolve somebody of *or* from: □ *They absolved us of* [or *from*] *blame.*

acquit I to acquit somebody of *or* on (a charge): □ *She was acquitted of* [or *on*] *all charges.* II to acquit somebody of (a crime): □ *She was acquitted of manslaughter.*

adjunct an adjunct to *or* of: □ *as an adjunct to* [or *of*] *the normal service.*

admit (to; of) see ADMIT.

affiliated affiliated to *or* with: organizations affiliated to [or *with*] *the union.*

affinity (with; for) see AFFINITY.

afraid I afraid of (something frightening): □ *I'm afraid of the dark.* II afraid for (something at risk): □ *I'm afraid for his safety.*

allied I allied with *or* to (another country, etc.): □ *Britain was allied with* [or *to*] *France in both world wars.* II (= connected) allied to: □ *The rise in crime is allied to the increase in poverty.*

alternate I to alternate between (two things): □ *Control of the council has alternated between Labour and the Conservatives for the past 20 years.* II to alternate with (another thing): □ *Joy alternated with sorrow.*

analogous analogous to *or* with: □ *This phenomenon is analogous to* [or *with*] *the reproductive* *process in animals.*

angry I angry about *or* at (something): □ *She was angry about* [or *at*] *the way they had treated him.* **II** angry with (somebody): □ *Are you angry with me?*

antidote an antidote to *or* for: □ *Alcohol should not be used as an antidote to* [or *for*] *depression.*

antipathy (an) antipathy to *or* towards: □ *a general feeling of antipathy to* [or *towards*] *the new manager.*

appropriate appropriate to *or* for: □ *language that is appropriate to* [or *for*] *the situation in which it is used.*

approval approval of *or* for: □ *They expressed their approval of* [or *for*] *our plan.*

arise to arise from *or* out of: □ *issues arising from* [or *out of*] *the discussion.*

assist to assist in *or* with: □ *He assisted her in* [or *with*] *her research.*

attempt I an attempt at (something): □ *Her first attempt at setting up a business ended in failure.* **II** an attempt on (somebody's life, a record, etc.): □ *He had survived two earlier attempts on his life.*

attribute (to, *not* with) see ATTRIBUTE.

averse (to *or* from) see ADVERSE OR AVERSE?

beg to beg (something) from *or* of: □ *She begged food from* [or *of*] *her neighbours.*

begin I to begin with (something): □ *The word 'knee' begins with the letter 'k'.* **II** to begin by (-ing): □ *He began by thanking the visiting speaker.*

benefit to benefit from *or* by: □ *Most old age pensioners will benefit from* [or *by*] *these changes in taxation.*

blow a blow on *or* to: □ *a blow on* [or *to*] *her left shoulder.*

book a book about *or* on: □ *a book about* [or *on*] *motor sport.*

born I (from the parents' point of view) born to: □ *Three daughters were born to them, but no sons.* **II** (from the child's point of view) born of: □ *He was born of wealthy parents.*

borrow (from, *not* off) see BORROW.

bridge a bridge over *or* across: □ *a bridge over* [or *across*] *the railway line.*

burden a burden on *or* to: □ *The unemployed are a burden on* [or *to*] *the taxpayer.*

care I (= feel affection) to care for *or* about: □ *Most people care for* [or *about*] *their family.* **II** (= like) to care for: □ *I don't care for foreign food.* **III** (= look after) to care for: □ *He cared for the wounded fox.* **IV** (= be concerned) to care about: □ *She doesn't care about the cost.*

cater to cater for *or* to: □ *The leisure centre caters for* [or *to*] *the needs of the local people.*

centre (on, *not* around) see CENTRE ON OR CENTRE AROUND?

chat to chat to *or* with: □ *chatting to* [or *with*] *his friend on the phone.*

cheat to cheat somebody of *or* out of: □ *She had been cheated of* [or *out of*] *her inheritance.*

clever I clever at (something): □ *He's not very clever at maths.* **II** clever with (a tool, one's hands, etc.): □ *She's clever with a needle.*

coat to coat something in *or* with: □ *Coat the fish in* [or *with*] *breadcrumbs.*

collaborate to collaborate in *or* on: □ *They have collaborated in* [or *on*] *a number of musicals.*

commensurate commensurate with: □ *a position commensurate with his abilities.*

communicate I to communicate with: □ *They communicated with each other through an interpreter.* **II** to communicate something to: □ *She communicated the news to her staff.*

compare (to; with) see COMPARE TO OR COMPARE WITH?

compete to compete with *or* against: □ *We found ourselves competing with* [or *against*] *three other companies for the contract.*

competent competent at *or* in: □ *Applicants must be competent at* [or *in*] *word processing.*

concerned (about *or* for; with) see CONCERNED.

conducive conducive to: □ *an environment conducive to mental concentration.*

confide I to confide in: □ *He confided in his sister.* **II** to confide something to: □ *He confided his problems to his sister.*

conform to conform to *or* with: □ *The results did not conform to* [or *with*] *our expectations.*

connect I (= join) to connect something to *or* with: □ *A narrow lane connects the farm to* [or *with*] *the village.* **II** (= associate) to connect something with: □ *The broken window may not be connected with the robbery.*

consist (of; in) see CONSIST OF OR CONSIST IN?

contingent contingent on: □ *The success or failure of the strike is contingent on these negotiations.*

convenient convenient for *or* to: □ *Come whenever it is convenient for* [or *to*] *you.*

conversant conversant with: □ *She is not yet conversant with the procedure.*

correspond (with; to) see CORRESPOND.

cover to cover something in *or* with: □ *The floor was covered in* [or *with*] *sawdust.*

criterion a criterion of *or* for: □ *the only criterion of* [or *for*] success.

culminate to culminate in: □ *The rebellion culminated in civil war.*

date to date from *or* back to: □ *This custom dates from* [or *back to*] *the 16th century.*
deal I to deal in (something bought and sold): □ *They deal in antique furniture.* **II** to deal with (a situation, problem, subject, person, etc.): □ *The police were called in to deal with the riot.*
defer to defer to: □ *She deferred to our wishes.*
desert to desert from (the armed forces): □ *He deserted from his regiment.*
detrimental detrimental to: □ *Smoking is detrimental to health.*
devoid devoid of: □ *The landscape is devoid of interesting features.*
die I to die of *or* from: □ *Thousands died of* [or *from*] *starvation during the drought.* **II** to die from (an injury): □ *He died from his wounds.*
different (from *or* to *or* than) see **DIFFERENT FROM, DIFFERENT TO, OR DIFFERENT THAN?**
disappointed I disappointed with *or* at (something): □ *She was disappointed with* [or *at*] *her results.* **II** disappointed in *or* with (somebody): □ *I felt that my parents were disappointed in* [or *with*] me.
disparity I a disparity between (two or more people or things): □ *the disparity between the upper and lower classes.* **II** a disparity in (size, age, income, etc.): □ *The disparity in their ages did not affect their performance in the tests.*
dissimilar dissimilar to *or* from: □ *The flavour is not dissimilar to* [or *from*] *that of yoghurt.*
dream to dream of *or* about: □ *I often dream of* [or *about*] *the house where I used to live.* □ *She dreamt of* [or *about*] *becoming a brain surgeon.*
due I due to (a cause): □ *The change in the weather may be due to global warming.* **II** due for (something owed, deserved, etc.): □ *I'm due for a pay rise in September.*
end I to end in *or* with: □ *words ending in* [or *with*] *'-er'.* **II** (= have as result) to end in: □ *Their marriage ended in divorce.* **III** (= finish) to end (something) with: □ *He ended his speech with a vote of thanks.*
endemic endemic in *or* to: □ *The disease is endemic in* [or *to*] *Africa.*
engrossed engrossed in: □ *She was engrossed in her work and didn't hear the doorbell.*
engulfed engulfed in: □ *The car was engulfed in flames.*
entangled I entangled in (something): □ *His fishing line was entangled in the seaweed.* **II** entangled with (another thing): □ *His fishing line was entangled with mine.* **III** (= involved in dif-

ficulties) entangled in: □ *become entangled in criminal activities.* **IV** (= involved in a difficult relationship) entangled with: □ *get entangled with some idle young man.*

entrance the entrance to *or* of: □ *the entrance to* [or *of*] *the theatre.*

equal (to; with) see EQUAL TO OR EQUAL WITH?

essential essential to *or* for: □ *Money is not essential to* [or *for*] *happiness.*

excel to excel at *or* in: □ *She excels at* [or *in*] *creative writing.*

expert I an expert on *or* in (a subject): □ *We need the advice of an expert on* [or *in*] *commercial law.* **II** an expert at *or* in (an activity): □ *He's an expert at* [or *in*] *problem-solving.*

explanation I an explanation for *or* of (an occurrence, situation, behaviour, etc.): □ *There's no scientific explanation for* [or *of*] *the phenomenon.* **II** an explanation of (something complicated): □ *an explanation of the theory of relativity.*

familiar I familiar to (somebody): □ *Her name is familiar to me.* **II** familiar with (something): □ *I'm not familiar with her poetry.*

fed up fed up with: □ *I'm fed up with his rude remarks.*

fight to fight with *or* against (an opponent, enemy, etc.): □ *The Cavaliers fought with* [or *against*] *the Roundheads.*

fill (in; out) see FILL IN OR FILL OUT?

free free of *or* from: □ *The path is free of* [or *from*] obstacles.

fret to fret about *or* over: □ *Don't fret about* [or *over*] *it.*

friend I a friend of: □ *a friend of Mary's.* **II** a friend to (somebody who needs help): □ *a friend to the needy.*

fuss a fuss about *or* over: □ *There's no need to make such a fuss about* [or *over*] such a trivial matter.

gamble I to gamble with (what is at stake): □ *Don't gamble with your health.* **II** to gamble on (what is uncertain): □ *I'm gambling on her accepting my offer.*

grieve to grieve for *or* over: □ *She grieved for* [or *over*] *the death of her horse.*

grounded I grounded on (a foundation): □ *The story is grounded on fact.* **II** grounded in (a subject): □ *The children are grounded in road safety.*

guilty I guilty of (a crime): □ *He was found guilty of manslaughter.* **II** to plead guilty to (a crime): □ *He pleaded guilty to all the charges.* **III** to feel guilty about (something): □ *She felt guilty about taking time off work.*

hanker to hanker after *or* for: □ *those who hanker after* [or *for*] *power.*

happy happy about *or* with: □ *Are you happy about* [or *with*] *the arrangements?*
hatred hatred for *or* of: □ *Her hatred for* [or *of*] *her father.*
hazardous hazardous to *or* for: □ *These sharp edges can be hazardous to* [or *for*] *young children.*
hear I (= receive news from) to hear from: □ *I've not heard from her for years.* **II** (= know about) to hear of: □ *I'd never heard of the disease before.* **III** (= find out about) to hear about *or* of: □ *I only heard about* [or *of*] *his promotion yesterday.*
identical (with *or* to) see IDENTICAL WITH OR IDENTICAL TO?
ignorant I ignorant of (a fact): □ *foreign tourists who are ignorant of the law.* **II** ignorant about (a subject): □ *I'm pretty ignorant about football.*
immune (to; from) see IMMUNE FROM OR IMMUNE TO?
impervious impervious to: □ *She is impervious to criticism.*
incentive (an) incentive to *or* for: □ *an incentive to* [or *for*] *their employees to work harder.*
indifferent (to, *not* about) see INDIFFERENT.
indignant I indignant at *or* about (something): □ *He was indignant at* [or *about*] *having to do the washing-up.* **II** indignant with (somebody): □ *She seemed indignant with me.*
inferior inferior to: □ *This novel is inferior to his last one.*
information information on *or* about: □ *Do you have any information on* [or *about*] *the company?*
infringement (an) infringement of *or* on: □ *an infringement of* [or *on*] *our privacy.*
insulate to insulate something from *or* against: □ *The cupboard next to the cooker is insulated from* [or *against*] *the heat of the oven.*
intended I intended as (something): □ *The message was intended as a warning.* **II** intended for (a person, a purpose): □ *The table is not intended for sitting on.*
interfere I (= meddle) to interfere with: □ *Don't interfere with my papers.* **II** (= intrude) to interfere in: □ *The police are reluctant to interfere in a domestic dispute.* **III** (= abuse sexually) to interfere with: □ *He denied interfering with the girl.*
involved I (= concerned; taking part) involved in *or* with: □ *a meeting of all the people involved in* [or *with*] *the project.* ***II** (= having a close relationship) involved with:* □ *She's involved with a married man.*
jealous jealous of: □ *He was jealous of her success.*
judging judging by *or* from: □ *Judging by* [or *from*] *the*

design, I'd say this chair was at least 50 years old.

land I to land somebody in (a situation): □ *You'll land yourself in trouble.* **II** to land somebody with (something unwanted): □ *I was landed with the job of clearing up the mess.*

learn I (= receive information) to learn of *or* about: □ *When did you learn of* [or *about*] *the accident?* **II** (= gain knowledge) to learn about: □ *We learnt about the Vikings last week.*

liable I (= responsible) liable for: □ *She is liable for their debts.* **II** (= susceptible) liable to: □ *He is liable to epileptic attacks.*

linger I (= be slow) to linger over: □ *He lingered over his breakfast.* **II** (= dwell) to linger on: □ *Don't let your mind linger on the unpleasant details.*

live I to live on (money, food): □ *We can't live on my wages.* **II** to live off (a source of income): □ *She lived off her parents for many years.*

love I love for (somebody): □ *his love for his children.* **II** love of (something): □ *her love of tennis.*

lust to lust for *or* after: □ *He lusted for* [or *after*] *fame.*

make to make something from *or* out of: □ *She made a model of the Eiffel Tower from* [or *out of*] *matchsticks.*

mediate I to mediate in (a situation): □ *An independent adviser was called in to mediate in the dispute.* **II** to mediate between (people): □ *Who will mediate between the union and the management?*

memory I a memory of (a particular thing): □ *I have no memory of the incident.* **II** a memory for (a particular type of thing): □ *I have a very poor memory for names.*

merge I to merge with *or* into (something else): □ *On the horizon, the sea appeared to merge with* [or *into*] *the sky.* **II** to merge with (another business, company, etc.): □ *Cadbury merged with Schweppes.* **III** to merge into (the combined group): □ *The three companies merged into one.*

militate to militate against: □ *His left-wing opinions militated against his appointment as headmaster.*

mixed up I (= involved) mixed up in: □ *Several of the president's aides were mixed up in the conspiracy.* **II** (= confused) mixed up with: □ *You've got Jane's telephone number mixed up with Sarah's.*

name I (in British English) to name somebody or something after: □ *He was named after his grandfather.* **II** (in American English) to name somebody or something for: □ *The airport is named for John F. Kennedy.*

native I (noun) a native of: □ *She's a native of Sweden.* **II** (adjective) native to: □ *The bird is native to Australia.*

nominate I (= propose) to nominate somebody for (a position, office, etc.): □ *He was nominated for the post of treasurer.* **II** (= propose) to nominate somebody as (the holder of a position, office, etc.): He was nominated as treasurer. **III** (= appoint) to nominate somebody to: □ *She was nominated to the board of directors.*

opinion an opinion of *or* about: □ *What's your opinion of* [or *about*] *their proposal?*

opposite (of; to) see OPPOSITE.

parallel parallel to *or* with: □ *The shelf should be parallel to* [or *with*] *the bottom of the cupboard.*

partake I to partake of (food, drink, etc.): □ *She partook of a glass of wine.* **II** to partake in (an activity): □ *I did not partake in the ceremony.*

persevere to persevere in *or* with: □ *They persevered in* [or *with*] *their efforts to dam the stream.*

pivot to pivot on: □ *Everything pivots on his response.*

possessed I (= having) possessed of: □ *He is possessed of an ability to communicate with animals.* **II** (= dominated) possessed by: □ *She was possessed by a desire for revenge.*

precondition a precondition of *or* for: □ *Freedom of speech is a precondition of* [or *for*] *true democracy.*

predispose to predispose somebody to: □ *His background predisposed him to a life of crime.*

prefer (to, *not* than) see PREFER.

prerequisite a prerequisite of *or* for: □ *A good education is not a prerequisite of* [or *for*] *a successful career.*

preside to preside at *or* over: □ *The chairman presided at* [or *over*] *the meeting.*

proficient proficient in *or* at: □ *Applicants must be proficient in* [or *at*] *French and German.*

proportion I in proportion to: □ *The cost of the project will increase in proportion to the time spent on it.* **II** out of proportion to: □ *The animal's head looks out of proportion to its body.*

protect to protect somebody or something from *or* against: □ *This vaccination will protect you from* [or *against*] *a number of tropical diseases.*

quest I a quest for: □ *The never-ending quest for truth.* **II** in quest of: □ *She travelled the world in quest of her missing brother.*

quibble to quibble about *or* over: □ *Let's not quibble about* [or *over*] *the details.*

rail to rail at *or* against: □ *Protes-*

ters railed at [or *against*] *the reform of the abortion law.*

rankle to rankle with: □ *Her attitude rankled with him.*

recoil to recoil from *or* at: □ *She recoiled from* [or *at*] *the prospect of meeting him again.*

reconcile I to reconcile something or somebody with: □ *I cannot reconcile this theory with scientific fact.* **II** to reconcile oneself to: □ *We must reconcile ourselves to a lower standard of living.*

reek I to reek of: □ *His breath reeked of alcohol.* **II** (in figurative use) to reek of *or* with: □ *The affair reeks of* [or *with*] *corruption.*

relation in relation to: □ *The price of these video games seems excessively high in relation to the cost of producing them.*

remind I (= cause to think of) to remind somebody of: □ *The smell of pine forests reminds me of my childhood in Scotland.* **II** (= cause to remember) to remind somebody about *or* of: □ *She reminded me about* [or *of*] *the promise I had made.*

renege to renege on: □ *They reneged on the deal.*

repentance repentance for: □ *repentance for her past misdemeanours.*

replace (with; by) see REPLACE OR SUBSTITUTE?

reproach to reproach somebody with *or* for: □ *She reproached me with* [or *for*] *my carelessness.*

resign I to resign *or* to resign from (a position, office, etc.): □ *She resigned (from) the presidency.* **II** to resign as (the holder of a position, office, etc.): □ *She resigned as president.*

respect I in respect of: □ *In respect of value for money, this package is the best buy.* **II** with respect to: □ *With respect to your letter of 24 July, ...*

responsible I responsible for (something): □ *The landlord is responsible for the maintenance of the building.* **II** responsible to (somebody): □ *The directors of the company are responsible to the shareholders.*

result I to result in (the effect): □ *Drug abuse resulted in her premature death.* **II** to result from (the cause): □ *Her premature death resulted from drug abuse.*

rob to rob somebody of: □ *The incident robbed him of his dignity.*

satire a satire on: □ *The novel is a satire on totalitarianism.*

saturate to saturate something with *or* in: □ *The rug was saturated with* [or *in*] *dirty water.*

scared I (adjective) scared of: □ *He's scared of spiders.* **II** (past participle) scared by: □ *We were scared by their threats.*

sceptical sceptical about *or* of: □ *I remain sceptical about* [or *of*] *her motives.*

sell to sell for *or* at (a price): □ *These houses normally sell for* [or *at*] *around £100,000.*

sensitive I (= affected by) sensitive to: □ *He is too sensitive to criticism.* **II** (= self-conscious about) sensitive about: □ *She is very sensitive about her large nose.*

separate separate from: □ *Keep raw meat separate from cooked meat.*

serve to serve as *or* for: □ *The sofa serves as* [or *for*] *a spare bed.*

share I to share in (something): □ *We shared in the household chores.* **II** to share something with somebody: □ *I shared the household chores with my flatmate.*

sick sick of (something boring or annoying): □ *I'm sick of hearing about your problems.*

similar similar to: □ *Their car is similar to ours.*

skill skill at *or* in: □ *The job requires considerable skill at* [or *in*] *dealing with difficult people.*

smothered smothered in *or* with: □ *The vegetables were smothered in* [or *with*] *cheese sauce.*

sorry sorry for *or* about: □ *I'm sorry for* [or *about*] *what I said yesterday.*

speak I (= address) to speak to: □ *He hasn't spoken to his daughter for years.* **II** (= have a conversation) to speak to *or* with: □ *I spoke to* [or *with*] *the manager on the phone.*

speculate to speculate on *or* about: □ *There's no point in speculating on* [or *about*] *what might happen.*

sponge to sponge off *or* on: □ *You can't sponge off* [or *on*] *your family for the rest of your life.*

strive to strive for *or* after: □ *Some minority groups are still striving for* [or *after*] *equality of opportunity.*

stumble to stumble across *or* on: □ *I stumbled across* [or *on*] *the solution to the problem.*

substitute (for) see REPLACE OR SUBSTITUTE?

suited suited to *or* for: □ *She's not suited to* [or *for*] *this type of work.*

superior superior to: □ *This wine is superior to the one we had in the restaurant.*

surprised (by; at) see SURPRISED.

susceptible (to; of) see SUSCEPTIBLE.

symbol I (= emblem) a symbol of: □ *An olive branch is a symbol of peace.* **II** (= sign) a symbol for: □ *A diagonal cross is the symbol for multiplication.*

tantamount tantamount to: □ *Her offer was tantamount to*

bribery.
think I (= ponder) think about: □*I've been thinking about your idea.* **II** (= formulate) think of: □*Can you think of a better idea?* **III** (= have an opinion) think of: □*What do you think of the idea?*
thirst to thirst for *or* after: □*They thirsted for* [or *after*] *revenge.*
tired tired of: □*I'm tired of waiting.*
tower to tower above *or* over: □*The cliff towered above* [or *over*] *him.*
tremble I to tremble at (something frightening): □*I trembled at the thought.* **II** to tremble with (fear, excitement, etc.): □*The children were trembling with fear.*
turn I (= change) to turn to *or* into: □*The snow had turned to* [or *into*] *slush.* **II** (= be transformed) to turn into: □*The frog turned into a handsome prince.*
uncertain uncertain of *or* about: □*She was uncertain of* [or *about*] *the terms of the contract.*
unfair unfair to *or* on: □*The present system is unfair to* [or *on*] *the self-employed.*
upsurge an upsurge in *or* of: □*an upsurge in* [or *of*] *enthusiasm for the project.*
use I to use something as (something): □*I use this cloth as a duster.* **II** to use something for (-ing): □*I use this cloth for dusting.*
variation I (= change) a variation in *or* of: □*The machine responds to variations in* [or *of*] *temperature.* **II** (= different form) a variation on: □*a variation on the usual theme.*
vital vital to *or* for: □*Their co-operation is vital to* [or *for*] *the success of the mission.*
war I a war with *or* against: □*wars with* [or *against*] *neighbouring countries.* **II** at war with: □*France was at war with Spain.* **III** to declare war on: □*Britain declared war on Germany.*
wary wary of *or* about: □*She's wary of* [or *about*] *giving her address to strangers.*
wonder I (= marvel) to wonder at: □*I wondered at his strength.* **II** (= speculate) to wonder about: □*I wondered about the reason for his departure.*
wring to wring something from *or* out of: □*They tried in vain to wring the truth from* [or *out of*] *her.*

prerequisite or **perquisite**? A *prerequisite* is a precondition; a *perquisite* is a benefit, privilege, or exclusive right: □ *A degree is not a prerequisite for a career in journalism.* □ *A company car is often regarded as a perquisite.*

prerequisite or **requisite**? Both these words may be used as nouns or adjectives. *Requisite* relates to anything that is required, necessary, essential, or indispensable; *prerequisite* relates to something that is required in advance: □ *Does the building have the requisite number of fire exits?* □ *The shop sells pens, paper, and other writing requisites.* □ *Physical fitness is prerequisite to/a prerequisite of success at sport.* See also PREREQUISITE OR PERQUISITE?

prescribe or **proscribe**? To *prescribe* is to lay down as a rule or to advise or order as a remedy; to *proscribe* is to condemn, prohibit, outlaw, or exile: □ *The union has prescribed a new procedure for dealing with complaints.* □ *Surrogate motherhood has been proscribed in Britain.* □ *Proscribing the doctor's habit of prescribing* (*Daily Telegraph* headline).

presently Some people object to the increasingly frequent use of the adverb *presently* in place of *currently*, *at present*, or *now*: □ *Mr John Smith, presently leader of the opposition.* □ *The company presently manufactures components for the electronics industry.*

pressure or **pressurize**? The verb *pressure*, which literally means 'apply pressure to', is frequently used in the figurative sense of 'coerce'. The literal meaning of the verb *pressurize* is 'increase the pressure in', but it is also used figuratively in British English.

prestige The noun *prestige*, denoting the high status, esteem, or renown derived from wealth or success, is usually pronounced [pres*teezh*].

prestigious The adjective *prestigious* is frequently used in the sense of 'having or conferring prestige': □ *new ways of raising money for the country's most prestigious opera house* □ *The company will shortly be relocating to prestigious new offices in the City.*

presume see ASSUME OR PRESUME?

presumptuous or **presumptive**? *Presumptuous* means 'bold', 'forward', or 'impudent'; *presumptive* means 'based on presumption or probability' or 'giving reasonable grounds for belief': □ *It's rather presumptuous of him to make such a request.* □ *This is only presumptive evidence.*

pretence, pretension, or **pretentiousness**? The noun *pretence* denotes the act of pretending; a *pretension* is a claim; *pretentiousness* means 'ostentation' or 'affectation': □ *She made a pretence of closing the door.* □ *He has no pretensions to fame.* □ *Their pretentiousness does not impress me.*

prevaricate or **procrastinate**? To *prevaricate* is to be evasive, misleading, or untruthful; to *procrastinate* is to delay, defer, or put off: □ *She prevaricated in order to avoid revealing her husband's whereabouts.* □ *He procrastinated in the hope of avoiding the work altogether.*

prevent When the verb *prevent* is followed by an *-ing* form in formal contexts, the *-ing* form should be preceded either by *from* or by a possessive adjective or noun: □ *They prevented me from winning.* □ *They prevented Andrew from winning.* □ *They prevented my winning.* □ *They prevented Andrew's winning.*

preventive or **preventative**? Either word may be used as an adjective or noun, but *preventive* is the more frequent: □ *preventive measures* □ *preventative surgery* □ *This drug is used as a preventive/preventative.*

pre-war This word is usually hyphenated, although some dictionaries list it as a one-word compound. See also HYPHEN 1.

prey see PRAY OR PREY?

price see COST OR PRICE?

prima facie This Latin phrase is used adverbially or adjectivally in the sense of 'at first sight', '(based) on first impressions', or 'apparently true': □ *Her argument seems reasonable prima facie.* □ *There is prima facie evidence to support his case.*

primarily Many users prefer to stress this word on the first syllable [*prīmărĕli*], but this is very difficult to say unless one is speaking slowly and carefully. The pronunciation with the stress on the second syllable [prīmerrĕli] is becoming increasingly common in British English, although it is disliked by many. It is the standard pronunciation in American English. See also STRESS.

prime Some people dislike the frequent use of the adjective *prime* in the sense of 'best', 'most important', 'principal', etc., especially when it is applied to something that is not of the highest quality, significance, or rank: □ *in prime condition* □ *the prime position* □ *a prime example.*

primeval This word, meaning 'of the first ages', is usually spelt *primeval* but in British English may also be spelt *primaeval*. See also -AE- AND -OE-.

principal or **principle**? These two spellings are often confused. The adjective *principal* means 'of the most importance': □ *the principal cause*; the noun *principal* refers to the head of an organization: □ *the principal of a college. Principle* is always a noun and refers to a fundamental truth or standard: □ *moral principles.* The adjectival form is *principled.*

principal parts The *principal parts* of a verb are the main inflected forms from which all the other verb forms can be derived. In English they usually include the infinitive, the present participle, the past tense, and past participle. The principal parts of *give*, for example, would be: □ *give, giving, gave, given.* Often the past tense and past participle are the same, and do not both have to be listed: □ *walk, walking, walked.* The present participle is not always included when it is derived regularly, as in: □ *know, knew, known.*

principle see PRINCIPAL OR PRINCIPLE?

prioritize The verb *prioritize*, meaning 'put in order of priority' or 'give priority to', is disliked by some users as an example of the increasing tendency to coin new verbs by adding the suffix *-ize* to nouns and adjectives: □ *The methods of increasing industrial output have been prioritized.* □ *Where women are, in fact, seen to prioritise their career, they are considered in some way 'unnatural', 'unfeminine' or 'on the shelf'*

(*The Bookseller*).

prior to Many people object to the unnecessary use of the phrase *prior to* in place of the simpler and more natural preposition *before*: □ *Players and singers rehearsed the works during the afternoon prior to performing them in the evening* (*Chichester Observer*).

prise or **prize**? For the meaning 'to force open', either spelling can be used in British English, but *prise* is more common: □ *In the end we managed to prise the lid off*.

pristine The use of *pristine* to mean 'spotlessly clean', 'pure', or 'as good as new' is acceptable to most users: □ *a pristine tablecloth* □ *He made the packet look untouched and in pristine condition* (*Daily Telegraph*).

privacy This word has two pronunciations: [*pri*văsi] and [*prī*văsi] in British English.

privatization or **denationalization**? Both these nouns refer to the transfer or restoration by a government of nationalized industries to private ownership: □ *the privatization of British Telecom* □ *the denationalization of the iron and steel industry* □ *Electricity charges are likely to rise by 15 to 20 per cent after privatisation to ensure that de-nationalisation is successful* (*Daily Telegraph*).

privilege This word, meaning 'special right or advantage', is often misspelt. Note particularly the second *-i-* and the first *-e-*. Remember also that there is no *d* as in *ledge*.

prize see PRISE OR PRIZE?

pro- see PER-, PRE-, OR PRO-?

proactive *Proactive*, a technical term in psychology, is entering general usage as a vogue word, meaning 'taking the initiative; acting in anticipation rather than reacting after the event': □ *a proactive approach to business* □ *a proactive role in the marketplace*. This word is disliked by many people and should not be overused in this sense.

probe In the headline language of popular newspapers the noun *probe* is often used in place of the longer *enquiry* or *investigation*: □ *Crucial questions the BBC poll probe must answer* (*Sunday Times*). See also JOURNALESE.

procedure or **proceeding**? The noun *procedure* denotes a way of doing something; the noun *proceeding* (or, more frequently, *proceedings*) means 'something that is done': □ *to follow the established procedure* □ *to take part in the proceedings.*

proceed see PRECEDE OR PROCEED?

proceeding see PROCEDURE OR PROCEEDING?

process The noun *process* is always pronounced with the stress on the first syllable, [*prō*ses]. (The pronunciation [*pros*es], with a short *-o-*, is largely restricted to American English.) The verb *process* is also stressed on the first syllable in most contexts; however, in the rare sense 'move (as if) in a procession': □ *They processed down the avenue,* the second syllable is stressed, [prŏ*ses*].

pro-choice see PRO-LIFE.

procrastinate see PREVARICATE OR PROCRASTINATE?

prodigal *Prodigal* means 'recklessly wasteful', 'extravagant', or 'lavish'. The use of the adjective *prodigal* to mean 'returning home after a long absence' is based on a misunderstanding of the word in the New Testament parable, and is disliked by some users. The use of the noun *prodigal* to mean 'returned wanderer' or 'repentant sinner' is acceptable to most.

prodigy or **protégé**? The noun *prodigy*, meaning 'marvel', is used to denote an exceptionally talented person, especially a child. A *protégé* is someone who receives help, guidance, protection, patronage, etc., from a more influential or experienced person: □ *one of Lord Olivier's protégés.*

produce or **product**? Both these nouns denote something that is produced. *Produce* refers to things that have been produced by growing or farming, whereas *product* usually refers to industrially produced goods: □ *farm produce* □ *the company's latest product.*

productivity The noun *productivity*, frequently used in industrial contexts, relates to efficiency or rate of production; it is not synonymous with *output*, which denotes the amount produced: □ *a productivity bonus* □ *The installation of new machinery will increase the company's productivity; employing more workers will only increase its output.*

professional The adjective *professional* is applied to people who are engaged in a profession or who take part in a sport or other activity for gain: □ *doctors, lawyers, and other professional people* □ *a professional golfer/musician.* The noun *professional* is used to denote such people.

professor This word is sometimes misspelt. Note the single *f*, *-ss-*, and the *-or* ending.

proffer see OFFER OR PROFFER?

profile The noun *profile* is widely used in the expression *keep a low profile*, meaning 'be inconspicuous or unobtrusive' or 'avoid attention or publicity': □ *The group has kept a low profile since the arrest of its leader.* This usage is disliked by some.

prognosis see DIAGNOSIS OR PROGNOSIS?

program or **programme**? Both these words may be used as nouns or verbs. In British English the spelling *program* is restricted to the computing sense of '(provide with) a series of coded instructions': □ *a computer program* □ *to program a computer. Program* is also the American spelling of the word *programme*.

prohibit see FORBID OR PROHIBIT?

project The word *project*, as a noun, meaning 'scheme or plan', is usually pronounced [projekt]. The alternative [prōjekt] is sometimes heard but is avoided by careful users.

pro-life The adjective *pro-life* is used to describe an organization, movement, etc., that supports the right to the maintenance of the life of the unborn. Those with *pro-life* views are in favour of limitations on the availability of legal abortions and a ban on experiments on human embryos. *Pro-life* is considered by some to be a euphemism for *anti-abortion. Pro-choice* may be considered a euphemism for *pro-abortion*.

prolific The adjective *prolific* means 'very productive'; it is applied to the person or thing that produces rather than to what is produced: □ *A prolific author, she* *writes two or three new novels every year.*

prone see LIABLE OR LIKELY?; PROSTRATE, PRONE, OR SUPINE?

pronouns *Pronouns* are words that are used to replace nouns or noun phrases to refer to something or someone: □ *I* □ *she* □ *him* □ *it* □ *you* □ *they*, etc. The main difficulty that arises with pronouns is in the use of the personal pronoun, where many people are confused between the subject and object forms. Such phrases as: □ *Everything comes to he who waits.* □ *It was up to Julia and I*, though incorrect, are frequently used. Remember that after verbs and prepositions, the object pronoun (*me, him, her, us, them*) should be used: □ *Everything comes to him who waits.* □ *It was up to Julia and me.* The confusion can be resolved by mentally changing the sentence slightly: □ *Things come to him* [not *he*]. □ *It was up to me* [not *I*]. Before verbs the subject pronouns (*I, he, she, we, they*) should be used: □ *I* [not *me*] *and my friend will come.* □ *She* [not *her*] *and her colleague are arguing.* See also I OR ME?

pronunciation The recommended pronunciation of English words found in dictionaries and grammar books is usually what is known as *RP* or *received pronunciation*, which more or less represents the speech of educated middle-class people from the South-East of England. Until comparatively recently, RP was regarded as 'correct' and other pronunciations were sometimes thought of as, if not actually incorrect, at least inferior. Most people now accept that there is no one standard form of English pronunciation which is correct. There is great regional variety within the United Kingdom and further variations in the speech of other English-speaking countries, and there is nothing incorrect about a pronunciation that is standard to a particular community or region.

propeller This word for a rotating device with blades is usually spelt with the ending *-er*, though *-or* is occasionally found.

proper nouns see CAPITAL

LETTERS; NOUNS.

prophecy or **prophesy**? These spellings and pronunciations are sometimes confused. The noun meaning 'prediction' is spelt *prophecy* and pronounced [*prof*isi]. The verb meaning 'utter predictions' is spelt *prophesy* and pronounced [*prof*isī].

proportion The noun *proportion* denotes a ratio; it is best avoided where *part*, *number*, *some*, etc., would be adequate or more appropriate: □ *The proportion of female students to male students has increased.* □ *Some* [not *A proportion*] *of his friends are unemployed.*

proportional or **proportionate**? The adjectives *proportional* and *proportionate* are virtually synonymous in the sense of 'in proportion': □ *a proportionate* [or *proportional*] *increase in spending* □ *the cooking time is proportional* [or *proportionate*] *to the size of the joint of meat.*

proposal or **proposition**? Both these nouns can mean 'something that is proposed, suggested, or put forward for consideration', but they are not always interchangeable: □ *the government's latest proposal/proposition* □ *That's an interesting proposition/proposal.* □ *an insurance proposal* □ *a business proposition.*

proprietary Note the spelling of this word, which is used to refer to goods sold under a particular trade name, especially the second *r*, the *ie*, and the *-ary* ending. The *a* is not always sounded in speech.

proscribe see PRESCRIBE OR PROSCRIBE?

prosecute see PERSECUTE OR PROSECUTE?

prospective see PERSPECTIVE OR PROSPECTIVE?

prostate or **prostrate**? The word *prostate* refers to a gland around the neck of the bladder in men and other male mammals. *Prostrate* means 'lying face downwards', 'exhausted' or 'overcome'; it is also used as a verb.

prostrate, **prone**, or **supine**? *Prostrate* and *prone* mean 'lying face downwards'; *supine* means 'lying face upwards'. In these senses the adjectives *prone* and *supine* are largely restricted to formal or literary usage, or to contexts where the distinction between 'face downwards' and 'face upwards' is particularly important or relevant. Elsewhere, the adjective *prostrate* (with its additional meanings of 'exhausted' or 'overcome': see PROSTATE OR PROSTRATE?) is more frequent than *prone* and may also be used in place of *supine* or in the general sense of 'lying flat': □ *She lay prostrate with exhaustion.*

protagonist Some people object to the frequent use of the noun *protagonist* to denote a supporter, especially a leading or notable supporter, of a cause, movement, idea, political party, etc.: □ *British Rail has been the chief protagonist of the pro-Tunnel view over recent years* (*The Guardian*). □ *I would find myself a protagonist of a movement to introduce sanctions on those who do not use these established trade tools* (*The Bookseller*). In such contexts *protagonist* may be better replaced by an appropriate synonym, such as *champion, advocate,* or *proponent.*

protégé see PRODIGY OR PROTÉGÉ?

protein Note the spelling of this word, especially the *-ein* ending. It is an exception to the '*i* before *e*' rule (see SPELLING 5).

pro tem The expression *pro tem* is a shortened form of the Latin phrase *pro tempore*, meaning 'for the time being' or 'temporarily': □ *Mr Jones will take charge of the sales department pro tem.*

proved or **proven**? *Proved* is the past tense of the verb *prove* and the usual form of its past participle in British English: □ *They (have) proved their innocence.* As a variant form of the past participle, *proven* is largely restricted to the Scottish legal phrase *not proven.* In British English it is more frequently used as an adjective: □ *a proven remedy.*

proverbial The cliché *the proverbial …* is often used when (part of) a proverb or other idiomatic expression is quoted: □ *It's like taking the proverbial horse to water.* □ *We found ourselves up the proverbial creek.*

provided or **providing**? The expressions *provided (that)* and *providing (that)* mean 'on the condition (that)':

□ *You may have a dog provided/providing that you look after it yourself.*

provident or **providential**? These two adjectives, both used in formal contexts, should not be confused. *Provident* means 'showing or exercising foresight' or 'thrifty'; *providential* means 'fortunate' or 'relating to divine providence': □ *They should have been more provident with their resources.* □ *A providential shower of rain brought the game to an end.*

providing see PROVIDED OR PROVIDING?

psychedelic The adjective *psychedelic,* describing hallucinogenic drugs or their effects, is sometimes spelt *psychodelic.* This spelling is acknowledged by some dictionaries but is unacceptable to many users, on the grounds that the adjective is derived from the word *psyche* rather than the prefix *psycho-*.

psychiatry The branch of medicine dealing with problems of the mind is known as *psychiatry.* Note the spelling of the first syllable: *psych-*, which is from the Greek *psychē* 'soul'.

psychological moment The phrase *psychological moment,* of German origin, is generally used with reference to the most appropriate time to produce the desired effect: □ *He waited until she had digested the news of his promotion and then, at the psychological moment, he proposed to her.*

publicly This word is frequently misspelt; there is no *-k-* before the suffix *-ly.*

pudding see DESSERT, SWEET, PUDDING, OR AFTERS?

punctilious or **punctual**? These two adjectives should not be confused. *Punctilious* is the more formal of the two and means 'scrupulously correct' or 'attentive to detail'; *punctual* means 'prompt; exactly on time': □ *He is very punctilious about etiquette.* □ *If you're called for an interview, be punctual.*

punctuation The primary purpose of punctuation is to clarify the writer's meaning. In speech the meaning is conveyed by the use of emphasis and pauses; punctuation has to serve the same purpose with written language.

Lack of punctuation or incorrect punctuation can lead to misunderstanding and ambiguity. See also APOSTROPHE; BRACKETS; CAPITAL LETTERS; COLON; COMMA; DASH; ELLIPSIS; EXCLAMATION MARK; FULL STOP; HYPHEN; ITALICS; PARAGRAPHS; QUESTION MARK; QUOTATION MARKS; SEMICOLON; SOLIDUS.

pupil or **student**? In British English the noun *pupil* denotes a child at school or a person receiving instruction from an expert; a *student* is a person who studies at an institute of further or higher education, such as a college or university: □ *a pupil at the local infant school* □ *a painting by one of Michelangelo's pupils* □ *while she was a student at Oxford.*

purposely or **purposefully**? *Purposely* means 'on purpose; intentionally' and usually refers to the reason for doing something; *purposefully* means 'in a determined way; with a definite purpose in mind' and usually indicates the manner in which something is done: □ *He purposely left his umbrella behind.* □ *She strode purposefully into the room.* The two adverbs are sometimes confused.

pusillanimous The adjective *pusillanimous*, used in formal contexts to mean 'timid' or 'cowardly', is sometimes misspelt. Note the *-ll-*, the single *-n-*, and the *-ous* ending.

putrefy This word, used in formal English to mean 'decompose' or 'rot', is sometimes misspelt. Note the ending *-efy* (like *stupefy*), in spite of the related word *putrid*.

pygmy or **pigmy**? Both of these spellings are acceptable, although the *y* spelling is preferred by some users as it shows the word's Greek origins, *pygmaios* 'dwarfish'.

Q

quality The word *quality* is often used adjectivally as a synonym for 'excellent' or 'of superior quality': □ *quality goods* □ *quality fiction* □ *a quality newspaper*. Some people object to this usage on the grounds that the noun *quality* does not always denote excellence: the quality of a product, service, etc., may be good, mediocre, or bad.

quality time The phrase *quality time* is a vogue expression applied to time spent in personal relationships, e.g., by working parents with their children; a comparatively small amount of time exclusively devoted to the needs and interests of the children: □ *an hour's quality time with the twins before they go to bed*.

quantum leap Many people object to the frequent use of the term *quantum leap* (or *quantum jump*) to denote a great change or advance: □ *Sir Geoffrey has failed to convince the South African Government that it must make the 'quantum leap' to negotiations with Mr Nelson Mandela and the African National Congress* (*The Guardian*).

quasi The Latin word *quasi*, meaning 'as if', may be combined with adjectives, in the sense of 'seemingly', 'partly', or 'almost', or with nouns, in the sense of 'resembling', 'so-called', or 'apparent': □ *quasi-religious* □ *quasi-official* □ *quasi-republics*.

quay This word for 'landing place' is sometimes misspelt. Although pronounced like *key*, note its totally different spelling.

queer The use of *queer* as an informal, often derogatory, synonym for 'homosexual', dates back to the early 20th century. In recent years it has been replaced by the word GAY, which is not derogatory.

query The verb *query* is best avoided where *ask* or *question* would be more appropriate: □ *'Where do you live?' she asked* [not *queried*].

question see BEG THE QUESTION; LEADING QUESTION; QUESTION MARK; QUESTIONS; RHETORICAL QUESTION.

question mark The primary use of the question mark is as a substitute for a full stop at the end of a sentence that is a direct question: □ *Where are you going?*, and at the end of a quoted question, within the quotation marks: □ *'Where are you going?' he asked.* It is not used for an indirect question: □ *He asked me where I was going.*

questionnaire This word is sometimes misspelt. Note the *-nn-*, unlike the single *n* in *millionaire*.

questions A *question* is a word, phrase, or sentence that asks for information and requires an answer (see also RHETORICAL QUESTION). Questions often begin with *how, what, when, where, which, who,* or *why*: □ *How did you find out?* □ *Where is it?* □ *Which one?* □ *Why?*, or with an inverted verb: □ *Is he old enough?* □ *Are you hungry?* □ *Must she?* □ *Will the car be ready tomorrow?* Direct questions are always followed by a QUESTION MARK. Indirect questions, which occur in REPORTED SPEECH, do not have a question mark at the end: □ *She asked me what I was doing.*

quick The use of the word *quick* as an adverb should generally be avoided in formal contexts: □ *Please reply quickly* [not *quick*] *to avoid disappointment.* □ *Come quick!*

quiet or **quieten**? Both these verbs may be used to mean 'soothe, calm, or allay' or 'make or become quiet'; in the second of these senses the verb is often followed by *down*.

quit or **quitted**? Either word may be used as the past tense and past participle of the verb *quit*.

quite In the sense of 'completely', 'totally', or 'entirely', the adverb *quite* is generally used with adjectives that cannot be qualified by *very*: □ *a quite excellent result* □ *a quite unnecessary remark* □ *It is quite* *impossible!* □ *The ring is quite worthless.* Used with other adjectives, *quite* usually has the meaning 'somewhat', 'fairly', or 'rather': □ *They are quite useful.* □ *The film is quite frightening.*

quitted see QUIT OR QUITTED?

quiz Some people dislike the use of the verb *quiz* in the sense of 'interrogate': □ *The police quizzed him about his involvement in the affair.* This usage is widely regarded as JOURNALESE.

quotation marks Quotation marks are used at the beginning and end of direct quotations: □ *He said, 'I'm going out now.'* □ *'All right,' she replied, 'but don't be late.'* Only the words actually spoken are placed within the quotation marks; they are not used in reported speech: □ *'I am tired,' she said.* □ *She said that she was tired.* However, in reported speech, one might use quotation marks in order to draw attention to the fact that the speaker has used certain words, particularly if one wished to dissociate oneself from the expression used: □ *He said he was in an 'ongoing situation'.* Quotation marks are used instead of italics for various literary and musical works (see TITLES). They are sometimes used by writers to indicate slang or as an apology for using a particular word or expression: □ *I gather my writing is thought to lack 'pizzazz'.*

quote The noun *quote* (short for *quotation*) and the plural form *quotes* (short for *quotation marks*) are best restricted to informal contexts: □ *It's a quote from Shakespeare.* □ *We'd better get a quote for having the fence repaired.* □ *Should the last sentence be in quotes?*

R

racism or **racialism**? Both these nouns are used in the sense of 'racial prejudice or discrimination', *racism* being more frequent than *racialism* in modern usage: □ *The company was accused of racism in its recruitment policy.*

rack or **wrack**? These two words are sometimes confused. *Rack* is used for a framework for storing or displaying things: □ *a luggage rack* □ *a shoe rack. Rack* is also used for the torturing frame: □ *on the rack.* As a verb *rack* means 'cause to suffer pain': □ *racked with uncertainty;* one also *racks one's brains*. The expression *rack and ruin*, 'a state of collapse', may also be spelt *wrack and ruin*; *nerve-racking*, 'causing great anxiety and tension', has the variant spelling *nerve-wracking*. *Wrack* is seaweed.

racket or **racquet**? Either spelling is acceptable for describing the implement used in sport for striking the ball: □ *tennis racket/racquet* □ *the game of rackets/racquets.*

rad The adjective *rad* and its full form *radical* are slang terms of approval used especially by young people: □ *a rad new video game.*

rainbow coalition The phrase *rainbow coalition* is a vogue expression of American origin, denoting a political alliance of minority groups (such as ethnic minorities, pressure groups, or minor political parties): □ *a rainbow coalition of New Agers, peace campaigners, and animal rights activists.*

raise or **raze**? The verb *raise* means 'move to a higher position': □ *He raised the trophy high*; *raze* means 'destroy completely': □ *The city was razed to the ground.* The two spellings should not be confused.

raise or **rise**? Both these

verbs mean 'move to a higher or upright position' or 'increase'. *Raise* is transitive, *rise* is intransitive: □ *She raised her arm.* □ *They may raise the price.* □ *I watched the smoke rise.* □ *The temperature was rising.*

raison d'être The phrase *raison d'être*, of French origin, is used in English to denote a reason or justification for existence; it is best avoided where *reason, explanation*, etc., would be adequate or more appropriate: □ *Helping the bereaved is the organization's raison d'être.* □ *The Prime Minister explained the reason* [not *raison d'être*] *for the government's change of policy.*

rang see RINGED, RANG, OR RUNG?

rapt or **wrapped**? These spellings are sometimes confused. The adjective *rapt* means 'engrossed or absorbed': □ *rapt with wonder* □ *They listened with rapt attention. Wrapped* is the past tense of the verb *wrap*, meaning 'enfold': □ *She wrapped the shawl round the baby.*

rara avis The phrase *rara avis*, denoting a rare or unusual person or thing, is often better replaced by the noun *rarity*.

rarefy This word, meaning 'make rare or less dense', is sometimes misspelt. Note the *-efy* ending, unlike *purify, intensify*, etc. The variant spelling *rarify* is acknowledged by some dictionaries but is best avoided.

rateable or **ratable**? Both spellings of this word are acceptable, but *rateable* is preferred by some users: □ *rateable value.* See SPELLING 3.

rather The adverb *rather* may be used with *would* or *had*, but *would* is more frequent in modern usage, *had* being rather formal: □ *They would/had rather watch television than listen to the radio.*

ravage or **ravish**? These two verbs should not be confused. *Ravage* means 'cause great damage to' and 'devastate'; to *ravish* is 'to delight or enrapture': □ *The country was ravaged by war.* □ *They were ravished by the beauty of the sunset.*

raze see RAISE OR RAZE?

re The use of the preposition *re*, meaning 'with reference to' or 'in the matter of', should be restricted to the heading or opening of a business letter: □ *Re: Interest rates for personal loans.*

re- The prefix *re-*, meaning 'again', should be followed by a hyphen in compounds that might be confused with existing or more familiar words. Such verbs as *re-sound*, *re-lease*, and *re-sign* (meaning 'sound again', 'lease again', and 'sign again'), for example, are thus distinguished from the verbs *resound*, *release*, and *resign*. See also REBOUND OR RE-BOUND?; RECOUNT OR RE-COUNT?; RECOVER OR RE-COVER?; RECREATION OR RE-CREATION? REFORM OR RE-FORM?; RELAY OR RE-LAY?; REPRESENT OR RE-PRESENT?; RESORT OR RE-SORT? The use of a hyphen in such words as *re-educate* and *re-election* is optional (see also HYPHEN 1).

reaction The noun *reaction*, which denotes a spontaneous or automatic response, is best avoided where *reply, response, answer, opinion*, etc., would be more appropriate: □ *On hearing the alarm his reaction was one of panic.* □ *We had hoped for a more favourable response* [not *reaction*] *from the committee.* □ *Please study these proposals and give me your opinion* [not *reaction*].

readable see LEGIBLE OR READABLE?

real Many people object to the frequent use of the adjective *real* in place of *important, serious*, etc., or simply for emphasis: □ *a real achievement* □ *a real problem* □ *the real facts* □ *in real life.*

realism or **reality**? *Reality* is the state of being real, or the state of things as they really are: □ *Daydreams are an escape from reality.* □ *We must face reality. Realism* is the acceptance of reality, a practical rather than idealistic attitude of mind: □ *Problems like this must be approached with realism and common sense.*

realistic The frequent use of the adjective *realistic* as a synonym for 'sensible', 'practical', 'reasonable', etc., is disliked by many users: □ *a realistic proposal* □ *a realistic alternative* □ *a realistic offer.*

reality see REALISM OR REALITY?

really The excessive use of the adverb *really* is best avoided, even in informal contexts. *Really* can often be replaced by a different intensifier, such as *very*, *extremely*, *thoroughly*, *truly*, etc., or omitted altogether: □ *It was really late when they arrived and we were really worried.* □ *Wait until the paint is really dry.* □ *She really hates her job.*

reason Careful users regard the tautological construction *the reason is/was because* as wrong, preferring *the reason is/was that* or a simpler paraphrase using *because* alone: □ *The reason for the delay is that* [not *because*] *there are road works in the town centre.* □ *The reason I opened the window was that* [not *because*] *there was a wasp in the room.* □ *I opened the window because there was a wasp in the room.*

rebound or **re-bound**? These two spellings are sometimes confused. The verb *rebound* means 'spring back': □ *The ball rebounded. Re-bound,* spelt with a hyphen, is the past tense and past participle of the verb *re-bind* (or *rebind*), meaning 'bind again': □ *The book has been re-bound.*

receipt This word, meaning 'written confirmation that something has been paid or received', is sometimes misspelt. Note the *-ei-* spelling, and the silent *p*. See also SPELLING 5.

receive This word is often misspelt. Note the *-ei-* spelling, which conforms to the rule '*i* before *e* except after *c*'. See also SPELLING 5.

recess The noun *recess* may be pronounced [ri*ses*] or [*ree*ses]. The first pronunciation, with the stress on the second syllable, is preferred by some users of British English, but the second pronunciation, stressed on the first syllable, is becoming increasingly frequent.

reciprocal see MUTUAL, COMMON, OR RECIPROCAL?

reckon The use of the verb *reckon* in place of *think*, expressing a personal opinion, is best restricted to informal contexts: □ *He reckons the other team will win.*

recommend This word, meaning 'praise or suggest as suitable', is often misspelt. Note the single *c* and *-mm-*.

reconnaissance This word, meaning 'exploration or survey of an area for military intelligence purposes', is often misspelt. Note the *-nn-* and *-ss-*.

recount or **re-count**? These two spellings are sometimes confused. The verb *recount* means 'narrate': □ *He recounted his experiences during the war.* The verb *re-count*, with a hyphen, means 'count again', and the noun *re-count*, which is used more frequently than the verb, means 'second count': □ *to demand a re-count of the votes.*

recourse, **resort**, or **resource**? Similarities in the sense, usage, form, and pronunciation of these words may lead to confusion. All three can refer to a source of help or an expedient: □ *Violence was our only recourse/resort/resource.* In the expressions *have recourse/resort to* and *without recourse/resort to*, *recourse* and *resort* are virtually interchangeable but cannot be replaced by *resource*. In the expression *as a last resort/resource* the nounds *resort* and *resource* are interchangeable but cannot be replaced by *recourse*.

recover or **re-cover**? These two spellings are sometimes confused. *Recover* means 'regain': □ *She recovered her health.* *Re-cover*, with a hyphen, means 'give a new cover to': □ *The firm re-covered the chair.*

recreation or **re-creation**? The spellings of these words are sometimes confused. *Recreation* means 'relaxation; leisure (pursuit)': □ *a recreation ground.* *Re-creation*, with a hyphen, is a word less frequently used and means 'a new creation': □ *the re-creation of the Wild West for the film set.*

recuperate The verb *recuperate,* meaning 'recover', is sometimes misspelt, a common error being the substitution of *-coup-* for *-cup-*, as in the verb *recoup*.

redouble or **reduplicate**? The verb *redouble* means 'increase' or 'intensify': □ *We redoubled our efforts.* The rarer and more formal verb *reduplicate* means 'repeat' or 'double'; it also has the specialized sense of 'repeat (a syllable)', as in the words bye-bye, papa, etc.

redundant Some people object to the frequent use of the adjective *redundant* in place of *unnecessary, superfluous, irrelevant, unimportant,* etc.: □ *Our second car will become redundant when my husband starts commuting by train.*

reduplicate see REDOUBLE OR REDUPLICATE?

refer The verb *refer* is stressed on the second syllable; the final *r* is doubled before *-ed, -ing,* and *-er*. In the noun *reference* the stress shifts to the first syllable, and the second *r* is not doubled.

referee or **umpire**? Both nouns denote a person who ensures that a game is played according to the rules and settles any disputes that arise during the course of the game. A *referee* supervises such sports as football, boxing, etc.; an *umpire* supervises such sports as tennis, cricket, baseball, hockey, etc.

referendum The noun *referendum* has two plural forms, *referendums* and *referenda*. *Referendums* is the more frequent in general usage.

reflective or **reflexive**? These two adjectives should not be confused. *Reflective* is used in the literal sense of 'reflecting light' or the figurative sense of 'thoughtful; contemplative': □ *a reflective stripe across the back of the jacket* □ *in a reflective mood. Reflexive* is a grammatical term (see REFLEXIVE): □ *reflexive verb* □ *reflexive pronoun.*

reflexive A *reflexive verb* is a transitive verb in which the subject and object are the same: □ *I washed myself.* □ *She hid herself behind a tree.* □ *He perjured himself.* □ *The directors awarded themselves large pay increases.* The pronouns *myself, yourself, himself, herself, itself, oneself, ourselves, yourselves,* and *themselves* are called *reflexive pronouns*.

reform or **re-form**? These spellings are sometimes confused. The verb *reform* means 'change by improvement': □ *plans to reform the tax system. Re-form,* with a hyphen, means 'form again': □ *After a lapse of ten years, the club decided to re-form.*

refrigerator Note the spelling of this word, particularly the *-er-* in the middle and the *-or* at the end. There is no *d* in *refrigerator*, unlike the informal short form *fridge*.

refute or **deny**? The verb *refute* means 'prove to be false'; *deny* means 'declare to be false': □ *He refuted their accusations by producing a receipt for the camera.* □ *He denied their accusations but was unable to prove his innocence.* The use of *refute* in place of *deny* is avoided by many careful users but nevertheless occurs with some frequency.

regard In the sense of 'consider' the verb *regard* should be used with the preposition *as*: □ *She regards her mother as her friend.* □ *This novel is regarded as the author's masterpiece.* Compare CONSIDER.

regardless see IRRESPECTIVE.

registry office or **register office**? Both these terms are used to denote the place where civil marriages are conducted and where births, marriages, and deaths are recorded. *Registry office* is the more frequent term in general usage, *register office* being largely restricted to formal contexts.

regrettably or **regretfully**? These two adverbs are sometimes confused. *Regrettably* relates to something that causes regret; *regretfully* relates to somebody who feels regret: □ *This year's profits are regrettably low.* □ *She regretfully turned down their offer.*

rein or **reign**? These spellings are sometimes confused. *Reins* are the leather straps that control a horse; a *reign* is the period of a monarch's rule: □ *pull at the reins* □ *the reign of King Henry VIII.*

reiterate The verb *reiterate* means 'repeat' or 'say or do repeatedly'; it should not be used with the adverb *again* (see also RE-).

relation or **relationship**? Both these nouns may be used in the sense of 'connection' but they are not interchangeable in all contexts: □ *Is there any relation/relationship between unemployment and crime?* □ *This evidence bears no relation* [not *relationship*] *to the case.* □ *What is his relationship* [not *relation*] *to the deceased?* The noun *relationship* is preferred for human connections, *relation* for more abstract connections.

relation or **relative**? Either noun may be used to denote a person connected to another by blood, marriage, or adoption: □ *Most of her relations/relatives are going to the wedding.* □ *I have a distant relation/relative in Canada.*

relative clause see CLAUSE; COMMA; THAT OR WHICH?

relatively The adverb *relatively* implies comparison; many people object to its use as a synonym for 'fairly', 'somewhat', 'rather', etc., where there is no comparison: □ *After the heat of the kitchen the lounge felt relatively cool.* □ *Our records are fairly* [not *relatively*] *up to date.*

relay or **re-lay**? These two spellings are sometimes confused. The verb *relay* means 'pass on': □ *to relay a message*. The verb *re-lay*, spelt with a hyphen, means 'lay again': □ *to re-lay a carpet.*

relevant This word is sometimes misspelt. Note particularly the second *e*.

reliable or **reliant**? The adjective *reliable* means 'dependable' or 'able to be trusted': □ *a reliable car* □ *Some of the author's sources are not very reliable.* The adjective *reliant*, meaning 'dependent', is chiefly used in the phrase *be reliant on*: □ *We were reliant on their assistance.*

relocate The verb *relocate*, frequently used in business and industrial contexts, is widely regarded as a pretentious synonym for 'move': □ *the latest major firm to relocate to Basingstoke* □ *Unemployment in the North is forcing many families to relocate.*

remedial or **remediable**? *Remedial* means 'intended as a remedy'; *remediable* means 'able to be remedied': □ *remedial treatment* □ *a remediable problem. Remedial* is also specifically applied to the teaching of slow learners: □ *remedial education.*

remembrance The noun *remembrance,* meaning 'the act of remembering', 'memory', or 'memento', is often misspelt, the most frequent error being the substitution of *-ber-* for *-br-*, as in the verb *remember.* Note also the *-ance* ending.

reminiscent This word is sometimes misspelt. Note particularly the *-sc-*, as in *scent.*

remission or **remittance**? Both these nouns are derived from the verb *remit. Remittance* is largely restricted to official contexts, in the sense of 'payment': □ *Please enclose this counterfoil with your remittance. Remission* has a wider range of uses and meanings, such as 'reduction in the length of a prison sentence', 'abatement of the symptoms of a disease', 'discharge; release': □ *the remission of sins.*

remit The noun *remit* is best avoided where *task, responsibility, brief,* etc., would be adequate or more appropriate: □ *The quality control function will also be part of your remit* (*Executive Post*).

remittance see REMISSION OR REMITTANCE?

renege The traditional pronunciation of this word, which means 'not keep (a promise, agreement, etc.)' is [r*ineeg*], but [r*inayg*] is also frequently used and is acceptable.

rent see HIRE OR RENT?

repair see FIX OR REPAIR?

repairable or **reparable**? Both these adjectives mean 'able to be repaired'; careful users apply *repairable* to material objects and *reparable* to abstract nouns: □ *The car is badly damaged but repairable.* □ *His loss is scarcely reparable.*

repellent or **repulsive**? *Repellent* and *repulsive* mean 'causing disgust or aversion'. *Repulsive* is the stronger of the two adjectives, both of which are ultimately derived from the Latin verb *repellere,* meaning 'repel': □ *His deformed body was a repellent sight.* □ *The partially decomposed corpse was a repulsive sight.* □ *The principles of Communism are repellent to some; the doctrines of Nazism were repulsive to many.*

repercussions The word *repercussions* is best avoided where *result, consequence, effect,* etc., would be adequate or more appropriate: □ *the repercussions of a ban on smoking in restaurants.*

repertoire or **repertory**? The noun *repertoire* principally denotes the musical or dramatic works, poems, jokes, etc., that a person or group is able or prepared to perform: □ *That song is not in her repertoire. Repertory* is also used in this sense, but is more frequently applied to a company of actors that presents a *repertoire* of plays at the same theatre: □ *a repertory company.*

repetitious or **repetitive**? The adjective *repetitive* means 'characterized by repetition'; *repetitious* means 'characterized by unnecessary or tedious repetition': □ *a repetitive rhythm* □ *repetitious arguments.*

replace or **substitute**? The verb *replace* means 'take the place of'; the verb *substitute* means 'put in the place of': □ *I substituted his painting for her photograph.* □ *His painting was substituted for her photograph.* □ *His painting replaced her photograph. Substitute* is always used with the preposition *for*; *replace* may be used with the preposition *with* or *by.*

replica Some people object to the frequent use of *replica* in place of *copy, duplicate, reproduction, model,* etc.: □ *He bought a plastic replica of the Eiffel Tower.*

reported speech Reported speech, also called indirect speech, differs from direct speech in a number of ways. In direct speech the actual words of the speaker are given, enclosed in QUOTATION MARKS in written or printed texts: □ *Mary said, 'I've lost my ring.'* In reported speech quotation marks are not used for this purpose: □ *Mary said that she had lost her ring.*

represent or **re-present**? These spellings are sometimes confused. *Represent* means 'act in place of': □ *The team will represent the whole school. Re-present*, with a hyphen, means 'present again'.

repress see OPPRESS, REPRESS, OR SUPPRESS?

repulse, repulsive see REPELLENT OR REPULSIVE?

reputable The adjective *reputable* should be stressed on the first syllable, [*rep*yuutăbl]. The pronunciation [ri*pew*tăbl], with the stress on the second syllable, is incorrect.

requisite see PREREQUISITE OR REQUISITE?

resin or **rosin**? *Resin* is a natural substance exuded by plants, insects, etc., or a synthetic substance that resembles natural resin. *Rosin* is a type of natural resin used on the bow of a stringed instrument to increase friction, on the hands of a gymnast to increase grip, etc.

resort or **re-sort**? The noun *resort* means 'place of rest or recreation': □ *seaside resorts.* The verb *resort* means 'turn to': □ *I hope he will not resort to violence.* The verb *re-sort*, with a hyphen, means 'sort again': □ *re-sort all the index cards.*

resort, resource see RECOURSE, RESORT, OR RESOURCE?

respectable, **respectful**, or **respective**? These three adjectives should not be confused. *Respectable* means 'worthy of respect'; *respectful* means 'showing respect'; *respective* means 'separate; several' (see RESPECTIVE OR RESPECTIVELY?): □ *In those days acting was not considered a respectable profession.* □ *a respectful silence* □ *Jane and Michael collected their respective children and went home.*

respective and **respectively** The words *respective* and *respectively* should be used only where there would be a risk of ambiguity or confusion in their absence: □ *The workers explained their respective problems to the shop steward.* □ *Toys and furniture are sold on the second and third floors respectively.* Without *respective*, the first example could imply that all the workers had the same problems; without *respectively*, the second example might suggest that toys and furniture are sold on both floors.

respite This word, meaning 'relief, delay': □ *no respite from the toil,* is often mispronounced. The stress falls on the first syllable, unlike *despite*, which has the stress on the second syllable.

restaurateur Note the spelling of this formal word for a person who runs a restaurant. There is no *n* as in *restaurant*.

restive or **restless**? The adjective *restive* means 'resisting control'; *restless* means 'fidgety' or 'agitated'. The use of *restive* in place of *restless* is disliked by careful users.

restrain see CONSTRAIN OR RESTRAIN?

resuscitate This word, meaning 'revive': □ *All attempts to resuscitate him with the kiss of life failed*, is often misspelt. Note particularly the *-sc-* in the middle of the word.

retread The noun *retread* denotes an old tyre with a new outer surface; it is synonymous with *remould*. Many people object to the metaphorical application of the word *retread* to people, such as politicians returning to parliament after a spell out of office or retired people returning to paid employment: □ *There will be a number of retreads in the new government.*

retro The prefix *retro-*, meaning 'backwards', is increasingly used as an adjective in its own right, describing fashions, styles, ideas, etc., that have been revived from the past: □ *the retro look/sound* □ *His latest film is unashamedly retro.*

return see RE-.

returner A *returner* is a person who returns to work after an extended period of absence from paid employment, such as a woman who resumes her career after spending a number of years bringing up her children: □ *Few employers are actually offering women returners a new deal ... but information on the subject is available.*

reveille This word may be pronounced [ri*val*i] or [ri*vel*i], the former being the more frequent pronunciation.

revenge or **avenge**? Both these verbs refer to the act of repaying a wrong. The person who *revenges* is usually the offended or injured party; a person who *avenges* is usually a third party acting on behalf of another: □ *I will revenge myself on those who cruelly humiliated me.* □ *He planned to avenge his brother's death by drowning the murderer's daughter.* □ *He avenged his murdered brother.*

revenge or **vengeance**? Both these nouns may be used in the sense of 'retaliation' or 'retribution': □ *The destruction of her parents' home was an act of revenge/vengeance.* Some users associate *revenge* with the subjective or personal act of revenging and *vengeance* with the objective or impersonal act of avenging (see REVENGE OR AVENGE?).

reversal or **reversion**? *Reversal* is the act of reversing; *reversion* is the act of reverting: □ *the reversal of this trend* □ *reversion to his former way of life*. The two nouns should not be confused.

reverse see CONVERSE, INVERSE, OBVERSE, OR REVERSE?

reversion see REVERSAL OR REVERSION?

review or **revue**? These two spellings are sometimes confused. *Review*, as a noun, is a 'critical appraisal': □ *a review of her latest novel* or a 'reassessment': □ *The minister ordered an urgent review of prison security*. A *revue* is a light theatrical show consisting of sketches, songs, etc.: □ *the annual Christmas revue*.

rhetorical question A *rhetorical question* is one which is asked for effect, and to which no answer is expected: □ *What is the world coming to?* □ *How can people behave like that?* The question is sometimes asked so that it can be answered immediately by the speaker: □ *Why are we on strike? I will tell you why ....*

rheumatism This word for an illness that causes pain in the muscles or joints is sometimes misspelt. Note particularly the first syllable *rheum-*.

rhinoceros The name of this animal is often misspelt. Note particularly the *rh-*, and the *c* in the middle of the word.

rhythm This word is frequently misspelt. Note particularly the first *h* and the *y*.

ribald This adjective, meaning 'coarse or crude': □ *ribald language*, is often mispronounced. The pronunciation is [ribăld].

ricochet This word, used to describe bullets, etc., that rebound, is usually pronounced [rikŏshay] although [rikŏshet] is also acceptable. There are alternative present and past participles: *ricocheting* [rikŏshaying] or *ricochetting* [rikŏsheting] and *ricocheted* [rikŏshayd] or *ricochetted* [rikŏshetid].

right or **rightly**? Both these adverbs may be used in the sense of 'correctly' or 'properly'. *Right* is generally placed after the verb, *rightly* before the verb: □ *Have I spelt your name right?* □ *He rightly stopped* *at the zebra crossing.* □ *You're not holding your fork right.* □ *She rightly held her fork in her left hand.* The phrase *If I remember rightly/right* is a notable exception to this rule.

rigor see RIGOUR OR RIGOR?

rigorous This word is sometimes misspelt. The *u* of *rigour* is dropped in front of the suffix *-ous*.

rigour or **rigor**? *Rigour*, meaning 'harsh conditions; severity': □ *the rigours of winter*, should not be confused in British English with the medical *rigor*: □ *rigor mortis*.

ring or **wring**? These two verbs are sometimes confused, being identical in pronunciation. *Ring* means 'make a resonant sound' or 'surround or mark with a ring'; *wring* means 'twist' or 'squeeze': □ *to ring a bell* □ *I asked her to ring any errors in red ink.* □ *to wring one's hands.*

ringed, rang, or **rung**? *Ringed* is the past tense and past participle of the verb *ring* in the sense of 'surround or mark with a ring': □ *He ringed all the words that had been misspelt.* □ *The birds have been ringed for identification. Rang* is the past tense and *rung* the past participle of the verb *ring* in the sense of 'sound (a bell)': □ *She rang the bell.* □ *The telephone has not rung.*

rip-off Derived from the slang verb *rip off*, meaning 'steal' or 'cheat', the noun *rip-off* is principally applied to overpriced goods or the practice of charging exorbitant prices: □ *This handbag is an absolute rip-off – it's not even made of real leather.*

rise see ARISE OR RISE?; RAISE OR RISE?

road or **street**? Generally the noun *road* is used to denote a thoroughfare between towns or cities or in the suburbs of a town or city; a *street* is a thoroughfare in the town or city centre: □ *a country road* □ *a one-way street* □ *the road to Brighton* □ *the streets of London* □ *a new housing estate on Park Road* □ *their Oxford Street store.* There are, however, numerous exceptions to this rule, especially in the naming of roads and streets.

rob, robbery see BURGLE, ROB, OR STEAL?

role Some people object to the frequent use of the

noun *role* as a synonym for 'place', 'function', 'position', 'part', etc.: □ *the role of religion in modern society* □ *a proven track record in a technical sales role* □ *A new manager is now sought to play a key role in determining the company's future strategy*. The noun *role* is principally used to denote the part played by an actor. In psychology and sociology it refers to the part played by an individual in a social situation: □ *role reversal* □ *role-playing*.

roofs or **rooves**? The plural of the word *roof*, 'covering of a building', is usually *roofs*, pronounced [roofs] or [roovz].

rosin see RESIN OR ROSIN?

roughage This word, meaning 'coarse food; dietary fibre', is sometimes misspelt. Note the *-gh-* in the middle of the word.

round see AROUND OR ROUND?

rouse see AROUSE OR ROUSE?

rout or **route**? The noun *rout* means 'overwhelming defeat' or 'disorderly retreat'; the noun *route* means 'road' or 'course': □ *They put the enemy to rout.* □ *The procession took a different route this summer*. The risk of confusion is greater when the words are used as verbs, especially in the past tense: □ *They routed the enemy.* □ *The procession was routed along a different road.*

rowlock This word, for the device in a boat that holds an oar in place, is usually pronounced [*rol*ŏk].

RSI The abbreviation *RSI* is short for *repetitive strain injru*; injury to muscles or tendons caused by repetitive action, such as using a computer keyboard: □ *Repetitive Strain Injury (RSI) is an umbrella term for a series of musculo-skeletal complaints now affecting the newspaper industry – among others* (*The Guardian*).

rubbish The use of the word *rubbish* as a verb, meaning 'criticize severely' or 'condemn as worthless', is disliked by many users and should be avoided in formal contexts: □ *The report rubbishes the new GCSE examinations.*

rung see RINGED, RANG, OR RUNG?

run-up Some people dislike the frequent use of the noun *run-up*, adopted from the field of athletics, to denote the period preceding an important event: □ *the last few days in the run-up to the general election* □ *The run-up to the anniversary of soldiers being deployed on the streets of Northern Ireland* (*BBC TV*).

rural or **rustic**? Both these adjectives relate to the countryside, country life, country people, farming, etc. *Rural* is used as a neutral opposite of *urban*; *rustic* has the connotations of simplicity, crudeness, quaintness, or lack of sophistication: □ *rural schools* □ *a rural setting* □ *rural areas* □ *rustic food* □ *a rustic cottage* □ *rustic manners*. Careful users maintain the distinction between the two words.

Russian or **Soviet**? The word *Russian* relates to the country of Russia, which formed the major part of the Soviet Union from 1922 to 1991, and its people: □ *the Russian composer Rimsky-Korsakov* □ *a Russian manufacturing company*. The word *Soviet* is used with reference to people and events of the years when the Soviet Union was in existence: □ *Soviet space missions* □ *a Soviet politician*.

S

's or **s'**? Possessive nouns are usually formed by adding *'s* to singular nouns, an apostrophe to plural nouns that end in *s*, and *'s* to irregular plural nouns that do not end in *s*: □ *Jane's pen* □ *the boy's father* □ *the directors' cars* □ *women's clothes*. In the possessive form of a name or singular noun that ends in *s*, *x*, or *z*, the apostrophe may or may not be followed by *s*. The final *s* is most frequently omitted in names, especially names of three or more syllables that end in the sound [z]: □ *Euripides' tragedies* □ *Berlioz' operas*. For words of one syllable *'s* is generally used: □ *Liz's house* □ *the boss's secretary*. Other cases depend on usage, pronunciation, etc.

sac or **sack**? These two spellings are sometimes confused. The noun *sac* is largely restricted to scientific contexts, where it denotes a baglike part of an animal or plant: □ *a fluid-filled sac*. A *sack* is a large bag used to hold coal, potatoes, etc.

saccharin or **saccharine**? The sweet powder that is used as a sugar substitute is spelt *saccharin*, without a final *-e*; *saccharine* is an adjective meaning 'excessively sweet': □ *The drink is sweetened with saccharin*. □ *a saccharine smile*.

sack see SAC OR SACK?

sacrilegious This word, which means 'showing disrespect towards something holy', sometimes causes problems with spelling. Note the position of the first *i* and *e*, which are in the opposite order in the word *religious*.

sake The noun *sake* is usually preceded by a possessive adjective or noun: □ *for their sake* □ *for Edward's sake* □ *for pity's sake* □ *for old times' sake*.

salable see SALEABLE OR SALABLE?

salary or **wage**? Both these nouns denote the money paid to employees at regular intervals in return for their services. A *salary* is usually paid monthly to professional people or nonmanual workers; a *wage* is usually paid weekly to manual workers or servants.

saleable or **salable**? Both spellings of this word are acceptable, but *saleable* is the more frequent in British English. See SPELLING 3.

salivary This word has two possible pronunciations. The more traditional pronunciation has the stress on the first syllable [*sa*livări]. The pronunciation [să*lī*vări], with the stress on the second syllable, is perfectly acceptable and is more frequently used.

salmonella This word is sometimes mispronounced. The correct pronunciation is [salmŏ*nel*ă].

salon or **saloon**? *Saloon* is the anglicized form of the French word *salon*. Both words entered the English language in the 18th century and have developed a number of individual meanings. *Salon* is most frequently found in the names of certain places of business, such as: □ *beauty salon* □ *hairdressing salon*. A *saloon* is a large room in a public house or on a ship: □ *We went into the saloon (bar)*; it also denotes a type of car: □ *the most popular saloon (car)*.

salubrious or **salutary**? *Salubrious* means 'wholesome' or 'conducive to health'; *salutary* means 'beneficial', 'causing improvement', or 'remedial': □ *a salubrious climate* □ *a salutary warning* □ *We decided to look for a more salubrious hotel.* □ *Spending a few days in prison can be a salutary experience for young offenders.*

same The use of *same* as a pronoun is best restricted to business or official contexts: □ *I enclose my passport, as requested; please return same by registered post.* This usage is widely regarded as COMMERCIALESE. Another pronoun, such as *it* or *them*, can usually be substituted for *same*: □ *He found an old blanket and used it* [not *same*] *to line the dog's basket.*

sanatorium A *sanatorium* is a medical establishment for the treatment and care of people, especially those suffering from long-term illnesses. Note the spelling of this word in British English, particularly the second *a* and the *o*. The spelling *sanitarium* is an American English variant.

sanction The noun *sanction* has two senses that appear to contradict each other. It may mean 'official authorization or permission': □ *The project has been given the sanction of the board of directors.* This use is largely restricted to formal contexts, and the noun is perhaps more frequently found in the plural form *sanctions*, referring to coercive measures taken against a state or institution: □ *economic sanctions against Iraq* □ *to impose political sanctions.*

sank, sunk, or **sunken**? The past tense of the verb *sink* is *sank* or *sunk*, *sank* being the more frequent. The usual form of its past participle is *sunk*, *sunken* being largely restricted to adjectival use: □ *The dog sank its teeth into the man's leg.* □ *One of the boats has sunk.* □ *We are diving for sunken treasure.*

sarcasm, sarcastic see IRONY.

sat see SITTING OR SAT?

sate, satiate, or **satisfy**? The verb *satisfy* means 'supply' or 'fulfil': □ *Her needs had been satisfied.* □ *This should satisfy their demands.* The verbs *sate* and *satiate* may mean 'satisfy fully', but are more frequently used in the sense of 'supply or fulfil to excess': □ *to satiate a person's appetite* □ *Television viewers are sated with imported comedy shows.* A person who is *satisfied* has had enough; a person who is *sated* or *satiated* has usually had too much. *Sate* and *satiate* are used in formal contexts and are largely synonymous, but *sate* is very rarely used as an active verb.

satire or **satyr**? *Satire* is the use of irony or parody to mock folly and evil in human behaviour, politics, religion, etc.; a *satyr* is a mythological creature in the form of a goatlike man, associated with lechery. The two nouns should not be confused in usage or pronunciation: *satyr* rhymes with matter, whereas the second syllable of *satire* rhymes with *fire*.

satisfy see SATE, SATIATE, OR SATISFY?

satyr see SATIRE OR SATYR?

says This word is sometimes mispronounced. The form of the verb *say* used in the present tense with *he*, *she*, or *it* is *says*, pronounced [sez].

scallop The standard pronunciation of this word, which means 'a shellfish with two flat fan-shaped shells', is [*skol*ŏp]. An alternative which rhymes with *gallop* is often heard, but avoided by careful users.

scam The noun *scam* means 'swindle', 'trick', 'racket', or 'hoax': □ *This* [the Enterprise Allowance Scheme] *was a government scam to get the unemployed off the register and pretend they were all setting up small businesses in the thriving enterprise culture instead* (*The Guardian*).

scant or **scanty**? Both these adjectives mean 'limited', 'barely enough', or 'meagre'. *Scant* is more formal and less frequent than *scanty*, being chiefly used in front of certain abstract nouns: □ *He paid scant attention to my words.* □ *She has scant regard for the law. Scanty* is used before or after a wider range of nouns: □ *Their knowledge is rather scanty.* □ *a scanty bikini* □ *a scanty collection of books.*

scarcely see HARDLY.

scarfs or **scarves**? Either *scarfs* or *scarves* is accept-able as the plural of the noun *scarf*, denoting a piece of cloth worn around the neck or on the head.

scarify The verb *scarify* should not be used in place of *scare*, to which it is unrelated in meaning and origin. *Scarify* tends to be used in formal contexts and means 'scratch or break up the surface of': □ *to scarify the skin before administering a vaccine* □ *to scarify the topsoil of a field.* In figurative contexts it is used in the sense of 'wound with harsh criticism': □ *a scarifying review.*

scarves see SCARFS OR SCARVES?

scenario The noun *scenario* is frequently used to denote a projected or imagined future state of affairs or sequence of events: □ *a scenario in which the super-*

powers would have recourse to nuclear weapons. Many people object to the frequency of this usage, especially in contexts where *plan, programme, scene, situation*, etc., would be adequate or more appropriate. The clichés *nightmare scenario* and *worst-case scenario*, both of which mean 'the worst thing that could happen', are also best avoided wherever possible.

sceptic or **septic**? The pronunciation of these two words is sometimes confused. A *sceptic* (American English, *skeptic*) is a person who has doubts about accepted beliefs or principles, and is pronounced [*skep*tik].

sceptical see CYNICAL OR SCEPTICAL?

schedule This word, meaning 'plan or timetable': □ *The train was behind schedule again*, is usually pronounced [*shed*yool] in British English.

schism The traditional pronunciation of this word, meaning 'separation into opposed groups', is [sizm], with a silent *ch*. The alternative pronunciation [skizm] is perfectly acceptable.

schizophrenic The adjective *schizophrenic* relates to the mental disorder *schizophrenia*, which is characterized by hallucinations, delusions, social withdrawal, emotional instability, loss of contact with reality, etc. The use of the adjective *schizophrenic* in the extended sense of 'inconsistent', 'contradictory', 'unpredictable', etc., is disliked and avoided by most users.

scone The pronunciation of this word is a favourite topic for debate; both [skon] and [skōn] are equally acceptable.

Scotch, **Scots**, or **Scottish**? All these adjectives mean 'of Scotland', but there are differences of usage and application between them. *Scottish*, the most frequent, is used in a wide range of contexts: □ *Scottish history* □ *a Scottish town* □ *Scottish Gaelic* □ *a Scottish name* □ *Scottish dancing* □ *a Scottish poet.* The adjective *Scotch* was formerly used for such purposes but is now restricted to a number of fixed phrases, in the sense of 'produced in Scotland' or 'associated with Scotland': □ *Scotch whisky* □ *Scotch broth* □ *Scotch mist. Scots* is usually applied to people: □ *the Scots Guards* □ *a Scotsman* □ *a Scotswoman.* The last two examples may be replaced by the noun *Scot*, which means 'a native or inhabitant or Scotland': □ *She married a Scot.* The collective name for the people of Scotland is *the Scots* or *the Scottish.* The noun *Scots* also denotes a variety of English spoken in Scotland. In some contexts two of the adjectives are interchangeable: □ *a Scots/Scotch pine* □ *a Scottish/Scotch terrier* □ *a Scottish/Scots accent.*

sculpt or **sculpture**? The verbs *sculpt* and *sculpture* are synonymous and virtually interchangeable in all contexts: □ *He sculpted/sculptured a copy of the Venus de Milo in marble.* □ *She paints and sculpts/sculptures in her attic studio.*

seasonal or **seasonable**? *Seasonal* means 'of or occurring in a particular season'; *seasonable* means 'suitable for the season' or 'opportune': □ *seasonal vegetables* □ *seasonal work* □ *seasonable weather* □ *seasonable advice.* The two adjectives should not be confused.

secateurs This word, meaning 'pruning shears', is sometimes misspelt. Note the single *-c-* and the *-eurs* ending.

second or **secondly**? see FIRST OR FIRSTLY?

second-guess The verb *second-guess*, of American origin, means 'predict', 'anticipate', or 'evaluate with hindsight': □ *On a scale of difficulty of one to 10, second-guessing the travel market this year is 12* (*The Guardian*).

secretary The word *secretary* is sometimes misspelt. Note the *-ary* ending, which is attached to the letters of the word *secret*.

seem When the verb *seem* is used in the negative, the word *not* (or other negative element) may be placed before or after the verb: □ *She didn't seem to understand.* □ *She seemed not to understand.* □ *The weather doesn't seem likely to improve.* □ *The weather seems unlikely to improve.* The use of *didn't seem, doesn't seem,* etc., is best avoided in formal contexts.

seize This word, meaning 'take eagerly or by force': □ *He seized the money and ran*, is sometimes misspelt. Note the order of the vowels *-ei-* which does not correspond to the usual '*i* before *e*' rule. See also SPELLING 5.

self The use of the word *self* as a pronoun is disliked and avoided by many users, even in informal contexts: □ *tickets for husband and self*.

self-starter The frequent use of the noun *self-starter*, especially in job advertisements, to denote a person with initiative who can work without supervision, is disliked by many users.

sell-by date This phrase literally means 'the date by which perishable goods should be sold', but it is increasingly used in figurative contexts, meaning 'no longer useful or effective; out-of-date'.

semantics, semiotics, or **semiology**? *Semiotics* (or *semiology*) is the study of the properties of sign systems, especially as used in human communication. *Semantics*, one part of semiotics, is the study of the meaning of linguistic signs. For example, discussion of the meaning of the words *book*, *the moon*, or *yellow* belongs to semantics, whereas the wider cultural aspects of raising one's eyebrows when people greet each other at a distance belongs to semiotics.

semi- see DEMI-, HEMI-, OR SEMI-?

semicolon The semicolon is a useful punctuation mark but, unlike many of the other punctuation marks, there is no occasion when its use is compulsory. It is mainly used between clauses that are linked by sense but are not joined by a conjunction, and that could each stand as a separate sentence: □ *I am very tired; I am also hungry.* □ *The night was dark; the rain fell in torrents.* It is frequently used before such phrases as *however, none the less, nevertheless.* The semicolon can be replaced by a comma, but in sentences where clauses already contain commas, the semicolon is often used to separate the clauses. It can also be used to establish subjects in a long list or series separated by commas.

semiotics, semiology see SEMANTICS, SEMIOTICS, OR SEMIOLOGY?

senior citizen or **old age pensioner**? Both these expressions are used with reference to people who are over the age of retirement. The expression *senior citizen* is considered a euphemism by most. The term *old age pensioner* specifically denotes a person who receives a state retirement pension.

sensible or **sensitive**? The most frequent meaning of *sensible* is 'having or showing common sense; not foolish; practical': □ *a sensible child* □ *sensible advice* □ *the sensible thing to do* □ *sensible shoes. Sensitive* means 'easily hurt or irritated', 'having awareness', 'delicate', or 'reacting to very small differences'.

sensual or **sensuous**? Both these adjectives relate to the gratification of the senses. Something that is *sensual* appeals to the body, arousing or satisfying physical appetites or sexual desire; something that is *sensuous* appeals to the senses, sometimes especially the mind, being aesthetically pleasing or spiritually uplifting.

sentences A *sentence* can be defined as 'a grammatically complete unit consisting of one or more words, which starts with a capital letter and ends with a full stop, question mark, or exclamation mark'.

sentiment or **sentimentality**? A *sentiment* is a feeling, emotion, attitude, or opinion: □ *anti-communist sentiment* □ *These are my sentiments on the matter. Sentimentality* is the state of being sentimental, with particular reference to excessive indulgence of the emotions.

separate This word is often misspelt. Note the vowels; the most frequent error is to replace the first *-a-* with *-e-*. It may help to associate the central syllable *-par-* with the central letters of the word *apart*.

septic see SCEPTIC OR SEPTIC?

sergeant The spelling of *sergeant* is often a source of error. A *sergeant* is a middle-ranking noncommissioned officer in an army, etc., or an officer in a police force. A *sergeant-major* is a noncommissioned officer of the highest rank. A *serjeant-at-arms* is an officer in a parliament; a *serjeant-at-law* a former rank of barrister.

serial see CEREAL OR SERIAL?

seriously The adverb *seriously* is best avoided where *very* or *extremely* would be adequate or more appropriate: □ *They seemed to be having a very* [not *seriously*] *good time.* □ *Her parents are extremely* [not *seriously*] *rich.*

service The verb *service* is best avoided where *serve* would be adequate or more appropriate: □ *A national organization has been formed to service the local groups.*

serviceable This word, meaning 'ready to be used; durable': □ *The television had been repaired and was now serviceable*, is sometimes misspelt. The *e* is retained before the suffix *-able* in order to retain the soft *c* sound.

session see CESSION OR SESSION?

sewed or **sewn**? Either word may be used as the past participle of the verb *sew*: □ *I have sewn/sewed a patch over the hole. Sewn* is often preferred to *sewed*, especially when the participle is used as an adjective: □ *a neatly sewn hem.*

sexism The use of sexist language can often be avoided by the substitution of neutral synonyms or simple paraphrases, without recourse to clumsy or controversial neologisms. Those opponents of sexism who coin such expressions as *to person the telephones* do little to further their cause. See also POLITICAL CORRECTNESS; HE OR SHE?; MAN; MS, MRS OR MISS?; WOMAN; PERSON; -ESS.

sexy *Sexy*, an informal adjective meaning 'arousing sexual interest' or 'sexually aroused', is increasingly used as a synonym for 'attractive', 'enjoyable', 'exciting', or 'fashionable' in contexts that are completely devoid of sexual connotations: □ *'Crime,' according to an independent television producer recently, 'is very sexy this year.'* (*The Guardian*).

Shakespearean or **Shakespearian**? This word, meaning 'of or having the characteristics of Shakespeare': □ *a Shakespearean sonnet*, may end with *-ean* or with *-ian*.

shall or **will**? The traditional

distinction between *shall* and *will* is that *shall* is used in the first person and *will* in the second and third persons as the future tense of the verb *to be* and that *will* is used to express determination, compulsion, intention, willingness, commands, promises, etc.: □ *I shall wash the dishes later.* □ *He will come back tomorrow.* □ *We will not obey you.* □ *They shall apologize immediately.*

shaved or **shaven**? *Shaved* is the past tense of the verb *shave* and the usual form of the past participle: □ *He (has) shaved off his beard. Shaven*, a variant form of the past participle, is largely restricted to adjectival use: □ *the shaven heads of the monks* □ *a clean-shaven young man.*

she see HE OR SHE.

sheared or **shorn**? *Sheared* is the past tense of the verb *shear*; *shorn* is the usual form of its past participle: □ *They sheared the sheep.* □ *They have shorn the sheep.* □ *You will be shorn of your power.*

sheikh The preferred pronunciation of this word, which means 'an Arab chief or ruler', is [shayk]. The alternative pronunciation [sheek] is not generally accepted.

shelf-life see SELL-BY DATE.

shibboleth The noun *shibboleth* is frequently used to denote a catchword, slogan, maxim, cliché, etc., especially one that is old-fashioned or obsolescent: □ *We were unimpressed by his speech, in which he did little more than repeat the old shibboleths of the party.*

shined or **shone**? *Shone* is the past tense and past participle for most senses of the verb *shine*; *shined* is restricted to the meaning 'polished': □ *The sun (has) shone all day.* □ *He shone his torch on the statue.* □ *They (have) shined our shoes.*

ship see BOAT OR SHIP?

shone see SHINED OR SHONE?

shorn see SHEARED OR SHORN?

should or **would**? In reported speech, conditional sentences, and other indirect constructions, the use of *should* and *would* follows the pattern of *shall* and *will* (as the future tense of the verb *to be*); *would* is always used in the second and third persons and often replaces *should* in the first person: □ *We* *said we should/would stay until Saturday.* □ *She thought you would fail.* □ *If you were in trouble I should/would help you.* □ *He would open the door if he had the key.* See also SHALL OR WILL?

shrank, shrunk, or **shrunken?** *Shrank* is the past tense of the verb *shrink* and *shrunk* the usual form of its past participle, the variant *shrunken* being more frequently used as an adjective: □ *He shrank from telling her the truth.* □ *My pullover has shrunk.* □ *A shrunken old woman stood in the doorway.*

sibling The noun *sibling*, which denotes a brother or sister, is a useful word that is unfortunately disliked by many users and largely restricted to formal contexts and sociological jargon: □ *the twins' relationship with their siblings* □ *sibling rivalry.*

sic The Latin word *sic*, meaning 'so' or 'thus', is used in printed or written text (often in a quotation) to indicate that an unlikely, unexpected, questionable, or misspelt word or phrase has in fact been accurately transcribed: □ *He spoke of a need for 'more thorough analysation [sic]' of the results.*

sick or **ill?** In British English to feel *sick* is to feel nauseated or queasy, to feel *ill* is to feel unwell: □ *She was sick yesterday* usually means 'she vomited yesterday'; □ *She was ill yesterday* means 'she was not well yesterday'.

sideline Some people dislike the increasing use of the verb *sideline*, meaning 'prevent from taking part' or 'put out of action': □ *In his warmest speech yet on European integration, Mr Major set out his determination not to allow Britain to be sidelined in Europe* (*The Guardian*). □ *A 100-day counter revolution to undo the Conservatives' local government reforms, including sidelining Thatcherite civil servants, is being prepared by Labour for immediate implementation if returned in April* (*The Guardian*).

siege This word, meaning 'the surrounding of a fortified place to force a surrender', is sometimes misspelt. Note the order of the vowels *-ie-*, which conforms to the normal '*i* before *e*' rule. See also

SPELLING 5.

significant The adjective *significant* means 'having meaning': □ *a significant detail* □ *a significant gesture.*

silhouette This word, meaning 'outline; shadow', is sometimes misspelt, the most frequent error being the omission of the silent *-h-*. Note also the *-ette* ending.

silicon or **silicone**? *Silicon* is an element that occurs in sand and is used in alloys, glass manufacture, and the electronics industry: □ *silicon chip. Silicone* is a compound that contains silicon and is used in lubricants, polishes, and cosmetic surgery: □ *silicone rubber.*

similar Note the spelling of this adjective, particularly the single *-m-* and *-l-* and the *-ar* ending.

similes A *simile* is a figure of speech which, like a metaphor, suggests a comparison or analogy, but a simile expresses the comparison explicitly and is usually introduced by *like* or *as*: □ *teeth like pearls* □ *wide as the ocean.*

simplistic The adjective *simplistic* means 'over-simplified' or 'naive'; it should not be used in place of *simple*: □ *a simplistic explanation of the theory of relativity* □ *a simple* [not *simplistic*] *explanation for her behaviour.*

simulate or **stimulate**? These two verbs are sometimes confused. *Simulate* means 'feign', 'imitate', or 'reproduce for the purpose of study, training, experiment, etc.': □ *to simulate indifference* □ *simulated leather* □ *The process is simulated in the laboratory. Stimulate* means 'arouse' or 'excite': □ *He stimulated his pupils' interest.* □ *a stimulating experience.* See also DISSEMBLE, DISSIMULATE, OR SIMULATE?

simultaneity The traditional pronunciation of this noun, derived from SIMULTANEOUS, is [simŭltă*nee*iti], although [simŭltă*nay*iti] is also heard. The American English pronunciation is [sīm-].

simultaneous This word, meaning 'happening at the same time', may cause problems with pronunciation. The usual pronunciation is [simŭl*tay*niĕs]. The American English pronunciation is [sīm-].

since see AGO OR SINCE? □; BECAUSE, AS, FOR, OR SINCE?

sincerely The adverb *sincerely* is sometimes misspelt. Note the *-cere-* in the middle, and the *-ly* (not *-ley*) ending.

sinecure The noun *sinecure*, meaning 'a job or position in which payment is received for little or no work', is often mispronounced. The correct pronunciation of this three syllable word is [sīnikewr]: the *-i-* is long, as in *wine*, and the first *-e-* is not silent.

sine qua non The expression *sine qua non*, which is largely restricted to formal contexts, denotes an essential or indispensable condition or requirement: □ *Mutual trust is a sine qua non of a successful marriage.*

singeing or **singing**? *Singeing* is the present participle of the verb *singe*, meaning 'burn slightly': □ *It is difficult to iron this blouse without singeing the lace.* The *-e* of *singe* is retained in *singeing* to keep the *-g-* soft and to distinguish it from *singing*, the present participle of the verb *sing*: □ *The birds were singing in the trees.*

singular or **plural**? As a general rule a singular verb is used with a singular subject and a plural verb is used with a plural subject. Problems arise when the subject is a noun or phrase that can be singular or plural and when a singular subject is separated from the verb by a number of plural nouns (or vice versa): □ *A list of the names and addresses of new members is* [not *are*] *available on request.* Such nouns as *audience, government, jury, crowd*, etc., and other collective nouns followed by *of* (*a bunch of flowers*) are used with a singular verb if the people or items in question are considered as a group and with a plural verb if they are considered as individuals. Any corresponding pronouns or possessive adjectives should agree with the chosen verb: □ *The audience were asked to remain in their* [not *its*] *seats.* Measurements, sums of money, percentages, etc., are used with a singular verb if they are considered as a single entity: □ *Four metres is all we need.* Two or more nouns joined with *and* are used with a plural verb unless they represent a single concept: □ *Gin and tonic is a popular drink.* Nouns and phrases joined to the principal subject with *as well as, together with, plus,* etc., are regarded as parenthetical; the verb agrees with the principal subject alone: □ *A valuable painting, as well as her engravings, was destroyed in the fire.*

siphon or **syphon**? This word, meaning '(draw off liquid by means of a) tube using atmospheric pressure', can be spelt with an *i* or a *y*.

Sir *Sir* is a polite term of address for a man: □ *Thank you very much, sir.* The word is usually written with a lower-case *s-* in such contexts, but as an impersonal salutation in LETTER WRITING it is always written with a capital *S-*: □ *Dear Sir.*

sitting or **sat**? The substitution of *sat*, the past participle of the verb *sit*, for the present participle *sitting* is found in some dialects of English: □ *They were sitting* [in some dialects *sat*] *in the garden.*

sitting room see LOUNGE.

situation In the sense of 'state of affairs' the noun *situation* often serves a useful purpose, but it should not be used to excess: □ *We discussed our financial situation with the bank manager.* □ *They are trying to improve the unemployment situation.*

sixth This word may be pronounced [siksth] or [sikth], although some people dislike the omission of the second [s] sound.

sizeable or **sizable**? Both spellings of this word are acceptable. See SPELLING 3.

skilful The adjective *skilful*, meaning 'possessing skill', is sometimes misspelt. The final *l* of *skill* is dropped in British English before the suffix *-ful*. In American English, the *-ll-* is retained: *skillful*.

slander see LIBEL OR SLANDER?

slang *Slang* is unauthorized language, often but not necessarily coarse, which stands in the linguistic hierarchy between general informal speech and the specific vocabularies of professional and occupational jargon. Innovative and dramatic, slang is the most ephemeral of language, continually coining new terms and discarding old ones, which are either abandoned to obscurity or transferred into the respectability of the standard language.

sled, **sledge**, or **sleigh**? All these nouns denote vehicles that are used on snow for transport or recreation. *Sledge*, the most frequent in British English, is replaced by *sled* in American English. *Sleigh* usually refers to a large sledge that is pulled by animals.

sleight The word *sleight*, most frequently used in the phrase *sleight of hand* ('dexterity in using the hands to perform conjuring tricks, etc.') is sometimes misspelt and mispronounced. Note the *-ei-* spelling and the pronunciation [slīt] not [slayt].

slough *Slough* is pronounced [slow], rhyming with *how*, in the sense 'swamp; state of hopeless dejection': □ *in the slough of despond*, and [sluf] when referring to the cast-off skin of a snake or the verb 'shed or abandon'.

slow The use of the word *slow* as an adverb should generally be avoided in formal contexts: □ *Time passes slowly* [not *slow*] *in prison.* □ *You'd better drive slow in this fog.*

smart In modern usage the adjective *smart*, meaning 'intelligent', is often applied to devices that use sophisticated electronic technology: □ *smart card* (a plastic bank card with an integral microprocessor) □ *smart house* (a house with computer-controlled heating, lighting, etc.).

smear The increasing use of the noun *smear* to denote a defamatory attack, often involving slander or libel, is disliked by many users: □ *Their allegations of professional misconduct are the latest in a series of smears.* □ *the victim of a smear campaign.*

smelled or **smelt**? Either word may be used as the past tense and past participle of the verb *smell*: □ *The cake smelled/smelt delicious.*

so The phrase *so that*, expressing purpose, is sometimes reduced to *so* in informal contexts. In formal speech and writing the word *that* should be retained: □ *The gate had been left open so (that) we could drive in.*

so-called The adjective *so-called* is generally used in an ironic sense, implying that the following word is inaccurate or inappropriate: □ *a so-called friend.*

sociable or **social**? *Sociable* means 'friendly', 'companionable', or 'convivial'; *social* means 'of society' or 'promoting companionship': □ *a sociable guest* □ *a sociable dinner party* □ *a social worker* □ *a social club.*

solidus The solidus is also known as the *stroke, slant, slash mark, oblique,* or *virgule*. Its main use is in separating alternatives: □ *A doctor must use his/her diagnostic skill in such cases.*

soluble or **solvable**? Either adjective may be used to describe something that can be solved: □ *a soluble/solvable problem. Soluble* is more frequently used to describe something that can be dissolved, especially something that dissolves easily in water: □ *soluble aspirin.*

somebody or **someone**? The pronoun *somebody* and its synonym *someone* are interchangeable in all contexts.

somersault Note the spelling and pronunciation of this word, which means 'acrobatic roll'. The first two syllables are pronounced like *summer*, but are spelt *somer-*; the last syllable is pronounced like *salt*, but spelt *-sault.*

-something Many people dislike the frequent use of the words *twentysomething, thirtysomething, fortysomething,* etc., with reference to people in their twenties/thirties/forties/etc. These words may be used as adjectives or nouns.

sometime or **some time**? These spellings are occasionally confused. *Sometime* is used as an adverb to mean 'at some point in time': □ *I'll come and see you sometime,* and as an adjective to mean 'former': □ *Sir Percy Cooper, the sometime President of the Yachting Association. Some time* means 'a period of time': □ *I need some time to think.* □ *I've been worried about her for some time now.*

sooner see HARDLY.

sophisticated The adjective *sophisticated* is frequently applied to machines or devices, in the sense of 'complex' or 'advanced': □ *Our client ... develops and manufactures sophisticated electrical and electronic* *products and systems* (*Sunday Times*).

sort of see KIND OF.

sound bite A *sound bite* is a segment of a speech, especially one made by a politician, specifically designed to be extracted for news reports and media coverage. Of American origin, the term is a vogue expression that is becoming increasingly common in Britain.

source The use of the word *source* as a verb, meaning 'find a source', is disliked by many users: □ *He had difficulty sourcing the material for his thesis.*

south, **South**, or **southern**? As an adjective, *south* is always written with a capital *S* when it forms part of a proper name: □ *South Africa* □ *the South Pole.* The noun *south* is usually written with a capital *S* when it denotes a specific region, such as the southern states of the USA: □ *The secession of the South precipitated the American Civil War.* In other contexts, and as an adverb, *south* is usually written with a lower-case *s*: □ *Many birds fly south for the winter.* The adjective *southern* is more frequent and usually less specific than the adjective *south*. It is written with a capital *S* when it forms part of a proper name.

Soviet see RUSSIAN OR SOVIET?

sowed or **sown**? Either word may be used as the past participle of the verb *sow*, but *sown* is the more frequent: □ *I have sown/sowed some more parsley in the herb garden.* The past tense of the verb *sow* is always *sowed.*

span see SPUN OR SPAN?

spatula The noun *spatula*, meaning 'flat-bladed utensil', is sometimes misspelt. Note that the word ends in *-a*, not *-ar* or *-er*.

-speak Some people object to the overuse of the suffix *-speak*, meaning 'jargon' or 'characteristic language', which is attached to nouns, proper names, or prefixes and is derived from the term *newspeak* coined by George Orwell in his novel *Nineteen Eighty-Four*: □ *computerspeak* □ *Thatcherspeak.*

spearhead The verb *spearhead* is best avoided where *lead* would be adequate.

speciality or **specialty**? *Spe-*

ciality is used in British English and *specialty* in American English to denote a special skill or interest or a product, service, etc., that is specialized in: □ *Wildlife photography is his speciality.* □ *Steak tartare is a speciality of the house.*

specially see ESPECIALLY OR SPECIALLY?

specialty see SPECIALITY OR SPECIALTY?

species This word is normally pronounced [*spee*sheez]. The alternative pronunciation [*spee*seez] is avoided by careful users.

spectrum The noun *spectrum* is best avoided where *range* would be adequate or more appropriate: □ *a wide spectrum of experience* □ *across the whole spectrum* □ *at the other end of the political spectrum.*

speeded or **sped**? *Sped* is the past tense and past participle of the verb *speed* in the sense of 'move or go quickly'; *speeded* relates to the sense of 'drive at excessive speed' and to the phrasal verb *speed up*, meaning 'accelerate': □ *We sped through the water.* □ *The days have sped by.* □ *He has never speeded on a motorway.* □ *The workers speeded up when the supervisor arrived.*

spelled or **spelt**? Either word may be used as the past tense and past participle of the verb *spell*: □ *Have I spelt/spelled your name right?*

spelling English spelling is notoriously difficult to learn, for native English speakers as well as foreign students. However, it is to some extent governed by rules, some of which are described below.

1 Doubling of consonants Final consonants are sometimes doubled when a suffix starting with a vowel is added. With single-syllable words this applies when the final consonant is preceded by a single vowel: □ *hit – hitting* □ *drop – dropped.* If the word has more than one syllable, the consonant is doubled if the last syllable is stressed and the final consonant is preceded by a single vowel: □ *refer – referred* □ *commit – committed.* Exceptions are words with a final *-l*, which is doubled even if the syllable is unstressed: □ *traveller* (but *traveler* in American

English); and □ *worshipped* □ *handicapped* □ *kidnapped* (not always doubled in American English) □ *leapfrogged* □ *jetlagged* □ *outfitter*. A final *-c* is not doubled, but is changed to *ck* before a suffix beginning with a vowel: □ *panic – panicked*.

2 y and i When a suffix is added to a word that ends in *-y*, the *y* becomes an *i* only if the preceding letter is a consonant: □ *silly – sillier* □ *hurry – hurried*. Exceptions are: □ *said* □ *laid* □ *paid* and in words where a suffix beginning with an *i* is added, such as *-ing*: □ *try – trying*.

3 Final -e When a suffix beginning with a vowel is added to a word with a silent final *-e*, the *e* is dropped: □ *rate – rating*. A growing trend is to drop the *-e-* before the suffixes *-able* and *-age*: □ *likeable – likable* □ *sizeable – sizable* □ *mileage – milage*. If the word ends in *-ge* or *-ce* the *e* is not dropped before *a* and *o*: □ *outrageous* □ *peaceable*. The *e* is not dropped if the suffix begins with a consonant: □ *excitement*, except *-ly* (see 4 below).

4 -ly suffix When *-ly* is added to a word it remains unchanged except for the endings *-ll* and *-le* which change to *-lly* and *-ly*: □ *nice – nicely* □ *full – fully* □ *noble – nobly*. Exceptions are: □ *truly* □ *duly* □ *wholly*.

5 ie and ei The rule '*i* before *e* except after *c*' applies to most words where the sound those letters represent is [ee]: □ *believe* □ *grief* □ *deceive* □ *ceiling*. *Caffeine, protein, seize, species, weir*, and *weird* are exceptions. When the sound represented is [ay] then *ei* is used: □ *beige* □ *reign*.

See also -ABLE OR -IBLE?; -AE- AND -OE-; AMERICANISMS; -ANT OR -ENT?; -IZE OR -ISE?; PLURALS; and individual entries.

spelt see SPELLED OR SPELT?

spend The use of the word *spend* as a noun, meaning 'amount spent' or 'amount to be spent': □ *an advertising spend of £20,000*, is disliked by many people and is best replaced by an appropriate synonym or paraphrase.

spilled or **spilt**? Either word may be used as the past tense and past participle of the verb *spill*: □ *He has spilt/spilled his coffee.* □ *The* *children spilled/spilt out of the school.*

spin doctor A *spin doctor* is a person employed by a political party, government department, etc., to present or interpret facts or events in a favourable light: □ *He received help from Scotland Yard's own spin doctors* (*The Independent*). The term is a vogue expression of American origin, which is becoming increasingly common in Britain.

split infinitive A *split infinitive* occurs when an adverb is inserted between *to* and the infinitive form of a verb: □ *to boldly go.* The practice is widely disliked but very widely used: □ *Captains on the bridge would be able to visually check what was happening on the car decks* (*The Guardian*).

spoiled or **spoilt**? Either word may be used as the past tense and past participle of the verb *spoil*: □ *The bad weather spoiled/spoilt our holiday.*

spontaneity The traditional pronunciation of this noun, meaning 'the quality of behaving in a natural, impulsive way', is [spontă*nee*iti] but the pronunciation [spontă*nay*iti] is probably more frequently heard.

spoonful Most users prefer to form the plural *-fuls*: □ *spoonfuls.* See -FUL.

spouse The use of the noun *spouse* in place of *husband* or *wife* is best avoided where the sex of the person is known: □ *The broadcaster Sue Baker and her husband* [not *spouse*] *were the guests of honour.*

spun or **span**? *Spun* is the past tense and part participle of the verb *spin* in modern usage; *span* is an archaic form of the past tense: □ *He spun the wheel.* □ *This yarn has been spun by hand.*

squalor This word, meaning 'dirtiness; wretchedness': □ *the squalor of the slums*, is sometimes misspelt. In both British and American English the ending is *-or* as in *tremor*, not *-o(u)r* as in *colour*.

squeaky clean The adjective *squeaky clean*, which originated in advertising, is often used in the figurative sense of 'beyond reproach' or 'above suspicion': □ *the squeaky clean image of this generation of pop-stars*

□ *The president must be squeaky clean.* Users of this expression should be aware of its possible derogatory connotations: there may be an implication that the person or thing so described is too good to be true.

stadiums or **stadia**? *Stadiums* is the more usual plural of the noun *stadium*, but either word may be used.

stalactite or **stalagmite**? *Stalactites* and *stalagmites* are tapering masses of calcium carbonate that form in limestone caves. A *stalactite* hangs from the roof; a *stalagmite* rises from the floor.

stanch or **staunch**? Either word may be used as a verb, meaning 'stop (the flow of)', *staunch* being more frequent than *stanch* in modern usage: □ *I staunched/stanched the flow of blood with a handkerchief.* □ *She staunched/stanched the wound.* □ *This offer is no remedy to recruitment and retention problems within our universities:* □ *It won't staunch the brain drain* (*The Guardian*).

standing or **stood**? The substitution of *stood*, the past participle of the verb *stand*, for the present participle *standing* is found in some dialects of English: □ *She was standing* [in some dialects *stood*] *in front of the mirror. Stood* is correctly used in the passive form of the transitive verb *stand*: □ *The bottle should be stood in a cool place for two hours.*

stank or **stunk**? Either word may be used as the past tense of the verb *stink*, but *stunk* is the only form of its past participle: □ *The room stank/stunk of cigarette smoke.* □ *These boots have stunk* [not *stank*] of manure since my visit to the farm last week.

state-of-the-art The adjective *state-of-the-art*, which relates to the current level of technical achievement, development, knowledge, etc., is disliked by some users: □ *Heart of the system is a state-of-the-art desktop copier with a host of time-saving features* (*Sunday Times*). □ *state-of-the-art computer technology.*

stationary or **stationery**? These two words are often confused. *Stationary* means 'not moving': □ *a stationary car*; *stationery* means 'writing materials': □ *office stationery*.

statistics see -ICS.

status In British English the word *status* should be pronounced [*stay*tŭs], with the first syllable like *state*. The pronunciation [*stat*ŭs], with the first syllable as in *static*, is an American English variant.

staunch see STANCH OR STAUNCH?

stay or **stop**? The substitution of the verb *stop* for *stay* in the sense of 'reside temporarily' or 'remain' is found in some dialects of English: □ *We stayed* [in some dialects *stopped*] *with my sister for a few days*.

steal see BURGLE, ROB, OR STEAL?

step- see HALF- OR STEP-?

stereo- This word has the alternative pronunciations [*ster*riō] and [*steer*iō], both of which are acceptable, although the former is more frequent in contemporary usage.

stiletto Note the spelling of this word, which refers to a woman's shoe with a high narrow heel, particularly the *-l-* and the *-tt-*.

stimulant or **stimulus**? Both these nouns are used to denote something that stimulates activity. *Stimulant* is specifically applied to drugs, alcohol, etc., whereas *stimulus* is a more general synonym for 'incentive': □ *Caffeine is a stimulant*. □ *They responded to the stimulus of competition*. A *stimulant* increases activity; a *stimulus* initiates activity.

stimulate see SIMULATE OR STIMULATE?

stimulus see STIMULANT OR STIMULUS?

stoical The adjective *stoical*, meaning 'resigned to or unaffected by suffering': □ *a stoical attitude to death*, is pronounced [*stō*ikl]. The *-o-* and *-i-* are pronounced separately, not as the *oi* sound of *soil*.

stood see STANDING OR STOOD?

stop see STAY OR STOP?

storey or **story**? These two spellings are sometimes confused. The word *storey*, meaning 'level of a building': □ *He lives on the second storey*. □ *a multi-storey car park*, is spelt with an *e*; the plural is *storeys*. A *story* means 'a tale': □ *Tell me a story*; its plural is *stories*.

straight or **strait**? The word *straight* is most frequently used as an adjective or adverb: □ *a straight line* □ *I went straight there.* It is sometimes used as a noun, meaning 'straight line or part': □ *the home straight* (of a racecourse). The word *strait* is an archaic adjective meaning 'narrow; restricted'; in modern usage it is most frequently found in the form of the plural noun *straits*, meaning 'difficult circumstances': □ *in dire straits.* In the sense of 'narrow channel', the noun *strait* (or *straits*) also occurs in proper names: □ *the Straits of Dover*.

straightaway or **straight away**? This expression, meaning 'without delay': □ *I'll be going to the shops straightaway*, may be written as one word or two.

straightened or **straitened**? These words are sometimes confused. *Straightened* means 'made straight': □ *The road has been straightened. Straitened*, which is derived from the archaic adjective *strait* (see STRAIGHT OR STRAIT?), means 'restricted': □ *in straitened circumstances.*

strait see STRAIGHT OR STRAIT?

straitened see STRAIGHTENED OR STRAITENED?

straitjacket and **straitlaced** A *straitjacket*, a constricting jacket used to restrain a violent person, and also in extended senses, 'something that restricts', may also be spelt *straightjacket*: □ *Eurotunnel will overnight make cross-Channel communications fast, efficient and dependable. A change from the straightjacket we're in now* (*Sunday Times*). In the same way, *straitlaced*, meaning 'puritanical', may also be spelt *straightlaced*: □ *a very straitlaced maiden aunt.* See also STRAIGHT OR STRAIT?

strata see STRATUM OR STRATA?

stratagem or **strategy**? A *stratagem* is a scheme, trick, or ruse; *strategy* is the art of planning a campaign: □ *to devise a new stratagem* □ *the strategy involved in a game of chess.*

stratum or **strata**? *Strata* is the plural form of the noun *stratum*: □ *from a different social stratum* □ *in one of the upper strata of the rock.*

street see ROAD OR STREET?

street- In such words and phrases as *streetwise* and *street credibility*, *street-* refers to the culture of young people, especially young working-class inhabitants of the inner cities: □ *a streetwise kid.* The meaning has recently widened to include the culture of those familiar with the latest trends, fashions, topical issues, etc.: □ *To be successful in the public relations industry, you need more than just street credibility.* □ *Ladas and Skodas snubbed as car thieves opt for 'street cred' (headline, The Guardian).* See also -CRED. *Street* is occasionally used as an adjective in slang usage in its own right, meaning 'accepted by young people, or those familiar with the latest trends, etc.': □ *He isn't street enough.*

strength This word is sometimes mispronounced [strenth]. The correct pronunciation is [strength], but the variant pronunciation [strenkth] is acceptable to most users.

stress Some languages have a fairly regular stress pattern but English stress patterns are varied and subject to change over time. As foreign words become absorbed into the English language they often change their stress to a more English-sounding one: □ *bureau* □ *chauffeur.* Two-syllable words are more likely to be stressed on the first syllable, but when a word serves as both a noun (or adjective) and a verb it is normally stressed on the first syllable as a noun (or adjective), but the second as a verb: □ *permit* □ *rebel.* Most three-syllable words have their stress on the first syllable. Words with four or more syllables usually have their stress on the second or third syllable. Individual words may be stressed in speech for emphasis (see also INTONATION).

stringed or **strung**? *Stringed* is an adjective derived from the noun *string*; *strung* is the past tense and past participle of the verb *string*: □ *a stringed instrument* □ *a twelve-stringed guitar* □ *His squash racket was strung by an expert.* □ *The children (have) strung decorations around the room.*

student see PUPIL OR STUDENT?

stunk see STANK OR STUNK?

stupefy This word, meaning 'bewilder or amaze', is sometimes misspelt. Note the ending *-efy* (like *putrefy*), in spite of the spelling of the related word *stupid*.

stupor This word, meaning 'a drowsy dazed state': □ *in a drunken stupor*, is sometimes misspelt. Note the final *-or*, as in *torpor*, rather than *-our*.

subconscious or **unconscious**? Both these adjectives mean 'without (full) awareness', but *subconscious* implies a greater degree of consciousness than *unconscious*: □ *a subconscious desire* □ *unconscious resentment*.

subject The *subject* of a clause or sentence is the noun, pronoun, or phrase that controls the verb (see also ACTIVE; PASSIVE). The subject usually precedes the verb, unless the clause or sentence is a question. In the sentence: □ *The dog buried the bone*, *the dog* is the subject. In the sentence: □ *Does he like them?*, the pronoun *he* is the subject.

subjective see OBJECTIVE OR SUBJECTIVE?

subjunctive The *subjunctive is the grammatical set ('mood') of forms of a verb used to express possibilities or wishes rather than facts. With most verbs the subjunctive form is its basic form minus the* *-s* ending of the third person singular, but *to be* has the past tense subjunctive *were*. The subjunctive is largely falling into disuse but survives in such idioms as: □ *be that as it may* □ *as it were* □ *far be it from me* □ *come what may*. The main use of subjunctives is in clauses introduced by *that* and expressing a proposal, desire, or necessity: □ *It is vital that she leave immediately*. The other use of subjunctives is in clauses introduced by *if*, *though* or *supposing*: □ *If you were to go, you might regret it*.

subordinate clause see CLAUSE.

subpoena This word, as a noun referring to a writ requiring a person to appear in court, is sometimes misspelt. Note particularly the *-oe-*. The pronunciations [sŭb*peen*ă] or [sŭ*peen*ă] are both acceptable.

subsequent see CONSEQUENT OR SUBSEQUENT?

subsidence The traditional pronunciation of this word, which means 'falling or sinking': □ *cracks* *due to subsidence*, is [sŭbsī-dĕns].

subsidiarity The noun *subsidiarity* is often used in the conext of the European Community, where it refers to the principle that political decisions should be made at the lowest level. Thus some issues may be dealt with by countries that belong to the EC rather than by the EC itself.

subsidiary The noun and adjective *subsidiary*, which means 'auxiliary; subordinate', is sometimes misspelt. Note that the word ends in *-iary*, not *-uary* or *-ary*.

substantial or **substantive**? Both these adjectives refer to the basic substance or essence of something, but neither is in frequent use in this sense. *Substantial* usually means 'of considerable size, importance, etc.': □ *a substantial improvement* □ *a substantial meal*. *Substantive*, a rarer word, is used to mean 'real; firm': □ *substantive measures to curb inflation.*

substitute see REPLACE OR SUBSTITUTE?

subsume The verb *subsume* means 'incorporate within a larger category or group' or 'classify under a general rule or heading'; it should not be used as a pretentious synonym for 'include' or 'contain': □ *The concept of a classless society is subsumed within the doctrine of Marxism.*

succeed see ACCEDE OR EXCEED?

successfully or **successively**? These two adverbs are sometimes confused. *Successfully* means 'with success'; *successively* means 'in succession': □ *The surgeons operated successfully.* □ *The sales figures fell for several months successively.*

such The use of the construction *such ... that* (or *such ... who*) in place of *such ... as* is avoided by careful users: □ *such tools as* [not *that*] *are needed for the job* □ *such people as* [not *who*] *are eligible for supplementary benefit.*

such as or **like**? *Such as* introduces an example; *like* introduces a comparison: □ *Dairy products, such as milk and cheese, should be kept in a cool place.* □ *Dairy products, like fresh meat, should be kept in a cool place.* □ *He directed several horror films, such as Dracula.*

□ *He directed several horror films like Dracula.*

suffer from or **suffer with**? *Suffer from* means 'have (an illness or disability)'; *suffer with* means 'experience pain or discomfort because of (an illness or disability)': □ *I suffer from hay fever.* □ *I have been suffering with my hay fever today.*

suffixes see PREFIXES AND SUFFIXES.

suit or **suite**? These two nouns should not be confused. A *suit* is a set of clothes, one of the four sets of playing cards, or an action in a court of law: □ *a trouser suit* □ *to follow suit* □ *a lawsuit. A suite* is a set of furniture, a set of rooms, or a musical composition with several movements: □ *to reupholster a suite* □ *the honeymoon suite* □ *a ballet suite.*

summon or **summons**? To *summon* is to send for, call upon, or muster; to *summons* is to serve with a legal summons (an order to appear in court): □ *I was summoned to the managing director's office.* □ *He was summonsed for speeding.*

sunk, **sunken** see SANK, SUNK, OR SUNKEN?

super- Some people object to the frequent use of the prefix *super-*, in the sense of 'surpassing all others' or 'to an excessive degree', to coin new nouns and adjectives: □ *a superbug that is resistant to most antibiotics* □ *those superfit people who put the rest of us to shame.*

supercilious This word, meaning 'haughty in a condescending disdainful manner', is sometimes misspelt. Note the single *c* and single *l*.

superlative see COMPARATIVE AND SUPERLATIVE.

supersede This word, meaning 'replace', is sometimes misspelt. The most frequent mistake is to confuse the *-sede* ending with the *-cede* ending of *precede*.

supervise *Supervise*, meaning 'oversee': □ *She supervised the plans for the party*, is sometimes misspelt; the *-ise* ending cannot be spelt *-ize*: see -IZE OR -ISE?

supine see PROSTRATE, PRONE, OR SUPINE?

supper see DINNER, LUNCH, TEA, OR SUPPER?

supplement see COMPLEMENT OR SUPPLEMENT?

suppose or **supposing**? Either word may be used to introduce a suggestion or hypothesis, *suppose* being preferred by some users in formal contexts: □ *Suppose/Supposing we sell the car?* □ *Suppose/Supposing the train is late.*

suppress see OPPRESS, REPRESS, OR SUPPRESS?

surprised *Surprised* is followed by the preposition *by* in the sense of 'taken unawares' and by *at* in the sense of 'amazed': □ *The thief was surprised by the owner of the car.* □ *I was surprised at her ignorance.*

surveillance This word, meaning 'careful observation', is usually pronounced [ser*vay*lĕns]. The pronunciation [ser*vay*ĕns], imitating the French original, sounds rather affected.

susceptible The adjective *susceptible* is followed by the preposition *to* in the sense of 'easily influenced or affected' and by *of* in the formal sense of 'capable' or 'admitting': □ *susceptible to flattery* □ *susceptible to hay fever* □ *susceptible of a different interpretation.*

suspect or **suspicious**? The word *suspect* may be used as a verb, noun, or adjective. *Suspicious* functions only as an adjective. In its adjectival sense of 'causing suspicion' or 'open to suspicion', *suspect* is sometimes virtually synonymous with *suspicious*: □ *a suspect/suspicious package* □ *The scheme sounds rather suspect/suspicious.* However, only *suspicious* can be used in the sense of 'feeling or showing suspicion': □ *The police were suspicious* [not *suspect*] *of her behaviour.* Similarly, only *suspect* can be used in the sense of 'possibly false or unreliable': □ *a suspect banknote* □ *The braking system is suspect.*

suspense or **suspension**? Both these nouns are derived from the verb *suspend*, meaning 'hang'. *Suspense* is largely restricted to the figurative sense of 'a state of uncertainty, anxiety, insecurity, or excitement': □ *Don't keep me in suspense any longer! Suspension* means 'the act of suspending' or 'the state of being suspended'; it is also used in the figurative senses of 'interruption; deferment; postponement' and 'temporary debarment or expulsion': □ *the suspension of an insurance policy* □ *The offending players face suspension from the team.*

The two nouns are not interchangeable in any context.

suspicious see SUSPECT OR SUSPICIOUS?

sustainable In modern usage the adjective *sustainable* has developed a specialized application to natural resources that can be renewed: □ *sustainable forests*, and to activities that do not damage the environment: □ *sustainable development*.

swam or **swum**? *Swam* is the past tense of the verb *swim*; *swum* is the past participle: □ *The dog swam to the shore.* □ *the lake where they had swum.*

swap or **swop**? Both spellings are acceptable for this informal word meaning 'exchange': □ *to swap stamps* □ *swop homes for a holiday. Swap* is the more traditional spelling, but *swop* is a frequently used variation.

swat or **swot**? These spellings are sometimes confused. *Swat* means 'strike with a blow': □ *to swat flies.* This word may also be spelt *swot*, although this spelling is disliked by many careful users. *Swot* is an informal word meaning 'study hard': □ *swotting for exams.*

sweet see DESSERT, SWEET, PUDDING, OR AFTERS?

swelled or **swollen**? Either word may be used as the past participle of the verb *swell. Swelled* is the more neutral form; *swollen* often indicates an undesirable or harmful increase or expansion: □ *The population has swelled in recent years.* □ *The disaster fund was swelled by a generous contribution from the mayor.* □ *His wrist has swollen to twice its normal size.* □ *The stream was swollen by the melted snow.*

swingeing Note the pronunciation and spelling of this word, which means 'severe': □ *swingeing cuts in public expenditure* □ *swingeing tax increases.* The word is pronounced [*swin*jing]; the *-e-* distinguishes it from *swinging* and indicates the softness of the *g*. See also SPELLING 3.

swollen see SWELLED OR SWOLLEN?

swop see SWAP OR SWOP?

swot see SWAT OR SWOT?

syllable A *syllable* is a unit of a word that contains a vowel sound or something that resembles a vowel sound. The words *by*, *tune*, and *through* have one syllable; the words *doctor*, *table*, and *open* have two syllables; the word *secretary* has three syllables if the *a* is not sounded and four syllables if the *a* is sounded.

syllabus The plural of this word, which means 'the subjects studied in a particular course', is usually *syllabuses*. *Syllabi*, pronounced [-bī], is the less frequent plural form.

symbol see CYMBAL OR SYMBOL?

syndrome Some people object to the frequent use of the noun *syndrome* in nonmedical contexts to denote any set of characteristics, actions, emotions, etc.: □ *She is suffering from the only-child syndrome.*

synergy In technical contexts the noun *synergy*, pronounced with a soft *g* sound [*sinĕ*ji], denotes the combined action and increased effect of two or more drugs, muscles, etc., working together. The introduction of the noun *synergy* into general usage is disliked by some: □ *Synergy, as business people know, is bringing several elements together to make a product greater than the parts* (Islwyn Borough Council advertisement). □ [of the Cadbury-Schweppes merger] *The growth of vending machines has provided the magic synergy which such mergers are always supposed to produce* (*The Guardian*).

synonymous Note the spelling of this word, particularly the vowel sequence *-y-o-y-o-*.

syphon see SIPHON OR SYPHON?

systematic or **systemic**? The adjective *systematic* means 'methodical; well-ordered; well-planned': □ *a systematic approach to the problem* □ *You must try to be more systematic.* A rare synonym of *systematic*, the adjective *systemic* is most frequently found in biological contexts, in the sense of 'affecting or spreading through the whole system, body, plant, etc': □ *a systemic disease* □ *a systemic fungicide.*

T

-t see **-ED OR -T?**
tactics see **-ICS**.
tag question see **QUESTIONS**.
take on board The informal phrase *take on board* means 'accept (a situation, new idea, etc.)': □ *This is a lesson everyone is having to take on board.* This vogue expression is disliked by some people and should not be overused.
tall see **HIGH OR TALL?**
target The noun *target* is now most frequently used in its metaphorical meaning of 'an aim or goal'. The verb form is more recent, and is often followed by *on* or *at*: □ *The advertising campaign is to be carefully targeted at the 18–25 age group.*
tariff This word is sometimes misspelt. Note the single *r* and the *-ff* ending.
task force A *task force* is a group of people formed in order to undertake a particular objective, usually of a military nature: □ *The captain led a task force to blow up the bridge.*
tasteful or **tasty**? These two adjectives relate to different senses of the word *taste. Tasteful* is applied to things that indicate good taste, in the sense of 'aesthetic discrimination'; *tasty* is applied to things that have a good taste, in the sense of 'flavour'.
tautology *Tautology* is the avoidable repetition of an idea already expressed in different words: □ *a new innovation* □ *a brief moment.* Many well-established English phrases contain tautologies: □ *circle round* □ *free gift* □ *join together* □ *all-time record*, etc.
tea see **DINNER, LUNCH, TEA, OR SUPPER?**
teach see **LEARN OR TEACH?**
team or **teem**? These two words are sometimes confused, being identical in pronunciation. *Team* is most frequently used as a noun, meaning 'group of

people (or animals) who work or play together': □ *a valuable member of the sales team* □ *the captain of the hockey team* □ *a team of oxen. Teem* is a verb, meaning 'pour' or 'abound': □ *It was teeming with rain.* □ *The village was teeming with tourists.*

technical or **technological**? *Technical* means 'having or concerned with special practical knowledge of a scientific or mechanical subject'; *technological* means 'using science for practical purposes' and is used particularly of modern advances in technical processes: □ *technical skills* □ *a technical college* □ *a technological breakthrough.*

techno- The prefix *techno-* relates to art, craft, technology, or technical matters. Some people object to its frequent use in the coining of new words in the sense of 'relating to high technology, especially computers'. *Techno-* may be used with or without a hyphen: □ *technophobia* □ *technofreak* □ *techno-politics.* See also HI-TECH.

technological see TECHNICAL OR TECHNOLOGICAL?

teem see TEAM OR TEEM?

tele- The prefix *tele-*, from a Greek word meaning 'far', is found in such words as *television, telephone, telescope,* etc. It is increasingly used in the senses of 'relating to television' or 'by telephone': □ *telebook* □ *telecast* □ *televangelism.* These neologisms are disliked by some people, despite the fact that most of them retain the original sense of 'far', since a thing transmitted by television or telephone must originate at a distance.

telephone see PHONE.

televise This word is often spelt incorrectly with a *z* instead of an *s*.

temerity or **timidity**? *Temerity* means 'audacity or recklessness'; *timidity* means 'lacking courage or self-confidence; easily frightened or alarmed'.

temperature *Temperature* can mean 'the degree of heat or cold as measured on, for example, a thermometer'; 'the degree of heat natural to the body'; and, as a synonym for *fever*, 'abnormally high body heat'. To *take someone's temperature* means 'to use a thermometer to find the person's body heat'.

temporary The adjective *temporary* may be pronounced as a three- or four-syllable word, with the stress on the first syllable: [*tem*prări] or [*tem*pŏrări]. The four-syllable pronunciation is preferred by some careful users.

temporize see EXTEMPORIZE OR TEMPORIZE?

tense The *tense* of a verb is a set of forms expressing distinctions of time. Some modern grammarians tend to say that fundamentally there are only two real tenses in English, the *present*: □ *It is hot today*, and the *past*: □ *It was cloudy yesterday*. The *future* is simply formed by the addition of *will* or *shall*, etc.: □ *It will be fine tomorrow*, and all other changes of tense are marked by using *be*, *have*, or both combined, with the past or present participle of the verb: □ *She is dancing.* □ *He was talking.* □ *I'll be thinking of you.* □ *They had ridden for three days.* □ *I shall have finished it by then.* □ *They had slept until noon.* □ *He had been praying.* □ *She has been working.* □ *They will have been travelling all day.* If there is more than one verb in a sentence, the tense of the subordinate clause(s) containing the other verb(s) often follow(s) the tense of the main clause containing the most important verb. This is by no means always the case, as clauses may refer to different times: □ *I believe I met him last week.* When the main clause is in the future, the verb of the subordinate clause is usually in the present: □ *I will look him up when I go to London.* When the main clause is in the past but the subordinate clause expresses some permanent fact, then that clause can be in the present. The present tense can be used to express the future: □ *I leave on Thursday.* The *present perfect* is generally used for expressing recent events or actions by adding *have* to the past participle of a verb: □ *You've already told me.*

terminal or **terminus**? Used as a noun meaning 'end or finishing point' these words are often synonymous. Both can mean the finishing point of a transport line, but in Britain *terminal* is used for airlines, *terminus* for railways, while either can be used for bus routes. *Terminal* as an adjective can mean 'of, at, the end' or 'leading to death': □ *a terminal illness.*

terminate *Terminate*, meaning 'bring to an end, form the ending of, close', is increasingly used in the context of ending employment. From speaking of *terminating someone's contract*, etc., some people have gone on to use *terminated* as a synonym for *dismissed*: □ *The workers were terminated when profits fell.*

terminus see TERMINAL OR TERMINUS?

terrible or **terrific**? *Terrible* can be used as a general term of disapproval or can mean 'very bad' or 'causing distress'. *Terrific*, on the other hand, expresses approval: □ *Chartres has a terrific cathedral.* Both can mean 'unusually great': □ *There's a terrible/terrific amount of paperwork here.*

tête-à-tête This compound, meaning 'intimate conversation between two people', is of French origin. Note the accents, which should not be omitted when the term is used in English texts.

than *Than* is used to link two halves of comparisons or contrasts: □ *Jack is taller than Jill.* □ *I am wiser now than I was at that time.*

thankfully As an adverb from *thank*, *thankfully* means 'in a thankful, relieved, or grateful way': □ *They received the good news thankfully.* It is also used to mean 'it is a matter of relief that': □ *Thankfully, he has survived the operation.*

thank you *Thank you, thanks, many thanks*, etc., are expressions of gratitude: □ *Thank you for a lovely evening.* They are also used in acceptance: □ *'Have a sweet.' 'Thanks, I will.'*, as a polite refusal in conjunction with *no*: □ *'Have a sweet.' 'No, thanks.'*, in a firm and less polite refusal: □ *I can manage without your advice, thank you very much*, and to show pleasure: □ *Now David's got a new job, we're doing very nicely, thank you very much.*

that *That* is used as a conjunction or relative pronoun to introduce various types of clause, and in some cases can be omitted, both in written and spoken English. As a conjunction it can usually be omitted:

□ *I'm sure (that) you're lying.* It cannot be left out when used with a noun: □ *the fact that grass is green*, or with certain verbs, usually of a formal nature, for example *assert, contend*. It must not be left out when its omission could lead to ambiguity: □ *I said last week you were wrong* might mean either 'I said that last week you were wrong' or 'I said last week that you were wrong'.

that or this? The difference between the pronouns *that* and *this,* referring to objects or people, is one of distance. *That* is further away from the speaker than *this*: □ *Give me that.* □ *Take this.*

that or which? Whether to use *that* or *which* depends on whether it appears in a defining or non-defining clause. *That* and *which* are both used in defining clauses: □ *the school that/which they go to.* Note that a defining clause is not preceded by a comma. In non-defining clauses, those conveying parenthetical or incidental information, only *which* can be used: □ *The programme, which was broadcast by the BBC, caused much controversy.* Non-defining clauses are always preceded by a comma and, unless at the end of a sentence, followed by one. On the use of *that* or *who/whom*, see WHO.

the *The* is the most frequently used word in the English language. Before consonants it is pronounced [dhĕ]; before vowels or an unaspirated *h* it is pronounced [dhee].

theft see BURGLE, ROB, OR STEAL?

their, there, or they're? These three words are sometimes confused. *Their* means 'of them or belonging to them': □ *their house*. *There* means 'in or to that place': □ *over there*. *They're* is a contraction of *they are*: □ *They're/They are always late.*

them or their? see -ING FORMS.

theme park A *theme park* is an amusement park in which the displays and entertainments are organized round one particular idea or group of ideas, e.g. space travel or the Wild West.

themself The reflexive pronoun *themself* is unacceptable to careful users, being associated with the controversial singular usage of *they, them, their,* etc. (see THEY): □ *Somebody has been helping themself to my whisky.*

thence *Thence* is a formal and almost archaic word with three meanings: 'from there, from that place': □ *We drove to York and thence to Scotland*; 'from that premise, or for that reason': □ *She proved that x was an even number and thence that it must be 42*; and 'from that time': □ *His wife died ten years ago and thence he has become a recluse.*

there see THEIR, THERE, OR THEY'RE?

there are see THERE IS OR THERE ARE?

therefore *Therefore* means 'for that reason, consequently, as this proves': □ *I dislike worms; therefore I avoid digging the garden.*

there is or **there are**? Normally, *there is* should precede a singular noun, and *there are* a plural: □ *There is a pine.* □ *There are cedars.* However, *there is* is widely used in various expressions where *there are* is formally correct.

they *They, them, their*, etc., are increasingly being used to refer to singular entities: □ *Anyone can apply if they have the qualifications.*

they're see THEIR, THERE, OR THEY'RE?

third or **thirdly**? see FIRST OR FIRSTLY?

this see NEXT OR THIS?; THAT OR THIS?

thoroughfare The noun *thoroughfare,* meaning 'way through', is sometimes misspelt and/or mispronounced, the most frequent error being the substitution of *through-* for *thorough-*.

though see ALTHOUGH OR THOUGH?

thrash or **thresh**? The verb *thrash* means 'flog or beat with repeated blows' or 'defeat': □ *He was thrashed by the headmaster.* □ *We thrashed the opposition. Thresh* means 'separate seeds of cereal from husks by beating'.

threshold Note that there is only one *h* in the middle of this word, unlike in the word *withhold*.

thus The slightly formal adverb *thus* means 'in such a manner, in the way indicated, consequently': □ *His father died in a hunting accident and he thus* *became a baron.*

till or **until**? Both words mean 'up to the time that, up to as far as': □ *I will work until I drop.* □ *Carry on till you reach the traffic lights.*

timidity see TEMERITY OR TIMIDITY?

titillate or **titivate**? Literally, *titillate* means the same as *tickle* but it is almost always used figuratively in the sense of 'stimulate or arouse pleasantly': □ *Her interest titillated his vanity. Titivate* is occasionally confused with *titillate*, but its meaning is 'tidy or smarten up': □ *I must titivate myself for the party.*

titles Generally the titles of literary works, musical works, works of art, films, etc., are set in italics or, in handwriting and typescript, underlined: □ I saw *King Lear* last night. □ She sang the title role in *Carmen.* □ Constable's *Flatford Mill.* The Bible and the names of its individual books are not set in italics, and neither are the Talmud, the Torah, or the Koran. Newspapers and periodicals are set in italics. Normally the definite article before a paper's name is not italicized: □ the *Daily Mail. The Times* and *The Economist* are exceptions. The titles of long poems are usually set in italics, but short ones set in inverted commas: □ Keats's *Endymion* □ Keats's 'To Autumn'.

to or **too**? These two spellings are sometimes confused. *To* is used with the infinitive and as a preposition; *too* is an adverb, meaning 'also' or 'excessively': □ *to go home* □ *Give it to me.* □ *too much noise* □ *Mary came too.*

together with *Together with* means 'in addition to': □ *The chairman of the company, together with three of the directors, has resigned.* Note that the verb *has* agrees with the singular noun *chairman*: the phrase introduced by *together with* does not form part of the subject of the sentence.

toilet, lavatory, loo, or **bathroom**? *Toilet, lavatory,* and *loo* are virtually interchangeable in British English: □ *I need the toilet.* □ *We're out of lavatory paper.* □ *Where's the loo? Bathroom* is used in American English as a synonym for *toilet*, but in Britain its main meaning is a room containing a bath but not necessarily a toilet. The use of *toilet* or *lavatory* is often considered a class marker in Britain. Upper- and middle-class people tend to use *lavatory*, while lower-middle and working-class people use *toilet* and regard *lavatory* as affected or impolite. *Loo* is classless.

tolerance or **toleration**? Both these words are nouns from *tolerate*, but *tolerance* is 'the capacity to tolerate', while *toleration* is 'the act of tolerating': □ *His tolerance is unlimited.* □ *Her toleration of his habits demonstrates her good nature.*

too see TO OR TOO?

torpor This word, meaning 'inactive condition', is sometimes misspelt. Note the final *-or*, as in *stupor*, rather than *-our*.

tortuous or **torturous**? *Tortuous* means 'twisting; winding' and, figuratively, 'complex, devious, or overelaborate': □ *a tortuous road* □ *a tortuous policy. Torturous* comes from *torture* and means 'inflicting torture; agonizing or painful': □ *a torturous illness.*

total *Total* is used as a noun: □ *The total was 115*, a verb: □ *Profits this year total one million pounds*, and an intensifying adjective suggesting completeness: □ *a total failure* □ *a total stranger.*

tourniquet This word, meaning 'a bandage tied tightly round an arm or leg to stop bleeding', may be pronounced [*toor*nikay] or [*tor*nikay] in British English.

toward or **towards**? In British English *toward* is a rare adjective meaning 'afoot', 'imminent', or 'favourable' or a variant of *towards*, the usual form of the preposition meaning 'in the direction of' or 'with regard to': □ *They walked towards the hotel.* □ *What are his feelings towards her?*

town see CITY OR TOWN?

town house A *town house* suggests an urban terraced house, usually with three or more storeys. However, when one speaks of someone's *town house* one can also mean a house in town belonging to a rich person whose main residence is in the country: □ *They used their town house for Veronica's ball.*

track record The phrase *track record*, meaning 'record of past performance', is frequently used as an unnecessary extension of the word *record* or synonym for 'experience', especially in job advertisements: □ *a sound track record in R&D* □ *a successful track record in sales and marketing*. Care should be taken to avoid overusing this expression.

trade names Trade names are names given to articles by their manufacturers. Some have become generic names for articles of their kind, even when the article does not actually bear the trade name in question: □ *Thermos flask* □ *Hoover* □ *Biro*. All nouns that are actually trade names should be spelt with an initial capital letter, although this is frequently overlooked. When the noun has given rise to a verb it is spelt with a lower-case initial letter: □ *He hoovered the carpet*.

trade union or **trades union**? The generally accepted singular noun is *trade union*, with the plural *trade unions*. There is no good grammatical reason for the use of *trades union* or *trades unions*, although both are frequently used. However, the official title of the TUC, the central association of British trade unions, is the *Trades Union Congress*, and this title should be used when referring to that organization.

trafficker This word is sometimes misspelt. The word *traffic* adds a *k* before the suffixes *-er*, *-ed*, and *-ing*: □ *drug traffickers* □ *illegal arms trafficking*. See also SPELLING 1.

trait This word may be pronounced [tray] or [trayt], although careful users prefer the first pronunciation.

tranche The noun *tranche* is best avoided where *section*, *group*, *portion*, or *instalment* would be adequate or more appropriate: □ *a tranche of the population*.

tranquillity This word, meaning 'peaceful state': □ *the perfect tranquillity of the lake*, is often misspelt. Note the *-ll-* and the final single *t*.

transient or **transitory**? Both words mean 'short-lived, lasting only a brief time': □ *It is just a transient/transitory phase*. The words are virtually interchangeable but have a slightly different feel about them. *Transient* often suggests passing by quickly, perhaps because of rapid movement from place to place: □ *transient summer visitors*. *Transitory* often carries a suggestion of regret about the way desirable things change or disappear: □ *the transitory nature of human love*. *Transient* is sometimes used as a noun to denote a person who stays for only a short time in any one place.

transitive see VERBS.

translate or **transliterate**? To *translate* is to express in a different language; to *transliterate* is to write or print using a different alphabet.

transparent This word has various pronunciations, all of which are acceptable. The most frequent in contemporary usage is [trans*par*rĕnt] but the pronunciations [trahns*par*rĕnt] and [trans*pair*ĕnt] are also heard. The *-s-* is sometimes pronounced with a *z* sound.

transpire *Transpire* means 'become known; come to light': □ *It later transpired that the President had known of the plan all along*. It is also widely used to mean 'happen or occur': □ *I will let you know what transpires*. This second use is disliked by many careful users, although it has a well-established history.

transport or **transportation**? *Transport* is used in British English both for the system and means of conveying: □ *public transport* □ *I have my own transport*. In American English *transportation* is often used: □ *the fastest form of transportation* □ *The goods were packed ready for transportation*, and this usage is now occasionally found in British English.

transverse or **traverse**? *Transverse* is an adjective meaning 'lying or set across; at right angles': □ *a transverse section*. *Traverse* is a verb meaning 'cross; go across' or a noun meaning 'way or path across'.

traumatic *Traumatic* is the adjective from *trauma*, which means 'a wound or injury' and it is still used in this sense in medical contexts: □ *traumatic fever*. However its main use is with the figurative meaning of 'causing great and deeply disturbing emotional shock': □ *a traumatic bereavement* □ *the traumatic effects of divorce* □ *the traumatic experience of a concentration camp.*

travel This word is sometimes misspelt. In British English the final *l* is doubled before the suffixes *-ed*, *-ing*, and *-er*: □ *well-travelled* □ *travelling fast along the motorway* □ *commercial travellers.*

traverse see TRANSVERSE OR TRAVERSE?

treble or **triple**? Both words can be used as a noun, verb, and adjective and are virtually interchangeable in meaning. However, *treble* is preferred by many careful users when the meaning is 'three times as great': □ *treble the sum,* and *triple* when the meaning is 'consisting of three parts': □ *a triple jump*. The words have distinctly different meanings in the context of music. *Treble* refers to a high-pitched voice or instrument, or a singer who performs at this pitch, whereas *triple* is used of rhythm: □ *a treble recorder* □ *triple time.*

tremor This word, meaning 'shaking or quivering action': □ *earth tremors*, is sometimes misspelt. Note the ending *-or*, not *-our*.

triple see TREBLE OR TRIPLE?

triumphal or **triumphant**? These adjectives are often confused. *Triumphal* is connected with the celebration of a victory, usually of a military nature: □ *triumphal arch. Triumphant* means 'victorious, exulting or rejoicing in success': □ *The team were triumphant.*

trivia *Trivia* means 'matters of very minor importance': □ *the trivia of village gossip.*

troop or **troupe**? These words are sometimes confused. A *troop* is a military unit or group of people or things: □ *troops of soldiers* □ *a Scout troop. Troop* is also used as a verb in informal English to mean 'move as a large group': □ *Then they all trooped off home.* A *troupe* is a group of actors or performers: □ *a troupe of travelling acrobats.*

trooping the colour To *troop the colour* is to parade the flag of a regiment ceremonially along the ranks of soldiers of that regiment. Written with capital initials, the phrase *Trooping* *the Colour* refers to the annual parade in London, usually attended by the Queen, the Prime Minister, and other dignitaries.

troupe see TROOP OR TROUPE?

truculent This adjective, which means 'sullenly or defiantly aggressive', is sometimes misspelt. Note the *-ucu-* and the *-ent* ending. The correct pronunciation is [*truk*yuulĕnt].

truism The narrower meaning of *truism* is 'a statement of self-evident truth, one containing superfluous repetition of an idea': □ *It is a truism to speak of single bachelors.* The word is more widely used to mean 'a statement of a fact that is too obvious to be thought worth stating': □ *the truism that stars are only visible at night.*

truly The adverb *truly* is sometimes misspelt. Note that the final *-e* of *true* is dropped when the adverbial suffix *-ly* is added.

try and or **try to**? The two expressions are virtually interchangeable: □ *Try and catch me!* □ *Try to tell the truth. Try and* is colloquial and is very frequently used; it is unacceptable only in formal written English.

tsar or **czar**? This word, the title of any of the former Russian emperors, is spelt *tsar*, *czar*, or, rarely, *tzar*. It is pronounced [zah].

turbid, turbulent, or **turgid**? *Turbid* means 'opaque; cloudy; muddy; dense': □ *a turbid pool.* The adjective *turbulent* means 'in a state of agitated movement or confusion': □ *turbulent seas* □ *a politically turbulent period of history.* The adjective *turgid* means 'swollen' or 'distended': □ *The turgid river had overflowed its banks.*

turbo- The prefix *turbo-* is applied to a machine that is driven by a turbine: □ *turbofan* □ *turbojet.* Its association with turbocharged cars, in which performance is improved by the use of a turbine, sometimes leads to a mistaken interpretation and application of the prefix in the sense of 'fast' or 'powerful': □ *a turbo model of a computer.* This extension of usage is best avoided.

turbulent, turgid see TURBID, TURBULENT, OR TURGID?

twelfth This word is frequently pronounced without the *f*, although careful users pronounce it [twelfth].

type of see KIND OF.

U

ultimate *Ultimate* is used mainly as an adjective meaning 'last, final, eventual': □ *the ultimate goal*, or 'fundamental': □ *ultimate truths*. As a noun it has traditionally simply meant 'something ultimate' or 'the extreme': □ *the ultimate in wickedness*. This last use is increasingly being extended, particularly in advertising and journalism, to mean 'the best possible; the most modern or advanced thing': □ *the ultimate in swimming pools* □ *the ultimate in high technology*.

ultra *Ultra* is an adjective meaning 'going beyond' or 'extreme' and is also used as a prefix with other words, either with or without a hyphen. In the sense of 'extremely' it is used in such words as: □ *ultra-modern* □ *ultra-radical*.

umbilical This word may be stressed on the second syllable [um*bil*ikl] or on the third [umbi*līk*l].

umpire see REFEREE OR UMPIRE?

un- see NON-.

unanimous *Unanimous* means 'of one mind; in complete agreement': □ *The committee reached a unanimous decision*. It can only be used when several people all agree about something, and cannot be used as a synonym for *wholehearted* or *enthusiastic* as in: □ *Many of the group were prepared to give the project their unanimous backing*.

unaware or **unawares**? *Unaware* is an adjective meaning 'not aware; not knowing about; not having noticed': □ *I was unaware that you were coming.* □ *He seemed unaware of the reaction he was causing*. It is occasionally used as an adverb, but the usual adverb is *unawares*, meaning 'unexpectedly, without warning', often in *caught unawares* or *taken* *unawares*: □ *The landslide caught the villagers unawares.*

unconscious see SUBCONSCIOUS OR UNCONSCIOUS?

under see BELOW, BENEATH, UNDER, OR UNDERNEATH?

under foot or **underfoot**? This term should be spelt as one word, not as two separate words: □ *It was rather wet underfoot.*

underhand or **underhanded**? Both *underhand* and *underhanded* are used as adjectives to mean 'sly; marked by dishonesty, trickery, and deception': □ *They used the most underhand/underhanded methods in their campaign.*

underneath see BELOW, BENEATH, UNDER, OR UNDERNEATH?

underprivileged *Underprivileged* has become a fashionable adjective to use in connection with those lacking the standard of income and opportunities enjoyed by other members of the society in which they live: □ *She started a clinic for underprivileged children.* □ *Many young criminals come from underprivileged backgrounds.* It is used as a noun as well as an adjective: □ *His concern for the underprivileged drew him towards social work as a career.*

undertone see OVERTONE OR UNDERTONE?

underway or **under way**? Careful users prefer to write this expression, meaning 'moving; in progress', as two words: □ *Preparations for the new project are now well under way.* The expression is, however, increasingly being spelt as one word.

undiscriminating see INDISCRIMINATE OR UNDISCRIMINATING?

undoubtedly *Undoubtedly, no doubt, doubtless, without (a) doubt* are all adverbs expressing that something is not disputed. However, *undoubtedly* and *without a doubt* express that idea much more positively and strongly than the other expressions: □ *She is undoubtedly the best student in her year. No doubt* and *doubtless* are much weaker expressions, often suggesting that the user is in fact not completely certain, or is even harbouring doubts: □ *No doubt he is very clever but I still can't understand what he is saying.*

unequivocally Note that the

adverb *unequivocally* has the ending *-ally*, not *-ably*. It is derived from the adjective *unequivocal*, meaning 'clear; plain'.

unexceptionable or **unexceptional**? *Unexceptionable* means 'inoffensive; not liable to be criticized or objected to': □ *His behaviour had been unexceptionable, so he could not understand how he could have offended his hosts. Unexceptional* means 'usual, normal, or ordinary': □ *The weather was unexceptional for the time of year.* It is, however, more frequently used to suggest that something is dull or disappointingly commonplace: □ *I had heard enthusiastic reports of his playing, but I found this an unexceptional performance.*

uninterested see DISINTERESTED OR UNINTERESTED?

unique *Unique* means 'being the only one of its kind': □ *Every snowflake has a unique pattern.* A thing is either unique or it is not, so careful users dislike such expressions as *so unique, rather unique, very unique*, etc., and something cannot be *more unique* or *less unique* than something else. *Almost* and *nearly* are the only modifiers generally acceptable with *unique*.

United Kingdom see BRITAIN.

United States, United States of America see AMERICA.

unmistakable or **unmistakeable**? Both spellings of this word are acceptable, but *unmistakable* is the more frequent in British English. See SPELLING 3.

unnecessary The adjective *unnecessary* is sometimes misspelt. Note the *-nn-* (from the addition of the prefix *un-* to the adjective *necessary*), the single *-c-*, and the *-ss-*.

unorganized see DISORGANIZED OR UNORGANIZED?

unpractical see PRACTICAL OR PRACTICABLE?

unprecedented A *precedent* is 'an earlier example or occurrence of a similar thing', so *unprecedented* means 'never having happened before; completely new or original': □ *His score was unprecedented in the history of cricket.*

unreadable see ILLEGIBLE OR UNREADABLE?

unrepairable see REPAIRABLE OR REPARABLE?

unsociable, unsocial see

ANTISOCIAL, ASOCIAL, UNSOCIAL, OR UNSOCIABLE?

until see TILL OR UNTIL?

unused Like USED, the word *unused* may be pronounced with the [s] sound of the noun *use* or the [z] sound of the verb *use*. In the phrase *unused to,* meaning 'unaccustomed to', *unused* is pronounced [un*yoost*]: □ *I am unused to driving on the righthand side of the road.* The adjective *unused,* meaning 'not being used' or 'never having been used', is pronounced [un*yoozd*]: □ *Many of the rooms are unused.* □ *Unused pills and tablets should be returned to the pharmacy for safe disposal.*

unwaged The adjective and noun *unwaged* refers to anybody who does not receive a wage or salary. Such people include the unemployed, full-time mothers or housewives, students, and old age pensioners: □ *The membership fee is £5 (or £3 for the unwaged).* The euphemistic use of the term *unwaged* in place of *unemployed,* with reference to those who are out of work and seeking employment, could be misleading and is best avoided.

unwanted or **unwonted**? *Unwanted* means simply 'not wanted': □ *She gave her unwanted clothes to the Oxfam shop. Unwonted* means 'out of the ordinary; unusual': □ *The drug gave him an unwonted feeling of euphoria.*

up-front Some people dislike the increasing use of the term *up-front,* meaning 'paid in advance, at the beginning, or as a deposit': □ *an up-front payment* □ *They want £500 up-front and the remainder in monthly instalments.* The term should not be overused, and is best restricted to informal contexts.

upon or **on**? These two words are synonyms and virtually indistinguishable in use: □ *She threw herself upon the sofa.* □ *He walked on the beach. Upon* has a more formal sound and, particularly in spoken English, *on* is more frequently used.

upward or **upwards**? In British English *upward* is principally used as an adjective, *upwards* being the usual form of the adverb meaning 'to a higher level': □ *an upward trend*

□ *to float upwards.*

upwardly mobile This is a very fashionable modern expression, used of ambitious, usually young, people who are moving into a higher class, income bracket, etc.: □ *These days the City is thought to be full of upwardly mobile men and women trying to enhance their status in society.*

urban or **urbane**? *Urban* means 'of a town or city': □ *Unemployment is higher in urban areas. Urbane* is used of someone who is sophisticated and polite, with a smooth and easy manner in any social situation: □ *He turned out to be an elegant and urbane man who charmed them all.*

urinal This word may be stressed on either the second syllable [yuu*rin*l] or the first syllable [*yoor*inl] in British English.

usable or **useable**? Both spellings of this word are acceptable, but *usable* is the more frequent in British English. See SPELLING 3.

usage or **use**? *Usage* is the way in which something, especially language, is used; the noun *use* denotes the act of using: □ *This book deals with problems of usage.* □ *in contemporary usage* □ *the use of wood as an insulator* □ *The photocopier is in use.* Careful users maintain this distinction between the two words, avoiding such phrases as: □ *a ban on the usage of hosepipes.*

useable see USABLE OR USEABLE?

used In the phrase USED TO, *used* is pronounced [yoost]. *Used* as an adjective, for example in: □ *used cars,* and as the past tense and past participle of the verb *use* is pronounced [yoozd].

used to *Used to* either means 'accustomed to': □ *I have got used to the noise by now,* or refers to a habitual action or situation in the past: □ *She used to play squash regularly.* Difficulties arise over negative and question forms of the phrase in its second meaning. In negative forms the more formal *used not to* or the more informal *did not/didn't use to* are both acceptable: □ *He used not to be so aggressive.* □ *She did not use to like fish.* Both *usen't to* and *didn't used to* are heard, but are avoided by careful users. In the question form the formal and rather old-fashioned *used X to?* and the less formal *did X use to?* are both correct: □ *Used there to be a lake in that wood?* □ *Did Henry use to visit you? Did X used to?* or *didn't X used to?* are frequently heard, though disliked by many careful users. As no form sounds completely natural and correct many people would reconstruct the sentence and say, for example: □ *Was there once a lake in that wood?*

user-friendly *User-friendly* is a term used in computing to describe software that is simple to use, being designed to assist the user and forestall any potential problems: □ *a user-friendly program.* The term is increasingly found in other fields, meaning 'easy to operate or understand', and describing electrical appliances, cars, etc.

utilize *Utilize* means 'use in a practical and effective, profitable or productive way': □ *They utilized every machine that was available.* It can also mean 'make good use of something not intended for the purpose': □ *She utilized her tights when the fan belt broke*; or 'make use of something that might be thought useless': □ *She utilized all the scraps for stuffing cushions.* The verb *utilize* is often used, particularly in business jargon, as a synonym for *use.* However, careful users restrict the word to the narrower senses described above.

V

vacant or **vacuous**? Both these adjectives mean 'empty', but they are not generally interchangeable in usage. The adjective *vacant* is most frequently applied to a flat, room, seat, post, etc., that is not occupied by a person or people: □ *a hotel with vacant rooms* □ *The post remained vacant for several months after her resignation.* The adjective *vacuous* is used in formal contexts often in the derogatory sense of 'apparently devoid of intelligence; inane; mindless': □ *a vacuous remark* □ *Modern pop music is vacuous, repetitive, and uninspiring.*

vacation In British English the primary meaning of the noun *vacation* is 'the period when universities and law courts are not officially working': □ *She went home for the Christmas vacation.*

vaccinate see INOCULATE OR VACCINATE?

vacuous see VACANT OR VACUOUS?

vagary The noun *vagary*, meaning 'whim', 'caprice', or 'unpredictable change': □ *the vagaries of the weather*, causes problems of pronunciation. In British English the noun is usually pronounced [*vay*-gări]; the pronunciation [vă*gair*i] is less frequent and may be regarded as an Americanism.

vain, **vane**, or **vein**? These three words are sometimes confused, being identical in pronunciation. *Vain* is an adjective, meaning 'conceited; excessively proud' or 'worthless; futile': □ *the vain parents of talented children* □ *a vain attempt to increase productivity. Vane* and *vein* are nouns. A *vane* is a flat blade moved by wind or water: □ *a weather vane*; a *vein* is a blood vessel, a thin layer of ore in rock, etc.

vantage see VANTAGE OR VANTAGE?

vaporize Note the spelling of the verb *vaporize*, meaning 'change into vapour'. The *-u-* of *vapour* is dropped before the suffix *-ize*.

variegated This word, meaning 'having different colours; diverse': □ *variegated leaves*, is sometimes misspelt. Note the *e* between the *i* and the *g*.

've see OF.

vein see VAIN, VANE, OR VEIN?

venal or **venial**? *Venal* means literally 'for sale' and it is used either of individuals who are capable of being 'bought' or corrupted, or of systems which operate by bribery and corruption: □ *Their legal system is so venal that criminals openly offer bribes in court. Venial* means 'pardonable; excusable' and is applied to minor faults and offences: □ *He was inclined to be thoughtless but that was a venial fault in one so young.*

vengeance see REVENGE OR VENGEANCE?

venial see VENAL OR VENIAL?

venison This word, meaning 'the meat of a deer', is usually pronounced [*venisŏn*] or [*venizŏn*], although the traditional pronunciation is [*venzŏn*].

venue The usual meaning of *venue* is 'the place where a meeting, event, or gathering happens': □ *We have not yet decided on the venue for the annual conference.*

verbal or **oral**? *Verbal* means 'expressed in words' while *oral* means 'relating to the mouth' or 'expressed in speech'. Something *verbal* can be expressed in either speech or writing. However, a *verbal agreement* is generally understood to mean one that is spoken and not written.

verbs Verbs refer to actions, occurrences, or existence. They vary in form according to the tense or mood used, usually in a predictable way but, with irregular verbs, in various different ways which need to be learned. Verbs differ in their functions. One distinction is between *transitive* and *intransitive* verbs. A transitive verb is one that needs a direct object, for example, *like*. One cannot just like; one has to like someone or something. Either it must take a direct object: □ *He likes chocolate*, or it can be used in the passive: □ *She is liked by* *everyone*. Intransitive verbs do not take a direct object. *Fall*, for example, is an intransitive verb. Some verbs can be used both transitively and intransitively in different constructions: □ *Can the boat sail? – She sailed the boat.* Some transitive verbs are *reflexive verbs*, where the subject and object are the same: □ *perjure oneself.* In this example the verb is always reflexive; one cannot perjure anyone or anything other than oneself. But some verbs are not always used reflexively: □ *I introduced myself to our hostess. – I introduced Chris to our hostess. Auxiliary verbs* are those used with other verbs, enabling them to express variations in tense, mood, voice, etc. The most frequently used auxiliaries are *be, have,* and *do*: □ *He is tired.* □ *I have finished.* □ *We did not agree. Be* is used to form the passive: □ *It was dicsussed.* Other auxiliaries include: *shall, should, can, could, will, would, may, might,* and *must*: □ *I shall accept the offer.* □ *You must stop immediately.* This second group of auxiliary verbs, which cannot be used as full verbs (unlike *be, have,* and *do*), are also called *modal verbs. Phrasal verbs* are verbs which include an adverb, preposition, or both: □ *give in* □ *throw away* □ *take to.* Many such verbs have meanings which go beyond the sum of their parts, for example *came by* as in: □ *I came by* [i.e. obtained or received] *that engraving in Venice.* New verbs are formed in various ways. One way is by converting nouns: He serviced her car (see NOUNS). A variation of this is the formation of compound verbs: □ *to rubber-stamp* □ *blue-pencil* □ *inflation-proof* □ *top-score* □ *fund-raise* □ *downgrade.* For other ways of forming new verbs see BACK FORMATION; -IZE OR -ISE?

vermilion The noun and adjective *vermilion*, meaning 'bright red', is sometimes misspelt. Note that *vermilion* has a single *-l-*, unlike the word *million*.

vertex or **vortex**? A *vertex* is the highest point or a point where two or more lines intersect; a *vortex* is the spiralling motion of a whirlpool or whirlwind or, metaphorically, an activity that one is drawn into like a whirlpool or whirlwind: □ *the vertex of a triangle* □ *the vortex of rebellion.*

very *Very* can be used as an intensifier before most adjectives and adverbs: □ *very unpleasant* □ *very efficiently*. However, before past participles *much* is used instead of *very*: □ *It was much improved*. The exception is when the past participle is used adjectivally: □ *She was very excited.*

veterinary This word causes problems with spelling and pronunciation. Note the *-erin-* and the *-ary* ending. The word is frequently pronounced [*vet*ĕnri], [*vet*ĕnĕri], or [*vet*rinri], although careful users insist on the pronunciation with five syllables [*vet*ĕrinĕri].

via *Via* means 'by way of' and is used when talking of the route for a journey: □ *They went to Australia via Hong Kong.* □ *Your best route would be via the M6.*

viable *Viable* means 'capable of living or surviving independently': □ *a viable foetus*. It can be used figuratively in this sense of new communities: □ *When the colony shows itself to be viable, it will be granted independence.*

vice versa This expression, meaning 'with the order reversed', is usually pronounced [vīsĕ *vers*ĕ]. Alternative pronunciations for the first word are: [vīsi] and [vīs].

vicious or **viscous**? *Vicious* means 'wicked' or 'ferocious'; *viscous* describes a liquid that is thick and sticky: □ *a vicious dog* □ *viscous paint.*

victuals This word, meaning 'supplies of food', is pronounced [*vit*lz].

vigorous This word, meaning 'healthy and strong', is often misspelt. Note that the *u* of *vigour* is dropped before the suffix *-ous*.

vilify Note the spelling of this verb, used in formal contexts to mean 'malign; defame', particularly the single *-l-*.

virtual reality *Virtual reality* is an interactive hypothetical environment created by sophisticated computer graphics and related technology: □ *ITV could be the first network to screen a game show using virtual reality,* the emerging technology in which users become immersed in, and interact with, a world generated by computers (*The Guardian*).

virus A *virus* is the causative agent of a disease, but the word is frequently used of the disease itself: □ *He's recovering from a nasty virus.*

vis-à-vis *Vis-à-vis* literally means 'face to face' and is most frequently used as a preposition to mean 'in relation to': □ *We shall have to change our policy vis-à-vis the law.* It also means 'opposite' or 'face to face with' and is sometimes used as a noun to mean 'someone or something opposite another; a counterpart'. It is also occasionally used as a synonym for *tête-à-tête*, meaning 'a private conversation between two people'.

viscous see VICIOUS OR VISCOUS?

visible There is a recent fashionable use of *visible* to mean 'in the public eye; well known': □ *He's one of the more visible cabinet ministers.* It can also be more or less synonymous with *having a high profile*, with the meaning of 'being in a position where one's actions are liable to become subject to public comment or notice': □ *The role of Director of Social Services is an increasingly visible one.* As some object to these uses of *visible*, care should be taken to avoid overworking this word.

visit or visitation? In its most frequent use *visit* is a verb meaning 'pay a call on, stay with as a guest, stay somewhere temporarily' and a noun meaning 'an act of visiting': □ *I will visit Venice when I am in Italy.* □ *He was on a visit to his daughter.* A *visitation* is an official or formal act of visiting: □ *The vicar's work includes the visitation of parishioners in hospital*, and is often found in humorous use, referring to an unwelcome visit: □ *I'm awaiting a visitation from the VAT man.*

vitamin The traditional British pronunciation of this word is [*vit*ămin].

voluntarily Careful users of British English stress this word on the first syllable [*vol*ĕntĕrili].

vortex see VERTEX OR VORTEX?

vowel A *vowel* is the sound represented by any of the letters *a*, *e*, *i*, *o*, and *u* in the English language. Compare CONSONANT.

W

wage, wages see SALARY OR WAGE?

wait see AWAIT OR WAIT?

waive or **wave**? These two words are sometimes confused. The verb *waive* means 'relinquish': □ *The judge waived the penalty; wave* means 'move to and fro': □ *wave goodbye* □ *The corn waved in the wind.* The noun *wave* means 'ridge of water'.

wake, waken see AWAKE, AWAKEN, WAKE, OR WAKEN?

wander or **wonder**? These spellings are sometimes confused. *Wander* means 'roam aimlessly': □ *He wandered through the streets; wonder* means 'be astonished at' or 'think about': □ *I wonder where she is.*

wannabee A *wannabee* is a person who strives to emulate another, especially a young fan who mimics a famous person in appearance, behaviour, etc.: □ *a horde of Madonna wanna bees.*

want As a verb the main meanings of *want* are 'to desire': □ *I want a bigger car*, 'to need': □ *That door wants mending*, and 'to lack': □ *The door wants a handle*. As a noun it means 'something desired; a desire for something; a lack' or is used as a synonym for *poverty*: □ *the want experienced by the unemployed. Want to* is often used in informal contexts to mean 'ought to': □ *You want to be more careful.*

-ward or **-wards**? The adverbial suffixes *-ward* and *-wards* are used to indicate direction. Both forms are equally correct, although *-wards* is usually preferred in British English and *-ward* in American English.

-ware or **-wear**? The ending *-ware* denotes goods of the specified type or material; the ending *-wear* denotes clothing: □ *glassware*

□ *computer software* □ *knitwear* □ *leather footwear.* The two endings are sometimes confused: □ *Dawn French, who is planning to open a knitware shop* (*The Bookseller*).

was see WERE OR WAS?

wastage or **waste**? *Waste* is used as a verb, noun, and adjective. As a noun its main meanings are 'squandering, using carelessly or ungainfully': □ *It was a complete waste of time and money*; or 'rubbish; unwanted material': □ *Get rid of all this waste. Wastage* is a noun meaning 'loss due to leakage, decay, erosion, evaporation, etc.' □ *the wastage of water from a reservoir* □ *Petrol stored in garages is subject to wastage.* Another meaning, usually occurring in the phrase *natural wastage*, refers to the loss of employees through resignation, retirement, or death.

wave, waver see WAIVE OR WAVE?

-ways see -WISE OR -WAYS?

we *We* is used to mean 'I and one or more other people': □ *We should get a divorce.* □ *Shall we all go for a walk?*

weal, wheal, or **wheel**? The noun *wheel*, denoting a circular object, is by far the most common of these three words: □ *the wheels of a bicycle* □ *a steering wheel* □ *a spinning wheel.* The nouns *weal* and *wheal* are interchangeable in the sense of 'raised mark on the skin (usually caused by a blow from a whip, cane, etc.)', *weal* being the more frequent: □ *The weals* [or *wheals*] *on his back suggested that he had been beaten.*

-wear see WARE OR WEAR?

weather, wether, or **whether**? These three spellings are sometimes confused. The noun *weather* (see WEATHER CONDITIONS) and the conjunction *whether* (see WHETHER) are far more common than the noun *wether*, which denotes a (castrated) male sheep.

weather conditions *Weather* means 'the condition of the atmosphere, especially in respect of sunshine, rainfall, wind, etc.' As the word contains *condition* in its meaning, careful users maintain that it is tautological to talk of *weather conditions*, as in: □ *The bad weather conditions stopped* *play.* □ *The freezing weather conditions in the North will not improve.*

weaved, wove, or **woven**? The usual past tense of *weave* is *wove*: □ *She wove the cloth herself.* □ *The spider wove its web. Woven* is the usual past participle of *weave*: □ *It was woven by hand.* □ *They were wearing woven garments.*

wed or **wedded**? The use of the verb *wed* in the sense of 'marry' is rather old-fashioned, formal, or literary; in modern usage it is chiefly found in newspaper headlines: □ *Doctor weds former patient.* Either word may be used as the past tense or past participle of the verb *wed*, meaning 'marry': □ *They wed* [or *wedded*] the following spring. □ *They were wed* [or *wedded*] by her uncle.

Wednesday The name of this day of the week is usually pronounced [*wenz*di], although careful users prefer to sound the *d* [*wednz*di] or [*wednz*day].

weigh or **weight**? To *weigh* is to measure the weight of something; to *weight* is to add weight to something: □ *The box weighs 3 kg.* □ *We weighted the tarpaulin with stones so that it would not blow away.*

weird This word, meaning 'uncanny or extraordinary', is sometimes misspelt. Note the *-ei-* spelling.

were or **was**? Difficulty is sometimes experienced in the use of the subjunctive form *were* in phrases expressing supposition. The basic rule is that *were* is used when the suggestion is of something hypothetical, unlikely, or not actually the case: □ *If I were you, I'd leave him.* □ *She talks to me as if I were three years old.* If the supposition is factual or realistic then *was* is used: □ *I'm sorry if I was rude.*

west, West, or **western**? As an adjective, *west* is always written with a capital *W* when it forms part of a proper name: □ *West Germany* □ *the West Country.* The noun *west* is usually written with a capital *W* when it denotes a specific region, such as the non-communist countries of Europe and America: □ *She defected to the West in 1986.*

wet or **wetted**? The verb *to*

wet means 'make wet': □ *Don't keep wetting your lips*, and 'urinate in or on something': □ *Children often wet their beds when they are anxious.* The usual past tense or participle is *wet*: □ *The baby has wet its nappy again.* However, in the passive, *wetted* is used. *The sheets have been wetted* is less ambiguous than *the sheets have been wet*.

wet or **whet**? These two spellings are sometimes confused. *Wet* means 'cover with moisture': □ *to wet one's lips*; *whet* means 'stimulate or sharpen': □ *whet someone's appetite*.

wether see WEATHER, WETHER, OR WHETHER?

wetted see WET OR WETTED?

wharfs or **wharves**? Either *wharfs* or *wharves* is acceptable as the plural of the noun *wharf*, denoting a place where ships dock for loading and unloading. *Wharves* is the more frequent form.

what A difficulty in the use of the pronoun *what* is whether it should be followed by a singular or plural verb. In general the rule is that when *what* means 'that which' it takes a singular verb, even if the complement is plural, and when it means 'those which' it takes a plural verb: □ *What we need is a ladder.* □ *What he likes best is expensive restaurants.* □ *I mentioned what I thought were the most important points.*

what or **which**? In a question, the use of *what* or *which* affects the interpretation of the meaning. *Which* chooses from a limited range of alternatives; *what* is used in more general enquiries.

whatever or **what ever**? If *ever* is used to intensify *what* the expression is written as two words in formal writing: □ *What ever* ['What on earth'] *did he say next?* In less formal writing, one word is sometimes used, but careful writers object to this usage. If *whatever* means 'no matter what', it is written as one word: □ *I'll write whatever I like.* □ *Whatever the weather he always wears a vest.* □ *There is no chance whatever of him winning.*

wheal, **wheel** see WEAL, WHEAL, OR WHEEL?

whence *Whence* is a formal, rarely used word meaning 'from where; from what place': □ *The monster returned to the swamp whence it had appeared.*

whenever or **when ever**? see WHATEVER OR WHAT EVER?

whereabouts The noun *whereabouts*, meaning 'place where somebody or something is', may be used with a singular or plural verb: □ *The whereabouts of the original manuscript remains* [or *remain*] *a secret.* □ *Her whereabouts are* [or *is*] *unknown.*

wherever or **where ever**? see WHATEVER OR WHAT EVER?

whet see WET OR WHET?

whether *Whether* can be used to introduce an indirect question: □ *He asked whether we were going.* Here it is synonymous with *if* but sounds rather more formal. *Whether* is also used to introduce alternatives or consider possibilities: □ *I wonder whether she'll come.* □ *I don't know whether it is correct.*

which see THAT OR WHICH?; WHAT OR WHICH?

whichever or **which ever**? see WHATEVER OR WHAT EVER?

while or **whilst**? As a conjunction *while* means 'during the time that; as long as' and it is also used to mean 'although; whereas': □ *I shall be doing his work while he's away on holiday.* □ *Elizabeth votes Labour while her husband votes Conservative.* *Whilst* has the same meanings but is rarely used; it tends to sound formal and old-fashioned.

whisky or **whiskey**? The alcoholic drink distilled in Scotland is spelt *whisky*, which is the more frequent spelling in British English. The alcoholic drink distilled in the USA or Ireland is spelt *whiskey*, the usual spelling in American English.

who The pronoun *who* is normally used in reference to human beings (*which* being used for nonhumans): □ *the man who runs the shop.* However, it is acceptable to use *who* in referring to animals, to countries in certain contexts, and to a group of people, especially when taking a plural verb: □ *cats who refuse to eat leftovers* □ *Iraq, who started the war* □ *the band who plays the loudest.*

who or **whom**? *Who* is used when it is the subject of a verb and *whom* when it is the object of a verb or preposition: □ *the boy who delivers the papers* □ *the woman whom you just saw* □ *the people to whom I was talking. Whom* is falling into disuse, especially in questions. □ *Whom did you give it to?* is formally correct but most people would now use *who*. As a relative pronoun, *whom* should still be used, when correct, in all but informal speech.

whodunit This word, used in informal contexts to describe a detective story, may be spelt *whodunit* or, less frequently, *whodunnit*.

whoever or **who ever**? see WHATEVER OR WHAT EVER?

wholly see HOLY, HOLEY, OR WHOLLY?□; SPELLING 4.

whom see WHO OR WHOM?

whoop This word, meaning 'express delight', as in: □ *Sally whooped excitedly*, is sometimes mispronounced. The correct pronunciation is [woop].

whose or **who's**? These spellings are sometimes confused. *Whose* means 'of whom' or 'of which': □ *the children, whose father had left them* □ *political parties whose ideas are old-fashioned* □ *Whose book is that? Who's* is a contraction of *who is* or *who has*: □ *Who's coming to dinner tonight?*

wicked Like BAD, the adjective *wicked* is used as slang term of approval, especially by young people: □ *His new bike is well wicked.*

wilful Note the spelling of this word, which has a single *l* in the middle and at the end in British English. In American English the *-ll* ending of *will* is retained in the spelling *willful*.

will see SHALL OR WILL?

window *Window* has various well-established metaphorical uses. It can mean 'something that allows people to see something they might otherwise not see': □ *The programme is a window on the closed world of the monastery*; or 'an opportunity to display something': □ *The exhibition is the annual window of domestic design.* A more recent use is 'a gap; an interval of time': □ *a window of opportunity*, though care should be taken to avoid overworking this expression.

-wise or **-ways**? The suffix *-ways* combines with certain abstract nouns to form an adverb meaning 'in (such) a way, direction, or manner': □ *sideways* □ *lengthways*. It has a more limited use than *-wise*, which can combine with various nouns to mean either 'in the position or direction of': □ *clockwise* □ *lengthwise* or 'in the manner of': □ *to walk crabwise*. The use of *-wise* to mean 'in respect of' in such expressions as: □ *moneywise* □ *weatherwise* □ *careerwise* □ *taxwise* □ *performancewise* is becoming increasingly popular, but is disliked by many people.

with When a singular subject is linked to something else by *with* it should take a singular verb: □ *The Prime Minister with senior members of the Cabinet has been considering the problem.*

withhold This word, meaning 'keep back', is sometimes misspelt. Note the *-hh-* in the middle of this word, unlike the word *threshold*.

woman As a general term for an adult female human being, *woman* is more acceptable than *female*, *girl*, or *lady*: □ *The prize was won by a woman from Brighton.* The noun *female* is best reserved for animals and plants. It may be applied to human beings when the question of age makes *woman* or *women* inappropriate: □ *He shares the house with five females: his wife and their four young daughters.* In most other cases it is considered inelegant, contemptuous, or offensive. As an adjective, however, *female* is more acceptable than *woman* or *lady*: □ *There are two female doctors and one male doctor at the local surgery.* □ *Female drivers do not have more road accidents than male drivers.*

A *girl* is a female child or adolescent. The term is often used as a synonym for 'woman' but is considered patronizing or disrespectful by some people in some contexts, especially when used by men.

The word *lady* has connotations of nobility, dignity, and good manners: □ *the Lady of the manor.* □ *She may be wealthy but she's no lady!* It is used in polite address, as in formal or official contexts: □ *This lady would like to speak to the manager.* □ *Ladies and gentlemen ....* However, it is sometimes regarded as a term of condescension, especially in such phrases as *the cleaning lady,* which may be replaced by *the cleaning woman* or, more simply, *the cleaner.*

As a general rule, *female, girl,* and *lady* are best restricted to contexts where *male, boy,* or *gentleman* would be used of the opposite sex. See also MAN; SEXISM.

wonder see WANDER OR WONDER?

woolly Note the spelling of this word: *-oo-* and *-ll-* in British English; *-oo-* and single *-l-* in American English. Similarly, the adjective *woollen* has *-ll-* in British English and a single *-l-* in American English.

worship The single final *p* doubles in front of most suffixes beginning with a vowel in British English: □ *worshipped* □ *worshipper* □ *worshipping.* American English retains the single *p. Worshipful* retains the single *p.*

worthwhile or **worth while**? The traditional rule is that this expression is written as two words after a verb and as one word in front of a noun: □ *It is worth while spending a little more money.* □ *a project that is worth while – a worthwhile project.*

would see SHOULD OR WOULD?

wove, woven see WEAVED, WOVE, OR WOVEN?

wrack see RACK OR WRACK?

wrapped see RAPT OR WRAPPED?

wring see RING OR WRING?

wrought *Wrought* is an archaic form of the past tense and past participle of the verb *work.* It is still used adjectivally in such expressions as *wrought iron.*

wysiwyg The term *wysiwyg,* used in computing and pronounced [*wiziwig*], is an acronym for *what you see is what you get*: the display on the computer screen is an exact representation of what will appear on the printout. The term is sometimes spelt *WYSIWYG* or *Wysiwyg*: □ *Offering full Wysiwyg (what you see is what you get), including the enhancements such as bold, italic, inverse, tone and outlines* (*Daily Telegraph*).

X

Xerox This word should be spelt *Xerox* if it is referring to the trademarked noun for a type of photographic copier or process. The verb, meaning 'copy on a Xerox machine', is spelt with a lower-case *x*.

Xmas *Xmas*, an abbreviation for *Christmas*, is used particularly in commercial contexts and newspaper headlines. The *X* derives from the Greek *chi*, the initial letter of *Christos*, the Greek for *Christ*.

X-ray or **x-ray**? The noun is nearly always written with a capital *X*; the verb is written with a capital or lower-case letter: □ *He had an X-ray/He was X-rayed* [or *x-rayed*] *after the accident.*

Y

yes and **no** In discussing affirmative or negative expressions one has the option of writing, for example, either: □ *She said yes to the offer* or: *She said, 'Yes' to the offer*. The latter carries more of an implication that the person actually used the word *yes* or *no*.

yet *Yet* has various meanings: 'up till now; so far': □ *It has not yet been decided*, 'even': □ *a yet greater problem*, 'in addition': □ *yet more presents*, 'at some future time': □ *We'll do it yet*, and 'nevertheless': □ *slow, yet sure*.

yoghurt The most frequent spelling of this word is *yoghurt*. Acceptable alternatives are *yogurt* and *yoghourt*. The usual pronunciation is [yogĕrt] in British English and [yōgĕrt] in American English.

yoke or **yolk**? These words are sometimes confused. *Yoke* means 'connecting bar or bond': □ *yoked oxen* □ *under the yoke of slavery*. A *yolk* is the yellow part of an egg: □ *Would you like your yolk hard?*

yoof *Yoof* is a phonetic respelling of the word *youth* (as pronounced by a Londoner), used with particular reference to contemporary youth culture: □ *Panels are a good idea, but they shouldn't all be authors who don't appeal to the 'yoof' culture* (*The Bookseller*).

you *You* is often used to mean 'people in general' in place of the slightly more formal *one*: □ *You certainly get a good meal at that restaurant.* □ *You hold a hammer like this.* □ *They* [i.e. 'The authorities'] *fine you on the spot if you've not got a ticket.* □ *It's really embarrassing when you forget someone's name.* □ *Dentists say you should clean your teeth at least twice a day.* Although *one* is less frequently used than *you* it is sometimes better to use *one* to avoid possible confusion as to whether the speaker is talking personally or generally. It is also important to be consistent in the use of either *you* or *one* throughout a single piece of writing.

you know The expression *you know* is used by speakers who are not sure about what they have just said or who are not sure what to say next: □ *I just wondered ... you know ... if you might like to come with me to the theatre.* The expression is frequently used with this function but is very widely disliked.

your or **you're**? These two words may be confused. *Your* means 'belonging to you': □ *your house* □ *your rights*. *You're* is a contraction of *you are:* □ *Hurry up, you're going to be late!* Note also the spelling of *yours*: □ *That's mine not yours*; the spelling with an apostrophe, *your's*, is wrong.

yuppie *Yuppie*, often spelt *yuppy*, is a North American coinage which came into frequent use in Britain in the mid-1980s. It stands for 'young urban (or upwardly mobile) professional' and is used to designate well-educated young adults, living in cities, working in well-paid occupations, and enjoying a fashionable way of life.

Z

zero The digit 0 has a variety of names. *Nought* (see also NAUGHT OR NOUGHT?) and (less frequently) *zero* are the general terms for this digit: □ *The number 1000 has three noughts* [or *zeros*]. □ *You've missed a nought off the end – it should be two hundred thousand, not twenty thousand.* In scientific contexts, and for expressing temperatures, etc., *zero* is preferred: □ *Water freezes at zero degrees Celsius. Zero* is also used in countdowns: □ *five, four, three, two, one, zero.*

zoology This word, referring to the biological study of animals, has two pronunciations. The more frequent pronunciation is [zoo*ol*ŏji], though careful users prefer [zō*ol*ŏji].

C000102992

THE *Little Book* — OF — ARTHURIAN WISDOM

In the same series

The Little Book of Angels

❖

The Little Book of The Bible

❖

The Little Book of Celtic Blessings

❖

The Little Book of Celtic Wisdom

❖

The Little Book of Iron John

❖

The Little Book of Love

❖

The Little Book of Native American Wisdom

❖

The Little Book of Zen Wisdom

THE

Little Book

OF

ARTHURIAN WISDOM

compiled by

John Matthews

ELEMENT

Shaftesbury, Dorset ✦ Rockport, Massachusetts

Brisbane, Queensland

Published in Great Britain in 1994 by
ELEMENT BOOKS LTD
Shaftesbury, Dorset

Published in the USA in 1994 by
ELEMENT, INC.
42 Broadway, Rockport, MA 01966

Published in Australia in 1994 by
ELEMENT BOOKS LTD
for JACARANDA WILEY LTD
33 Park Road, Milton, Brisbane, 4064

Front and back cover: Photograph reproduced by permission of P. Kent
Designed and created by:
The Bridgewater Book Company / Ron Bryant-Funnell
Picture research by Vanessa Fletcher
Textural photographs by Sarah Bentley
Printed and bound in Great Britain by:
William Clowes Ltd, Beccles, Suffolk

British Library Cataloguing in Publication data available

Library of Congress Cataloging in Publication data available

ISBN 1-85230-565-7

For Stuart, Alison & Aoife Littlejohn

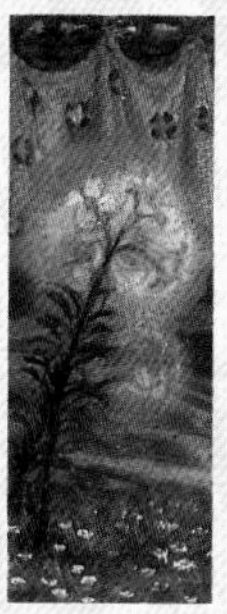

INTRODUCTION

THE MYTHS of King Arthur and the Knights of the Round Table came into being during the medieval period and rapidly spread throughout most of Europe. Based on a mixture of half-remembered stories of a sixth century hero and his warriors, and the folk-lore and traditions of the Celtic peoples, they soon became the favourite reading of the literate, and the most frequently requested stories told in halls and villages throughout the land.

There is indeed much wisdom in the Arthurian world. It ranges in kind from the earthy wisdom of challenging otherworldly figures like the Green Knight, Lady Ragnell and the Lady of the Lake, to the high wisdom of Merlin and the mysterious lore of the Grail. These themes, together with the lore of chivalry and the love of women, are of prime importance within the Arthurian world.

There is so much in the huge body of Arthurian literature that any selection of quotations taken from it must necessarily leave out more than it includes. I make no secret of the fact that I have opted for favourite passages which, in more than twenty years reading about this subject, have come to mean a great deal to me. I hope that readers will find things here which are both unfamiliar (or familiar) and inspiring, and that it may encourage them to delve deeper into the wonderful world of the Arthurian Tradition.

JOHN MATTHEWS

The Wisdom of Merlin

MERLIN . . . approached the king, and said to him; 'For what reason am I introduced into your presence?' 'My magicians' answered Vortigern, 'advised me to seek out a man that had no father, with whose blood my building is to be sprinkled, in order to make it stand. 'Order your magicians,' said Merlin, 'to come before me, and I will convict them of a lie.' The king ordered the magicians to come and Merlin spoke to them after this manner: 'Because you are ignorant what it is that hinders the foundation of the tower, you have recommended the shedding of my blood for cement . . . . But tell me now, what is there under the foundation . . . ? The magicians at this began to be afraid, and made him no answer. Then said Merlin . . . 'Command your workmen to dig into the ground, and you will find a pond which causes the foundations to sink'.

Presently they found a pond deep under ground, which had made it [the tower] give way. Merlin after this went again to the magicians, and said, 'Tell me . . . what is there under the pond?' But they were silent. Then said he again to the king, Command the pond to be drained, and at the bottom you will see two hollow stones, and in them two dragons asleep.'

The king made no scruple, and therefore ordered it to be drained: which done, he found as Merlin had said; and now was possessed with the greatest admiration of him. [1]

S VORTIGERN . . . was sitting upon the bank of the drained pond, the two dragons, one of which was white, the other red, came forth and began a terrible fight. After this battle of the dragons, the king demanded Merlin . . . to tell him what it portended. Upon which, bursting into tears, delivered what his prophetical spirit suggested to him . . .

'Woe to the red dragon, for his banishment hasteneth on. His lurking holes shall be seized by the white dragon, which signifies the Saxons . . . but the red dragon denotes the British nation, which shall be oppressed by the white . . . [But] at last the oppressed shall prevail, and oppose the cruelty of foreigners. For a boar of Cornwall shall give his assistance and trample their necks under his feet . . .[2]

Sweet appletree, of luxuriant growth!
I used to find food at its foot,
When, because of a maid,
I slept alone in the woods of Celyddon,
Shield on shoulder, sword on thigh.
Hear, O little pig! listen to my words,
As sweet as birds that sing on Monday –
When the sovereigns come across the sea,
Blessed be the Cymry, because of their strength . . .

Sweet appletree, growing by the river,
Who will thrive on its wondrous fruit?
When my reason was intact
I used to lie at its foot
With a fair wanton maid, of slender form.
Fifty years the plaything of lawless men
I have wandered in gloom among spirits.
After great wealth, and gregarious minstrels,
I have been here so long not even sprites
Can lead me astray.[3]

ING [ARTHUR] sat in a study, and bade his men fetch his horse as fast as ever they might. Right so came by him Merlin like a child of fourteen year of age, and saluted the king, and asked him why he was so pensive. I may well be pensive, said the king, for I have seen the marvellest sight that ever I saw. That know I well, said Merlin . . . Also I know what thou art, and who was thy father, and of whom thou were begotten . . . That is false, said King Arthur, how shouldst thou know it, for thou art not so old of years to know my father? Yes, said Merlin, I know it better than ye or any man living. I will not believe thee, said Arthur, and was wroth with the child. So departed Merlin, and came again in the likeness of an old man of fourscore year of age, whereof the king was right glad for he seemed to be right wise.

What are ye, said Arthur, that tell me these tidings? I am Merlin, as I was he in the child's likeness. Ah, said King Arthur, ye are a marvellous man . . .[4]

He who speaks from the grave
Knows that before seven years
March will die.

I have drunk from a bright cup
With fierce and warlike lords;
My name is Myrddin, son of Morvran.

I have drunk from a goblet
With powerful warlords;
Myrddin is my given name.

When the black wheel of oppression
Comes to destroy exhausted Llogres
Defence will be bitter and sustained.
The White Mount will see sorrow
A long regret to the people of the Cymry.

Protection won't be found
From the Boar of the Hosts,
Even in the heights of Ardudwy
Or the Cymry's secret ports . . . .[5]

AS THEY RODE, Arthur said, I have no sword. No force, said Merlin, hereby is a sword that shall be yours, and I may. So they rode till they came to a lake, the which was a fair and broad, and in the midst of the lake Arthur was ware of an arm clothed in white samite, that held a fair sword in that hand. Lo! said Merlin, yonder is that sword that I spake of. With that they saw a damosel going upon the lake. What damosel is that? said Arthur. That is the Lady of the Lake, said Merlin; and within that lake is a rock, and therein is as fair a place as any on earth, and richly beseen; and this damosel will come to you anon, and then speak ye fair to her that she will give you that sword. Anon withal came the damosel to Arthur, and saluted him, and he her again. Damosel, said Arthur, what sword is that, that yonder the arm holdeth above the water? I would it were mine, for I have no sword... Well! said the damosel, go ye in yonder barge, and row yourself to the sword, and take it and the scabbard with you . . . Sir Arthur and Merlin . . . went into the ship, and when they came to the sword that the hand held, Sir Arthur took it up by the handles, and took it with him, and the arm and the hand went under the water . . . (6)

Listen, little pig,
Don't sleep yet!
Rumours reach me
Of perjured chieftains,
And tight-fisted farmers.
Soon, over the sea,
Shall come men in armour,
Two-faced men,
On armoured horses,
With destroying spears.
When that happens,
War will come,
Fields will be ploughed
But never reaped . . .

Listen, little pig,
O pig of truth!
The Sybil has told me
A wondrous tale.
I predict a Summer full of fury,
Treachery between brothers.
A pledge of peace will be required
From Gwynedd,
Seven hundred ships from Gynt
Blown in by the North wind.
In Aber Dyn they will confer.(7)

Taliesin had come to see Merlin the prophet who had sent for him to find out what wind or rainstorm was coming up, for both together were growing near and the clouds were thickening. He [Merlin] drew the following illustrations under the guidance of [the Goddess] Minerva . . .

UT OF NOTHING the Creator of the world produced four elements that they might be the prior cause as well as the material for creating all things when they were joined together in harmony: the heaven which he adorned with stars and which stands on high and embraces everything like the shell surrounding a nut; then he made the air, fit for forming sounds, through the medium of which day and night present the stars; the sea which girds the land in four circles, and with its mighty refulgence so strikes the air as to generate the winds which are said to be four in number; as a foundation, he placed the earth, standing by its own strength and not lightly moved, which is divided into five parts, whereof the middle one is not habitable because of the heat, and the two furthest are shunned because of their cold. To the last two he gave a moderate temperature and these are inhabited by men and birds and herds of wild beasts.[8]

ND THEN MERLIN came to Perceval and to Blayse his master, and he took leave of them and told them that Our Lord did not wish that he should show himself to people, yet that he would not be able to die before the end of the world; 'but then I shall enjoy the eternal joy, and I wish to make a lodging outside your palace and to dwell there and I will prophesy whatever Our Lord commands me. And all those who will see my lodging will name it the *esplumoir* (or moulting cage) of Merlin . . .'[9]

THE ROUND TABLE

EARKEN UNTO ME with favour and keep silence and I will tell you a tale both noble and true of the prince-like men of the Round Table who excelled in chivalry and were noble chieftains in their deeds; they were wise men at arms, valiant in action, holding shame always in dread; kind men and courteous they were, learned in courtly manners . . .[10]

MERLIN made the Round Table in tokening of roundness of the world, for by the Round Table is the world signified by right, for all the world, Christian and heathen, repair unto the Round Table; and when they are chosen to be of the fellowship of the Round Table they think them more blessed and more in worship than if they had gotten half the world . . . When Merlin had ordained the Round Table he said, by them which should be fellows of the Round Table the truth of the Sangreal should be well known . . .[11]

RTHUR never heard speak of a knight in praise, but he caused him to be numbered of his household . . . Because of these noble lords about his hall, of whom each knight pain himself to be the hardiest champion, and none would count him the least praiseworthy, Arthur made the Round Table . . . It was ordained of Arthur that when his fair fellowship sat to meat their chairs should be high alike, their service equal, and none before or after his comrade. Thus no man could boast that he was exalted above his fellow, for all alike were gathered round the board, and none was alien at the breaking of Arthur's bread.[12]

HEN THE KING stablished all his knights, and them that were of lands not rich he gave them lands, and charged them never to do outrageously nor murder, and always to flee treason; also, by no means to be cruel, but to give mercy unto him that asketh mercy, upon pain of forfeiture of their worship and lordship of King Arthur for evermore; and always to do ladies, damosels, and gentlewomen succour, upon pain of death. Also, that no man take no battles in a wrongful quarrel for no law, nor for no world's goods.(13)

First he was found faultless in his five wits.
Then he failed not in his five fingers.
And all his trust on earth was in the five wounds
Suffered by Christ on the cross . . .
So that when the knight was placed in the melée,
His thought was ever upon them
above all other things.
And so it was that all his strength he found
In the five joys that the fair Queen of Heaven had in her child.
And for this cause that the knight had made to be painted
Her image in comely fashioned on the greater half of his shield,
So that when he looked upon it, his valour never failed him.
Now the fifth five that this knight excelled in were
Frankness, and fellowship above all others,
His cleanness and courtesy never were crooked,
And compassion, that surpasseth all else.
These five pure virtues were fixed in this knight
More firmly than in any other.[14]

EARLESSLY and unhesitatingly Geraint dashed forward into the mist. And on leaving the mist he came into a large orchard; and in the orchard he saw an open space, wherein was a tent of red satin; and the door of the tent was open, and an apple-tree stood in front of the door of the tent; and on the branch of the apple-tree hung a huge hunting horn . . . and there was no-one in the tent save one maiden sitting in a golden chair, and another chair was opposite to her, empty. And Geraint went in . . . and sat down therein.[15]

The Love of Fair Ladies

The month of May was come, when every lusty heart beginneth to blossom, and to bring forth fruit; for like as herbs and trees bring forth fruit and flourish in May, in like wise every lusty heart that is in any manner a lover, springeth and flourisheth in lusty deeds. For . . . like as winter rasure doth alway arase and deface green summer so fareth it by unstable love in man and woman. For in many persons is there no stability, for we may see all day, for a little blast of winter's rasure, and none shall we deface and lay apart true love for little or naught, that cost much thing; this is no wisdom nor stability, but is feebleness of nature and great disworship . . .

The old love was not so; men and women could love together seven years . . . and then was love, truth, and faithfulness; and lo, in likewise was used love in King Arthur's days.[16]

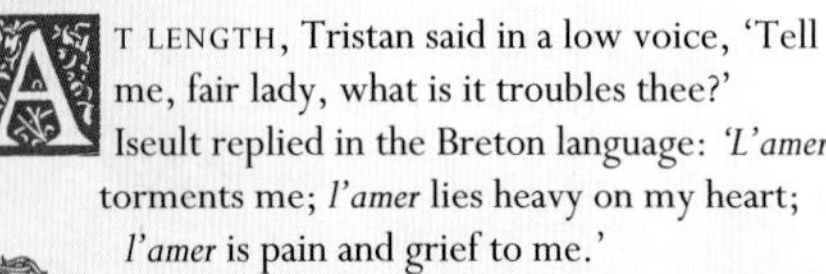

AT LENGTH, Tristan said in a low voice, 'Tell me, fair lady, what is it troubles thee?' Iseult replied in the Breton language: *'L'amer* torments me; *l'amer* lies heavy on my heart; *l'amer* is pain and grief to me.'

And Tristan knew not what to think, for in the Breton tongue, the words *l'amer* have three meanings. There is *l'amer,* bitterness; there is *la mer,* the sea; there is *l'amer,* which means love. Of these three meanings there was one which he dared not think of; he set Love, their common lord and master, their mutual comfort and desire, and spoke only of the other two.[17]

HE, who loves lightly, may make her lover pray for long, so that she may hide how often her feet have trodden the pathway with another friend. But the honest dame, when she has once given her heart to a friend, will not deny his wish because of pride. The rather she will find her pride in humbleness, and love him again with the same love he has set on her. So they will be glad together, and since none will have knowledge or hearing of the matter, they will rejoice in their youth.[18]

Then Tristan rose and spake, Alack,
Sweet love Iseult wake up anon,
We have been trapped and spied upon!
The King knows all that we have wrought
Goes now to fetch his lords from court;
In company he will us take,
To judge and burn us at the stake.
Sweet heart, I must depart from thee;
Thy life is in no jeopardy . . . .

To far off lands in bitter woe,
For thy love's sake I fain must go.
Leave all my joy, become a stranger,
Renounce delight and follow danger . . . .[19]

I WOULD LIKE to make a brief mention of the friendship that was struck up in private between the moon and the sun. Do you know of whom I want to tell you? The man who was chief of the knights and honoured above them all should indeed be called the sun. I refer to my lord Gawain . . . And by the moon I mean she who is so uniquely endowed with good sense and courtly ways . . . her name is Lunete.[20]

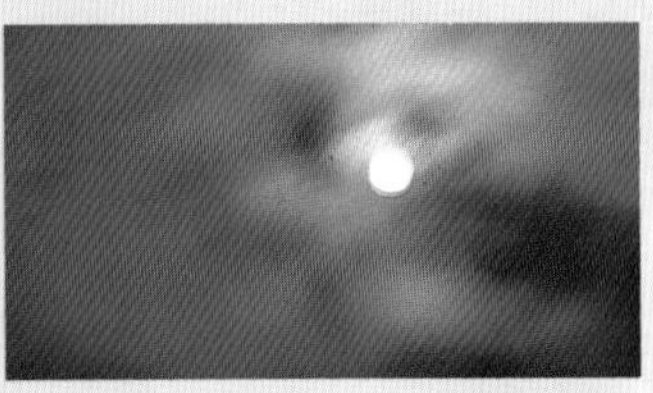

N HER CHAMBER, Iseult lay sleepless . . . suddenly, through the open window where the moonbeams moved, came the voice of a nightingale. Iseult listened to the loud bird-throat that charmed the night, and the tones rose plaintively and such that there exists no cruel heart, no murderer's heart that would not have been touched. The Queen wondered: 'Whence comes this melody?' Suddenly she understood 'It is Tristan! Thus in the wood of Morois, he used to imitate song-birds for my delight. He is leaving; this is his last adieu. How he laments, like the nightingale when he takes leave at summer's end, in very sadness. Friend, never again will I hear your voice!'(21)

UST AS THE WISE MASTER teaches young children, my lady the queen teaches and instructs every living being. From her flows all the good in the world, she is its source and origin. Nobody can take leave of her and go away disheartened, for she knows what each person wants and the way to please each according to his desires.[22]

N THE EVENING . . . [Peredur] entered a valley, and at the head of the valley he came to a hermit's cell, and the hermit welcomed him gladly, and there he spent the night. And in the morning he arose, and when he went forth, behold a shower of snow had fallen the night before, and a hawk had killed a wild fowl in front of the cell. And the noise of the horse scared the hawk away, and a raven alighted upon the bird. And Peredur stood, and compared the blackness of the raven and the whiteness of the snow, and the redness of the blood, to the hair of the lady that best he loved, which was blacker than jet, and to her skin which was whiter than the snow, and to the two red spots upon her cheeks, which were redder than the blood upon the snow appeared to be . . .[23]

THE WISDOM OF THE GRAIL

THE HIGH BOOK of the Grail begins in the name of the Father, the Son and the Holy Spirit. These three are one substance and that substance is God, and from God comes the noble story of the Grail; and all those who hear it must be attentive and forget all their baseness, for those who hear it with their hearts will find it most profitable, because of the worthy men and good knights whose deeds you will hear recalled.[24]

Here is the Book of thy Descent.

Here begins the Book of the Sangreal,

Here begin the terrors,

Here begin the miracles.[25]

HE KING and all the estates went home unto Camelot . . . and every knight sat in his own place as they were toforehand. Then anon they heard cracking and crying of thunder . . . In the midst of this blast entered a sunbeam more clearer by seven times than ever they saw day, and all they were alighted of the grace of the Holy Spirit. Then began every knight to behold other, and either saw other, by their seeming, fairer than ever they saw afore . . . Then there entered into the hall the Holy Grail covered with white samite, but there was none might see it, nor who bare it. And there was all the hall filled with good odours, and every knight had such meats and drinks as he best loved in this world. And when the Holy Grail had been born through the hall, then the holy vessel departed suddenly, that they wist not where it became . . .[26]

THE GRAIL appeared at the consecration in five forms, but they should not be revealed, for the secrets of the sacrament none should tell save he whom God has granted grace. But King Arthur saw all of the transubstantiations, and last appeared the chalice; and the hermit who was conducting the mass, found a memorandum upon the consecration cloth, and the letters declared that God wanted his body to be sacrificed in such a vessel in remembrance of him.[27]

ANCELOT kept on till he reached a chamber of which the door was closed and locked. He put his hand on the door and tried to open it, but in vain; he even made a great effort, but he could nothing to effect an entrance, then he listened, and heard a voice chanting so sweetly that it seemed to be the voice rather of some heavenly, than of a mortal creature . . . [then he] saw the door of the chamber open, and through it there shone as bright a light as if the sun were lodged therein . . . When he saw this, he was very happy, and felt such a desire to see whence this brightness came, that he forgot all else.(28)

HEN LOOKED THEY and saw a man come out of the Holy Vessel, that had all the signs of the passion of Jesu Christ, bleeding all openly, and [he] said: My knights, and my sergeants, and my true children, which be come out of deadly life into spiritual life, I will now no longer hide me from you, but ye shall see now a part of my secrets and of my hidden things: now hold and receive the high meat which ye have so much desired. Then took he himself the Holy Vessel and came to Galahad; and he kneeled down, and there he received his Saviour, and after him so received all his fellows; and they thought it so sweet that it was marvellous to tell. Then said he to Galahad: Son, wottest thou what I hold betwixt my hands? Nay, said he, but if ye will tell me. This is, said he, the holy dish wherein I ate the lamb on Sheer-Thursday. And now hast thou seen that thou most desired to see, but yet hast thou not seen it so openly as thou shalt see it in the city of Sarras in the spiritual place.[29]

OW AT THE YEAR'S END, and the self day after Galahad had born the crown of gold, he arose early, and came to the palace, and saw to-fore them the Holy Vessel, and a man kneeling on his knees in likeness of a bishop . . . and then he arose and began the Mass of Our Lady. And when he came to the sacrament of the Mass, and had done, anon he called Galahad, and said to him: Come forth the servant of Jesu Christ and thou shalt see that thou hast much desired to see. And then he [Galahad] began to tremble right hard when the deadly flesh beheld the spiritual things. Then he held up his hands toward heaven and said: Lord, I thank thee, for now I see that that hath been my desire many a day. Now, blessed Lord, would I no longer live, if it might please thee, Lord. And therewithal the good man took Our Lord's body betwixt his hands, and proffered it to Galahad, and he received it right gladly and meekly . . .[30]

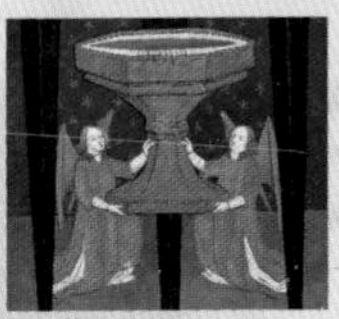

HE CASTLE [of the Grail] had been far from any people and it seemed a rather strange place, and when it had turned to ruins, many people in the neighbouring lands and isles wondered what could be there, and some were tempted to go and look . . . The news travelled to every land, but no-one . . . dared go there save two Welsh knights, who had heard about it . . . and full of excitement they entered the castle. They stayed there for a long while. And when they left they lived as hermits, wearing hair-shirts and wandering through the forests, eating only roots; it was a hard life, but it pleased them greatly, and when people asked them why they were living thus, they would reply:

'Go where we went, and you will know why.'(31)

The Passing of Arthur

Gone is Sir Gawain! his good fight is o'er
No man may aid him, pity 't is the more!
Gone is Sir Gawain! who did rule aright,
From Gower to Guernsey, many a noble night,
Wales and Glamorgan's gallant knights and true
For sorrow 'stonied, joy no more they knew . . .

Matchless on mold that man was reckoned e'er,
That was Sir Gawain good, the gladest knight
And the most gracious to whom God gave light.
Happiest in arms, the hardiest of his hand,
In hall most courteous who 'neath Heaven did stand
The while he lived as lordliest leader known
And many lands his lion courage own . . . .[32]

HEN WENT Sir Bors unto Sir Ector, and told him how lay his brother, Sir Lancelot, dead… And when he beheld Sir Lancelot's visage, he fell down in a swoon. And when he waked, it were hard any tongue to tell the doleful complaints that he made for his brother. Ah Lancelot, he said, thou were head of all Christian knights, and now I dare say, said Sir Ector, thou Sir Lancelot, there thou liest, thou that were never matched of earthly knight's hand. And thou were the courtliest knight that ever bare shield. And thou were the truest friend to thy lover that ever bestrad horse. And thou were the truest lover of a sinful man that ever loved woman. And thou were the kindest man that ever struck with sword. And thou were the goodliest person that ever came among press of knights. And thou were the meekest man and the gentlest that ever ate in hall among ladies. And thou were the sternest knight to thy mortal foe that ever put spear in rest . . . .[33]

Methought in woodland wild was I astray.
And wist not whither I should take my way,
For wolves, wild swine, and wicked beasts, methought,
Walked in that wilderness, my harm sought;
And loathly lions, from their teeth so white
Did lick the blood of many a noble knight.
I thro' the forest fled, where flowers waxed high,
For fear of foul things I did espy;
I gained a meadow, mountains closed it in,
None merrier on mid-earth a man might win . . .

❖

In that fair dale, down from the clouds, did 'light
In diapered weeds, a duchess duly dight,
In silken surcote, changly hued, and made,
Down to the hems with broideries o'er-laid . . .
A wheel she whirled with these her hands so white,
In fashion quaint she turned it as she might . . .
And to that wheel arow, see, kings do cling
Each with a crown that doth asunder spring . . .

❖

With slender hands she lightly lifted me
Sceptre in hand, she set me in the chair,
Then with a comb she lightly combed my hair,
That the crisp curls were from the crown outspread,
A diadem, fair dight, set on my head;
Then offered me an orb, where bright stones shone . . .

❖

Thus for an hour she led me to and fro
With all the love and liking a maid might show;
But at the midday, lo! her mood did change,
When I upon her cried, she knit her brow;
'By Christ who made me, King, be silent now!
Sped is they sport, thy life shalt lose, I trow,
In lordship and delight hast lived enow!'
About she whirls the wheel, and I, withal,
Whirled undermost, was shattered with the fall.
My chin was chopped asunder with the chair,
For chill I've shivered since so I must fare,
Then, all dream-weary, did I wake, I wis –
Read thou my woe, and say what meaneth this![34]

❖

AND I WILL fare to Avalun, to the fairest of all maidens, to Argante the queen, an elf most fair, and she shall make my wounds all sound; make me all whole with healing draughts. And afterwards I will come again to my kingdom, and dwell with the Britons with mickle joy.[35]

HE ISLAND OF APPLES which men call 'The Fortunate Isle' gets its name from the fact that because it produces all things of itself, the fields there have no need of the ploughs of the farmers and all cultivation is lacking except what nature provides . . . There nine sisters rule by a pleasing set of laws those who come to them from our country. She who is first of them is more skilled in the healing art, and excells her sisters in the beauty of her person. Morgen is her name, and she has learned what useful properties all the herbs contain, so that she can cure sick bodies . . . Thither after the battle of Camlan we took the wounded Arthur, guided by Barinthus, to whom the waters and the stars of heaven were well known. With him steering the ship arrived there with the prince, and Morgen received us with fitting honour . . .[36]

THUS OF ARTHUR I find no more written . . . nor more of the very certainty of his death I never read, but thus he was led away in a ship wherein were three Queens . . . Queen Morgan le Fay . . . the Queen of Northgalis . . . the Queen of the Waste Lands . . .

Yet some men say in many parts of England that King Arthur is not dead, but had by the will of our Lord Jesu into another place; and men say that he shall come again . . . I will not say it shall be so, but rather I will say: here in this world he changed his life. But many men say there is written upon his tomb the verse: *Hic Jacet Arthurus, Rex Quondam, Rexque Futurus.* [Here lies Arthur, King that was, King that shall be].[37]

Sources

1. Geoffrey of Monmouth, *The History of the Kings of Britain*. Trans. by J.A.Giles in *Old English Chronicles*, G. Bell, 1910.
2. Geoffrey of Monmouth.
3. *The Avallanau of Myrddin*. Translated by J. Matthews.
4. *Le Morte d'Arthur* by Sir Thomas Malory, New York: University Books, 1961.
5. 'A Fugitive Poem of Merlin in His Grave.' Translated by John Matthews.
6. Malory.
7. *The Oianau*, trans. John Matthews.
8. Geoffrey of Monmouth, *Vita Merlini*, trans. J.J.Parry, University of Illinois, 1925.
9. *The Romance of Perceval in Prose*, trans. D. Skeels, University of Washington Press, 1966.
10. *Morte Arthure*, trans. J.L. Weston, in *Romance, Vision & Satire*, David Nutt, 1912.
11. Malory.
12. Wace, *The Roman du Brut*, trans. by E.Mason in *Arthurian Chronicles*, Dent, 1912.
13. Malory.
14. *Sir Gawain & the Green Knight*, trans. E.J.B.Kirtlan, C.H.Kelly, 1912.
15. 'Gereint, Son of Erbin', trans. Lady C. Guest, *Mabinogion*, Dent, 1937.
16. Malory.
17. 'Tristan of Thomas', trans. D.L. Sayers in *Tristan in Brittany*, Benn, 1929.
18. Marie de France, Lay of Gugemar, trans. E. Mason, in *Medieval French Romances*, Dent, n.d.
19. *Tristan of Thomas*.

20. Chrétien de Troyes, *Yvain*, trans. by W.W.Comfort in *Arthurian Romances*, Dent, 1914.
21. *The Romance of Tristan and Iseult* by Joseph Bedier. Trans. by Hilaire Belloc.
22. Chrétien de Troyes, *Perceval*.
23. 'Peredur' in *Mabinogion*.
24. *Perlesvaus*, trans. N. Bryant, D.S. Brewer, 1978.
25. 'Prologue to Perlesvaus' in *The Grail, Quest for the Eternal*, by J. Matthews, Thames & Hudson, 1981.
26. Malory.
27. *Perlesvaus*.
28. *Quest of the Holy Grail*, trans. W.W. Comfort, Dent, 1926.
29. Malory.
30. ibid.
31. *Perlesvaus*.
32. *Morte Arthure*.
33. Malory.
34. *Morte Arthure*.
35. 'Layamon, Brut', trans. E.Mason, *Arthurian Chronicles*, Dent, 1912.
36. Geoffrey of Monmouth, *Vita Merlini* .
37. Malory.

ACKNOWLEDGEMENTS

The publishers would like to thank the following for permission to reproduce their illustrations:

Birmingham Museum and Art Gallery – pages 8, 26, 44
E.T. Archive, Newschwanstein Castle – pages 20, 22, 38
E.T. Archive, Victoria & Albert Museum – page 38
Fine Art Photographic – pages 6, 10, 28
King Arthur's Great Halls, Tintagel – pages 11, 12, 32,
Laing Art Gallery, Newcastle upon Tyne, Tyne and Wear Museum – page 14
Tate Gallery, John Webb – page 4